Patriarch and Folk

Patriarch and Folk
The Emergence
of Nicaragua
1798–1858

E. Bradford Burns

Harvard University Press
Cambridge, Massachusetts
London, England
1991

This book is printed on acid-free paper, and its binding materials
have been chosen for strength and durability.

Library of Congress Cataloging-in-Publication Data

Burns, E. Bradford.
Patriarch and folk : the emergence of Nicaragua, 1798–1858 / E.
Bradford Burns.
p.   cm.
Includes bibliographical references (p.   ) and index.
ISBN 0–674–65796–9
1. Nicaragua—History—To 1838.   2. Nicaragua—
History—1838–1909.   I. Title.
F1526.25.B87   1991
972.85—dc20
90-23892
CIP

To the heroic people of Nicaragua, who have known
turbulent times and persevered

Acknowledgments

In a poem written in the early 1980s, "What Kind of a Country Is This?" Romano de Sant'Anna mused,

> I live in the twentieth century.
> I'm off to the twenty-first,
> Still the prisoner of the nineteenth.

His pithy historical summary of modern Brazil also characterizes Latin America.

As I began to think about the dramatic events of Nicaragua, a country which periodically during the last century and a half has monopolized international headlines, I searched the annals of the past to find explanations for the high global profile of this small nation. In that search, the intriguingly hazy, shrouded, and mysterious first half of the nineteenth century challenged me. Simply put: what happened and why and with what consequences? I set out to explore those questions. *Patriarch and Folk* is the result. I conclude, like the Brazilian poet, that the events of that distant period determine these crucial years as the twentieth century dissolves into the twenty-first. Nicaragua, like Latin America, is more than the creation of its past: it is a prisoner.

Exploring nineteenth-century Nicaraguan history provided at least a dual experience.

Repeated visits to Nicaragua, the opportunity to travel extensively within it, and the joy of savoring a variety of unique experiences there exhilarated me. The Nicaraguans are a generous, hospitable, exciting people, whose kindness remains deeply impressed on my memory. They taught me a great deal. They expanded my consciousness and under-standing.

A much quieter sort of experience arose from the research and writing, intellectually invigorating but sensually less stimulating than those lively sojourns in Nicaragua. Fortunately, even the solitude of scholarship must be broken with human contact. Many people helped and guided me. The conceptualization, research, and writing could not have been possible without their contributions.

For the pertinent questions they asked and the comments they made about the conceptualization of this book, I am grateful to Karl Bermann, Florencia E. Mallon, Alexander Moore, Mario Rodríguez, Charles L. Stansifer, and Thomas W. Walker. I am specially indebted to Elizabeth Dore, José Moya, and Ralph Lee Woodward, who read an early draft of the manuscript and made valuable suggestions. A colleague at UCLA, Larry Lauerhass, provided bibliographic support and enlightenment. Judy Sandoval supplied me with a copy of E. G. Squier's report on the Nicaraguan debt, which she found at Tulane University. Joan Palevsky provided encouragement. A much appreciated Guggenheim Fellowship permitted a year of uninterrupted research. I thank Provost Raymond L. Orbach of UCLA for generously facilitating a sabbatical for that research. Richard Smyzer lent a helping hand when the complexities of the word processor overwhelmed me. Aida D. Donald of Harvard University Press boosted my morale.

The Nicaraguans were generous. Alfonso Vijil gave me free run of his impressive library on the Nicaraguan past. At both the National and the Central American universities, I learned from discussions with historians. Jorge Eduardo Arellano helped me to understand nineteenth-century Nicaragua. Fidel Coloma González received me warmly at the Rubén Darío National Library. Many and treasured were the conversations with Nicaraguans such as Dr. Fernando Silva, poet, novelist, and pediatrician, from which I gained insights into the people of Nicaragua. I thank all of them.

They contributed. We confabulated. I confected. The interpretations, like the errors, are mine.

E. Bradford Burns
Muscatine, Iowa

Contents

Patriarch and Folk

Introduction

From the violence — always endemic and often erupting among the patriarchs of the dominant families, the folk communities, and the foreigners—emerged Nicaragua. The painfully prolonged process of transition from colonial status to incipient nation-state lasted six decades, 1798–1858. The dates mark, at the starting point, the first cogent statement by the Nicaraguan patriarchal elites of their vision of a vibrant commercial future, the logical consequence of an abundant nature and unique geography, and, at the end, the first signs of the emergence of a viable nation-state. Anarchy characterized the decades between them.

The economic decline of the Spanish empire in the late eighteenth century encouraged a small group of merchants and landowners to cherish a vision of prosperity through agrarian exports that could occur within a Nicaragua freed of colonial restraints. Those local patriarchs urged the use of Nicaragua's unique geography to create a prosperous transit route or canal, the much desired link between the Atlantic and Pacific oceans. That alluring vision of commerce accompanied by agrarian exports has never tarnished. For two centuries it inspired hopes and, occasionally, action. Anarchy thwarted early efforts to realize that vision and, for that matter, to establish the nation-state.

The complex period encasing the disintegration of colonial empires and the establishment of nation-states is also one of conflict of basic values in nineteenth-century society. Throughout Latin America, the newly emerging governments drew heavily from the ideas of the European Enlightenment, novel ideas of contractual governance that contrasted dramatically with both local and imperial experiences. Adjustments to the innovations varied. Brazil made the transition to nationhood quickly because the presence of Prince Pedro facilitated a genetic, patriarchal continuity alongside a contractual accommodation—a case unique in the Western Hemisphere. Nicaragua represented the other extreme, a prolonged, troubled transition from such a patriarchal governance to the contractual state. The most significant step in that transition did not occur until 1857 and 1858.

In the Spanish colonial system throughout the Western Hemisphere, the city symbolized imperial power. In each region one city dominated. As the examples of Mexico City, Guatemala City, Lima, Santiago, and Buenos Aires demonstrate, the concentration of social, economic, and political power set a pattern still characteristic of urbanization and authority in Latin America. Nicaragua represented an unusual example of urban ambivalence. Two relatively equal cities vied for dominance, a rivalry that intensified in the nineteenth century until 1857.

The disintegration and then disappearance of the crown's authority removed inhibitions from the increasingly bitter political and economic rivalry between the patriarchs of León and Granada, the two principal urban centers and virtual city-states by the advent of Central American independence in 1821. Their constant warfare devastated Nicaragua between the early 1820s and the mid-1850s. Ending that cycle of self-destruction, the National War, 1856–57, cleared the way to begin the construction of a nation-state.

Nicaragua entered independence with an economic and social balance between the folk with their inwardly oriented, self-sufficient, agrarian communities and the patriarchs, whose wider, more outward vision encompassed international trade. For nearly half a century the balance wavered but remained. During that period, fragile institutional structures characterized Nicaragua. Even the Roman Catholic Church and the military—vigorous institutions elsewhere in Latin America—exerted minimal influence. No caudillo emerged until 1858. In a society of weak institutions and leaders, the patriarchal family and the folk community filled the void, playing vibrant, although at times conflicting, historical roles.

The large and economically vigorous Indian populations of Nicaragua—and to a lesser degree the growing number of mestizos—manifested no interest in creating a Europeanized nation-state. Respecting their own past, they found satisfaction within the local community. They enjoyed virtually unrestricted access to land. From their local experience, they drew their values. Ironically, the anarchy that engulfed Nicaragua protected the local folk societies from undue disruption of tradition. Disorder served their goals.

The patriarchs increasingly looked outward to the world beyond Central America. They wanted to promote international trade. With varying degrees of enthusiasm, they drew their values from the Enlightenment that had swept through the North Atlantic nations and into Central America. They hoped to establish a Europeanized nation-state, or a reasonable approximation thereof. Concurrently and contradictorily, those patriarchs felt a good deal of comfort within their localized city-state structures, a historically sanctioned status deeply rooted in the long colonial past. Although their local jealousies promoted anarchy and frustrated efforts to create the nation-state they professed to want, the rival elites never looked to secession.

Realities, both within and without Nicaragua, eventually forced the patriarchs to subordinate to an incipient nation-state their loyalties to the city-states. A common struggle, first against the folk (1845–1849) and then against foreign intruders (1855–1857) in addition to the prospects of coffee prosperity suggested by the Costa Rican model, diminished their internecine armed struggles. By 1857 the elites disengaged sufficiently from the past to forge a new, quite radically different Nicaragua, one, ironically, that threatened their own patriarchal preferences. Envisioning an increasingly material future linked to the North Atlantic capitalist marketplace, they accepted and expressed new values. European progress impressed the Nicaraguan patriarchs. They hoped to emulate that progress, but to do so cost money. That money could be earned from agrarian exports. The export crops required land and labor, two necessities which forced the patriarchs to confront the folk who farmed some of the lands needed for export crops, and who could—and must—supply the labor. The patriarchs determined to redefine to their greater advantage the mechanisms of rural social control so as to impose their new values.

If the folk did not need the patriarchs, the large landowners and merchants most emphatically needed the folk to be able to realize their vision. The elite tipped the social balance in their favor in 1849 after suppressing protracted popular rebellions. Victory permitted them to impose their economic and political agenda, but that had to be deferred until after they defeated the major foreign threat, the North American adventurer William Walker (1855–1857). Those two victories united the warring patriarchs, who finally understood their goals and values harmonized rather than conflicted. The days of the folk societies were numbered.

During the final decade of the age of anarchy, 1849–1858, three major realms of relationships were defined: among the patriarchs, between the patriarchs and the folk, and between Nicaragua as a client state and the United States as the new metropolis. In the long and bitter struggle among the patriarchs—which is to say between the two city-states of León and Granada—a devastating civil conflict and a brutal international war virtually erased the power of each and promoted Managua as the political center of a more unified elite and nation. The triumph over the filibuster William Walker marked the demise of the city-states. The patriarchs resolved their problems with the folk communities by defeating the popular rebellions of 1845–1849 and by increasing the powers of their more effective central government after 1857 to begin the process of dismantling those communities. Finally, in their extremely important relations with the outside world, the patriarchs substituted the United States for Great Britain as the metropolis, thus charting a new course through the stormy seas of international relations

A dynamic of conflicting values characterized early Nicaraguan national society. The patriarchs succeeded in resolving the conflict in their favor. In a relatively brief time span, 1849–1858, they triumphed internally and externally in a remarkable tour de force. Their victory, they believed, opened the nation's doors to opportunity and progress. They trumpeted their success as the victory of civilization over barbarism. Investing the state with new power, they radically reshaped Nicaragua to accommodate their economic vision. They set the nation on a new course, one of structural upheaval for the rural folk. Along that newly charted course, the patriarchal elites dispossessed the folk of much of their land and impoverished them culturally and economically. The imposed progress benefited the few at the expense of the many. Social, economic, and political imbalance increasingly characterized Nicaragua. The dramatic events after 1979 are but one upheaval in the stormy historical course set between 1849 and 1858.

City-States: Rivalry Begets Anarchy

Vision

As the Spanish empire in the New World faltered at the end of the eighteenth century on a course that led it to disintegrate in the early nineteenth, some prominent patriarchs of Nicaragua conjured up a vision of a lively commercial future for their impoverished region. "This miserable and abandoned kingdom would be reborn and flourish . . . if overseas commerce could be conducted through the San Juan River and Lake Nicaragua."[1] Thus did merchants and landowners of the fertile Rivas area reply in 1798 to a royal order for information explaining the stagnation of the Nicaraguan economy. Their report to the Marqués de la Hornaza voiced a common complaint among large planters, ranchers, and merchants that the only authorized trade route, a circuitous one via Guatemala City and then through the Honduran port of Omoa, was too long, hazardous, and costly to promote Nicaraguan trade. Furthermore, in the opinion of those frustrated entrepreneurs, greedy merchants in Guatemala City controlled the route and reaped unreasonable profits. That combination inhibited commerce and hobbled the economy. Those Nicaraguans pleaded for royal permission to open the shorter water route across their province to the Atlantic, the direct access they sought to external markets for the abundant products with which a generous nature had blessed their land.

The document of 1798 forcefully enumerated Nicaraguan goals just at the time discontent rocked the Spanish empire and the economic pace of Atlantic trade accelerated. It both summarized conditions of the moment and heralded hopes for the future.

The worthy fathers of Rivas were not the first to fantasize about living at the center of a thriving international commercial route. During the long colonial period, an occasional voice expressed hope that a transisthmian trade route would enliven the local economy. Such voices multiplied in the last decades of the eighteenth century. The governor of Nicaragua in 1788–89 argued in favor of opening the San Juan River to trade, and the Spanish merchant Juan de Zavala embraced "the great project" of direct trade between Nicaragua and Spain via the San Juan. As a merchant residing in Granada, 1790–95, he had sufficient time and the firsthand knowledge to formulate trade plans which he promoted in Spain until his death in 1800. [2]

Local entrepreneurs planned and pleaded. A logical transportation route to spur trade and unlock the natural wealth of their fertile land obsessed them. A very important aspect of their scheme was that locals would control the route and earn the profits. Invigorated trade would transform Nicaragua from poverty to prosperity, from a forgotten backwater of empire to a bustling lane of commerce between the two oceans. Nicaragua's moribund economy only made the merchants' and landowners' vision all the more alluring.

As the nineteenth century dawned, Nicaragua's scant trade was more local than international. Statistics for the year 1800 revealed that 69 percent of Nicaraguan exports went to other parts of Central America and only 31 percent outside of it. [3] The reality of a stagnant economy confined to Central America contrasted with the glowing economic vision that mesmerized the Nicaraguan patriarchs, those great "fathers" who dominated extensive families at the local social and economic pinnacles. They believed their province's unique geography ordained a special commercial role for Nicaragua.

Agriculture and cattle raising dominated the economy at the opening of the nineteenth century. Land was wealth, and most Nicaraguans owned at least some of it. The province was self-sufficient in food, producing it abundantly and cheaply. Craftsmen and artisans turned out the simple manufactured items required by a majority of the 159,000 inhabitants. Fully three-quarters of that population could be found along a western or Pacific axis linking El Viejo to Rivas and traversing Chinandega, León, Managua, Masaya, and Granada, an area encompassing less than one-quarter of the province of Nicaragua. For most of its inhabitants, the province provided a self-sustaining economy: simple, rustic, locally oriented. The inwardly oriented folk communities did not share the vast economic vision of the principal landlords. They traded in local markets, so international commerce threatened rather than attracted them.

Two cities, Granada and León, dominated the modest economic activity of the province. León, the more populous, contained approximately 32,000 inhabitants in 1823. It not only served as the political, educational, and religious center but also as a commercial hub. It commanded local commerce and also traded with Honduras, El Salvador, and Guatemala

Nicaragua

and with the West coast of South America through the port of Realejo. Granada, with a population of 10,233, ranked as the premier merchant city, commanding the outlet to the Atlantic Ocean across Lake Nicaragua and down the San Juan River, dominating the fertile lands around Masaya and Rivas, and penetrating the rapidly expanding cattle economy of Chontales. Both cities distributed the trickle of imports. Some textiles, liquors, iron tools, perfumes, medicines, and chinaware entered the province, but few consumers demanded or could afford them. Forbidden but alluring, some English contraband trade existed despite imperial mercantilist laws.

At the end of the eighteenth century, one yearly account of exports totalled 569,000 pesos and revealed three dominant categories: cattle (100,000 pesos), indigo (160,000), and cacao (220,000). Sugar, tar and pitch, woods, mules, horses, cheeses, corn, and cotton made up most of the rest.[4] These modest figures explained the crown's neglect of Nicaragua to concentrate on such regions as Mexico, a traditional exporter of great mineral wealth, and, increasingly, Buenos Aires, whose exports rose impressively in the eighteenth century. For the Nicaraguans, Spanish mercantilist policies imposed prohibitions and offered few opportunities for economic growth and none for economic development. Jaime Wheelock Román characterized the economic system imposed by Spain on Nicaragua as a "virtually closed subsistence economy."[5]

By the end of the eighteenth century, a tendency toward greater land concentration appeared. Cattle ranches in particular grew both in number and size and dominated the northern and central zones: Nueva Segovia, Chontales, and Boaco. A few families of León and Granada owned most of them.[6] Those ranches could propagate and expand with relative ease because they required few laborers. In general, workers were scarce and control of them precarious.

During the colonial period, the Spaniards forced the Indians to provide labor through imperial institutions such as the *repartimiento*, a temporary allotment of Indians by the crown to fulfill specific work contracts. The Indians preferred to work their own lands, and Spanish demands created social tension.[7]

Occasionally, as at El Viejo in 1759 and at Jalteva in 1769, the Indians vigorously protested what they considered to be excessive demands.[8] The few Spaniards increasingly sought to employ *ladinos* (also termed *mestizos*, the mixture of European and Indian), who, by the eighteenth century, constituted a population of growing significance. Some sources estimated that they outnumbered the Indians.[9]

As a rule, the ladinos hesitated to identify with the Indians, wishing to escape both forced labor (the repartimiento) and the payment of tribute, imposed by the Spaniards on the Indians but not on the ladinos. The least defined segment of society, the mestizos occupied all economic positions from that of the most menial day laborer to, occasionally, the owner of good-sized estates.[10] They often claimed vacant lands and impinged on Indian communities.[11] Mestizos played a particularly important role in the military, whose ranks they filled except for the highest offices monopolized by the Spaniards or "whites" born in Nicaragua, the creoles.[12] As the ladino population increased, the number of Spanish men marrying mestizas also rose. Children from such marriages passed as Spaniards so long as they adopted European behavior patterns and renounced their ethnicity.[13] The emerging importance of the ladinos by the end of the eighteenth century, as well as the trend toward land concentration, heralded socioeconomic changes whose impact would be fully felt only with the creation of the nation-state after the mid-nineteenth century.

Despair characterized the Nicaraguan economy during the final decades of the eighteenth century and the first two decades of the nineteenth. Stagnation alternated with decline. Strong competition from Venezuela and Ecuador, growers of excellent cacao, decimated Nicaraguan markets. Invigorated cattle production in El Salvador reduced Guatemalan demands for Nicaraguan cattle. A combination of European wars, locust plagues, higher taxes, and increasing competition eroded indigo production. Spanish trade monopolies, the low prices paid by the Guatemalan merchants, rising taxes, delayed payments, unreliable fleet sailings, further restricted Nicaragua's export economy. The once prosperous shipyard at Realejo began to decline after 1752, and it never regained its economic prominence as a shipbuilding center in the Americas.[14]

The economic gloom darkened after 1800.[15] The complaints of the merchants and landowners of Rivas thundered across the black skies of Nicaraguan discontent. The merchants and landowners of Granada echoed them. Governor Crisanto Sacasa spoke for the leading families. To flourish, Nicaragua had to export, he emphasized; to export, Nicaragua required freedom of commerce. Granadan notables, whether of liberal or conservative political persuasions, applauded. Not surprisingly, Sacasa played a significant role in the Nicaraguan independence movement.[16] His contemporary Pedro José Chamorro, a resident of Granada and owner of a cattle ranch and cacao plantation, castigated the Guatemalan merchants, charging that they always "impeded" the commerce of Nicaragua, subordinating Nicaraguan economic welfare to the interests of the merchants and bureaucrats in Guatemala City.[17] They blamed Guatemala for most of their economic woes. The logic of Granada's geographical location demanded the opening of Lake Nicaragua and the San Juan River to the Atlantic trade. The landowners and merchants found Guatemala to be as adamant as Spain in keeping that route closed. From the colonial period until the dissolution of the Central American Federation in 1838, tensions between Nicaragua and Guatemala over real and perceived conflicts of economic interests remained high.[18] Chamorro's accusations both reflected and intensified them.

The deputy from Nicaragua José Antonio López de la Plata, projected the "economic vision" vividly in the Spanish Cortes in 1812–13: "The Province of Nicaragua, because of its rich resources and geographic position, holds the greatest hopes of participating in a Universal Commerce."[19] The objectives of the Province of Nicaragua, as de la Plata outlined them to his fellow deputies, were to open the San Juan River to commercial traffic and trade, to develop the mineral and agrarian resources of the north-central highlands, and to separate the province from Guatemalan control.[20]

Nicaraguans increasingly reiterated those demands. Pedro Chamorro joined other provincial delegates in León in 1814 to petition the crown to separate the Province of Nicaragua and Costa Rica from Guatemala and raise it to the rank of an intendency. The petition repeated arguments all too familiar by that date, but coming after decades of disappointing responses or no responses from Madrid and Guatemala City, its tone reeked of petulance. The document melodramatically depicted the prevalent poverty. Its major message emerged in these three sentences: "What a contrast exists between the natural fertility, wealth, and abundance of these Provinces and the poverty misery, and depression in which they presently are submerged. . . . The principal cause is the subjection to and dependence upon Guatemala, so far away . . . that we feel abandoned. The only way for us to achieve prosperity is to be independent of Guatemala."[21] That independence would permit use of the San Juan River route, consistently regarded as the avenue to Nicaragua's prosperity.

While the demands of the local notables served immediate goals, they also carried a transcendental message. They pointed to the enigma of poverty amidst potential wealth, a problem that troubled the Nicaraguans in 1814 and still characterizes most of Latin America in the late twentieth century. Stating in unequivocal language the economic and political problems with Guatemala, the document of 1814 foretold the inevitable disintegration of Central America into separate states. As a kind of proto-nationalistic manifesto, it spoke for a small, seemingly cohesive group that found the larger political unit, the Kingdom of Guatemala, to be oppressive. The petition to the monarch in favor of local interests remains an impressive document in the "nation-forming process" of Nicaragua.

Whether the changes advocated could have enriched the region is questionable. Indeed, subsequent history may be interpreted as a negative response. The economic emphasis the patriarchs placed on export agri-culture reflected a colonial mentality more linked to a dependency contin-uum than to an innovative path to economic development and inde-pendence. The petitioners reaffirmed Nicaragua's role as a supplier of raw material and agrarian products but added their intention to use its unique geography to serve as a global highway for commerce.[22] That vision excited foreigners who encouraged Nicaragua to play the supplier/service role.[23]

In his useful *Bosquejo Político, Estadístico de Nicaragua Formado en el Año 1823* (A Political and Statistical Outline of Nicaragua in the Year 1823), the last Spanish colonial governor of the province, General Miguel González Saravia, lent his prestige to the local yearning for the San Juan route and the economic prosperity it promised Nicaragua. Further, he concluded that opening that route created a virtual canal across the isthmus: "Transportation by water from the Atlantic up the San Juan River and across Lake Nicaragua to Granada and by road from there to Realejo, why would anyone need a better or more effective canal between the two oceans?"[24] His pages recited the familiar litany of potential wealth.

The Rivas document, the 1814 petition to the monarch, and the *Bos-quejo Político* reveal a continuity of thought over the quarter of a century leading into Central American independence. All three articulated a cheerful confidence in a prosperous future on the strength of the potential wealth of Nicaragua, its benign climate and rich soil, its mineral resources and rare woods, its favorable location for transportation and trade. They accented the centuries-old longing for a canal or at the very least a transit route to connect the two oceans. They sought a greater local control over the province's economic destiny. Obviously such control would enhance local prosperity, but the authors judiciously argued that it would enrich the crown. In the following decades locals and foreigners alike joyously sang the theme of the "vision of prosperity." The Nicaraguan nationalist Fruto Chamorro proclaimed in the *Mentor Nicaragüense* in 1841: "Our country is destined to be, sooner or later, the emporium not just of this continent but of the entire world."[25] Hundreds of variations on that theme filled the press and oratory, echoed and reechoed across the decades. The most perceptive of the foreign visitors prior to 1870, Ephraim George Squier, concluded, "For, in Nicaragua, and there alone, has Nature combined those requisites for a water communication between the seas, which has so long been the dream of enthusiasts, and which is a desideratum of this age, as it will be a necessity for the next. There too has she lavished, with a bountiful hand, her richest tropical treasures; and the genial earth waits only for the touch of industry to reward the husbandman a hundredfold with those products."[26] Alas, while the vision of prosperity might have served to promote a philosophical unity among the Nicaraguan patriarchs, it also attracted the attention of foreigners far less altruistic than Squier, adventurers who besieged hapless Nicaragua in their own pursuit of the vision.

The three documents from the late eighteenth and early nineteenth centuries attest to a kind of historical and economic consciousness engendered by isolation and hope. Neglect rendered Nicaragua separate, distinctive. Isolation, neglect, and the hopes raised by agricultural fertility and favorable geography conferred individuality on the region and a common experience on the inhabitants. The local patriarchs at any rate shared a common vision of economic improvement engendered by local autonomy. A pride in the potential wealth of their region bespoke a sense of nativism, a regional patriotism, perhaps even an embryonic nationalism. In this particular Nicaraguan case, the determination of the elites to resolve their economic crisis and their optimistic vision of the region's future offered a study of the pursuit of trade and commerce as an incentive for nationalism.

The determined goal to expand trade subtly subsumed a double and difficult transition. The large landowners and merchants manifested, consciously or unconsciously, a willingness to convert themselves into a more "modern" bourgeoisie. They were equally willing to convert their isolated province into a "modern" nation, partly by competitively entering into the capitalist export marketplace and partly by providing the capitalist world with a transit route to link the oceans. These transformations would affect the entire Nicaraguan population. After all, the vision could not be realized without the participation of the humble majority. The decision to modernize also predestined independence and nationhood, since the goal could not be achieved within the confines of a disintegrating Spanish empire, nor, apparently, within the framework of a squabbling Central American union dominated from Guatemala City.

While the merchants and landowners believed that limited trade opportunities were the primary problems confronting Nicaragua, the Bishop of León, Juan Cruz Ruiz de Cabañas, saw others in the late eighteenth century. He signaled the scant population scattered across vast terrain as a major barrier to raising the quality of life. "The eternal solitude of the haciendas, ranches, and farms" impeded the influence of Church and State and encouraged "fatal ignorance and unbridled lust . . . the idleness and laziness so common in those unhappy regions." The good bishop recognized the challenge to the Church of scattered populations and few clergymen. He lamented the low level of culture and society and even decried the "lack of public schools."[27] However, fearful of the winds of change blowing at gale force in Europe, he cautioned "his very beloved brothers and children" to beware of the ideas propagated by the French Revolution.[28]

Breezes of the Enlightenment wafted gently across Nicaragua. The bishop's concern with public education, even in a modest and Roman Catholic form, suggests a presence of the new ideas in religious thinking. Despite the bishop's worst fears of French influences, they existed, albeit among that tiny percentage of the population who knew how to read. In a festive public speech in 1865 commemorating Nicaragua's independence, Juan de la Rocha hailed Jean-Jacques Rousseau as its intellectual father.[29] However heady the ideas of Rousseau, they played a secondary role to the vision of economic prosperity pursued by the patriarchs.

Division

Serious divisions rent society, primarily vertical ones between the ruling families and the people; but secondary divisions, such as the geographic isolation of the peoples of the Atlantic coast from those along the Pacific, also bedeviled Nicaragua. A powerful force in unifying the economic thought of the patriarchal elites, the vision of prosperity, failed to bridge a vertical political division between the two major cities, León and Granada. Although they could agree on a desire to promote exports and to encourage an isthmian transit route, the leading citizens of the two cities differed over who would oversee such an economic expansion and how.

They also could agree to break the colonial ties with Spain, but who would then rule and how troubled them. Fundamentally, the differences between the dominant citizens of Granada and León bespoke their concern over who would benefit more from economic and political changes. To match their city's economic vigor, the patriarchs of Granada coveted the political power long monopolized by León. Political upheaval in Central America after 1811 offered them an unusual opportunity: some institutional fluidity after centuries of predictable Spanish rule.

The frustrations caused by a long economic recession, the Spanish American independence struggles after 1808, and the strains of European wars during the Napoleonic period loosened the bonds uniting the Spanish empire.[30] By 1817, Central Americans had succumbed to the temptations of trade with eager English merchants, and the Spanish crown was virtually powerless to prevent it. The political and economic control of Guatemala City over the rest of Central America, always difficult because of poor communications and abysmal roads, weakened. The efforts of the Bourbon monarchs to centralize power failed. For a unique moment in Central American history, no metropolis held sway.

Nicaraguans understood the novelty. Talk of independence dominated the conversations among the patriarchal elite. At the beginning of the 1820s, Orlando Roberts, a British merchant temporarily held prisoner in Nicaragua by the Spaniards on charges of engaging in contraband trade, listened to a local priest and his friends discussing politics over drinks:

> He [the priest] observed, that he hoped the day was not far distant when Managua and the Interior of Central America, would be better known to my countrymen, and everyone seemed to speak freely of the state of the country, deplored the commercial and other restrictions under which they laboured; and it was evident that the worthy *cura*, who is a native Creole, and his friends, wished well to the cause of independence, and anticipated a great, and certain change in the political government of Central America. . . . Some of the gentlemen present expressed their hopes, that the trade would soon be more open; that British goods of almost every description were much wanted; and the towns in the vicinity of the Lakes of Nicaragua and León would consume and pay for a very large quantity.[31]

The elite was eager to pursue an independence which, many expected, would improve their economic and political position. The much larger and very economically diverse ladino population chafed under the restrictions of institutions which did not fully encompass or benefit them. After three centuries of colonial rule, society had engendered within itself the potential for transformation.[32]

As the authority of the captain-general and *audiencia* in Guatemala City faltered, the door to political power for the local creoles swung open. The *cabildos* or municipal governments, in which the creoles had gained political experience, served as the legal instrument of political change. The conclusion of Miles L. Wortman for the early independence period in Central America, that "Each cabildo considered itself autonomous," perfectly described the Nicaraguan political reality.[33] Local perspectives replaced the imperial view. Such perspectives fragmented first the Viceroyalty of New Spain and then the United Provinces of Central America, offering the extreme example of the territorial disintegration that the rest of Latin America hoped to avoid in the transition from Iberian colonies to independent nations. The Spanish-speaking Americans failed to escape it. Brazil provided the only example of a former Iberian viceroyalty that moved into nationhood without disintegrating. In fact, from 1822 to 1909, Brazil grew in territorial size.

During the struggle for independence, Granada took advantage of the confusion to challenge León. The challenge intensified their rivalry, set a disastrous political precedent for succeeding decades, and contributed to the bleak economic pattern for the next half-century. In December of 1811, first León and then Granada deposed the Spanish authorities in their midst. When royalist forces arrived from Guatemala early in 1812 to quell the rebellions, León immediately capitulated. Granada resolved to resist, although the resistance was brief. The crown rewarded León for its surrender and harshly punished the Granadans for their resistance. They resented their abandonment by León to the mercy of the royal forces. The resentment further embittered relations between the two cities.

Guatemala declared Central America's independence on September 15, 1821, setting off a quick reaction of contradictory events within Nicaragua. León declared its independence of both Spain *and* Guatemala; Granada renounced Spanish rule but maintained its link to Guatemala. Less than a month later, León accepted Iturbide's Plan of Iguala and joined the Mexican Empire. León remained under the influence of three important Spanish officials of the colonial past: the governor, the bishop, and the commander of the troops.[34] Granada, under the control of the local creoles, opposed the annexation. Momentarily supportive of that opposition, officials in Guatemala City created a Junta Gubernativa Subalterna in Granada, thus conferring on that city a political status it coveted.

León saw its old, well-established political monopoly threatened. Apprehensions further fanned the flames of rivalry. Shortly thereafter, bowing to the military pressure from Mexico, the Guatemalans accepted the Plan of Iguala and annexed Central America to the Mexican empire of Iturbide.

The consistently opposed political loyalties of León and Granada deteriorated into civil war. The fall of Emperor Iturbide and the declaration of Central America's independence from Mexico on June 29, 1823, did not end that increasingly bitter civil conflict in Nicaragua. Because of civil war, the local patriarchs failed to organize Nicaragua as a state within the Central American federation until 1826, and then only after Manuel José Arce arrived leading federal forces. He disbanded the local armies and exiled recalcitrant leaders. Passions without principles—to borrow the judgment of the nineteenth-century Nicaraguan historian Tomás Ayón—propelled Nicaraguan politics.[35] The foreign visitor Carl Scherzer blamed the "miserable squabbles" on the jealousies between León and Granada over "the privileges of government."[36]

A tiny urban elite (with intimate rural links) guided the Province of Nicaragua to independence from Spain within the larger and equally complex framework of Central American politics. Those privileged leaders hoped to increase local political power and economic benefits. In pursuit of their economic vision, they experienced more frustrations than satisfactions as participants in the United Provinces of Central America, 1823–1838. Their suspicions and resentments of the Guatemalan aristocracy and merchants made them increasingly uncomfortable within an isthmian union dominated from Guatemala City. Nicaragua was the last of the five Central American states to regularize its status within the United Provinces and the first to leave it.

In or out of the Central American union, divisions continued to rend Nicaragua. The underpopulated territory showed every sign of disintegration. León and Granada were more separate than unified. On the Atlantic coast, the Mosquito Kingdom fell under English protection, denying any Nicaraguan government, León or Granada, the opportunity to exercise sovereignty over its vast and unmarked terrain. Foreign economic enclaves in the Atlantic region, interested primarily in mining and logging, further isolated that underpopulated area from the Pacific region, the capital (wherever that might be at the moment), and the populated area of the nation. The enclaves traded directly with foreign markets and remained outside all except nominal control or claims of the Nicaraguan government. The southwestern province of Guanacaste seceded to join Costa Rica in 1824. Time deepened rather than mitigated Nicaragua's divisions. That reality shaped the first three-and-one-half decades of Nicaraguan national history.

The regional division was the most threatening. Virtual city-states, León and Granada frustrated national unity. Although they shared language, religion, and cultural heritage, they maintained separate political and economic identities. Even the Church and the military, institutions that by their very nature seemed national in scope, succumbed to localism in outlook and action. The priests echoed the sentiments of the city-state where they resided. The nonprofessional, partisan army could as easily support as subvert the national government. Political leaders raised new armies as quickly as possible for the campaign of the moment. The intellectuals, who otherwise might have provided the emotional cement of nationality, were no less divided.

Creating a nation-state from agrarian based city-states would require an elite with sufficient consensus to control the formal mechanism of government (the state) with some degree of authority over the entire geographic area it claimed to govern (the nation). Nicaragua, during the period 1821–1857, lacked that reasonably unified elite. The top people bickered at the expense of unity and stability. The first head of the State of Nicaragua, Supreme Chief Manuel Antonio de la Cerda, complained to the Nicaraguan Constituent Assembly of the "public arguments" among politicians and parties and of the municipal governments "contributing to disorder." At the same time, he informed the federal government in Guatemala City that the local Constituent Assembly fomented disorder. In his opinion, the resulting confusion caused "delay in achieving our consolidation."[37] José Nuñez, acting supreme chief in November 1834, fretted in a message to the legislature over the absence of order and obedience, concluding, "Ambition now occupies the place of patriotism."[38] Such complaints and observations multiplied over the decades as the executives realized they exercised slight power beyond the city in which they resided and almost none beyond the region their city dominated.

Both rival city-states counted on their hinterland inhabitants for political support. Granada exercised control over the departments of Granada (the Oriente) and the Meridional or Rivas, and a part of Matagalpa, whose joint population totalled approximately 135,000 in a national population estimated to be 257,000 in 1846; while León held sway over the departments of Nueva Segovia, the Occidente or León, and part of Matagalpa, whose combined population numbered approximately 122,000.[39] Such regionalism perpetuated an already badly disarticulated economy. Each region maintained self-sufficiency in food production; each was more closely linked to its foreign markets, via its own ports, than to one another.[40] Physical impediments contributed to the perpetuation of that

Departments of Nicaragua, 1826

division. Paul Levy observed as late as 1870, "The communications are so imperfect that each department is almost obliged to live its own life."[41]

Fragility characterized a nation that seemed to exist more in theory than in reality. For all practical purposes, no effective central government existed. George Byam, a temporary British resident, observed in 1840,

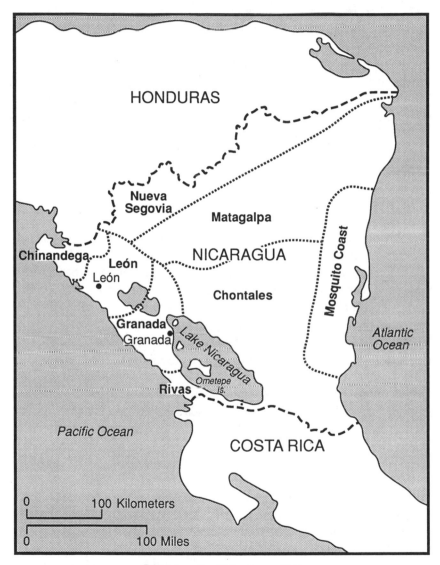

Departments of Nicaragua, 1858

"To say that there is any government is absurd; and yet the number of official proclamations that are constantly being issued, would lead most persons to believe that the government was excessively active, indeed too much so."[42]

Thus far, explanations of the regional bifurcation seem to be unsatisfactory. The search for them must begin with the reality of the well-established behavioral patterns of modest agrarian societies within the territorial configuration known as Nicaragua. Clearly, the patriarchs felt comfortable within localized and historically sanctioned city-state structures. The roots of the rivalry between Granada and León burrowed deeply into the past. At least one scholar argues a pre-Columbian basis for the regional strife.[43] Most place the origin within the colonial period.[44] Germán Romero Vargas concluded that the eighteenth century witnessed well-delineated political polarization between the two.[45]

Whatever might be the source of the rivalry, economics and politics propelled it in the nineteenth century. While León served as the political, religious, and educationa[l] ██████████████████ joyed a distinct economic advantage. Fro██████████████████ aragua, it could trade across that body of ██████████████████ er to the Atlantic. Historically, wheneve██████████████████ nants and landowners of Granada enjo██████████████████ When it was closed, the Nicaraguans ██████████████████ traband. After independence, San Juan ██████████████████ pal port, and Granada controlled both ██████████████████ as well as the customs duties, Nicarag██ primary source of income.[47] While data on tariffs collected prior to 1858 remain scarce, the figures for 1852 are partially available and provide a glimpse of an advantage Granada enjoyed. In that year, tariffs collected in San Juan del Norte amounted to $50,506 pesos (more often than not the peso approximated the dollar in value) and in San Juan del Sur, also within Granada's sphere of influence, $7,839 pesos. León collected only $16,964 in tariffs from the port under its influence, Realejo.[48] The two city-states considered proximity to tariff collection a distinct fiscal advantage. Furthermore, they competed intensely for access to foreign trade.

Psychological explanations might also account for the different behavior of the rival cities after independence. León, the seat of colonial government for the province, had maintained much closer ties to Guatemala City and Madrid. The trauma of independence prompted that city-state to break more radically with the Spanish past; thus, to welcome the ideas of the Enlightenment more enthusiastically. Furthermore León became the seat of foreign merchants after independence. Their very presence bespoke a contact with a Europe other than Spain. For its part, Granada by 1821 had settled comfortably into its role as a center of creole and ladino cultures. Local merchants and landowners dominated trade and production. With a past less associated with Spain and Guatemala and more attuned to the Nicaraguan environment, Granada might have had less reason to break radically with it.

The regional split into two city-states very often suggests ideological differences as well as political and economic causes. In fact, Nicaraguan historiography ascribes monumental importance to the ideological conflicts between the city-states. Pablo Antonio Cuadra, for one, wrote a poetic essay contrasting the two: East and West, Granada and León. While he did not specify the exact causes of that duality, he conveyed the "feeling" the Nicaraguans have of its existence, its influence, and above all else, its contradictions. [49] Most Nicaraguan historians, such as Pedro Joaquín Chamorro, Zelaya, point to the division between León and Granada as a key to understanding the political turmoil during the decades after independence. [50] Even in 1919, one intellectual, Mario Sancho, could exclaim, "León and Granada! I don't believe you will find two cities in the world more different in appearance or two peoples more different in their characteristics."[51] Actually, urban rivalries disturbed the tranquility of other Central American nations as well, although none suffered the prolonged rivalry and agony that rent Nicaragua. [52]

In an oft-repeated scenario, the Leónese waved the banner of liberalism, while the Granadans defended the barricades of conservatism. Political philosophy was made to bear the responsibility for civil wars. It challenged, shaped, and thwarted history. Writers used the contradictory ideologies as a kind of *deus ex machina* to move men and armies. The evidence does not always support this convenient explanation of ideology as prime mover.

First, division between the two city-states wid... abstract ideals but more likely because ... during the independence and posti... prompted action. León strove to retain ... León wanted *to conserve*, despite its em... Granada sought to improve, which is to s... cial and political positions (although it re... Conservative party).

Second, men subscribing to the Liberal and Conservative party labels resided in both cities. Some moved from one city to the other. Family linkages between the two existed. José de Vidaurre migrated from Cádiz to Granada in mid-seventeenth century. His offspring married into prosperous and well-established families in both Granada and León and later throughout Central America.[53] Crisanto Sacasa (1774–1824), sole heir to haciendas and businesses in Granada, where he dominated local politics, married Angela Méndez, daughter of one of the principal families of León.[54] The distinguished de la Rocha family amply illustrated family ties between the city-states. Gregorio de Pomar de la Rocha, a native of Granada, married Mercedes Zapata of León in the eighteenth century. Their son Nicolás de la Rocha Zapata was born in León (1774) and died there (1846). However, he lived part of his life in Granada and participated in the independence movement in that city. He married Josefa Sandoval y Vado, related to well known Granadan families. They had four daughters and four sons. One of the sons, Jesús de la Rocha, was born in León (1812) and died in Granada (1881). In the service of various governments, he resided in both cities as well as in Managua. He married twice, the first time to a woman of León and the second to a Granadan. Most of his life and activities were associated with Granada. His brother Juan Eligio was born in Granada (1815), studied and taught at the University of León, and served as mayor of León (1865). He lived for some time in Masaya. Much of his political life was associated with León, where he died in 1873. Pedro Francisco was born in Granada (1820) and died in León (1881). He attended universities in both cities. The fourth brother, Luís, also circulated among León, Managua, and Granada. Supreme Director José Laureano Pineda, (1851–1853) provides one final example. His mother was born in Granada, his father in León. The elites exhibited a certain degree of spatial mobility.

Third, while sharply differing attitudes toward the temporal powers of the Roman Catholic Church clearly separated Liberals from Conservatives in other parts of Central America, most notably in Guatemala, that distinction remained muted in Nicaragua. A few tense moments erupted between Church and state in the pre-1858 period, but good will and cooperation generally characterized the relationship. Both parties officially supported the Roman Catholic Church. The constitutions of 1826 (Liberal), 1838 (Liberal), and 1858 (Conservative) proclaimed Roman Catholicism as the official religion; the constitutions of 1838 and 1858, as well as the constitutions of 1848 and 1854 written by the Conservatives but not promulgated, all pledged the government to protect the Church. For their part, churchmen served prominently in Liberal and Conservative governments alike. Although the Roman Catholic Church obviously was a nation-wide institution, the individual religious tended to support the city-state in which they resided.

Fourth, no party structure existed. The so-called parties held neither conventions nor meetings; they boasted of no formal organization, no statutes, and no platforms. The closest the Conservatives ever came to enunciating a party platform came in a 1853 report of the Minister of Relations during the government of Supreme Director Fruto Chamorro: "The first reason to establish government is to guarantee liberty and property; the second is to unify resources and forces to defend against foreign attack; the third is to promote development and encourage prosperity."[55] At the beginning of a devastating civil war in 1854, the leading figure of the Liberal Party, Máximo Jerez, issued a proclamation of the goals for. which León and the Liberals fought. Although purporting to be a five-point program, the manifesto can be reduced to two: respect for property and defeat of the Conservatives. Since the Conservatives honored the concept of private property, that goal affirmed a similarity, not a difference, between the two parties. In reality, then, the Liberals fought to replace the Conservatives. They waged a war more for power than principle, a truth characterizing most of the bitter, bloody party strife.

Political power conferred economic advantages. The very economic vision that had encouraged independence perpetuated a historic regional rivalry after Spanish control ended. An economic and consequently a political rivalry existed despite commonalities and despite a degree of patriarchal family mobility between city-states.

Devoid of much substance, mind-numbing platitudes usually characterized both Conservative and Liberal political manifestos before the early 1850s. Their positions deserve the pithy political observation on nineteenth-century Brazilian politics by the Visconde de Albuquerque: nothing is so much like a Conservative as a Liberal in power. No leaders emerged to inspire either party until the 1850s, when Máximo Jerez spoke for the Liberals and Fruto Chamorro for the Conservatives. Otherwise the parties identified with the brief tenures of weak executives whose impacts all too often were negative. Chief of state de la Cerda equated "personalities" with "party spirit" in 1825.[56] At the same time the Dutch diplomat Jacobo Haefkerns judged politics to be more personal than philosophical: "One thing is certain: if the parties try to disguise their conduct under the rubric of politics, the true cause of the disorders can be found in personal rancors and hatreds. . . . To personal hatred can be added the local resentments by which the inhabitants of one town consider those of another as their natural enemies. While it is true that these same phenomena and other seeds of discord were present in all associations, in no place were they so strongly expressed as in Nicaragua."[57] A quarter of a century later, the traveler Carl Scherzer likened Nicaraguan politics to "a petty family quarrel" devoid of principle. [58]

Attempts to discover philosophical underpinings of politics suggest nonetheless that most men of the elite had been influenced by the concentric waves of foreign intellectual influence lapping at the shores of isolated Nicaraguan tranquility. At least acquainted with the broad outlines of Enlightenment thought, public men of both parties seemed receptive to its more moderate political and economic orientation. The experience of the United States in winning independence, defining itself politically, and growing economically impressed the Nicaraguans. The more radical ideas of the Enlightenment and the impact of the French Revolution reached Nicaragua in large measure through the new programs of the Guatemalan Liberals during the 1830s. Too radical to be practical in the social structure of nineteenth-century Nicaragua, they startled the self-proclaimed leadership. In short, then, while the politicians drew from the vast well of foreign experiences, all drank sparingly of its waters. Perhaps some of them heeded the advice of their last Spanish governor, Miguel Gonzalez Saravia: "Sublime theories and the quest for perfectibility lead to trouble."[59]

The literate and propertied men active in Nicaraguan politics, whether they claimed to be Liberals or Conservatives, agreed, however tacitly, upon a modest program which can be considered in the broadest terms of the Enlightenment to be vaguely liberal for early nineteenth-century Latin America and most certainly liberal for Nicaragua. They favored a written constitution that limited the powers of the chief executive by requiring him to share them with a legislature and judiciary, permitted greater freedom of trade, advocated public education, and accepted a formal equality of all men before the law. The elites paid at least lip service to some form of Central American union. They lauded progress, by which they meant greater trade and Europeanization accompanied by public order. They advocated a "democracy of reason," which, when decoded, signified that only propertied and literate males could participate, a standard nineteenth-century concept and practice. Throughout the Western world of that time, the few governed in the name of and, supposedly, for the benefit of the many. The *Mentor Nicaragüense* endorsed such a rational basis for government in 1841: "These elections are majestic and as such they ought to be accompanied not by a tumultuous, insolent, and unchecked liberty but by a moderate, rational, and restrained liberty, the true liberty of free and educated patriots and not the type of liberty that degenerates into licentiousness and profligacy."[60] Although the newspaper spoke with a Conservative accent, this statement harmonized, all rhetorical flourishes notwithstanding, with Liberal thought.

Further insight into evolving Nicaraguan political thought came from the prolific pen of Pedro Francisco de la Rocha. He advocated an "enlightened patriotism" in 1847:

It is necessary that this new force, that this double political and harmonizing element follow the natural direction of its constituent elements: order and freedom ought to be the two poles. . . . The simultaneous cooperation of the proletariat and the enlightened [individuals] strengthens political ties and maintains the unity of the State. Civilization educates and property conserves. Hand in hand, both lead to culture and progress. We must move forward with changes that address our needs. . . . The needs are many: to promote commerce, industry, and agriculture, freeing them of the shackles and obstacles that hinder their expansion and improvement; to establish schools to teach the sciences and arts, schools adapted to our own particular circumstances.[61]

His thoughts originated among the tiny intellectual elite; they carried a distinctly Conservative flavor; yet those who bore the party label of Liberal did not really disagree. Whatever the points of economic and political philosophies that might have separated them, the patriarchal elites forged an official nation and government characterized by institutions and ideas heavily influenced by the North Atlantic experience and quite divorced from the local experience of the folk majority.

The elite proudly accepted its role as the transmitter of the European Enlightenment into Nicaragua. Europe shone as the sun of progress, and the elite basked in its rays. Speaking in León, supposedly the Liberal citadel, Juan Eligio de la Rocha, with strong ties to Conservative politics, paid homage in 1865 to the Enlightenment and its influence in Nicaragua. Senõr de la Rocha counted liberty as his nation's major heritage from the Enlightenment.[62] His assertion probably meant political "liberty" from Spanish rule, or the liberties the elites enjoyed, or the liberty to exploit the natural wealth of Nicaragua. At any rate, Liberals and Conservatives alike enjoyed and lauded all those liberties.

The Physiocrat Doctrine extracted from the Enlightenment complemented the vision of prosperity held by the elites of both parties. Physiocracy, "the rule of nature,"encouraged the accumulation of wealth in a laissez-faire fashion through the skillful exploitation of natural resources. The concept that wealth derived from the land favored agriculture; it exalted farmers as the primary producers of wealth. Under this doctrine, the government's duty was to ensure for its citizens the freedom to exploit the natural wealth. Neither Liberal nor Conservative questioned the validity of Physiocracy. Quite the opposite, they eagerly endorsed it, yearning to enter the beckoning European or North American marketplaces with the tropical products—cacao, sugar, cotton, indigo—they boasted Nicaragua could produce in abundance. They opted to exercise what they considered to be their "comparative advantage." Perhaps without verbally indentifying the economic mechanism, they subscribed to the "complementary division of labor." They would trade their foods and raw resources for the enticing consumer items Europe seemed to manufacture so well. That their dreams would result in the nightmares of an export-dominated economy, dependency, and a declining quality of life for the majority was beyond their ability to predict or even to understand. From the more limited perspective of the ruling class, Physiocracy promised to bestow wealth on its members, enhancing their economic well-being if not that of their nation. Despite their theoretical acceptance of Physiocracy, the elites faced monumental barriers to economic prosperity before 1858, not the least of which was political turmoil. Alberto Lanuza has summarized ably and realistically the major economic characteristics of the period as regional rather than national, consisting of subsistence agriculture, the self-sufficiency of the traditional hacienda, a weak market economy, and a lack of direction.[63]

Liberals and Conservatives alike assumed the duty to introduce civilization into their new nation. Civilization clearly signified to them the enlightened Europe of technological advances and comfortable life-styles for the bourgeoisie, increasing wealth, and impressive cities. Defenders of civilization, the men of the elite rushed to the barricades to combat "barbarism." This simplistic reduction of history to a struggle between civilization and barbarism enjoyed tremendous popularity throughout nineteenth-century Latin America. The Argentine intellectual and politician Domingo Faustino Sarmiento composed in 1845 the most cogent statement of the theme in his ever popular *Civilización y Barbarie: Vida de Juan Facundo Quiroga (Life in the Argentine Republic in the Days of the Tyrants: or Civilization and Barbarism)*. The thesis, the progress of the Europeanized city and its duty to introduce civilization into the primitive, barbaric countryside, echoed throughout Latin America. The Nicaraguans also repeated it. In a speech before the Constituent Assembly in 1847, Supreme Director José Guerrero reminded his distinguished audience: "There has been a struggle between the ideas originating in the Enlightenment and the backward customs that tenaciously oppose their implementation."[64] Those "backward customs" referred to neither political party. Nicaragua was in the midst of popular uprisings threatening the property rights of the elites. The Supreme Director as well as the deputies in the Assembly thought they heard the roar of barbarism from the countryside before the gates of their civilized cities.

Political commentators later in the nineteenth century tended to reflect the partisan struggles and particularly the flamboyant rhetoric of the pre-1858 era. Anselmo H. Rivas claimed that the Conservative alone stood for "peace   "[65] With   al pontificating, he contributed to par   ves never hesitated to rebel. They fou   hold power. They advocated peace and   y as the Liberals did. In a more lucid mo   is is that until now there have not been,   rue political parties that struggle for the   Liberal editor and political commentat   il now, the names Conservative and L   agua."[67]

Nonetheless, it was true that from the 1830s onward, rationally or not, liberalism, whatever it meant, was associated with León; conservatism, however that might be defined, was identified with Granada. In seeking to identify political differences between the two parties, Jorge Edwardo Arellano associated the Conservatives with issues favoring political "order" and drawing on the traditions of the colonial past, and the Liberals with issues of political "liberty" and drawing on the ideas of the Enlightenment.[68]

Probably the fundamental political and economic questions awaiting resolution in the first half of the nineteenth century concerned, first, how much of the pattern of the colonial past would be disturbed and how quickly. Over several centuries, that pattern emerged from difficult compromises of Indo-Afro-Spanish life styles, an accommodation between conqueror and conquered, elite and folk, the realty of an impoverished, forgotten backwater province and local hopes for prominence and prosperity. While probably not totally satisfactory to any of the groups, the compromises had worked to a certain point, and all easily recognized the resultant pattern. Too sudden a change, apprehensions of such changes, or even perceptions of change could disturb society. After independence, apprehensions and perceptions far outdistanced actual change, but even so, the combination of independence, apprehension, and perception destabilized society. The second question concerned the political instability of the Spanish monarchy during the opening decades of the nineteenth century, and the resulting inability to resolve the questions of who should govern and how. Those two questions profoundly disturbed the tranquility of these newly independent peoples.

The elites wrote constitutions that were supposed to address those fundamental questions. The historian searching for some meaningful distinction between the Liberals and Conservatives will find discussions of the constitutions the most fruitful field to cultivate. The constitutions of the United Provinces of Central America (1824), the state of Nicaragua (1826), and the nation of Nicaragua (1838) bore the influences of the European Enlightenment and told of the experience of the United States. In one fundamental matter, they paid respect to the landowning patters of the colonial period, which meant that they recognized collective ownership of land, an important protection for the folk community. Though those constitutions existed more in theory than in practice, they served as the litmus test, truly separating the Liberals from the Conservatives.

The Liberals wrote and defended all three as bulwarks against tyranny and protectors of freedom. The Conservatives attacked them and tried twice, in 1848 and again in 1854, to substitute another charter for that of 1838. They blamed the constitutions for Nicaragua's political anarchy. In 1847 Supreme Director José León Sandoval noted, "This melancholy state of our political life is what has determined the Nicaraguan people to reform the Constitution of 1838."[69]

The Conservatives charged the constitutions failed to invest the executive with sufficient power and provided too much to the legislature. Political bickering between the two branches substituted for action. Further, they believed the Constitution of 1838 should have lodged military power in the president rather than in a virtually independent commander-in-chief. They judged the political power to be too diffuse. They advocated greater power for the executive, including the role of commander-in-chief, and a longer term of office, a four-year instead of a two-year administration. Lauding private ownership of land, the Conservatives wanted to remove constitutional protection from collective ownership. Hoping in 1854 to rewrite the constitution in order to centralize power in the executive, Supreme Director Fruto Chamorro informed the Constituent Assembly he convened that the 1838 document provided

> excessive extension of individual guarantees and extreme limitations on public power. . . . This weak and extremely precarious authority in Nicaragua has been the plaything of the parties, a joke for those who would disturb public order, and the taunt of the malcontents. The destruction and prostration of public power stimulates the audacity of the ambitions; it has eroded among us any respect for law and weakened social bonds. . . . We need . . . to strengthen the principle of authority, so deprecated and maligned among us. We can accomplish this end by conferring consistently greater and more power on the executive. Furthermore, it is essential to surround the executive with greater pomp and majesty to command respect and to attract admiration due that high office. [70]

Arriving at that same conclusion, the Chargé d'Affaires of Peru, Felipe Barriga Alvarez, observed, "In general, the Constitution of Nicaragua, desiring to avoid any abuses of power, has curtailed much of the power of the Chief Executive, leaving that office weak."[71]

The pervasive foreign influences over the constitutions of 1826 and 1838 gave the Conservatives the opportunity to criticize them as exotic and ill-suited to Nicaragua. A contemporary critic of the Constitution of 1838 pointed out that it failed to speak to local realities: "Enough of books and models. . . . Nicaragua needs a constitution that reflects our customs, habits, needs, the education of the inhabitants, their heterogeneity, the distances separating them, and a thousand other circumstances that are obvious. Our legislators should honor these realities; they ought to make laws suitable to our nation. The time for experiments is over."[72] Decades later, Anselmo H. Rivas came to the same conclusion. Illusions substituted for reality in his opinion. He awarded the Liberals high marks for "proclaiming fancy theories and ideas borrowed from the French Revolution," but criticized them for not taking "into account the character of our people and the nature of colonial education." He concluded sarcastically, "The result of these ideas was the creation of laws and constitutions appropriate for Plato's Republic."[73] Many twentieth-century Nicaraguan scholars have agreed with the assessment of José Coronel Urtecho that the study of those nineteenth-century constitutions, including those written by the Conservatives, lies more in the realm of the history of ideas than of political realities.[74]

The temptation to borrow ideas born of the experience of other countries and to ignore local realities was not unique to Nicaragua in the nineteenth century. Latin Americans have sought models in England, France, the United States, and the Soviet Union, and even at the end of the twentieth century flirt with the economic models of Taiwan, South Korea, and Japan. Leaders who were bold or confident enough to be original were not only ignored but ridiculed. The examples of Guatemala under Rafael Carrera, 1839–1865, and Paraguay under José Gaspar Rodríguez de Francia, 1814–1840, two nations that looked inward to resolve the perplexing problems faced by all the new nations, were rare indeed in nineteenth-century Latin America. The Europeanized intellectuals scorned both experiments as barbarian. Curiously, one political essay published in Nicaragua's *Registro Oficial* in 1847, during a Conservative administration, praised President Carrera, attributing his success and Guatemala's well-being to a highly centralized government rooted in local realities rather than in European theories.[75] The temptations to ape Northern Europe and the United States are easily explained. The elites rejected a Spain that seemed backward to them, a Spain that had retarded, in their view, their progress. Through books, conversations, imported goods, and visits, they had been exposed to the remarkable progress of Europe north of the Pyrenees. They admired, envied the progress. Unable to replicate it, they contented themselves by cloaking their newly formed governments with the exotic fabric of foreign constitutions and crowning them with a brilliant diadem of European philosophy. Because those laws and thoughts had created the marvels of Europe, they might work their magic in the Americas, too.

Under the awesome masquerade existed some very basic institutions inherited from a long colonial past. Those institutions—the Church, the land ownership patterns, the patriarchal family, the concentration of economic and political power in the hands of a few, the privileges and benefits accruing to the socially favored—passed into the national period virtually unaltered and seemingly unalterable. Looking at the remarkable continuity of those institutions, it is easy to concur with the conclusion of Nicaraguan historian Amaru Barahona: "Independence itself was nothing more than a proclamation devoid of any effective content."[76] The elites were inextricably linked to those institutions; they drew their satisfactory life style from them. No matter what rhetoric they might mouth, they were not about to divest themselves of their privileges. They did not. In all fairness, however, independence did bring about significant changes in the labor systems. The new governments abolished Black slavery and terminated Indian tribute. The latter measure reduced an already tenuous labor supply.

For good or for bad, a major institution of the colonial past was gone: the crown. In rejecting the monarchy, independence created a vast political vacuum. Into it rushed the winds of political conflict. And in Nicaragua, possibly more so than in any other nation in the New World, those winds blew with gale force. The first challenge to nation-building in Nicaragua was to resolve the political conflict over who would rule and how, extremely difficult questions for people whose practical experiences with "genetic" governance, the monarchy, far outweighed their knowledge of and experience with contractual governance, the republic.

Not only did a wide cultural gulf separate the patriarchal elite from the folk, but the general population itself broke up laterally into myriad local societies, all similar but all separate. Historically, the Indians, who vastly outnumbered the patriarchal elites, professed more loyalty to the local community than to the more abstract Spanish empire. They had sworn allegiance to a distant king and nominally accepted Roman Catholicism; but their life-styles, for the most part, were their own, unique amalgamations of Spanish, African, and Indian—the dominant—contributions. The Indians looked inward to the community. After independence they continued to maintain that loyalty to the community, and seemed indifferent to an abstract national entity, Nicaragua. They did not possess nor did they develop much national consciousness, an awareness of belonging to a nation combined with the idea that such a membership was desirable. From their point of view, the nation offered them nothing, the community everything. Consequently, the Indians shared none of the elite's vision of a nation-state, or even of the city-state, and of expanded commerce. They preferred to adhere to their own value system, to enjoy their own cultural traditions, and to grow their subsistence crops with just enough surplus for the local market. Unlike their counterparts in many other regions of Latin America, they often succeeded in avoiding forced labor on haciendas and plantations. Labor, wage or coerced, was hard to find in Nicaragua, a reality that challenged plans for an export economy.

The ruling class drew from a European experience of which the people had only the vaguest, if any, knowledge. One contemporary Nicaraguan estimated that at the time of independence only one person in a thousand knew how to read and write; only one in a hundred understood the doctrines of Roman Catholicism and the rest hopelessly confused it with superstitious beliefs; most of the population did not speak Spanish; and few had even the most elementary knowledge of political life and were unable to understand the words fatherland, constitution, laws, public treasury, legislature, etc. Discussions of equality, like debates over civil rights and responsibilities, aroused more incredulity than enthusiasm. Associating public authority with demands, punishments, taxes, and military service, the vast majority harbored more fear than respect for governments.[77]

Nicaragua had a multiethnic and multiracial population. In 1823, Miguel González Saravia estimated that two-fifths of the population was Indian; more than two-fifths, ladino; and less than one-fifth, European.[78] A quarter of a century later, putting the total population at approximately 300,000, E. G. Squier divided it into 18,000 Blacks, 30,000 Europeans, 96,000 Indians, and 156,000 mixed, largely ladinos.[79] Paul Levy thought the composition of the population in 1870 was 0.5 percent Black, 4.5 percent European, 40 percent ladino, and 55 percent Indian.[80] These "statistics" are consistent only in estimating a small number of Europeans and a large number of Indians, with a very high index of the mixing of the two. The number of Blacks in the more populous Pacific coast was small. African slavery had never been a significant institution in Nicaragua.[81]

Not all of the Europeans were members of the patriarchal elite, although all of them seemed to harbor pretensions to that position. From the creoles came most of the landowners, merchants, and professionals. Most of them lived in towns or cities. Most of the ladinos adopted or were in the process of adopting European ideas and customs. They preferred their European over their Indian heritage. Independence conferred on them a greater social flexibility. They challenged the Indians for land and the patriarchs for position. Some of the ladinos, those more distant from León and Granada, lived in their own folk communities whose cultures mediated in varying degrees Indian and European contributions.

Within the principally Indian communities, the traditional styles of life of pre-Columbian origins predominated. The Indians rarely accepted full Europeanization, although some cases have been identified. Tomás Ruiz, an Indian born in Chinandega in 1777, was one of those exceptional cases. Under the patronage of Bishop Juan Félix de Villegas, he studied in the seminaries of León and Guatemala City. After his ordination, he earned degrees in canon and civil law and taught at the University of San Carlos in Guatemala City and the University of León. The experience at San Carlos exposed the young priest to the ideas of the Enlightenment. Spanish officials repeatedly refused to promote him to higher Church offices, probably more because of his Indian blood than because of his exposure to the Enlightenment. Caught up in the political tumult of the second decade of the nineteenth century, Ruiz figured as one of the early leaders in both the Central American and Nicaraguan independence movements, for which he spent six years in prison. He died in 1819 and remains a fascinating example of the integration of an Indian into the European institutions. [82]

The extremes of European and Indian institutions defined and perpetuated two differing social patterns, one patriarchal with strong neocapitalist preferences, and the other folk and communal. During the long colonial period and throughout the first half-century of Nicaraguan independence they coexisted, however uneasily. Those two patterns defined the behavior, values, and "world view" of nearly all the Nicaraguans. They also divided society.

No one perceived the horizontal division of Nicaraguan society better than George Byam, who resided there in 1839 and 1840. Most of the time he spent living in the countryside among the folk. He cogently described the dual society. The turbulence of politics absorbed the attention and activity of the few, generally the city dwellers. The majority, "the quiet steady demeanour of the great mass of the people,"stood apart from the turmoil. [83] "In truth, these revolutions, like many other agitations, are invariably got up for the personal profit of a few, and at the expense of the great majority." [84] Byam saluted "the dwellers in the woods and forests; generally honest and inoffensive, but bold and hardy, they seem to care as little for revolutions as revolutions do for them. 'Remote from cities,' they lead a rather uncertain, precarious life, but, with a little hard work for a short time in the year, they can assure subsistence to their families. An acre of forest land, cleared, burnt, and fenced, is sure to produce an abundant crop of maize; and if a few join together in felling and fencing . . . the work is better and quicker done, and the produce divided." [85] He concluded that such a rural Nicaragua "is altogether . . . superior to the townspeople, both physically and morally." [86]

Divisions between the city-states and among the populations shaped nineteenth-century Nicaraguan history. They provoked struggle. The elite of León and Granada fought each other to exercise political power. The elites and folk struggled over the way and degree that power would be exercised. When the folk perceived elite incursion into or threats to their life style, they physically resisted; it proved difficult to coerce them to work, for example. Historians have not yet fully considered the consequences of the social tensions between the folk and the patriarchs.

The ideological differences separating the Liberals and Conservatives—and they appear less than previously claimed—have been identified with regional rivalry: Granada's challenge to León. The struggles of the late colonial period solidified the regional rivalries; the conflicts of the early independence period strengthened the regional solidarity. One supreme director, Fruto Chamorro, succinctly summed up Nicaragua's dynamic: "The struggles in reality were between the East [Granada] and the West [León] for predominance."[87] To the victor went whatever power and prerogatives the impoverished nation afforded.

The local elites understood that the state apparatus could be used for their own benefit to distribute privileges, lands, jobs, prestige, and authority. It conferred some power on them. At any rate, for all its many and great weaknesses, the state apparatus was a rich resource in a poor nation. Thus the spoils of politics held a mighty attraction.

Once in office, the supreme directors promptly, and correctly, blamed "localism" as the major source of unrest and, consequently, of their inability to govern. Typically, José León Sandoval spoke in 1847 of "Restless men who, not content with the order of things now established, encourage the spirit of localism which blinds those who succumb to it and does not let them see the abyss into which they are about to plunge."[88] A ministerial report in 1853 lamented, "Nothing exists but our misfortune. Our blind experience encourages miserable caudillos and localism, in which one man fights another, one family opposes another, one town attacks another, all with such a variety of different interests that we will never be able to form a state."[89] Unwilling to accept responsibility for the problem, the party in power inevitably blamed the other party. While some of Nicaragua's outstanding historians during the last century correctly diagnosed the source of political chaos as the rivalry of the two major cities, they did not hide their own sympathies for one or the other.[90] Contemporary historians tend to be more sweeping in their analysis. Humberto Belli writes, "The reality of a traditional society fragmented by local loyalties condemned to failure the efforts to create a Nation-State characterized by representative democracy."[91] During the period 1821–1857 no dominant national elite replaced the competing local oligarchs.

The ordinary people, as Byam astutely observed, contributed minimally to the formal process of nation-building, if it is possible to describe the anarchy of the period as such. Pompous generals from León and Granada dragooned many to serve in the armies. All too often the peasants and urban workers gave their lives for causes that mystified them. When they could, those folk preferred to turn away from the strife that characterized the elitist formation of national Nicaragua.

Meanwhile, despite common goals favoring trade and economic prosperity, Europeanization and progress, and the rule of order and reason, the elites failed to impose peace, order, and effective governance. Surveying the history of his country during the middle of the nineteenth century, Belli concluded, "The nation did not exist either structurally or psychologically."[92]

Anarchy

Disturbed by the political tumult at mid-century, the Conservative intellectual Pedro Francisco de la Rocha concluded, "[Our politics] defy all social sense. By arming the people against each other, they bring to the surface the worst aspects of society. They give license to people to kill each other. Unbridled liberty and absolute equality have enslaved the Fatherland. . . . Our existence as a nation is threatened; the bases of society are eroding. The absolute independence of these states has given rise to anarchy."[93] If anarchy can be defined as the condition of lawlessness and political disorder due to the absence of effective government, then de la Rocha concluded correctly. The authority of the government barely reached beyond the city in which the officials resided. Carl Scherzer, traveling in Nicaragua, experienced that reality. He carried a letter of recommendation from the supreme director. To his amazement, the German found it to be worthless. When a puzzled Scherzer "asked the Prefect of Matagalpa whether the President's letter of recommendation did not make every other unnecessary, he answered, "'Ah! the President is a long way off. The nearest authority is always the best!'"[94] Elusive political power had diffused—or even disappeared.

Anarchy characterized Nicaragua from the very late colonial period until the mid-1850s, while in much of the rest of Latin America during the first half-century after independence strong political leaders, the *caudillos*, emerged to impose order and to govern imperiously, even if temporarily. Nicaragua experienced no such leadership before 1858.

Like the rest of Latin America, Nicaragua enjoyed little preparation for nationhood. Three hundred years of monarchy enbodied the genetic nature and transfer of power, leaving the people ignorant of the contractual basis for power for which independence opted. The centralization of power notable in the colonial experience of Mexico or Peru or in the late colonial experience of Brazil and Argentina was weak in Central America and especially so in Nicaragua. The crown did little more than minimize rivalries between León and Granada and maintain order. A weak colonial government signified low imperial demand for products from the Province of Nicaragua. Isolation and neglect resulted from such disinterest. Consequently, Spanish institutions rested lightly upon the colony, despite the intentions of the Bourbon kings of the eighteenth century to centralize, modernize, and, in general, improve the efficiency of the bureaucracy.

Perhaps partly because of their long isolation, doubtless because of their suspicions of the Guatemalan merchants as avaricious, the local notables identified with the province and later the state and then the nation of Nicaragua, rather than with the vast, and to them amorphous, Spanish empire or a Central America beholden to Guatemala. The economic vision of a transisthmian route, commerce, and agrarian exports guided the otherwise fractious patriarchal elites through destructive decades as they fumbled to forge the Nicaraguan nation. The bitter rivalry between Granada and León, never prompted either to advocate secession. They fought each other to dominate the entire territory, not to balkanize it.

Yet disunity among the patriarchal elites and between them and the folk remained the historical reality. As one major consequence, it deprived Nicaragua of the bureaucratic infrastructure and deference to unity needed to create the modern, Europeanized nation-state idealized by the patriarchs. The *Rejistro Oficial* blamed disunity on the lack of "a national spirit," while de la Rocha lamented that "The people are deprived of any spirit of Nationalism, which is the soul of any State."[95]

De la Rocha, whether he realized it or not, shared concerns with a distant contemporary, John Stuart Mill. Both reflected and wrote on the nature of government and nationality. Although Mill never mentioned Nicaragua, some of what he had to say applied to the situation there. Mill defined the nation as a "union among people of common sympathies which do not exist between them and any others—which make them cooperate with each other more willingly than with other people."[96] Mill particularly warned that strong local loyalties prevented effective government or even the formation of the nation.[97] That warning was appropriate for Nicaragua. The "first lesson of civilization" in his judgment was obedience, and to teach obedience, he conceded, some situations called for a strong leader.[98] "The sentiment of nationality," discipline, obedience, and authority were necessary to consolidate the nation, according to Mill. De la Rocha had reached the same conclusions in 1847, as he wrestled with the question of the formation of a nation-state in Nicaragua.[99]

The concept of the nation as a defined geographical unit with an effective government mutually agreed upon by at least a part of the governed was vague and contrary to the experience of the Nicaraguans. They had never experimented with political contracts until the 1820s. At most, a small . . . and always sharply divided . . . elite imposed one or more such contracts of their own devising, but beholden to the ideas of the European Enlightenment, on an unsuspecting population. The legitimacy of such a compact depended on the ability of the elites to force its acceptance or gain public acquiescence in it. Yet the elites themselves remained dubious about the type of state they had created or wanted to create. Divisions and doubts hindered their ability to impose the contract, to gain recognition of the state, and to unify the nation. None of those conditions encouraged nation building. De La Rocha argued that neither the nation nor the state existed and, therefore, anarchy was inevitable.[100]

The anonymous but ubiquitous editorial writer S. C. dipped his pen into the inkwell of sarcasm to write a scathing critique of Nicaraguan institutions in the mid-1840s. More than unsuitable, they were a disaster since they bred anarchy. S. C. concluded that "ten or twelve" men with some knowledge, however imperfect, of history and politics read about what happened elsewhere and decided that Central America should declare its independence. The very word awoke dreams in them. They believed that they spoke for all Central Americans or at least that all Central Americans thought as they did. "They felt themselves able to govern and be governed by means of a political system created by other men for other countries which operated under incomparably different circumstances." Other Central Americans, their disciples, also numbering ten or twelve, followed those leaders blindly. Such was the manner by which a democratic republic emerged on the basis of "absurd and extravagant abstractions." People ignorant of democracy and republics elected equally unqualified men to govern them:

In this manner, our leaders were selected: he who knew nothing about legislating was to govern in a political system that he did not even understand;

he who did not know how to count was to manage the public finances, and what is more to improve them; he who did not even know his neighbors in the next village was to direct our foreign relations; he who did not know how to read and write was to sit as judge and pass judgment on others; he who knew nothing about armies and only the river that passed by his town was to arrange for armies and navies; he who barely was able to make local crafts and simple artifacts was expected to compete with the industrial capacity of the advanced nations. In short, the ignorant were called to deliberate and the impotent to command and to create. One can easily understand the results.

In the National Congress as well as in the assemblies of the respective States, the seeds of discord planted by the elections grew. Bad laws were passed; new governmental plans were discussed; there was opposition, cliques, fanatical parties. They resorted to violence, providing yet another kind of lesson for the people. The rival politicians told the people what and whom they should hate; they told them that it was necessary to destroy by armed force; to imprison, to exile, and to execute their own men. Learning their lessons, the people expressed hatred and served as the instrument to destroy, to imprison, to exile, and to assassinate without knowing really why or to what end. They told the people that they had enemies and that to defeat them it would be necessary to lay waste the fields, to burn houses, and once having defeated that enemy to place him outside the protection of the law, to rob and murder him, without understanding why and for what purpose. Enlightened by such excellent lessons, the people created their own strong ambitions. They interpreted in the most absurd and extravagant way their social rights and duties. That educated, active, and insensitive group which had taken charge of politics was unable to provide positive examples. Quite the contrary, they set negative patterns. Obscure demagogues appeared; they thrived on disorder. Morality was forgotten. Robbery, theft, fraud, and trickery substituted for work and industry. Anarchy reigned from its throne of chaos. [101]

S.C. offered one of the most pessimistic views of the failure of the nation-building process.

Before 1858, the cannons of war seldom fell silent long enough to provide the peace Nicaraguans required to engage in nation-building. Foreign interventions, first, by the English and then the North Americans, menaced the newly independent Nicaraguans, and they quite rightly judged those threats as the most insidious. The foreigners wanted territory; William Walker would have obliterated the nation. Regional Central American wars erupted with numbing frequency. They threatened governments, not nations. More often than not, they tipped the scales in favor of one side or the other in the almost constant local civil wars. The only threat capable of galvanizing León and Granada into common action prior to 1856 appeared to be popular uprisings. Those escalated in the late 1840s, frightened the patriarchs, and brought them together, at least momentarily, in the effort to defeat the challenge from below. The multiple levels of war created, in the words of José D. Gámez, "an anarchical and divided country whose soil ran red with the blood of its sons."[102] United States Minister John Hill Wheeler compared the chaos of Nicaragua to the Scotland of Macbeth, "This lovely country . . . is devastated by the furious passion of man. Like Ross of Scotland, Nicaragua may say:

> Alas, poor country,
> Almost afraid to know itself. It cannot
> Be call'd mother, but our grave: where nothing
> But who knows nothing is once seen to smile,
> Where sighs, and groans, and shrieks that rent the air
> Are made.[103]

Although less literary in his conclusion, Carl Scherzer concurred with Wheeler: "the elements of revolution and anarchy appear as inexhaustible as the combustible matter beneath its volcanic soil."[104]

Economic stagnation, vertical and horizontal social divisions, the resultant political turmoil, and war frustrated the formation of a nation-state. Lacking political experience and consensus, the elites struggled to seize and exercise power. Divided, they failed to maintain law and order. To the contrary, through their civil wars they contributed to their erosion, and hence served as active agents of anarchy. Supreme Director José León Sandoval warned, "Far from realizing the great destiny Nature intended for it, Nicaragua goes backward, headed toward its own destruction."[105]

The search for the causes of anarchy has evoked a variety of responses from and not a few debates among Nicaraguans. The causes most frequently mentioned center on Nicaragua's lack of preparation for independence, the novelty of the republican experience, the virulent "localism," the selfish politicians or demagogues, party strife, economic backwardness, the struggle of civilization against barbarism, a Nicaraguan propensity for violence, and class conflicts.

The attempt to explain the long period of anarchy, 1821–1857, ignited a lively historical debate. Traditional historiography regards the centuries of colonial rule as tranquil, in sharp contrast with the turmoil of independence and subsequent anarchy. Both José Coronel Urtecho and Pablo Antonio Cuadra elegantly idealized the colonial past, emphasizing what they regarded as its positive characteristics. Cuadra's classic collection of interpretive essays, *El Nicaragüense* (The Nicaraguan), somewhat reminiscent of the more famous study of colonial Brazil, *The Masters and the Slaves* by Gilberto Freyre, emphasized a "dialogue" between the Spaniards and the Indians over the course of nearly three hundred somewhat idylic years. From that "dialogue" emerged the Nicaraguan, the blend of two cultures. In his *Reflexiones sobre la Historia de Nicaragua* (Reflections on the History of Nicaragua), Coronel Urtecho comes to a similar conclusion. Peace and order reigned. People apparently accepted their given place in society. The Church mediated any disputes that arose. Their pages project an ideal society, a past lamentably lost.[106] To anyone subscribing to the thesis of a harmonious colonial society, the decades after 1811 came as a shock. Without warning, horizontal and vertical divisions of society appear. The abrupt change from tranquility to anarchy, harmony to hate, peace to war, order to chaos begs explanation.

In searching for the explanation, some scholars question these assumptions of a somnolent colonial society. Jaime Wheelock Román, Ileana Rodríguez, and Rodolfo Cardenal, among others, believe violence, not dialogue, characterized that past.[107] The Indians received the Spanish conquerors with arrows. The Spaniards responded with cannon fire. Slavery and rebellion were the dialogue of the sixteenth century. If in 1522 there were a half-million Indians in the area now designated Nicaragua, less than 12,000 remained a quarter of a century later. The first bishop, Antonio Valdivieso, was murdered because he tried to defend the Indians. Rebellions and buccaneer raids pepper the past. Jaime Wheelock claims, "Spanish colonialism in Nicaragua did not know one moment of peace."[108] The revisionists find that the date 1821 marks no magical change in behavior. The violence characterizing the colonial past continued to dominate the national period, although the monarchy may well have checked some of it, an inhibition the partisans of León or Granada did not experience after the separation from Spain. Nor does Juan Carlos Solórzano Fonseca judge 1821 to be a radical break with the past. He explains the chaos of the nineteenth century as a natural consequence of a failure to deal with societal changes that had been occurring throughout the eighteenth. Among such changes, he cites the growing population in which the ladino replaced the Indian as a new majority, the greater concentration of land in the hands of the patriarchs, and the deepening resentment of the control exerted by Guatemalan merchants and bureaucrats.[109] Perhaps these modern revisionists take their cue from the perceptive Pedro Francisco de la Rocha, who, mired in the anarchy of the 1840s, saw its origins in the Spanish colonial system, an unusual view for a conservative intellectual in Latin America. A "vicious colonial regime" subjugated Nicaragua for the good of Spain, he wrote. "We were weighed down by the oppressive yoke of social and political backwardness." An independent Nicaragua struggled to overcome that imposed backwardness.[110]

The revisionists' emphasis on the violence of the colonial period places the anarchy of the early national period into a broader context. They suggest an historical continuity denied by the traditional historiography. Conquest and rebellion, opposites that had not been reconciled, took on their nineteenth-century forms: the struggle of León and Granada for power and the rebellion of the folk against the patriarchs to prevent further encroachments into their societies.

Contrary positions taken by the two preeminent cities on the questions involving independence eventually ignited the tinder of municipal rivalry into the fires of civil wars. They ravaged Nicaragua in the 1820s. At one time in 1823 and 1824, four different governments located in León, Granada, Managua, and El Viejo claimed legitimacy, vivid testimony to the lack of political unity attending the emergence of independent Nicaragua.

León bore the brunt of the wars. Armies professing Conservative allegiances lay siege for four months to the former colonial and then state capital in 1824. Eventually they triumphed and celebrated their victory by sacking the city. One eyewitness to the devastation later recalled:

> Look, I was only twelve years old, and my mother and all the members of the family had hastily barricaded ourselves in the ruins of our once lovely home. Shut up in our hideaway, we could hear the most fearful noises. These were not hallucinations but reality. The sounds of bugles ordered the attack; the shouts of the officers in command rang out; the wounded screamed in pain; those feeling the bayonet or sword yelled for mercy; desperate cries from women echoed; flames crackled; buildings collapsed. . . . Those nights tormented all the people of León.[111]

Robert Glasgow Dunlop reported that the siege and sacking had reduced the city, "formerly one of the finest in the new world," to rubble.[112] After that civil war, the political labels Liberal and Conservative were applied respectively to León and Granada.[113] No matter how murky they might have been, those political associations remain a distinctive part of Nicaraguan history or, some might suggest, lore.

The federal government of the United Provinces of Central America intervened frequently in an effort to pacify the turbulent state. It dispatched José Milla in January of 1824, and when he failed, General Manuel Arzu in September. He enjoyed no greater success than his predecessor. General Manuel José Arce arrived with an army in early 1825 to impose a fleeting peace. In April of that year, the State Constituent Assembly elected Manuel Antonio de la Cerda as the chief of state and Juan Argüello as the vice-chief. De la Cerda resigned a few months later, and relations between him and Argüello deteriorated into a long, bitter civil war that ended with the public execution of de la Cerda in late 1828.

As preludes, first the destruction of León and then the war of Cerda and Argüello rang up the curtain on the tragedy of anarchy that would be acted out on the Nicaraguan stage for more than three decades. A study by José Coronel Urtecho reveals that between 1821 and 1857 twenty-five years of anarchy and civil war interlaced with twelve of peace, truce, or exhaustion: 1821, 1822, 1823, 1826, 1831, 1835, 1836, 1840, 1841, 1843, 1847, and 1852.[114] During the entire period, Nicaragua's nomadic government wandered from León to Granada to Masaya to Chinandega to Rivas, and to Managua.[115] No other government in Latin America moved so frequently. Its peripatetic nature bespoke its lack of authority as well as the pervasive localism.[116]

Disputes over where it should sit repeatedly raised political tensions, even ignited armed struggles.[117] At certain periods, chiefs of state came and went with bewildering rapidity. In 1849, three different men held the office of supreme director and in 1851, four. In total for the period between 1825 and 1854, twenty-five chief executives tried to govern.[118]

In late 1829, the new Liberal president of Central America, General Francisco Morazán dispatched the Honduran Dionisio Herrera to León to pacify the state and to assure Liberal ascendancy there. Entering Nicaragua in April of 1830, Herrera announced his intentions: "I have been sent to you by the Supreme Federal Government to conciliate your quarrels, to pacify the State, to organize it, to reestablish order and the government of law, to end your misfortunes, and to stop civil war, the cause of all your troubles."[119] Most Nicaraguans welcomed his words. They believed, like Agustín Vijil, that "only the presence of Señor Herrera could bring the benefits of peace and harmony to Nicaragua."[120] The federal government had set an impossible agenda for Herrera. An astute executive, he minimized but did not eliminate armed conflict. A resurgence of violence in 1833 caused *La Opinión Pública*, in support of Herrera, to denounce civil war as "the monster that attacks and devours" and "contrary to the teaching of our Holy Religion."[121] Before Herrera left at the end of 1833, he strengthened the position of the Nicaraguan Liberals, but he bequeathed no legacy of peace. Perhaps the major consequence of his administration was the political domination León and the Liberals enjoyed for a decade and a half, 1830–1845.

As the federal union disintegrated, León and the Liberals ushered Nicaragua into its national independence, unencumbered by any ties or responsibilities to the rest of Central America. On April 30, 1838, a constituent assembly declared Nicaragua to be free, independent, and sovereign. Liberals and Conservatives, León and Granada, welcomed the new status.[122] In November, the assembly promulgated a constitution that showered liberties on the inhabitants; in keeping with this spirit, its primary goal was to preclude any dictatorial government, military or civilian. To achieve that noble end, the Constitution of 1838 carefully separated the powers of government, strengthening the legislature at the expense of the executive and making the commander of the army as independent as possible from the executive. Designated the supreme director, the executive was limited to a two-year term. The constitution was significant for a number of reasons, possibly foremost of which was its ability to separate the Liberals from the Conservatives. Much of the political history between 1838 and 1858 centered on the Liberals' defense of the document and the Conservatives' efforts to replace it.[123] Five successive senators temporarily occupied the executive office until the elections of March 1841 selected Pablo Buitrago of León as the first supreme director.

A particularly brutal civil war in late 1844 climaxed with the second sacking of León in January 1845. León had become involved in the broader Central American struggle between the Liberals and the Conservatives. By the mid-1840s, the isthmian political pendulum had swung to the side of the Conservatives. Nicaragua remained the only nation governed by the Liberals. The Conservative president of El Salvador, General Franciso Malespín, allied with Honduras invaded Nicaragua to capture exiles who supported the former Liberal president of the defunct United Provinces of Central America, Francisco Morazán. Granada saw in those events its own opportunity to check the dominance of León. Together with the towns of Managua and Rivas, Granada set up a provisional government and dispatched troops to join with those of El Salvador and Honduras in siege and then in the virtual destruction of León, a holocaust equal to that of 1824. Granada, thanks to outside help, checked the power of its rival and opened the door to political power.

In early 1845, on the ruins of León, Granada succeeded in electing its candidate, José León Sandoval, to the directorship, the first Conservative to hold the executive post. Like all occupants of that office, Sandoval belonged to the political and economic elite. In Granada, he frequented "La Tertulia," an exclusive, informal, and regular gathering of a handful of civic leaders who made the city's political decisions. Sandoval's enterprises combined commerce and agriculture. He owned a shipping business on the San Juan River, raised cattle, and grew a variety of products for the market. His cacao hacienda on the eastern shores of Lake Nicaragua was reputed to be immense. Sandoval's vision of the future of the country did not differ much from that of his Leonese peers, but of course he had a different place of residence, and in the Nicaragua of the nineteenth century residence was everything.[124]

Sandoval experienced the same problems as his Liberal predecessors in imposing authority. Order eluded him. In a speech before the Legislative Assembly in 1846, its president, Norberto Ramírez, reiterated the political concerns that had long troubled Nicaragua: "The absence of national order and the false pleasures of exaggerated freedom have broken all the threads of the fabric of unity, even within families, and have produced the most complete and disastrous anarchy. Each wants to enjoy a liberty without restrictions; none wants to obey the law or the authorities; and each wants to be the tyrant over the others. This behavior will destroy everything."[125] At the same time, one of the official newspapers complained there were not enough well-educated citizens to fill all the government positions properly.[126] The Conservatives, like the Liberals, were finding Nicaragua impossible to govern.

Supreme Director Sandoval promptly moved the capital from León to the east: Granada and Masaya. The Granadans obviously approved; the Leonese objected. Increasingly, politicians advocated a permanent capital for the nation midway between León and Granada. With a neutral city as the capital, they hoped to dampen the fires of rivalry which all recognized as a major impediment to national unity and the formation of the nation-state. Some thought of Managua, approximately halfway between the rivals, as the logical location for the capital. The government raised the status of Managua to the dignity of a city in 1846.

One innovation that suggests the growing complexity of government was that Sandoval replaced the general minister who assisted the supreme director with a cabinet of three: war, treasury, and internal and external relations. Inevitably, that first Conservative supreme director summoned a constituent assembly to write a new constitution, but it failed to complete its task during his administration. His successor, José Guerrero, more Liberal than Conservative in his inclinations, did not pursue the matter. He never promulgated the constitution the assembly proffered in 1848.

The Conservatives did not return to power until 1851, with José Laureano Pineda as supreme director. Under his administration Managua became, at least in name, the new and permanent capital in 1852. The government thus hoped to radiate impartiality, to distance itself both physically and figuratively from the dominant city-states.

The tight and important elections of 1853 demonstrated how the indirect electoral system worked. Propertied males selected 490 electors. Each elector cast two votes, one of which had to be for a candidate living outside his district. Table 1 shows the plethora of candidates of whom only five showed any chance of winning. The close election failed to award a majority to either the Liberal candidate from León, Francisco Castellón, or the Conservative from Granada, Fruto Chamorro. Since none received a majority, the legislature had to elect one from the top three.[127] It invested the executive power in the hands of the Conservative ideologue Fruto Chamorro. Most Nicaraguans viewed his election as the "definitive victory" of Granada over León.[128]

Born in Guatemala in 1806, Fruto Chamorro was an illegitimate son of a prominent Nicaraguan. As a young man he studied philosophy, law, and mathematics at the university of San Carlos. Upon the death of his father, the widow called the son to Granada to take charge of the extensive family estates and businesses. Young Fruto succeeded in revitalizing the family economy and entered politics in 1836 as a deputy in the Nicaraguan state legislature. Thereafter, politics and public life absorbed most of his time. Among other positions, he served as a deputy in the constituent assemblies of 1838 and 1848, a senator (1839–1842), president of the Department of the Oriente Board of Education (1843), a delegate to the confederation of El Salvador, Honduras, and Nicaragua (1844), the prefect and military governor of the Department of the Oriente (1845; 1849–1851), Minister of the Treasury in the Sandoval government (1845–1847), and Minister of War (1851). In 1841–42 he edited an extremely important early newspaper, the *Mentor Nicaragüense*, whose motto read, "We were not born just to serve ourselves but also to serve the Fatherland." The newspaper denounced Nicaraguan elections as exercises in "disorder."[129] It often boasted of the great future in store for Nicaragua: "By every circumstance, this people is called, sooner or later, to serve as the great

Table I. Electoral Districts and Their Votes for Supreme Director, 1853

Candidate	León	Chinandega	N. Segovia	District Matagalpa	Rivas	Masaya	Jinotepe	Granada	Total
Fruto Chamorro			42	44	42	53	55	60	296
Francisco Castellón	83	49	14	1	39	6		1	193
Juan J. Ruíz					51	53	54	33	191
José Sacaza	3	49	48	46			1	10	157
Rosalio Cortéz	65					5			70
José M. Hurtado					12			1	13
Pedro Aguirre	10								10
Perfecto Altamirano				1				6	7
Liberato Abarca								7	7
Juan Guerra					6				6
Hermenejildo Zepeda			4						4
Pío Bolaños				3					3
Carlos Bolaños	3								3
Policarpo Zelaya					3				3
Pedro Zeledón					1	1			2
Ramón Morales	1							1	2
Ponciano Corral					2				2
Narciso Chavarría				1				1	2
Julio Jeres				2					2
Francisco Guerra					1				1
Gilberto Gallar					1				1
Pedro Hurtado					1				1
Clemente Santos				1					1
José León Sandoval	1								1
Ubaldo Palma					1				1
Gregorio Bolaños				1					1
Double votes cast	166	98	108	100	160	118	110	120	980
Electors participating	83	49	54	50	80	59	55	60	490

Source: Gaceta Oficial de Nicaragua (Granada) April 30, 1853.

merchant not just for this continent but for the entire world."[130] Chamorro's political philosophy favored a strong central government dominated by the executive as the only way to establish peace and order in Nicaragua: "It is necessary to strengthen the principle of authority so shaken and scorned among us. This goal can be accomplished by conferring on the executive greater power, authority, and consistency." This belief guided him throughout nearly two decades of politics.[131] In his comfortable home in Granada, Chamorro and his family hosted for many years a lively political *tertulia*, one of those informal parlor gatherings that combined social conviviality with political and intellectual discussions. Nicaraguans considered the Chamorro tertulia as the nucleus of the Conservative Party.

The short, pudgy, bald Chamorro, a man described as "conscious of his position and ability . . . withal quite prepossessing," assumed office during a rare hiatus of peace and prosperity, as unusual as it was welcome in the age of anarchy.[132] His inauguration, however, heightened political tensions. He went at once to the topic that interested him most: "I understand that my foremost duty is to maintain order, as this is the primary objective of society and the only way it can assure the happiness and prosperity of its citizens, I will try with all the power you have placed in my hands to fulfill that duty, to fulfill it in such a way that the Nicaraguan people will not suffer the harm caused by the disturbance of order. I will follow the wise rule of law that prescribes preventing the crime rather than the curing of it."[133] How he planned to prevent disorder before it happened intrigued the Nicaraguans. The supreme director gave no clue as to his methods. His pledge to enforce order, decidedly the major objective he set for himself, raised both expectations and apprehensions. His Liberal foes interpreted "the conservation of order" as a code phrase meaning the greater centralization of power in Granada.[134]

The most ideologically inclined executive to take office in the republic up to that date, Charmorro had frequently expressed his convictions. People expected him to infuse them into governance. He did not disappoint them. Consistently, he had voiced his opposition to the Constitution of 1838 and his desire to promulgate a new one. That obsession worried some of his compatriots. It could trigger trouble. Although an able and intelligent man, in some respects he lacked the light hand of political savvy. His uncompromising determination as Minister of the Treasury in 1845 to tax and regulate *aguardiente* had set in motion the popular rebellions that shook the country for nearly four years.

Chamorro's first weeks in office looked promising for agriculture, business, and commerce. He prepared laws to encourage road building, and not coincidentally, three petitions to encourage transportation had come from merchants in León and Granada, demonstrating a unity of economic interests where political harmony was missing. They urged the construction of roads but particularly favored the establishment of scheduled steamship service among the Central American ports for purposes of trade.[135] A law issued on May 5, 1853, created the Consulado de Comercio "to protect and encourage all forms of commerce." Its principal objectives included the construction of custom houses and wharfs, the improvement of ports and roads, and the promotion of commerce. The supreme director promulgated a law on May 9 to encourage coffee culture by offering monetary rewards to anyone growing the beans on a commercial scale. He increased the number of rural judges so that land and labor disputes could be more expeditiously settled. To stimulate the economy further, he established a rural fair and market at Candelaria. Those economic measures suggested the goals Chamorro hoped to accomplish. Events did not favor their execution.

On May 16th supreme director threw down the gauntlet to the Liberals. He arranged for the Conservative-dominated legislature to pass a law calling for elections to a constituent assembly, injecting the volatile issue of a new constitution into the political agenda. No issue carried more political charge or aroused more political emotion than that of the constitution. The Conservatives firmly believed the Constitution of 1838 invested too much power in the legislature and in the military commander and too little in the executive. Attributing anarchy to the institutional weakness of the office of chief executive, they favored a new constitution that would amplify his powers. The Liberals argued just as passionately that the division of power enshrined in the constitution saved Nicaragua from dictatorship and tyranny. With barely six weeks in office, Supreme Director Chamorro exacerbated political tensions. As subsequent events amply demonstrated, on May 16 he charted the course for an unprecedented political disaster, guaranteeing the very chaos which on April 1 he had sworn to avoid.[136]

The legislature gave the executive the option of when to set the elections for the constituent assembly. Chamorro made no immediate move to do so. Speculation fired an always overheated political caldron. But not until June 22 did the government announce the dates, July 31 and August 28, for carrying out the two-step electoral process to select delegates to the assembly, which would not meet until January of 1854.

To his credit, during that time span Chamorro funneled funds into León for several local projects, hoping at least to neutralize opposition in that Liberal bastion. The strategy failed. The city remained cool toward the Conservative supreme director. In November 1853, Chamorro revealed that he possessed "secret information" of a plot among Liberals to overthrow his government. He resolved to act decisively to "prevent" the anticipated disorder and attempted to arrest the Liberal leaders, all of whom had been elected to serve in the forthcoming constituent assembly. Most fled into neighboring Honduras. Only Máximo Jerez fell into the government's hands.

At that time, Jerez and Castellón ranked as the top Liberal leaders. Jerez was the ideologue. Born in 1818 to a modest family, he was able to get the best education León offered, including university degrees in law and philosophy. In 1843 he served as secretary with a Nicaraguan mission to Europe protesting British claims to the Mosquito coast. This experience turned the young Nicaraguan mystic into a Positivist. New ideas, experiences, and sights enveloped him. He concluded that Europe would show no respect for the individual small nations of Central America; only their unification could confer the strength needed to protect the isthmus from further interventions. Upon his return to León, he vigorously advocated a Central American union. His economic and political ideas changed; he embraced the Liberal cause. In the late 1840s, Jerez strengthened the ideological profile of the Liberal party. His spirited defense of the Constitution of 1838 made for inevitable conflict with Fruto Chamorro. The presence of two strong, able, and determined leaders, one at the head of each party, boded ill for the always fragile peace within Nicaragua. To share the common vision of the fatherland was to agree upon the goal, but the parties were farther apart than ever on the common means to reach it. Arrested in 1854 on charges of sedition, Jerez demanded access to the secret evidence that the supreme director claimed to hold. Instead, the government allowed him to leave for exile in Honduras, where he joined the other Liberals.

For his part, Chamorro stoutly defended his action against the Liberal leadership as necessary to maintain the peace and order he had sworn to enforce. He decried the activities of the Leonese Liberals: "Insurrection is rebellion; it is an unjustifiable crime that the supreme law of social cohesion condemns to energetic repression."[137] He pointed out correctly that the fratricidical wars had wearied the Nicaraguan people. They "dishonor us in the eyes of foreigners." The Nicaraguans, Chamorro claimed, "have concluded that the only means to participate in the march of progress characteristic of the century in which we live is to make a unanimous effort to achieve internal peace within our nation."[138] Chamorro never made public his secret evidence. If he expected his actions to calm the nation, he exposed himself as a poor judge of human nature. As 1853 closed with the persecution of the Liberal leadership, Minister Solon Borland sensed an impending crisis, "However calm and quiet the surface of affairs may be at any given time, there is no question but that instability is the characteristic of everything here; and the most complete change at any moment would not surprise anyone."[139] The minister surveyed Nicaragua as essentially a troubled land that stood before the world "in ruin and in rags."[140] Although the political leaders of both city-states were unaware of the danger as 1854 opened, Nicaragua teetered on the brink of extinction.

Penury and Plenitude

Two distinct economies reflected the vertical division of Nicaraguan society. The ranches, plantations, and haciendas looked outward, however wistfully, toward international markets. This segment of the economy, dominated by the patriarchs, drew hope from the vision of Nicaragua as an international emporium of tropical products and a transportation thoroughfare between two oceans. The export economy had never performed well, largely because Nicaraguan products were not in great demand worldwide and because of stiff competition from more efficient producers. The landowners lacked access to technology and capital. They had few transportation options, best characterized as irregular, unreliable, and hazardous. Potentially, the land was their principal source of wealth. In practice, though, the lack of ready labor was the major obstacle to the realization of the wealth their large estates promised. Their aspirations for wealth remained frustrated; their desires to acquire European consumer items were unfulfilled. To their disappointment, they led modest lives in a land they deemed potentially prosperous.

The patriarchs, knowingly or not, subscribed to Physiocrat ideas. The articulate Pedro Francisco de la Rocha provided insight into the Physiocrat nature of their economic vision. He summed up bright goals during the dark days of economic decline:

> Industry is the daughter of agriculture, and together they can provide ample production. They advance the positive activity of the popular masses joined

by intelligent and hardworking immigrants. Then, capital invests; savings accumulate; new routes of communication bring civilization and facilitate transportation; commerce unites people and raises values; the formation of new companies multiplies capital, broadens the spirit of enterprise, inspires social and political order; and finally liberty propelled by such powerful forces expands, gaining additional strength from international trade now facilitated by the steamship. Our narrow, sterile, senseless petty politics will be destroyed by these grand forces. . . . Without population, industry, and capital, we are unable to exploit our natural wealth. We also need roads, the arteries of civilization, in order to take full advantage of our natural wealth. As Don León Alvarado concluded, our national progress cannot occur from within because of our lack of resources and lack of business education. Our progress will be the complex result of our rapid assimilation of foreign influences and input, favored, encouraged, and sustained by our laws and authorities. [141]

The author's views ignore the fundamental question of labor scarcity, focusing on foreign ideas rather than on local conditions. Like the plans of many Latin Americans at mid-century, his too are shaped by North Atlantic sources. Such plans evinced not only a ready admission of economic dependency but threatened to bind the economy even more tightly to outside influences. De la Rocha effectively outlined much of Nicaraguan economic history.

In 1868, the naturalist Thomas Belt conceptualized Nicaragua in terms of three longitudinal zones: the East with its forests, producing woods and rubber for export; the Central with its grassy savannas for grazing cattle, mules, and horses; and the West with its fertile soils "where all the cultivated plants and fruits of the tropics thrive abundantly." In particular, he mentioned indigo, sugar, cacao, tobacco, and coffee, all exports. He viewed the economic combination of those three zones as a potential "Garden of Eden." [142] Belt's classification and judgment echoed the assessments of decades past. Orlando Roberts, traveling across Nicaragua in the early 1820s, positively assessed what he saw of the economy. The warehouses he visited in Granada contained "valuable productions of the country, such as indigo, cochineal, sarsparilla, cocoa, hides, barks, etc.," all ready for export through San Juan del Norte. [143] G. A. Thompson noted in the mid-1820s that the province's principal products were indigo, cacao, wheat, cattle, and woods. [144] In 1846, Baron A. von Buelow confirmed that list but added cotton, sugar, and tobacco. He may well have been the first to mention coffee. He also included minerals: gold, silver, and copper. [145] The foreign observers paid particular attention to export products. After all, those products, the most obvious sources of wealth, would link their own countries with Nicaragua. The patriarchal elite, too, stressed those products with a potential export sale.

The two centers for the export-import trade were, not surprisingly, León with its Pacific port of Realejo and Granada with its Atlantic port of San Juan del Norte and, in the 1850s, its Pacific port of San Juan del Sur. When Roberts arrived in León in the early 1820s, he found a German merchant already prospering there:

> His house was a large building, surrounded by a square cuadra of ware-houses, the under part nearly filled with bales of cocoa, indigo, cochineal, sarsaparilla, pearl oyster shells, or mother of pearl, tortoise-shell, barks, gums, and various other articles, with some European goods. He said he had been established in the country nearly eight years. . . . I found him busily employed receiving a quantity of cocoa, which had arrived from Massaya on the backs of eighty mules: it was reweighed and examined with great care: the quality was excellent. . . . He paid for most of these things in European goods, on which he had an enormous profit.[146]

English merchants from independence onward handled the export-import trade of León and Realejo. The principal company was directed by John Foster, British vice-consul in Realejo and Thomas Manning in León, and also included Walter Bridge and Jonas Glenton. Its main business was exporting woods—mahogany and brazilwood enjoyed a high demand and price—and indigo.[147] The English merchants lent money to the Nicaraguan government in exchange for the tobacco monopoly and the income from the customs house in Realejo.[148] They also enjoyed an import monopoly on the Pacific coast.[149] They invested in land, and their plantations grew export crops: tobacco, indigo, and cotton.[150] To increase their cotton production and reduce expenses, they introduced new machinery to clean, process, and bale it.[151] In turbulent Nicaragua, those merchants enjoyed the protection of the British government.[152] They provided an impressive study of the European entrepreneur in action. Their example as well as their access to capital, technology, and markets helped to introduce Nicaraguans to modern capitalism.

Whereas the English dominated in León, they encountered real competition among the merchant-landowner elite of Granada. Shrewd locals virtually monopolized the export-import trade up and down the San Juan River and held their own at the freewheeling port of San Juan del Norte. Passing through that port in mid-1849, Ephraim George Squier observed,

"Nearly all of the imports and exports of Nicaragua, and a considerable part of those of Costa Rica, pass through here; and here also reside the agents of the foreign houses engaged in trade with this portion of the continent. In fact, so far as commercial facilities are concerned, it is far the most important point between New Granada and Mexico."[153] The Granadan merchants maintained their presence despite the varied fates of their principal port.[154] In November 1850, the English declared San Juan to be a free port and changed the name to Greytown. The Nicaraguans protested vigorously. In the succeeding decade, military and political events kept the port bubbling in turmoil, but it still handled more trade than the Pacific ports, and Granada controlled that commerce.[155] Table 2 indicates the trade handled by San Juan del Norte and Realejo in 1841, a year during which they almost evenly divided the exports.

The Granadans also owned the mines, gold and silver being the primary minerals. The two most important mines, La Libertad and Santo Domingo, were in Chontales, but production in these and in other, much smaller ones seems to have declined during the period of anarchy. Squier reported that while the mountains of Nueva Segovia, Matagalpa, and Chontales contained gold, silver, copper, iron, and lead, the values of ores extracted in the 1850s probably did not exceed a quarter of a million dollars in value a year.[156] Starting in the 1860s those mines came under foreign ownership, particularly English.[157]

Until mid-century all commerce with England—whose merchants played the dominant role in Nicaragua's import-export trade throughout the 1821–1858 period, handling the trade as it left Nicaragua if not always within the country—was by sailing ship, either around the tip of South America or through the Caribbean. In 1848 the Royal Mail Steam Packet Company inaugurated a monthly steamship service between Southampton and San Juan del Norte. By 1850, as a result of the discovery of gold in California, U.S. ships made regular calls at San Juan del Norte and Realejo, later at San Juan del Sur. Regular steamship traffic became thereafter a sure and swift link between Nicaragua and the two metropolises vying for domination. It bound the patriarchal producers more tightly than ever to the international capitalist marketplace.

In charting the economic cycles of the decades of anarchy, Alberto Lanuza concluded that Nicaragua and Central America declared their independence of Spain during a period of prolonged economic depression. Nicaragua enjoyed a modest recovery in the 1820s and international trade increased during the first half of the 1830s. Indigo purchases recovered;

Table 2. Exports, 1841, Atlantic and Pacific ports.

Export	San Juan del Norte (Atlantic)	Realejo (Pacific)	Total value of exports (pesos)[a]
Brazilwood (hundredweight)	2,094	4,448	2,617.50
Other wood (*varas,* 2.8 ft.)	—	25,788	—
Raw cotton (hundredweight)	—	1,357	—
Processed cotton (bales)	—	450	—
Cattle hides	21,722	5,004	32,588.
Deer hides	1,988	103	1,242.50
Indigo (pounds)	139,461	27,900	139,461.00
Cacao (bales)	1	4	36.00
Brown sugar (25 lb. cakes)	—	75	—
Corn (sacks)	—	171	—
Cheese	—	100	—
Beans (2.5 bushels)	—	8	—
Costa Rican coffee (pounds)	1,871	110,000	467.75
Tobacco (hundredweight)	—	18	—
Cattle horns	—	6,000	—
Balsam (jars)	—	45	—
Metal ores (hundredweight)	—	200	—
Ginger (boxes)	—	2	—
Pepper (hundredweight)	—	50	—
Tortoise shell (pounds)	122	—	366.
Tiger skins	13	—	9.75
Total Sum			176,783.50

Source: Redactor Nicaragüense (León), February 2, 1842.

[a]When the value of an export is not given, it is because port authorities included the value with another export.

brazilwood exports boomed, rising from 200 tons in 1832 to 5,000 in 1834, before falling to 1,162 in 1836. A general trade decline began that year and continued to around 1851. [158] *The Mentor Nicaragüense* lamented in 1841 that commerce had been paralyzed for four years. [159]

Von Buelow provided vague trade statistics for 1846: exports of 223,009 piastras and imports of 294,039 (approximately 5 piastras equalled 1 peso). More trade passed through San Juan del Norte (123,000 piastras of exports and 174,039 of imports) than Realejo (100,000 piastras of exports and 120,000 of imports). San Juan del Norte shipped out woods, indigo, hides, and 50 *quintales* of coffee. Realejo exported woods, indigo, hides, and cotton.[160] Robert G. Dunlop, a visitor to Realejo in the mid-1840s, described it as "merely a collection of mud huts." One of its two churches was in "complete ruin, and the other, through entire, is without a curate or any officiating priests."[161] When Jacob D. B. Stillman passed through Realejo in 1850, he encountered evidence of past grandeur but present economic and physical decline.[162] According to Dunlop, trade was "yearly declining." He listed as the exports in 1844: "400 or 500 bales of cotton, principally sent to Costa Rica for the manufactures of that state; about 1,000 tons of Brazil wood, principally sent to Great Britain and the United States of America; a small quantity of chancake (the crude juice of sugar-cane boiled till it crystallizes), sent to Chili; about 1,000 bales of indigo, the quality being the best of any produced in the republic; and a few hundred bales of Granada cocoa sent to the states of San Salvador and Honduras."[163] Adolphe Boucard recorded livelier export activity in the port in 1852 with woods, sugar, tobacco, and cotton leading the exports. Realejo also exported foods: corn, rice, beans, eggs, fruit, and honey.[164] Dunlop visited the port shortly after a bitter civil war devastated the region; Boucard was there just before another would take its toll.

At mid-century, Squier depicted the national economy in gloomy terms: "The merchants of the country are impoverished and bankrupt, the revenues of the government merely nominal, and the little foreign commerce that remains, hardly worth the trouble of estimating."[165] However, a brief economic revival seems to have resuscitated the merchants, planters, and government. After a year in Nicaragua, Squier detected increased economic activity which he attributed to good relations with the United States and rising demands from California. He estimated a 33 percent rise in land under cultivation.[166] The British vice-consul in Realejo corroborated Squier's conclusions: "Almost every article of its produce for exportation has advanced one hundred per cent in value, by the increased demand to supply San Francisco and Panama markets in addition to the transit across the country."[167] Then, just as abruptly, a civil war beginning in 1854 and the subsequent National War of 1856–57 triggered another decline from which there was no recovery until 1864. Tables 3 and 4 provide a general synopsis of the economic trends. At best, however, the information available for such tables comes from partial or approximate figures.

Duties on exports and imports provided a principal source of government revenue, as did monopolies on the sale of gunpowder, stamps, and alcohol.[168] Unfortunately, income seldom equaled expenditures, always

Table 3. Nicaragua Exports and Imports (in thousands of dollars).

Year	Exports	Imports
1800	596	390
1837	230	385
1838	305	366
1839	205	160
1841	167.8	150
1851	1,010	525
1861	285.4	751.6
1862	289.3	853.3
1863	595.2	324.2
1864	1,112.4	953.2

Source: Alberto Lanuza Matamoros, "Comercio Exterior de Nicaragua," *Estudios Sociales Centroamericanos* (San José), pp. 119 and 123. Another set of statistics, not always in accordance with these, will be found in Thomas and Ebba Schoonover, "Statistics for an Understanding of Foreign Intrusions into Central America from 1820s to 1930," *Anuario de Estudios Centroamericanos* (Costa Rica), 15:1 (1989), pp. 114 and 116.

forcing the government deeper into debt.[169] In 1845, for example, expenditures amounted to $257,589 pesos (one peso equals approximately one dollar), while income totalled $157,487, resulting in a deficit of $100,102 pesos. That year the government budgeted $146,000 pesos for the army. In the budget for the fiscal year ending in June 1851, income totaled US$122,682; expenditures, US$173,646; leaving a deficit of US$50,964 (table 5). The military absorbed US$108,615 of the budget.[170] Military expenditures regularly drained the treasury. In emergencies the government relied on forced loans from citizens and foreigners, and on its shaky credit.

The total external and internal indebtedness of the state in 1851 stood at approximately US$574,869, an impressive figure considering the small population and the treasury's modest income. In addition, approximately

Table 4. Leading Nicaragua Exports as Percentages of Total Exports, 1841–1871.

Year	Value of Exports (thousands of US$)	Indigo	Precious Metals	Hides	Cotton	Rubber	Woods	Coffee
1841	167.8	83.1	0.0	14.8	0.0	0.0	1.5	0.4
1851	1,010.0	7.9	39.6	1.2	0.0	0.0	15.8	3.0
1864	1,112.4	8.6	9.1	17.2	47.9	8.8	2.0	1.2
1865	1,155.0	16.9	12.3	8.9	47.1	4.6	2.5	2.6

Source: Alberto Lanuza Matamoros, "Estructuras Socioeconómicas, Poder y Estado en Nicaragua (1821–1875)," cited by Ralph Lee Woodward, Jr., "Central American from Independence to c. 1870," in Leslie Bethell, *Cambridge History of Latin America,* vol. III, *From Independence to c 1870* (Cambridge University Press, 1985), p. 504.

US$100,000 in governmental promissory notes circulated. The foreign debt, US$350,000, represented the share of the total indebtedness of the United Provinces of Central America negotiated by President Manuel José Arce in 1825 with Barclay, Herring, and Richardson of London and assigned to Nicaragua after it seceded in 1838.[171]

The municipalities also faced financial challenges. Granada counted 2,006 pesos in its coffers in 1841, while it budgeted $2,275 for expenses. The largest single item, $372 pesos, paid the teachers' salaries, although salaries for all other government officials, when added up, exceeded that amount.[172] All the governments struggled vainly in financial quicksand.

A hodgepodge of foreign coins circulated. The government occasionally tried to infuse some order in the monetary chaos by issuing tables of comparative values. It also tried to maintain a bimetallic standard of sixteen silver pesos to one gold ounce, but Gresham's law worked as convincingly in Nicaragua as elsewhere: silver promptly drove gold out of circulation. Silver coins of one type or another sufficed for most transactions. Barter was common. At times cacao beans substituted as a form of specie. Von Buelow reported, "It is common for the farmers to pay for their goods in the city with cacao, using it as if it were money."[173] According to Squier, four cacao nuts were worth approximately one U.S. cent.[174]

Currency, budgets, and exports were relevant to but one of Nicaragua's economies, the precarious Europeanized one inspired by a Physiocrat blueprint. Alongside that rickety structure flourished a remarkably successful domestic folk economy, concerned with feeding the population daily and supplying its simple needs.

Table 5. Nicaraguan Revenues and Expenditures for the Year Ending June 3, 1851.

Category	Amount (in US$)
Revenues	
Duties on imports, San Juan del Norte	50,003
Duties on imports, Realejo	7,575
Other revenues, including aguardiente monopoly	65,104
Total	122,682
Expenses	
Diplomacy	2,000
Executive branch	17,508
Miscellaneous	18,932
Civil service	26,591
Military	108,615
Total	173,646
Deficit	50,964

Source: "Squier Notes On the Nicaraguan Debt."

The second economy, the subsistence agriculture of the peasants and rural communities, and also to a certain extent of the ranch, plantation, and hacienda, grew sufficient food for farmer and family with some surplus for the local market and even for export. It functioned well except during the most catastrophic periods of civil war.

Judgments of the performance of the Nicaraguan economy have concentrated on export sales, a conscious or unconscious reminder of the colonial status accorded Latin America. The mercantilist preoccupation with the export economy crossed from the colonial past into the national present unquestioned by the ruling class, not only preserving but eventually exaggerating old economic patterns. Wrongly but inevitably, export sales gaged progress. After all, they facilitated imports. Those imports, largely European consumer items, measured the degree of Europeanization taking place, the triumph of civilization over barbarism. Furthermore, the taxes on imports—and exports as well—buttressed an always shaky, often insolvent treasury, helping to finance the economic infrastructures, roads, for example, and to maintain the political superstructure, an army, for example. An ability to export and import promoted modernization and nation-building, both desired by the patriarchal elite. A perceived link among exports, economic development, and a modern nation-state explains the skewed nature of economic studies and economic histories.

Export economy held scant interest for the folk, however, who produced for themselves and the local market. Little tempted by European consumer goods and with their own measurements of success and well being, they looked inward to the local community. In their own terms, they enjoyed the plenitude Nicaragua offered. Most important for their well-being, they had access to land. That access guaranteed food, while also reinforcing a value system and a style of life that had evolved over a millennium.

In relation to its small population, Nicaragua was a large country, with territorial claims reaching far above 50,000 square miles. It boasted of rich soil. With regard to the size of the population, census figures were hardly more than guesses and varied widely. The figures in Table 6 are acceptable approximations. The population was not well distributed. In 1815 approximately 72 percent lived on that Pacific axis stretching from Chinandega through Rivas, a concentration that rose to 76 percent by 1846. During those same years, the population increased at an annual rate close to 1.2 percent, slightly higher than the overall Latin American rate of 0.9. The Department of Granada grew fastest, at approximately 1.8 percent a year, and contained nearly a third of the nation's population.[175] Between 1778 and 1867, the population doubled—and it doubled again during the next forty years.[176] Squier concluded in 1861 that Central America's population was growing faster than other regions of the Western World. [177]

Despite a *relatively* rapid growth, the population remained small in ratio to the land size, even along the more populous Pacific coast. Table 7 suggests the ratio of population to land. Abundant land was available to farm. The landowning patterns included government land, Church land, land held by Indian communities, the *ejidos* belonging to villages, towns, and

Table 6. Estimated Population of Nicaragua, 1820–1870 (in thousands).

			Year		
1820	1830	1840	1850	1860	1870
186	220	242	274	278	337

Source: Ralph Lee Woodward, Jr., "Central America from Independence to c. 1870," p. 478.

cities, and privately held land of all sizes. Something like 80 percent of the land was "property of the state," which meant it lay vacant.[178] The amount of land under cultivation was small, yet sufficient to feed the population. [179] Abundant land and scarce labor constituted the major economic reality of nineteenth-century Nicaragua. Anyone who really wanted to farm the land could get access to some. Consequently most people chose to work for themselves, primarily in subsistence agriculture, rather than seek employment on plantations and ranches. Landowners desperately sought laborers, and by Latin American standards paid dearly for them. Debt peonage and forms of forced labor were unusual.

At first glance, Nicaragua seemed to have an unusually high urban population. The explanation lay in the integration of town and country.

Reflecting both Indian and Iberian pasts, many of the rural workers and landowners, large and small, lived in villages, towns, and cities, going to the fields in the morning and returning to their urban homes in the evening. Squier reported that many walked "two, four, and six miles daily to labor in their fields."[180] He recalled that he had to hire a guide to lead him out of Masaya to the road to Granada because "the foot and mule paths diverge in a thousand directions from every principal town, all so nearly alike that it is impossible for the stranger to tell one from another." These were the paths many inhabitants trod to get from the town to their fields. Indeed, as Squier rode out in the evening he "met hundreds of Indians, of both sexes, young and old, coming in from the fields, each bearing a small load of wood, corn, plantains, or other articles of consumption. They were all in excellent humor, and saluted us gayly."[181] The towns mixed merchants, artisans, professionals, bureaucrats, clergy, and urban proletariat with landowners, farmers, peasants, and rural proletariat.

In those towns, handicrafts and artisans flourished. Masaya never

Table 7. Estimated Population Density, 1820–1870 (population per square kilometer).

	Year					
Region	1820	1830	1840	1850	1860	1870
Nicaragua	1.26	1.49	1.64	1.85	1.88	2.78
Central America	2.79	3.14	3.57	4.06	4.53	5.24

Source: Ralph Lee Woodward, Jr., "Crecimiento de Población en Centro América durante la Primera Mitad del Siglo de la Independencia Nacional," *Mesoamérica,* 1 (1980), p. 230.

failed to elicit praise from foreign travelers for the variety and quality of its "manufactures." Praising the inhabitants as "industrious," Squier inventoried some of the locally manufactured items he found for sale in 1849: "cordage, hammocks, saddles, cotton cloth, *petates* or mats, hats, shoes, in short, all the articles of common use in the country, are produced here, besides large quantities of *dulces* (sweetmeats and jellies)."[182] The animated Masaya market fired the American diplomat's imagination. The local artisans flourished within a varied milieu. Squier conveyed the variety in this vivid passage:

> Here were women seated on little stools beside snow-white sheets, or in the center of a cordon of baskets, heaped with cacao or coffee, starch, sugar, and the more valuable articles of common use; here a group with piles of hats of various patterns, hammocks, cotton, yarn, thread of pita, native blankets, *petates*, and the other various articles which Yankees call "dry goods;" here another group, with water jars, plates, and candlesticks of native pottery; there a *sillero* or saddler exposed the products of his art, the *zapatero* cried his shoes, the *herrero* his machetes, bits for horses, and other articles of iron; girls proclaimed their *dulces*, boys shouted parrots and monkeys, and in the midst of all a tall fellow stalked about bearing a wooden clock from Connecticut in his arms.[183]

In 1853, when Mrs. Henry Grant Foote stopped in Masaya, she admired the "exceedingly fine, pretty" straw mats, an excellent substitute for carpets in the tropics. "They are entirely manufactured by the Indians, who seem to be extremely expert with their hands. Their carved bowls, made from the tree gourds, are beautiful and curious, considering the only tool employed is a common pen-knife."[184] A few years later, Peter F. Stout observed the same items for sale that Squier had inventoried and noted, "Masaya was celebrated particularly for its manufactures."[185] On craft industries in general, he commented, "Hats, shoes, saddlery, fancy articles, earthenware, and pottery, are manufactured, though not to a very great extent. The artificers in gold and silver in Nicaragua are extremely ingenious and skillful, and exhibit great taste and experience in the manufacture of ornaments."[186] Among the observers of Masayan industry, Charles Parke alone described a home whose owner had installed a printing press, and his eighteen-year-old daughter worked as the typesetter.[187] Very significantly, those craftspeople and artisans produced simple items suitable to the needs of the local population. They sold in the local or regional markets. They did not produce for export. The distinction is simple but significant in explaining the relative wellbeing of the folk.

The foreign travelers delighted in describing the urban marketplaces and cataloging their wares. Those markets played immensely important economic roles, as centers of internal trade. Their roots burrowed into the Indian past.[188]

Political turmoil, the vagaries of international demand, and the hazards and uncertainties of transportation exacted far less toll from subsistence than from export agriculture. Further, internal trade patterns and activities remained more constant than external ones.[189] Except for periods during the harshest of the civil wars or remote areas without regular surpluses, food abounded.

Orlando Roberts, in his journey from Granada to León in the 1820s, positively assessed what he saw of the subsistence sector. He reported the markets of Granada to be "abundantly supplied with beef, pork, poultry, cheese, and milk" at "very reasonable" prices, as well as "a great variety of excellent fish, and waterfowl from the lake." [190] As he rode from Granada to Managua and then on to León, the Englishman passed through "well-cultivated" acreages of corn, plantains, bananas, and cacao. The extensive grassy plains near León fed "numerous herds" of cattle and horses.[191] The well-stocked Leonese markets rivaled those of Granada. They were "abundantly supplied with beef, pork, fish and fowls; and all the varieties of fruit and vegetables."[192] He remembered hearty meals at minimal cost in León:

> Shortly after daybreak half a pint of excellent chocolate or strong coffee, with a slice or two of bread; about nine o'clock a breakfast of fish, flesh, or fowl, and sometimes all these; to which was added an omelet, tortillas, and excellent wheaten bread, with claret or aguardiente—about noon a soup composed of boiled beef and vegetables and a saucer of sweetmeats, for those who chose them, ushered in a dinner consisting of the same materials as the breakfast, after which a cup of strong coffee prepares them for their siesta. . . . About nine supper was served—thus ending the day.[193]

Obviously it was a well fed day for Roberts and the officers whose mess he shared in the León garrison.

Dunlop left a different impression. Visiting Nicaragua after the sacking of León in the civil war of 1845, he reported, "Nicaragua is even in a more miserable condition than any of the other states. . . . Agriculture, and all sorts of industry, are at an end in every part of the state except Granada and its neighborhood."[194] Since Granada had triumphed in that civil war, it was spared the devastation of León and other towns. The buoyant subsistence economy apparently recovered because, as von Buelow recorded in 1846, "All the necessities of life are cheap. The humblest class enjoys in abundance the most necessary foods: corn, plantains, all kinds of fruits and vegetables, pineapples, rice, beans, chickens, eggs, and venison."[195] Three years later, John Baily corroborated the abundance and low cost of food.[196] Corn flourished, and as the ingredient for the tortilla it was the staff of life. The green stalks were fodder for horses and cattle. Carl Scherzer reported, "The maize, which is just carelessly thrown into the ground, returns five hundred fold, and there are three harvests in the year."[197] "It is easy to cultivate the land," von Buelow marvelled. He complimented the Nicaraguans on the "magnificent" state of cultivation and then added, "It is hard to understand how they achieve these results with such little and negligent work."[198]

At mid-century Squier provided details of an ample diet. Tortillas and beans were the essentials, ubiquitous, on every table. He advised travelers that in every Indian hut the menu was as simple as it was constant: *"Hay tortillas, frijoles, frijolitos, frijolitos fritos, y huevos*—tortillas, beans, little beans, little baked beans, and eggs."[199] The popular menu also included rice, plantains, and cheese. Pork, beef, and poultry were abundant, although not necessary a daily item on the working-class table. Fruit was available for the picking.[200] Commenting on the region around Realejo in 1851, the awed Lucien McLenathan Wolcott also admired the abundance and availability of fruit.[201] According to Squier, the Nicaraguans began the day sipping a cup of chocolate or coffee and ended it with a cup of chocolate or *tiste*, parched corn ground with chocolate and sugar and mixed with water. They nibbled on sweets, all readily available, Squier reported: "The vendors of 'dulces,' generally bright Indian girls, gaily dressed, and bearing a tray, covered with the purest white napkins, and temptingly spread upon their heads, pass daily from house to house."[202] Squier concluded that in Nicaragua even "the poorest wretch need not go hungry."[203] No one recorded signs of hunger. A few lame or blind beggars appeared in the accounts of travelers, who mentioned them as an unusual occurrence.[204]

After mid-century, more indications of prices exist. Squier gave some idea of the prices in the marketplaces: a pair of chickens: cost three to six cents in U.S. currency; six cents' worth of plantains could sustain a small family for a week; a bushel of corn was twenty cents; a hundred weight of rice cost $1.50 to $2.00. The daily wage of a working man was approximately twelve and one-half cents.[205] William Walker's newspaper, *El Nicaragüense*, contains a rather different picture of the products for sale in Granada and the U.S. dollar prices in 1855 and 1856. Beef sold for six cents a pound; chickens cost thirty cents each (the impressive five-fold increase in five years probably reflected the demand created by a large concentration of U.S. mercenaries in Granada); a pound of rice was five cents; beans, $1.50 a bushel; a pair of Nicaraguan shoes cost $3.00, while imported ones fetched $43.00. The paper noted, "All articles of Nicaraguan fruits, such as bananas, plantains, oranges, mangoes, coconuts, limes, etc. etc. are cheap and very plentiful, in fact they can scarcely be given away." The list of prices, while interesting, is probably somewhat inflated. The presence of Walker and his army drove prices upwards. The newspaper itself evinced this process: "Servants' wages in private houses for native are $3.00-$5.00 per month; foreign $9.00-$10.00. . . . Rents have materially advanced during the last month to nearly double and in some instances more than double previous demands. Comfortable houses formerly at $20 per month now rent for $50. Large houses have advanced from $60 and $100 to $90 and $150."[206] Probably two price scales existed in Granada in the mid-1850s, one for the free-spending Yankees and another for the locals.

The total value of the products sold or bartered annually in the local markets is unknown; the amount and value of foods consumed in households before surpluses reached the market places have not even been estimated. Economic history concentrates exclusively on foreign exports. The unbalanced assessments of economic performance make it difficult to assign a value comparison between internal and external trade and to calculate total production. Still, several tentative conclusions should be considered. Nicaragua experienced a late national consolidation, as well as a late integration into capitalist world markets. Both occurred—and not coincidentally—during the last third of the nineteenth century. During the period 1821–1858 the known activities of the internal and external markets suggest that the internal market was more active and probably more lucrative in very modest terms for more people. The internal market suffered fewer interruptions, fewer fluctuations, and less foreign participation. With the exception of a few brutal periods of civil war, the internal market functioned regularly and well. Very importantly, subsistence agriculture in conjunction with the internal market network provided Nicaraguans with a decent and regular diet.

Oblique observations from foreign travelers suggested that the Nicaraguan folk ate better than the masses in the burgeoning North Atlantic industrial cities. At the same time, the life-style of the patriarchal elite remained modest by any North Atlantic standards. The situation enforced a kind of brute egalitarianism which the patriarchs would alter to their own benefit. Local markets served both folk and patriarchs, to the profit of each sector, however modestly. Production for and participation in the international markets enriched patriarchs and foreigners but marginalized (even threatened) the folk. The local markets tended, on the one hand, to amalgamate populations locally and regionally, while, on the other, they contributed further to regional compartmentalization.

Determinedly optimistic, the patriarchs maintained their economic vision. Occasionally they even demonstrated an ability to cooperate for the sake of enhancing their economic positions. In 1853 merchants of León and Granada united to petition the supreme director to establish a steamship line that would provide regular scheduled service between Nicaraguan ports and those of the other Central American republics.[207] They realistically understood that much of their international trade was with their neighbors and wanted to develop it.[208] The requested steamship line, like many other projects, failed to materialize. They boldly petitioned for tax reductions, always promising that lower taxes, or exemptions such as those obtained in 1835, would stimulate a flagging economy.[209] The accumulating failures of agroexports by the mid-1850s were impressive. With an occasional exception, exports of agricultural products failed to grow, even though Nicaragua began to serve as a major interoceanic transit route after 1849. The patriarchs were unable to attract or acquire capital, to recruit labor, to arrange transportation *suitable for their goals*, and to provide order and stability. Still, the vision never blurred.

Despite immense problems, Nicaragua probably was more economically independent—which is to say, obviously, less dependent—during those politically turbulent decades than it would be at any time thereafter. The nation was poor in the material terms of Europe—some foreign visitors thought it primitive—but everyone ate. The next two chapters will discuss the slippery subject of the well-being and satisfaction of the population prior to indiscriminate economic growth, burgeoning exports and imports, progress, modernization, deepening dependency, and the complexities of wealth and power.

· II ·

Father: The Patriarchal Nature of Society

Patriarchy

Scandal rippled through the ranks of Nicaragua's high society in 1851. Alejandro Manning, youngest son of Don Tomás, the richest merchant of León and possibly of Nicaragua, had run off with Francisca Sanzón.[1] They "married clandestinely" in El Viejo, where an obliging "innovator" priest blessed the union.[2] The marriage without parental consent affronted the fundamental mores of the period. The outraged father of the groom demanded an annulment.[3] He took his case to the archbishop in Guatemala City and to the municipal government of León. The son hired a lawyer. The challenge to the deeply rooted patriarchal system set tongues wagging.

Wistful suggestions circulated that love should triumph over paternal disapproval. Someone even dared to speculate that times might be changing. In defense of Alejandro, some accused Señor Manning of class prejudice, a refusal to accept the marriage because Señorita Sanzón came from a "proletarian family."[4] The political and economic realities of class struggle threatened to complicate the social question. But however intriguing the implications of the economic difference between the young husband and wife might have been, they were not the real issue in mid-nineteenth-century Nicaragua.

Attention focused on filial disrespect. In marrying Francisca without the permission of his father, Alejandro defied paternal authority. The challenge to patriarchy disturbed society. A broadside appeared in the streets to defend "the good father against an ungrateful son." It pointed out that the introduction of "the principles of liberty and equality into Nicaragua had not been meant to alter public morality and permit an attack on paternal authority." The broadside warned, "Young people, you are obliged to respect your father whose will is law in domestic society. . . . This obligation falls on all social classes. It is a common and invariable rule founded on principles of religious morality and social harmony. . . . Public order rests on the respect due the father and on the subsequent peace and tranquility of the family."

The anonymous authors—they signed themselves "The Students of Confucius"—would have none of the arguments of class struggle. At the same time they censured those "innovators" who would "disturb the peace and quiet of our families and demoralize our youth with erroneous and seditious doctrines." The lengthy broadside mounted a spirited defense of patriarchal principles; God, society, and time had ordained them.[5]

Although the dispute centered on patriarchal authority, a tangential issue also disturbed the public. Marriage, the legal creator of new families, stood as the very foundation stone of a patriarchal society. The sacred institution served vital civil functions. The Church, the state, and the patriarchs regarded it as much too important to serve the romantic and impulsive whims of youth. Viewed from that angle, the actions of Alejandro and Francisca subverted society.

Amidst the anarchy of Nicaragua, convincing arguments could be mustered to explain the presence, persistence, significance, and dominance of patriarchy. The Students of Confucius correctly indicated that more than a marriage was at stake: patriarchy was the issue. In a much broader sense, so was the nation. Whatever its faults, the patriarchy also served a significant sociopolitical need, providing a substratum of order in a politically fragmented country. Like the folk community with which it shared these qualities of social cohesion, patriarchy prevented the disintegration of society. The strength of the institutions of the patriarchate and the folk community resulted from the singular lack of other strong institutions, a historical reality since the sixteenth century.

As the Spanish monarch's authority collapsed after 1811 and disappeared after 1821, the threads of unity among Nicaraguans frayed. No institutional structures and no psychological solidarity existed to insure the creation of a viable nation-state on either an isthmian or local level. Contrary to the experiences throughout much of Latin America, no caudillo emerged to consolidate the state and substitute personal strength for the missing or feeble political institutions. Furthermore, centripetal social, economic, and political trends polarized the inhabitants around Granada or León, contributing nothing to the task of nation-building.

Unlike the countries that had fought for their independence, Nicaragua had no military to act, however arbitrarily, as a repository for perceived national glory, a motor for unity, and the effective mechanism for governance. The armies that formed to fight each other during the half-century of municipal rivalries were at best ragtag collections of either unwilling conscripts or overly eager villains given to loot, rape, and terror. Their scurvy appearance inspired equal reactions of fear and laughter. Thomas Belt pitied the lot of the Indians, who, when wars broke out, were "driven about like cattle and forced into armies that are raised."[6] The officers won their rank more by social standing or rapacity than military ability.[7] They competed to confer sonorous titles on themselves. Generals abounded, and the most daring promoted himself to Field Marshal.

Nothing even remotely resembling a professional army existed. While the makeshift forces could cause trouble, consume impressive quantities of aguardiente, terrorize the innocent, and deplete the treasury, they never constituted a national institution capable of imposing unification and governing the land. In 1850 the government published the first regulations to organize and standardize a national army, a modest intent to institutionalize if not exactly professionalize the military.[8] The publication evoked strong protests. Critics accused the government of increasing military power at the expense of civilian.[9]

Even the Roman Catholic Church—such a powerful social, economic, and political force elsewhere in Latin America—was impoverished, understaffed, and, during at least two critical periods, divided. The hierarchy, including Bishop Nicolás García Jerez, opposed independence, while many priests such as Antonio Monino, Tomás Ruiz, and Benito Miguleña, actively supported it.[10] The bishop confronted not only a divided Church but taut tensions with the newly emerging state. Resultant pressures on the recalcitrant royalist to embrace independence prompted him to abandon his see. Bishop García Jerez retired to Guatemala City in 1824, where he died the following year.

From the date of the death of Bishop García Jerez until his own death nearly a quarter of a century later, José Desiderio de la Quadra (1786–1849) administered the diocese, first as Governor of the Bishopric and after 1832 as *Vicar Capitular*. Born into a modest Nicaraguan family, Quadra studied in León. He had been to other parts of Central America and had served in Managua, Matagalpa, and Jinotega, in addition to León. In 1825, he sat in the Nicaraguan Constituent Assembly. Thus, unlike men who preceded or followed him, he knew intimately the region he administered. A poet as well as rector of the University of León, Vicar Capitular Quadra shepherded the Nicaraguan Church through exceedingly difficult years. Amid the whirlwind of civil conflict, the Roman Catholic Church stood quietly, shunning overt political involvements. Neutrality within the state and harmony within the Church were achievements for which Quadra received praise.[11] They were unusual in Central America during the nineteenth century.

If Desiderio de la Quadra exemplified the churchmen who combined various high civil and religious posts, Pedro Solís (1773–1852) offered an even better example of that practice. In a country of few educated men, members of the elite had to play multiple roles. Born into an impoverished family, orphaned at a tender age, Solís received his education through the Roman Catholic Church, studying philosophy as well as civil and cannon law. He spent some years in Guatemala where he was ordained in 1798. A Liberal and a nationalist, he rallied to the cause of independence in 1813 and subsequently gained an impressive record of appointed and elected civil positions. He served as a deputy in the constituent assemblies that wrote the constitutions of 1826 and 1838; he was a deputy in the state legislature in 1827 and the Chamber of Deputies in 1842; he sat on the bench; he served as general minister to the supreme director in 1839; in 1842, 1843, and 1849, he handled diplomatic negotiations with El Salvador, Costa Rica, and Great Britain. Meanwhile, he rose through the ranks of the Church hierarchy to become Dean of the Cathedral in León by 1850. Gregorio Juárez summed up the thoughts of the throng of mourners at Solís's funeral in 1854: "You were the last torch that an indulgent God provided us from a past age in order to illuminate our present thought."[12]

Pope Pius IX named Jorge de Viteri y Ungo, a Guatemalan and the first Bishop of El Salvador (1843–1846), to the vacant Nicaraguan see after the death of Quadra.[13] Bishop Viteri came to his new post after a stormy career in El Salvador. His blatant interference in politics had resulted in his expulsion in 1846. In Nicaragua, the new bishop promptly fell into the bubbling cauldron of political struggles. He challenged the state in 1852 over the always contentious subject of national patronage, in that particular case over the right of the bishop to appoint a priest to a parish without government permission.[14] His propensity to meddle in political matters prompted an old friend, the Minister of Foreign Relations of Guatemala, Manuel Francisco Pavón, a member of one of Central America's most distinguished, richest, and powerful families, to advise the bishop to exercise caution in troubled Nicaragua. As Minister Pavón put it, "A scalded cat flees even from cold water."[15]

After Viteri's death in 1853, Bernardo Piñol y Aycinena, a Guatemalan, was named bishop in 1855, but because of war he was not consecrated until 1859. He inherited the Church-state imbroglios of his predecessor and a serious split in the already enfeebled Church. This was the result of William Walker's armed intervention of 1855–1857. Some of the priests, including the highly influential Agustín Vijil, morally, financially, and politically supported the foreign intervention. Others such as Rafael Villavicencio, fought the Protestant usurper "in defense of the Faith" and in the name of the Fatherland.[16]

Nicaragua confronted a startling reality: the absence of institutions capable of unifying the nation. Guatemalan Minister Pavón queried his friend Tomás Manning as to why the military and the Church did not ally to put an end to anarchy. Obviously he had not grasped the differences between Guatemala and Nicaragua. More to the point, he blamed squabbling lawyers for Nicaragua's plight: "Lawyers do not know how to govern. They have brought anarchy to Central America. . . . They are crazy, if not downright evil."[17] In contrast to the Guatemala of Pavón where political power was highly concentrated, clearly visible, and very effective under the lengthening administration of Rafael Carrera, a tremendous power vacuum threatened Nicaragua with continued disorder, even disintegration.

Whatever monumental problems the country faced, society did not disintegrate. Its strength lay in the family, arguably the strongest institution in pre–1858 Nicaragua.[18] The predominantly patriarchal family filled the political vacuum in some measure and proved to be a major force preserving a society under stress. Diana Balmori, Stuart F. Voss, and Miles Wortman posit the fruitful thesis that "notable families" created complex social, economic, and political networks, which "may be the pivot around which Latin American history moved from the late colonial period through the early twentieth century." They concluded that the family, always an important institution in Latin America, became the "strongest organization" in a society with weak state structures.[19] Speaking in more universal terms, the French historian André Bourgière noted, "It appears that whenever the state no longer wields enough power to act and to protect its people, the family expands, assumes control of every aspect of the individual life, and becomes a bastion. Whenever the state becomes stronger, the family shrinks, loosens the effective ties it had imposed on the individual, who then is more readily integrated into society as a whole."[20] These theses offer a useful means to understand the Nicaraguan past during its most chaotic period.

The colonial experience had conditioned Nicaraguans to view the political order in terms of family symbols, identifying authority with the domination of father over family. God, king, and father constituted the hierarchy. The cross and the crown intertwined with, reinforced, and legitimized patriarchal patterns.[21] God had conferred power on Adam, the first father and the origin of all kings. The Bible defined and hallowed the genetic patriarchy with its concepts of duty, obligation, values, authority, and, ultimately, political organization.[22] In addition to the Biblical support for patriarchy, the classical authors—Socrates and Aristotle, for example—argued in its favor and likewise linked family and polis.[23]

The philosophical construct of patriarchal authority also originated in part in traditional Mediterranean family structures which vested full authority in parents, particularly in the father. That example characterized the early Roman family. Patrilineal, that family was large, robust, stable, embracing into a single unit two, three, sometimes four generations. The father was priest (in the practice of ancestor worship), the only "legal" person in the family, and the owner of all the property. He exercised total power over the children.[24] Such ideas and behavioral patterns characterized Nicaraguan polity and society during the long colonial period. The intrusion of the Enlightenment confused, even challenged them.

By the opening of the nineteenth century, a few Nicaraguans joined the growing ranks of Latin Americans who questioned the genetic origins of political power. They advocated independence from the Spanish monarchy, a break with the past. They accepted the persuasive ideas of the European Enlightenment regarding government as a contract of consent among men, an agreement with limitations and restrictions. The notion that political power would derive from a contract rather than through inheritance marked a sharp political break with the past. Declaring independence proved to be relatively easy in comparison with forging an acceptable political contract. Nicaraguans spent thirty-five tragic years in search of such a contract, and most would claim the search lasted considerably longer.

The strong patriarchal family structure complicated the search for contractual government. While the sanctity of the patriarchal family united Nicaraguans in the nineteenth century, the broadening of that concept to political governance on a national level divided them. Few questioned the social authority of the family patriarch, but the repudiation of the monarchy had undermined the political authority of the patriarch. It weakened the genetic arguments for governance. The acceptance of the republic of the Enlightenment infused contrary arguments to favor contractual government. Contradictions between genetic patriarchal authority and contractual republican agreement could not be ignored. Not surprisingly, those contradictions continued during the *official* exercise of contractual political power. Despite constitutional prescriptions, Nicaraguans tended to exercise political power on a personal basis in a patriarchal style. The blur between family and national matters remained characteristic of Nicaragua.[25] So did the confusion between social and political institutions. Both contributed to uncertainty, which in turn fostered unrest and violence among the patriarchs over the concept of contractual agreement, the extent of it, and how democratic it would be.

The ideological disputes among Nicaraguans, reputed to be the political differences between León and Granada, involved the degree to which patriarchy and democracy, the genetic and the contractual, would shape the government. The two city-states represented different directions for the political contract—and, in the final analysis, for patriarchy. At least in theory, Granadans adhered more faithfully to the principles of patriarchy, while the Leonese seemed to profess more interest in contractual experiments, differences that would be easy to exaggerate. Whatever the degree of disagreement, it promoted anarchy. Yet even in the bitterness of debate and conflict, few Nicaraguans openly questioned the supreme role of the father in the family, social patriarchy.

While Nicaragua's political institutions changed from a hereditary monarchy to an elected chief executive, the patriarchal family remained relatively constant and vigorous.[26] The most influential figures of the colonial past had been landowners and merchants. If anything, independence strengthened their position. A few "new" families gained recognition and thus prestige and power, among them a small group of foreigners who played a disproportionately significant economic role. José Coronel Urtecho concluded that a small number of "leading families" demonstrated remarkable ability to adapt to changing conditions across time and consequently to retain power. He ascribed to them a strength greater than any other institution. With some exaggeration, he concluded, "The history of Nicaragua to a large degree has been the history of families."[27]

The notable families were not the only ones to provide organizational strength in a disorganized state. The stability and strength of the humble family—most emphatically in the Indian communities—also contributed to continuity, orientation, and local order. The patriarchal structure permeated those families as well.[28] The family unit stood supreme, whether among the patricians or the plebes, in all its complexities of marriage, kinship, God-parentship, duty, and obligation. It offered the haven of continuity, provision, security, and order in the tempest of political disorder.

Heir to Biblical and Roman traditions on the one hand and complementary Indian traditions on the other, the Nicaraguan family in the nineteenth century was emphatically hierarchical. From the apex, the father ruled. Juan Manuel Mendoza recalled nineteenth-century patriarchalism as "unlimited" in its powers. So long as the father lived, sons of any age or distinction obeyed him. "Married sons continued their submission to him as though they were still minors living at home. They received the same punishment and bore the same responsibilities and enjoyed no independence."[29]

"Father" could be a complex term signifying many kinds of relationships and evoking many emotions.[30] Obligations balanced rights. Father guided, disciplined, loved, instructed, and cared for members of the family. He protected; he provided; he served as the family mediator with the outside world. After independence, father was the "citizen" who participated in national life, a role limited to the fathers of more privileged families. To the *pater familias* the members of the extended family owed devotion, loyalty, obedience, and service. An aphorism commonly repeated in Nicaragua was "the father is God on earth."[31] As a patriarch, he often extended his sway from the immediate family to more distant kin, servants, workers, and perhaps others with whom he might establish some kind of patron-client relationship. But even the immediate, as distinguished from the extended, family could be impressively large. Twice married, Jesús de la Rocha (1812–1881) boasted of 82 children, most of them born out of wedlock. The patriarchs were known to take sexual liberties with the women in the family service and those who lived on the estates.[32] Relatives and in-laws often clustered around the patriarchal home. Speaking of his host and his wife in Juigalpa in 1872, Thomas Belt recalled that "a number of relations lived with them, including the mother of the hostess and two of her brothers." He added, "I noticed that the wealthier Nicaraguans are rather proud of having a lot of relations hanging about and dependent on them."[33]

Patriarchy manifested a strong ideology of gender in which women played subordinate roles. They enjoyed few rights and had limited access to institutions. Many more males than females attended primary schools.

The few women who learned to read and write could not attend any institution of higher learning. They did not vote or hold office, but neither did any other women in the world at that time. The Constitution of 1838 defined their status as "inhabitants" but denied them citizenship and offered only limited access to the courts. In 1845, Señora Josefa Quiñónez, wife of a deceased chief of state, could not give testimony in a court of law without her second husband's permission. In that particular case, the husband permitted the lawyer to transmit the questions through him to Doña Josefa.[34] In some cases women were restricted to the house, sallying forth to attend religious services under the careful eye of a trusted servant or relative.[35] Squier commented that the upper-class women of León "are very attentive to their devotions, but beyond their daily visit to the churches, rarely go out of doors." He did admit to a major exception: in the early evenings they might pay informal visits to friends or relatives.[36] Despite limited access to education, the women displayed "great quickness of apprehension and a readiness in good-natured repartee," according to Squier.[37]

While visiting a large hacienda at Olama, Belt learned that patriarchal customs required great circumspection in treating the women of the household. It would not do to offer a chair to the sister of the owner, a Nicaraguan friend advised him. Such courtesy to the lady would probably be misinterpreted by the family. Among the household rituals, "the master has some chocolate brought to him by his sister, who waited upon him. The wife, the sister, and the daughter in the departments seldom sat down to their meals with the master of the house but attend upon him, like servants."[38]

Among the elites, marriages were arranged.[39] The woman entered marriage a virgin and remained faithful to her husband thereafter. Society expected her to be a devoted wife and a loving mother. She was a devout Roman Catholic, the better to enhance the spirituality expected of her. In every way, she was expected to complement her husband.[40] Visiting the patriarchal and "hospitable mansion" of Don Hypólito Prato in Managua in 1854, Carl Scherzer recalled the hostess: "his wife, a stately, portly dame, played her part of hostess with much decorum, and with a sort of geniality not common among New Spanish."[41]

In my research I encountered only a single document written by a woman, a patriotic poem published in 1854.[42] I found little written about women. An essay entitled "The Education of Women" appeared in 1850 to explain the principal duties patriarchal society expected of the women as mother and to emphasize that her role continued as a grandmother. The essay would limit a woman's education to matters of the heart, omitting the mind.[43]

The rituals of death also reflected the patriarchal society. Of the approximately thirty obituaries I read, only one was for a woman, Margarita García, the wife of Minister Jesús de la Rocha. It praised the very characteristics esteemed in a patriarchal society: "Gifted with all of those qualities one might hope for in a good wife and mother, she knew how to carry out her duties. She was a religious woman who personified virtue. . . . Always at the side of her husband and children, she enjoyed inspiring the former and educating the latter." The obituary depicted the ideal model for woman, wife, and mother. It said as much about patriarchal society as about Margarita García.[44] Indeed, the very publication of the obituary served as a significant document approving and strengthening the patriarchal system. It prescribed as well as recorded the perfect behavior for the woman.

The same observation holds true for the unique "Intimacies of My Conjugal Love for María Josefa Narváez," by Gregorio Juárez.[45] The title conveys a nineteenth-century choice of words, somewhat more titillating to subsequent generations. Juárez, a distinguished politician and intellectual during the age of anarchy, married the sixteen-year-old María Josefa (his second wife) in 1833. She died in 1871, after bearing fourteen children of whom seven survived. Juárez provides—once again we only have the male viewpoint—unusual details about their meeting, courtship, and marriage. The emphasis again falls on the desired qualities of innocence, faithfulness, and religiosity, on her spirituality, generosity, and beauty, on her roles as mother and wife. However, this testimony also reveals the close companionship between this husband and wife, tells how they spent some of their time together, and records the times María Josefa accompanied Gregorio on official trips and in other official duties. The grief expressed by the bereaved husband impresses the reader. The document stands as an emotional tribute, a statement of profound love. Like the obituary of Margarita García, it depicts an ideal: an ideal marriage, an ideal relationship between man and woman, and the idealization of roles within a patriarchal society. Lest any doubt remain about the relationship of this document to the patriarchy, Gregorio Juárez concluded his tribute with a salute to it: "I want Nicaraguan history to preserve the memory of the period in which the patriarchal customs of our forefathers still reigned." He proudly boasted of those customs. In this particular situation, they comforted him. But in 1871 he also sensed that modernity threatened them.[46]

Not all the women of the upper class fit neatly within the patriarchal patterns. Some instances of matriarchy may also be cited. Carl Scherzer wrote of the woman rancher from Segovia who sold cattle and hides. He met the elderly lady on the road as she returned from Granada with twenty-one unladen mules, a "heavy purse," a daughter, and a large retinue of servants and muleteers.[47]

Moreover, various prevailing Indian customs contradicted the European-inspired pattern of patriarchy. The Indian women of Masaya, for example, retained their property after marriage.[48] Patriarchy characterized the Nicarao Indians but not the Chortegan.[49]

Marriage could be one means of upward mobility for the man. In the village of Diriamba in the mid-nineteenth century, Enrique Baltodano (1827–1899), poor and illiterate, married Dolores Parrales, a literate daughter of a landowning father. Enrique received land from his new father-in-law, worked it diligently, and became prosperous by village standards. His wife read to him, particularly from the newspaper, and he repeated to his friends in conversation what he had learned from her reading. He acquired a local reputation as a political activist. In this particular case the woman provided not only land, thus wealth, but also intellectual stimulation.[50] In due time Don Enrique shone as one of Diriamba's most distinguished citizens—and most powerful patriarch![51]

Whatever official discourse or homage to the Enlightenment might suggest, the reality was that the family and not the individual composed the base of society. Senator José Argüello Arce spoke of a nation composed of families although he referred, as others did, to the hierarchy of *pueblo, familia, individuo*.[52] Understanding the extreme importance of the family as the major means to stabilize society during the period of political anarchy, many Nicaraguans raised their voices to protect it. The Friends of Progress, in 1849, termed "morality, property, and family" the basis of society.[53] Similar ideas appeared in the *Eco Popular*.[54] These arguments sprang from conscious or unconscious fears that immorality might weaken the family, the most vital institution of order and stability. Immoral behavior that threatened the sanctity of the home was condemned. To extirpate immorality would strengthen the family and, thus, order and stability. A scandalized Pedro Francisco de la Rocha cataloged those immoralities in 1847: marital infidelity, wife abuse, insolence, and crime. He claimed all were increasing.[55] Like others before and after him, he denounced liquor as a major threat to the family.

Drunkenness and the evils thereof received considerable attention from the guardians of public and family morality. *Chichi*, a kind of light beer, was made from maize; the fermented juice of the wine-palm provided another light alcoholic beverage. The strongest drink, aguardiente, the "fire water" brewed from sugarcane, apparently enjoyed near universal popularity. One of the very few negative comments the observant Alexander von Buelow recorded about the Indians concerned their propensity for drunkenness, a vice he readily blamed on European influence.[56] An editorial in the *Mentor Nicaragüense* railed against the "evil of drunkenness."[57] In a testimony dated December 23, 1845, Father José Alvarado condemned aguardiente as a cause of fights and danger to the family since husbands "drink up their weekly wages and even sell household items and the clothes of their wives to buy more aguardiente with the result that wives and children have no food."[58] Fruto Chamorro condemned the hard liquor as "the fertile source of immorality and crime," lamenting that youth, women, and old people as well as working men imbibed all too freely to become "deprived of the very reason that made man similar to his Creator."[59] To these and other guardians of private and public morality, inebriation seriously threatened the well-being of the family; and in their cultural, social, and political environment the family offered stability amid chaos, order amid anarchy. It stood as the major barrier against social disintegration. In 1852 the politician Francisco Díaz Zapata, disturbed by crimes that "scandalize reason, morality, and civilization," proposed new legislation to combat them. However, the real deterrent to such crimes, in his opinion, was "the veneration of parents," the strong patriarchal family. To rehabilitate juvenile delinquents, it would be necessary to encourage parents to punish wayward children effectively.[60]

Father Agustín Vijil spoke out forcefully in support of a strong family. He noted that promiscuity might produce more children but the family took better care of them. Furthermore, "Only marriage can preserve society and guard morality." In classical patriarchal tradition, Father Vijil saw the family as the basic, indeed the fundamental and indispensable, unit of society. An intimate relationship existed between the family and the town, the later being a natural extension of the former. The town fathers could enhance the lives of inhabitants by beautifying the plazas and prohibiting the throwing of garbage and trash into the streets. They ought, however, to forbid all bathing between the equinox of September and the solstice of December. The idea that this was unhealthy, current in the West in mid-nineteenth century, was wholly against the Indian custom of frequent bathing. Vijil often referred to the municipal and central government officials as "the Fathers of the Fatherland."[61] If the elites had failed to come to a political consensus, they did reach a social one: the importance of the family.

The Iberian and Indian traditions and religious doctrine reinforced one another regarding the sanctity of the family and the dominant role the father played within that family. Those traditions and attitudes continued during the period of independence and anarchy. When Bishop Juan Cruz Ruiz de Cabañas addressed his Nicaraguan flock in a Pastoral Letter in 1795, he referred to Biblical patriarchy and emphasized exclusively the paternal role within the family:

> What man is better able to instruct his numerous family of children and servants in Religion, in the customs and demands of social, civil, moral, and religious life, than an active and hard-working laborer, an opulent landowner, a simple shepherd, and the inhabitant of the countryside who righteously look after the well being of their farms and herds? In him, you find the true Israelite, who without having lived in the cities or in the large urban centers knows the true God and understands the religion of his parents. He is a good man, a civic, political, and honored man without having abandoned the simple life and an honest but difficult occupation. He is a useful man, who without education in philosophy knows nature, her productive plants and animals, an important man to society who makes decisions in peace and justice without any of the pretensions of our learned wisemen. In short, I speak of the father of the family who without schools instructs his children and servants; he teaches them Religion and its ceremonies, the holy Law of God and its meanings, the marvels of our Lord. He passes on to his numerous descendants precious knowledge, sacred and profane, the very things he learned thanks to the zeal, vigilance, and care of his superiors.[62]

Those remarks summarized the attitudes of one of the two most influential social institutions, the other being the family itself. Such attitudes, coupled with the Church's constant emphasis on the Fifth Commandment, to "Honor thy Father and thy Mother," commended patriarchy; they enhanced tradition. The patriarchy and the Church buttressed each other.

Nearly a half-century later, the *Mentor Nicaragüense* revealed the continuity and strength of that patriarchal tradition well into the national period of Nicaraguan history. It published a long letter supposedly written by a father to a son who had just been elevated to the office of chief-of-state. Obviously the letter enunciated a political philosophy, but significant for this discussion is the degree to which it complements the patriarchal approach to governance suggested earlier by the bishop. First the father educates the son in his responsibilities. Second, those responsibilities draw on religion and custom much more than on the ideas of the Enlightenment. Governing is a *duty* to be accepted with the understanding that it entails heavy responsibilities, many obligations. "The unfortunate, the widow, and the orphan look to you, if not to remedy their ills, at least to alleviate them through compassion and humaneness, with loving counsel or, if necessary, with a sympathetic denial." The son is to seek "the love and respect of the people" whom he, in turn, will love as "sons and daughters." An interplay must exist between command and obedience, law and its observance. The father instructs the son to impose peace and order. Law and hierarchy are sacred. Disorder must be terminated without the "slightest hesitation."[63] Thus the father, the respected elder, the patriarch, prepares his son for his duties. The father's advice harmonized with that of Bishop Ruiz de Cabañas, underlining the basis of religious doctrine in patriarchal governance.[64] The pattern of the father transmitting wisdom directly to the son, who in turn integrates that advice into his political role, was apparently a well established one, both in Western history in general and in Nicaraguan history in particular. A biography of José Laureano Pineda, one of the nation's supreme directors, states, "His primary education he received directly from his father," not at all an unusual statement in the biographies of prominent men of the period.[65] Its frequent repetition contributed the definition of both patriarchy and politics.

In an effort to reconcile the genetic and contractual contradiction, the Constitution of 1838 conferred political power on the patriarchs, guaranteeing their ascension and domination. It made a distinction between inhabitants, that is, people living within the boundaries of the nation (Article 17), and citizens, men born within the boundaries or naturalized, of twenty years of age or older—or eighteen if married or with a "degree"— and either owners of a specified amount of property or professionals (Article 18). It restricted the vote and public office to citizens. Elections were indirect. To elect deputies to the assembly and the office of supreme director, citizens voted for electors who in turn selected members of the lower house and the executive. To elect senators, the citizens voted for electors who, in turn, selected another group of electors to name the senator. A limited electorate and indirect elections were common in Europe and the Americas in the nineteenth century. Clearly, in an impoverished

society such as Nicaragua where few legally met the property requirements, where political participation and decision-making concentrated in
two cities, and where an understanding of the law resided in a tiny minor-
ity, the process favored elite males who had some understanding of how a
complex, Europeanized political system functioned or should function. In
disproportionate numbers those elite males were large landowners or
merchants, all patriarchs.

The Constitution of 1858 essentially repeated those political provisions
of its Liberal predecessor that conferred political power on the already
powerful patriarchs. The second constitution went further to enhance the
patriarchy. Article 10 authorized the government to "suspend the rights of
a citizen for showing ingratitude toward his parents"! The constitution
thus equated citizenship with fulfillment of filial duty. Drawing on the Fifth
Commandment, the constitution rooted itself in the fundamental source
of patriarchalism.

In accordance with the propensity to combine familial and political
patriarchy, the *Rejistro Oficial* addressed the governmental leaders as
"honorable fathers of the State."[66] Ideally, the Nicaraguan senators were
expected to play the same role as the Roman senators, serving as
"Fathers of the Fatherland."[67] After a fire swept through Masaya in early
1852 destroying the homes of 327 Indian families, the government
reacted to the catastrophe as a part of its "paternal concerns.'"[68] These
reference were no mere figures of speech. Society, in particular the patriarchs, took them literally. The politicians themselves acknowledged their
patriarchal role. In an essay of 1847 Pedro Francisco de la Rocha praised
Supreme Director José León Sandoval for "his paternal presence."[69]
Supreme Director Norberto Ramírez termed his own government "paternal" in 1849.[70] The *Gaceta de Nicaragua* observed that Supreme Director
José Laureano Pineda had been a good husband and father and chief-
of-state, linking familial and political patriarchy.[71] In his inaugural address
of 1853, Supreme Director Fruto Chamorro notified his listeners, "I
consider myself as a loving but rigid father of the family who through pleasure and obligation always seeks the welfare of his children and only by
necessity and with a heavy heart punishes them when they require it. . . .
I will maintain the peace but like a good father of the family I will punish
the wayward son who disturbs it."[72] Chamorro returned to those themes
nine months later when rebellion threatened the peace he hoped to maintain: "All of the peoples form for me one single family and over each person I exercise my paternal solicitude."[73] When Granadan merchants

directed a petition to Supreme Director Chamorro in 1853, they responded obediently to his symbols of public discourse by addressing him as "the Father of the Nicaraguan people."[74] Likewise, an undated *Oración Suplicatoria* (a petition) addressed Chamorro as "Father of the Fatherland Fruto Chamorro."[75] The examples of invoking patriarchal duty and of identifying (and self-identifying) political leaders as patriarchs abound for the post 1846 period. Greater availability of documentation for that period, however, may explain the clustering of such examples.

Patriarchal practices extended beyond the age of anarchy into the remainder of the century. Writing in the early 1870s, Paul Levy, whose account of Nicaragua in the nineteenth century is among the most thorough, concluded, "Generally the customs of Nicaragua have a patriarchal character."[76] Widely spread and accepted, patriarchy has given rise to a number of theories to explain the Nicaraguan past, in terms of "society as the enlargement of the family."[77] No one has better adapted that theory for the study of nineteenth-century Nicaragua than Humberto Belli. From the hypothesis that societal values sanctioned the patriarchal family within which the father exercised absolute control, Belli drew the following implications for Nicaraguan history: an approbation of authoritarianism and personalism; limitations on compromise, dialogue, freedom, democracy, and equality; and a buttress to regionalism, that is, the rivalry between León and Granada.[78] Patriarchs resisted conceding powers to an impersonal and bureaucratic state. The family remained strong partly because the state was weak; the state remained weak partly because the patriarchs failed to come to a political consensus. Despite the inherent theoretical contradictions between the genetic family patriarchy and the contractual state, the state enforced and reflected the patriarchal norms of the family and the patriarchs participated in and controlled the state. Contradictions spawned confusion. Together, they help explain the difficulty Nicaragua experienced in its governance.

While Nicaragua suffered an extreme degree of anarchy and institutional weakness over an extended period, it was by no means unique within nineteenth-century Latin America in its political reliance on the family and patriarchy. Mark D. Szuchman convincingly presents Argentina as an example of "the logic of the link between domestic and political patriarchy."[79] Patriarchy offered newly emergent Argentina "a time-honored and widely recognized principle of authority to be used in lieu of an institutional apparatus."[80] Familiarity with patriarchal behavior—and conversely lack of familiarity with the newly imported European political theories, the ideas springing from the Enlightenment of others—made possible a consensus among elites and masses. Patriarchy offered many Argentines "a nonconstitutional consent and a non-articulated contract that operated under patriarchy for the best of reasons: they provided the most easily recognizable form of rule to the greatest number of people and they generated a mentalité toward authority that was very comfortable to the Iberian historical context."[81] Much less tersely but equally cogently, Gilberto Freyre argued the contributions of patriarchy to the formation of Brazil.[82] Brazil, unlike either Argentina or Nicaragua, enjoyed well-defined political institutions from independence onward; indeed, the vast scale of the South American giant required the mesh of patriarchy and monarchy to buttress unity and to facilitate governance. Most significantly, in the persons of Emperor Pedro I and Emperor Pedro II Brazil experienced genetic continuity, the core of patriarchalism, and did not have to rely on contractual government (although it did have an imperial constitution), whose conceptualization and execution have bedeviled the Latin Americas since independence.[83]

With deep historical, religious, legal, and intellectual roots, the patriarchal family flourished in Nicaragua. Because upper-class father enjoyed the rank of citizen, he not only exercised authority within his family but represented the family in the larger society of the nation. He set the tone for the family, society, and nation. Anarchy limited the effectiveness of his wider governance, but, then, he perpetuated the anarchy.

Haciendas, Plantations, and Ranches

Fruto Chamorro is a good example of the patriarchs whose wealth came from land and commerce and was the basis of their social prominence and political strength. [84] Since the land produced the items for commerce, it was of the two the more important source of wealth. From the comfortable family home in Granada, Don Fruto administered several cattle ranches and the very important family cacao plantation, "Las Mercedes," at Nandaime. The family fortunes depended on the productivity of those lands. Apparently Don Fruto administered them well—and in the manner of a patriarch. Maintaining friendly relations with the other merchants and landowners of the Granada region, he successfully expanded his socio-economic patriarchy to the political realm. Family wealth facilitated his successful political career.

Wealth was relative, just as political power prior to 1858 was never absolute. By European standards, the Nicaraguan elite lived modestly in their simple society. George Byam, who resided in the León region in 1839–40, testified that despite their lands members of the elite were "very poor." They found it difficult to sell their products; prices were low and barter was common; wages were high; and capital for improvements was scarce. Byam concluded that the landowners "having no sure sale of their herds and indigo, are generally very poor, as regards the possession of money, or even as to being able to obtain what in Europe would be considered not the comforts, but the necessities of life."[85] In 1855, Carl Scherzer paid a visit to the hacienda "El Dulce Nombre de Jesús" along the road between Rivas and Granada. Its owner, Tiburcio Chaparia, was, according to Scherzer, "an opulent man," possessing more land than a European noble, and which produced abundantly. Yet "his house was in such a simple and rough style, as many of our poor would be ashamed of."[86] The observations of both Byam and Scherzer corroborate other testimonies of the modest life styles of the elites. But, other evidence suggests that the privileged may have been more provident than was usually acknowledged. In a nation starved for capital, E. G. Squier, the U.S. diplomat in León in 1849, described an arresting instance of such foresight. Fearful of a rebellion, the local notables rushed to Squier's quarters to entrust him with their liquid wealth, a sum that astonished the young diplomat: "I will venture to say, more than a hundred thousand dollars in gold was brought to my room, within a space of two hours, and chiefly by persons who were not suspected of having an extra medio in the world. Experience had taught them the necessity of keeping a sum of ready money at hand, in event of revolution; and also of keeping it so completely concealed, as not to excite suspicion of their possessing it."[87] Squier's revelation indicated a thrift among the elites seldom commented upon. Still, while the perspicacious Paul Levy seems to repeat the obvious in 1870, his conclusion highlights in the broadest sense a major barrier between the elites and the fulfillment of their vision: "This society has one fundamental problem: it is poor."[88]

To overcome that poverty, the elites hoped to expand exports. They raised three primary commercial crops during the period of anarchy: indigo, cacao, and sugar. Each required capital investment. Consequently, while the large estates might not have a monopoly over cultivation or sale of these products, they tended to monopolize processing.

The indigo estate of Señor Hurtado one the nation's senators, nestled in a verdant valley near Brito on the Pacific coast. Like all the patriarchal landowners, he possessed individual title to his estate. His country house, in which the family resided occasionally, was spacious, built of adobe with a tile roof. The growth and particularly the processing of first-rate indigo (a blue dye that had already been in use in pre-Columbian America) required considerable attention. A dam across a stream furnished the water power to drive machinery, turning a wheel in one of two large masonry vats. In the larger, bundles of indigo plants soaked until the water fermented and the clear sap from the green leaves turned blue. The workers then drew the fermented water into the lower vat, where the wheel constantly churned it until the coloring matter curdled. The water was poured out, and the residue of pulp granulated. Spread flat on sheets, the blue dyestuff dried in the sun. When Squier visited that indigo plantation in 1849, civil disorder had taken its toll of Nicaraguan production. It had fallen to a fifth of its once best harvests; many estates had been abandoned.[89] Carl Scherzer reported in the mid–1850s that while once Chinandego, León, Rivas, and Granada had produced 750,000 pounds of indigo, many fields lay unworked and "desolate."[90]

The cacao tree, indigenous to the Americas, required seven years to bear the pod containing the bean. The delicate tree needed care during these non producing years. Any aspiring entrepreneur had to possess capital, labor, land, and, very important in this case, the time to wait patiently for that first crop. However, once producing, a healthy tree bore pods twice a year for thirty to fifty years with considerably less tending. Nicaragua produced excellent cacao. Since Nicaraguans drank much chocolate themselves, they could export only during years of abundant harvests, and then just a small percentage of the beans. Bad harvests forced importation from Guayaquil (Ecuador) of the indispensable chocolate.

Near Granada, José León Sandoval, who served as supreme director in 1845–1847, owned a plantation. His house, surrounded with palm and fruit trees, crowned a hill with views of Granada and Lake Nicaragua. He maintained a diversified estate: cattle, plantains, corn, indigo, and cacao. The graceful twenty-foot cacao trees and their sheltering shade trees gave the appearance of a park with broad walks extending in every direction. Workers gathered the pods, separated the beans from the husks, "surated" or fermented the beans, and spread them on skins to dry, turning them to prevent molding. After the drying, they sorted and packed the beans for marketing.[91] The region around Rivas alone was reputed to have had as many as 700 cacao estates in 1817.[92] Yet by 1855 only 40-50 working cacao plantations remained, with an average of 40,000 trees each, a total of approximately two million fruit-bearing cacao trees.[93]

Near El Viejo Chinandega, Bernardo Venerio owned two fine sugar plantations and a third which produced indigo. The Venerio family enjoyed a reputation as one of the wealthiest, most socially prominent, and most political influential in the country. The cane grew luxuriantly on the estates, and Don Bernardo harvested two crops a year, enough to keep the water-driven sugar mill turning all year. The fields required replanting every ten to fourteen years. Fully nine-tenths of the land lay fallow. The family manufactured aguardiente for local consumption and a crude brown sugar, *chanaca*, for the national market as well as for export.[94] In the late forties, the Venerios modernized the manufacturing of sugar and aguardiente by importing the latest machinery from England via Cape Horn.[95] Their estates were virtually self-sufficient in food.

When Squier visited one of the Venerio sugar plantations at mid-century, he sat swinging gently in a hammock on the second floor verandah of the white-washed, tile-roofed *casa grande*, gazing out upon an emerald, bucolic scene. He mused idyllically on "the charms of hacienda life—that aimless, dreamy existence, undisturbed by ambition and envy, and separated from the struggle of conflicting interests . . . without a wish ungratified, making the most of the present, and careless of the future."[96] The young American penned magnificently Romantic prose. He fell victim to the sweet illusions of a quiet, warm afternoon in an Edenic scene. In reality hacienda owners, particularly ones as successful as the Venerios, confronted problems of labor recruitment and retention, security and safety, civil war and social turbulence, machinery maintenance, capricious weather, marketing, the envy of competitors, and the fears of neighboring small farmers. Fretting over interest payments, scarcity of capital, wage demands, unpaid bills, debts, prices, and the irregularities of transportation, local and international, encroached upon the charms of hacienda life. The plantations obviously provided rewards; but amid the political chaos of Nicaragua, they also entailed risks, challenges, headaches, and, with mounting frequency, failure.

Ranching played an increasingly important economic role. Although cattle could be found everywhere on the Pacific side of the country, Nicaragua also experienced a rowdy cattle "invasion" advancing eastward across the central savannas. Already active in the seventeenth century, the advance guard of the cattle frontier were the *campistos*, men who hunted the wild cattle. [97] Acoyapa, founded prior to 1683 but not designated a city until 1862, was the urban center of the sprawling Chontales region that covered the territory from the eastern shore of Lake Nicaragua to the Mosquito territory on the Caribbean, the informal frontier. Julius Froebel visited Acoyapa in 1850 and estimated the population, including the surrounding country, to be around 2,600.[98] About two decades later, Thomas Belt, also a visitor, guessed it to be two thousand. Lawyers, merchants, and ranch owners, all of Spanish or ladino descent, lived in the city. Indians and blacks composed the lower classes.[99]

In the early 1820s Orlando Roberts observed "immense herds of cattle and horses," as well as mules, grazing the eastern shores of Lake Nicaragua.[100] By mid-century cattle populated Chontales. Cattle ranching required relatively few workers, a distinct advantage in chronically labor-short Nicaragua. From the cattle came cheese, tallow, hides, and jerky beef for the local markets and export. Fresh meat and milk also entered the local markets. Cattle were driven as far away as San Miguel, El Salvador, for sale in the extremely important annual November fair and also to Costa Rica.

Froebel trekked to the easternmost edge of the cattle frontier in 1850, where he was the guest of a certain Don Tomás S. "The small habitation . . . was exceedingly clean, and nicely built of bamboo-reeds, to the exclusion of almost any other material. Even the furniture—consisting of a table, some benches and bedsteads—was composed of the same." Don Tomás manufactured cheese. Froebel remembered, "As far as my eyes could reach from the habitation of Don Tomás, the savanna was covered with herds."[101] Squier visited the cattle ranch "Pasquiel," near the Rio Tipitapa. Owned by a wealthy resident of Granada, Federico Derbyshire, it was considered to be "one of the largest and most valuable" in Nicaragua. The only buildings consisted of two very large roofs supported by posts located in the center of a stockade of posts. The manager and his family lived in one corner, a small fenced off space, while animals shared the rest of the space under that roof. It also sheltered some rough machinery and equipment to make cheese.[102] Subsistence agriculture, the usual corn and beans, provided the few inhabitants of Chontales with the food they needed.

Wherever cattle roamed, cowboys flourished. The Nicaraguan frontier boasted of its *vaqueros*. Belt often watched them in action and described them as "wonderfully adroit in throwing the lasso; when riding at full speed, they throw it over the horns of the cattle, or the heads of the horses."[103] Few in number, the vaqueros conquered space to make the cattle industry flourish.

By mid-century, cattle provided one of the principal sources of wealth. [104] Further, as the cattle frontier advanced into Mosquito territory, it strengthened Nicaragua's claims to that underpopulated region over which Great Britain exercised a "protectorate" to the vehement protests of the Nicaraguans. Cattle in Nicaragua—as in the United States and Brazil—contributed to the consolidation of territorial claims. In that way, cattle raising became a foundation stone in the arduous construction of the nation-state.

While these descriptions depict prospering haciendas, plantations, and ranches, others equally valid paint a gloomy picture of abandonment, ruin, and decay. The economic insecurities and warfare took an increasingly heavy rural toll from the patriarchs. The times conspired against prosperity. Whatever the patriarchs possessed came from the haciendas, plantations, and ranches or from trade generated by their products. Such wealth was modest, although perhaps impressive within the Nicaraguan context. The Nicaraguans, even the wealthy ones, were money-poor. No opulence characterized any Nicaraguan family; conversely, at the other end of the economic spectrum, oppressive poverty was minimal, at least in the population axis between Chinandega and Rivas.

The Premodern City

In one sense, the countryside subordinated the towns and cities: they depended on its products. Yet in another sense, the urban prevailed over the rural. Within the confines of the modest cities of León and Granada, the patriarchal elites made political decisions that stirred a brew of discontent and rivalry. The civil strife bubbling in the urban caldron overflowed into the countryside, sweeping away hopes for economic prosperity. The city opened the door to modernity, only a narrow crack prior to 1858 but still sufficient for the "winds of progress" to penetrate. The new ideas from Europe and the United States were a challenge to tradition, more prevalent and tenacious in the countryside than in the city.

During the period of anarchy, an unusually high percent of the population lived in cities and towns of five hundred inhabitants or more. One estimate is as high as fifty percent. [105] An informal and incomplete tabulation of urban populations at mid-century by E. G. Squier (Table 8) adds up to 114,000 in a total population of approximately 250,000. [106] Since no accurate population statistics exist for the years prior to 1858, all figures are estimates and consequently vary. Despite variations, one generalization seems valid: a surprisingly high degree of urbanization characterized Nicaragua.

The major towns dated from the colonial period. Francisco Hernández de Córdoba founded first Granada and months later León in 1524. Earthquake damage prompted the citizens of León to move the city to its present site in 1610.

Large or small, the city represented a logic in Spain's imperial expansion: the power of a consolidated monarchy and the vigor of an incipient capitalism. Symbolizing the power of the empire, the city served as the primary instrument of imperial control. It centered on an open square. [107] The rigid grid pattern of streets signified order. Around the central plaza grouped the principal church, government buildings, major merchants, and the houses of those whose prestige was commensurate with the location. The more imposing the architecture the better it served imperial policy. In those cities resided the makers, enforcers, and judges of the monarch's laws. From the cathedral or the churches, the bishop or priests watched over the dispersed flocks of the faithful. The merchants directed local trade and participated in overseas commerce. The hierarchical order of the city as one moved from the imposing plaza outward to the humble suburbs enforced a colonial code of preference and authority. The Spaniards and their descendants lived on or near the plaza. That highly concentrated area, the residency of the patriarchate, served as the functional center.

If the city center reflected Spanish imposition of purpose, life styles, and architecture, the suburbs mirrored the Indian. The Indians lived in simple thatched huts, constructed in a traditional and nearly unvarying

Table 8. Approximate Urban Populations, 1850.

Town	Population	Town	Population
León	30,000	Chichigalpa	2,800
Masaya	15,000	Souci	2,500
Managua	12,000	Matagalpa	2,000
Chinandega	11,000	Somotillo	2,000
Granada	10,000	Nagarote	1,800
Rivas	8,000	Realejo	1,000
Segovia	8,000	Telica	1,000
Chinandega El Viejo	3,000	Posoltega	900
Pueblo Nuevo	2,900	Acoyapa	500

Source: E. G. Squier, Nicaragua, p.648.

style, surrounded by ample yards, the *solares*. They spread over a large area, attached to the city, yet also close to their fields. They brought their produce from farm to solar to plaza, making the cities virtually self-sufficient. The city thus mixed Europeanized and indigenous ways of life. It combined Spanish and Indian contributions. Mediating the extremes were the ladinos, a significant and growing population in each town and city.

Fittingly, the cities that were symbols of Spanish authority, ladino aggressiveness, and Indian persistence—an intriguing combination of order and subversion—became, by the early nineteenth century, the focal point of discontent and disorder. The citizens rejected Spanish authority, but disagreed about how to replace it. At least in theory, the structures of the colonial city clashed with the neocapitalist vision the patriarchs projected, but then the patriarchs themselves seemed to be, from many angles, contradictions of the capitalists they professed to want to be.

Figure 1. Granada. The central plaza vibrated with commercial and social activities in the mid-nineteenth-century, with carts, oxen, and horses as the main means of transportation. Abode walls, tile roofs, and wooden pillars and railings typify the building materials used to construct the city center. Lithograph source: *Meyer's Universum, oder, Abbildung und Beschreibung des Sehenswerthesten und Merkwurdigsten der Natur und Kunst auf der ganzen Erde* (Hildburghausen: Druck und Verlag vom Bibliographischen Institut, 1848–1852).

Orlando Roberts, who passed through Granada during its final days under the Spanish flag, described it as a classic colonial city: "One side of the great square is chiefly formed by the principal church; a large monastery and a convent make up the greater part of another side; the guard house, and a soldiers barracks, a third; and the principal shops in town, front the church, and complete the square."[108] He recalled that many of the houses in the central core were three stories high. In 1855, Scherzer contrasted the humble suburbs with the plaza and its "certain grand solidarity of character in its architecture."[109] Julius Froebel noted, "In the population of the suburbs and of the scattered habitations of the environs of Granada, the Indian element is predominant in part even exclusive."[110] The most important Indian suburb of Granada was Jalteva, with a history deeply rooted in the pre-Columbian past.

León, too, reflected the duality: modest suburbs and a more substantial center. John L. Stephens, visiting León in 1840, was critical of the approach to the city: "The suburbs were more miserable than anything I had yet seen."[111] Squier observed more gingerly in 1849, "In León, as in

Figure 2. León. This mid-nineteenth-century approach to the city shows Indian dwellings along the road. The origins of the domestic architecture reached back into the pre-Columbian past. Lithograph source: *Meyer's Universum, oder, Abbildung und Beschreibung des Sehenswerthesten und Merkwurdigsten der Natur und Kunst auf der ganzen Erde* (Hildburghausen: Druck und Verlag vom Bibliographischen Institut, 1848-1852).

Granada, the dwellings on the outskirts of the city are simple cane structures, covered with thatch, but sometimes plastered with mud and roofed with tiles."[112] These travelers praised the strength and beauty of the central section. Roberts found it "on the whole handsome . . . second in wealth and population to Guatemala [City]."[113] Later, Stephens was more enthusiastic: "It had an appearance of old and aristocratic respectability, which no other city in Central America possessed. The houses were large and many of the fronts were full of stucco ornament; the plaza was spacious, and the squares of the churches and the churches themselves magnificent."[114] Cobblestones paved the streets in the center which contrasted with the dusty (or muddy) lanes of the suburbs. The enormous cathedral of San Pedro, completed in 1743, dominated the plaza and the city for that matter. At its side, on a corner of the plaza, stood the bishop's palace and adjoining it the Tridentine College of San Román. The government palace, the garrison and barracks, and shops completed the inventory of buildings surrounding the plaza. A candle burning in a tin lantern over each door illuminated the narrow streets in 1850.[115] The large Indian population concentrated in the suburb of Subtiava, also of preconquest origin.

While a grander style reflected the greater importance of León and Granada, nearly all the towns followed a similar basic urban pattern. In describing Masaya, Scherzer spoke of the Indian inhabitants in "poor cottages" surrounding the town, the large church "stands in the middle of the square that serves as a market place," and the comfortable houses of the creoles compose the center of Masaya. "The walls of the houses here are thick and solid; the roofs of tile; and many have verandahs and balconies towards the street. Those of the opulent creoles frequently posses spacious courts and galleries supported on pillars, and many remind you of those in Andalusia."[116] Even the distant frontier towns followed the pattern. Juigalpa, although its population numbered only 800 in 1865, had a plaza on which stood the church, the priest's house, a presidio, a small hotel, and stores.[117] Acoyapa boasted of a large plaza with a "stucco-fronted church occupying one side." The principal stores and houses of the local notables filled the other three sides.[118]

Three types of housing predominated in the towns. A majority of the citizens inhabited simple cane huts, thatched with grass of palm leaves, with bare, earthen floors. Other inhabitants plastered over the canes, white-washed the walls, and crowned their houses with tile roofs. The wealthiest built their houses of large adobe bricks, two feet in length by eighteen inches in breadth by a foot in height, made of mud and hay. Their white-washed walls rose one or two stories around large courtyards, often filled with trees and flowers and occasionally containing a fountain. The roofs were tiled and the windows had iron bars or ornamental grating and shutters.

These housing types suggest the presence of three urban classes: the elites with their with their solid abode houses near the main plaza, the humble folk with their cane huts on the urban outskirts, and people who fit neither of those easily defined categories. Wedged precariously between the two extremes, neither rich nor poor, they lived in their houses of plastered walls. Scherzer gave some indication of the possible size of the elite population in both major cities. In 1855 he estimated that the population of León, including the neighboring Indian villages, did not exceed 30,000 of whom approximately 1,500 were creoles, and it is in that group the elites could be found.[119] He gave the population of Granada as 15,000 and added: "The Spanish Creoles, though their number scarcely amounts to 1,200, still retain all the advantages of wealth and political influence. . . . The president of the state, the ministers, generals, and officers of rank, magistrates, priests, ambassadors, and almost all official persons, are Creoles; that is of Spanish descent; or, at least, endeavor to pass for such, and carefully conceal the smallest mixture of Indian blood that may have polluted the pure Castilian fluid."[120] Although creoles could be found in all the towns, they concentrated in León and Granada for obvious economic and political reasons.

The commercially oriented towns contained an increasingly heterogeneous population, not just in race and ethnicity—the New Spaniards or creoles, ladinos, Indians, blacks, and sambos—but also in occupation. Almost all the wealthy families were landowners and merchants. Their houses more often than not contained warehouses, and nearly every one of them had a shop attached to the house, often presided over by the wife.[121] There were smaller merchants, too. Priests, a few teachers, soldiers, government bureaucrats, and a handful of professionals appeared in modest numbers. Roving peddlers and stationary sellers populated the markets and streets. Urban craftsmen plied their skills and wares. The farmers, peasants, and rural workers who dwelt in the towns completed the variety. Nonetheless, despite that apparent variety, the *Mentor Nicaragüense* divided society into two groups only: those who served the nation with their strength and those who served it with their brains.[122] The traveler Bedford Pim used another criterion for division: "the barefooted and the shoe-wearing. The former are lower class. . . . The shod-class—though they may be poor as church-mice, and as black as coal—regard themselves as the upper ten thousand, and look down upon the shoeless multitude with patronizing contempt."[123] In a superficial manner, Pim made a significant observation. Wearing shoes announced a social message; it declared a cultural preference. It indicated the role a ladino opted to play. To wear shoes signified Europeanization, a symbolic acceptance of the norms of elite behavior. To forego them meant adherence to local, traditional values. That distinction become increasing important as the push to modernize gained momentum.

As best as can be gleaned from the faulty statistics, urban Nicaragua grew impressively during the last decades of the colonial period and the early years of independence, only to decline during the mid-nineteenth century. The numbers in Table 9 suggest that trend. Although the population of the city of León was considerably larger than that of Granada in the national period, the larger city-state of Granada was more populous than that of León.[124] The stagnation and sometimes decline of the urban population between 1846 and 1867 reflected the bitter civil war and the catastrophic National War of the 1850s. In the national period, both León and Granada had been sacked and destroyed. León suffered partial destruction in 1824 and again in 1845. "Perhaps no city in America has suffered more from war than León," lamented Squire.[125] In 1849 he saw "The great cathedral . . . surrounded by entire squares of ruins of what were once palaces. . . . Entire streets, now almost deserted, are lined with the remains of large and beautiful edifices, destroyed in the civil wars."[126] The ink was hardly dry on Squier's lament before a worse disaster befell Granada. In November of 1856, William Walker ordered General Charles Frederick Henningsen to destroy Granada, because his forces could no longer hold the city against the allied armies of Central America. In a seventeen-day orgy of destruction, the filibusters blew up and set fire to the city. Proud of his fiery devastation, Henningsen left a sign flapping in the smoky breeze: "Aquí Fué Granada" (here was Granada).

Clearly the cities of Nicaragua—in particular the two rivals—did not prosper in the anarchy they perpetuated. It was more than mere symbolism that the formation of the nation-state did not occur until after their destruction. Nor did the government bureaucracy of the incipient nation-state concentrate in either of those city-states but rather in Managua, somewhat, although not totally, removed from the bitter rivalries of the past. Regardless of its disadvantages, Managua enjoyed a reputation as a

Table 9. Population of Major Nicaraguan Cities, 1778–1867 (in thousands).

	Year		
City	1778	1846	1867
León	7.6	25	24
Granada	8.2	10	10
Managua		12	2-7
Masaya	6	15	12
Chinandega		11	8
Matagalpa		2	
Rivas	6	8	8
All-Nicaragua totals	150	250	258

Source: David Richard Radell, "An Historical Geography of Western Nicaragua: The Spheres of Influence of León, Granada, and Managua" (Ph.D. diss., University of California, Berkeley, 1969), p. 233.

"new" and "neutral" city, less rooted in the tradition of conflict and therefore better able to lead Nicaragua into the future.

Education and Intellectuals

Education divided rather than consolidated Nicaragua. In the period of anarchy, literacy distinguished the patriarchs from the folk, as it later separated the ruling class from those they dominated. Schools existed for the "shod" or "booted" segment, those whom the *Mentor Nicaragüense* expected to serve society with their brains. The most affluent families also could hire tutors. Eventually, two universities gained a tenuous existence, one in León, and the other in Granada. Needless to say, these institutions enrolled the sons of the patriarchal elites but they also provided a means of social mobility for a select number of impoverished youths who somehow managed to gain admission. They contributed to the distinct personalities of the city-states, thus widening the divisions within the ranks of the elites. Operating two universities in a country which could not afford one squandered precious public funds. At the same time, few schools taught the "shoeless," those expected by the *Mentor Nicaragüense* to serve society with their brawn. In every sense education mirrored the dual society and, what was more, contributed to widening the cleavages among the patriarchal elites and between them and the folk.

The turmoil of the 1820s prevented anyone from seriously addressing the issues of education. Chief of State Dionisio Herrera imposed sufficient order to be able to propose the first comprehensive educational plan in 1831. Denouncing as scholastic the modest educational facilities inherited from Spain, he charged that they inhibited the development of an independent nation. He wanted to replace them with the practical ideas emanating from the Europe north of the Pyrenees. Herrera urged a new curriculum emphasizing foreign languages, mathematics, chemistry, agriculture, science, geography, and history as well as the fine arts. He suggested hiring European teachers.[127] The legislature of 1836 responded tardily with the first public education law mandating the primary school curriculum: reading, writing, arithmetic, Christian doctrine, and an introduction to the federal and state constitutions. At the opposite end of the educational spectrum, it created *escuelas universitarias* (university schools) in both León and Granada, a law of questionable utility in an already divided state. Often a single university could forge a unity of mentality and bonds of camaraderie among elites. Before independence, the sons of privileged Brazilians, for example, studied together at Coimbra University, a common experience credited with creating a reasonably homogeneous intellectual elite that in its turn contributed to national unity. The university laws of 1836 seemed determined to emphasize the separation between León and Granada. A law of 1840 decentralized all public instruction, requiring each department to create a board of public education to oversee local education.[128]

The political reality of a decentralized system of education contradicted the intellectual aspirations to use education as the tool to sculpt nationality. The *Mentor Nicaragüense* in 1841 repeatedly emphasized the importance of education for the nation's future. This was a belief to which the elites paid homage, but the concept served more as a goal for the future than a mandate for the present. Only some people understood the relationship between education and the creation of the modern nation-state. Education could infuse a sense of nationality, commonality, patriotism, love of the fatherland, and the shared experience. In a raging sea of anarchy, it could serve as a beacon beckoning the population to the shores of order. Nationality among heterogeneous peoples required a conscious commitment. Education could transmit the ideas and ideals about the reality the elites sought to create, the nation-state of their perceptions. Education could forge unity, bringing Nicaraguans to a consciousness of themselves and of the benefits of nationhood. Not being innate characteristics, nationality and nationalism result from processes that social learning and habit can accelerate. Schools could play a vital role in those processes.

Everywhere in Latin America, the elites put their faith in education to mold unity, to contribute to nation building, to instill civilization, and to ensure progress. In 1845 the Argentine Domingo F. Sarmiento affirmed that only education could redeem the barbaric masses, and the leaders of the hemisphere applauded. In 1902, the Brazilian Euclydes da Cunha excused the brutal military destruction of the folk community at Canudos, Bahia, on the grounds that the army's victory facilitated the introduction of education into the barbaric backlands; few national leaders dissented. More often than not, budgetary restrictions frustrated plans for educational expansion. Despite the rhetoric, the aspirations, and the hopes, education remained the domain of the privileged few in nineteenth-century Latin America. Nicaragua was no exception.

Pedro Francisco de la Rocha stood out as unique in his understanding of the importance to Nicaragua of education's ability to homogenize the population. Primary education in particular served to incorporate the folk into the elite culture, since the curriculum reflected the elite's bias toward European behavior, ideas, and tastes. At the same time, he was acutely aware of the dangers posed by the government's greater attention to university education.

Limiting higher education to a privileged few followed well-delineated elitist patterns by no means exclusive to Nicaragua during the first half of the nineteenth century. In general, education reinforced the reality of a class society, although, on occasion, in unusual cases, education promoted some mobility. The *Mentor Nicaragüense* openly reflected on the concept of inequity in education: "A farmer needs instructions on how to be a citizen and farmer, not to be a judge or a political leader; an artisan needs the proper education to avoid vice and to love virtue and the Fatherland, to respect the laws and to become a better artisan, but not to govern the Fatherland or to influence the government. Finally, public education must be universal, all classes of society must participate, but not in the same way. In short, education must be universal but not uniform, public but not common."[129] This short quotation twice mentioned the Fatherland. Education was to instill a love for it among all students but to prepare only a handful, neither the farmer nor the artisan but most certainly the sons of the elites, to govern. To use the words and sense of the Constitution of 1838, the "inhabitants" of the nation would dwell on and work the land, while the "citizens"—the elite and propertied, the patriarchs—would govern it. Those citizens comprised "the men of reason" about whom the Argentine intellectual Esteban Echeverría discoursed so convincingly in 1838. His *Dogma Socialista* proclaimed that only the "prudent and rational" part of the population, that is, the educated elite, should govern. "Democracy, then, is not the absolute despotism of the masses or of the majority; it is the rule of reason."[130] Nicaraguan political philosophy sprang from and contributed to the wider currents accepted throughout Latin America. Nothing remarkable characterized that concept of the elite monopoly of power. Yet it's immediate failure—the lack of political consensus, the anarchy, the economic decline—should have sobered the privileged sufficiently to see that their own best interests were not being served.

Education did not serve all the privileged. Very few girls attended primary school. The universities admitted none. Creole males dominated education. They predominated in the primary schools, could afford the time and money to take those Latin courses which served as a kind of university preparation, and they monopolized the universities. Almost all the young men matriculating in the universities studied law and philosophy. Medicine was a poor third choice; the few chairs of medicine often stood vacant. The universities offered no engineering or science options. Jerónimo Pérez (1828–1884) entered the University of Granada in 1842, one of eighty students studying philosophy with Dr. Rosalio Cortez and law with Dr. Francisco Barberena. He received his degree in philosophy in 1844 and in 1852 his law degree. Academically he distinguished himself as a historian. Landowner of a farm near Masaya, his natal city, he spent most of his long career in the government: mayor of Masaya, director of the first tobacco factory (government-owned), director of various government publications, a legislator, minister of the interior, and diplomat. He was the brother-in-law and confidant of President Tomás Martínez. [131] His successful career reflected an early reality of the educational system in general and the universities in particular: they prepared the students primarily to serve the government. The perspicacious Pedro Francisco de la Rocha detected a danger: "The young people are not trained for anything else but a government job, and although the number of employees far exceeds the needs of the country, it is insufficient for the many who want such employment."[132] In short, he, like others, blamed part of the anarchy on the excess numbers of lawyers and philosophy graduates eager to displace others in governmental office. Too many students for the few jobs available fueled the fires of frustration consuming public order. [133]

In 1850 Minister Sebastián Salinas also raised his voice to criticize the educational system. Public education suffered from scanty funding. University education failed to speak to national needs. The two universities taught Spanish grammar and Latin, philosophy, and canon and civil law. Granada gave instruction in French and English; León offered courses in medicine. Both ignored mathematics and sciences. Salinas concluded that the restricted curricula handicapped the youth and harmed the nation. [134] Minister Jesús de la Rocha repeated those criticisms in 1853. [135] The patriarchs wanted to open a transit route across the isthmus and to promote the building of a canal. Not one Nicaraguan had the education to undertake either project or even to discuss the projects scientifically and intelligently with foreigners eager and prepared to build a transit route for their own goals.

Foreign visitors recorded negative impressions of Nicaraguan education. Squier reported in 1850 large sections of the country, Chontales and Nueva Segovia, without schools. Teachers received no training. Schools were few and in the largest towns overcrowded. They had no texts, no paper, no pens, and no equipment. Students recited their lessons in unison. "The lesson is repeated after the master, simultaneously by the whole school, and it is difficult to say which shouts it the loudest, the master or the scholars; but it is always easy to tell the proximity of the schoolhouse, from the noise." [136] At most the teachers taught reading, writing, arithmetic, and something about Christian morality. No schools existed in the countryside. Squire did visit one "cane-built" house of a priest where the housekeeper "had about her some fifteen or twenty little children collected from the poorest families, to whom she taught reading and writing." [137] Such a scene was all too exceptional, the very reason it attracted Squier's attention.

In a governmental report in 1853, Minister Jesús de la Rocha provided a census of primary education: the Department of the Oriente had 964 students enrolled in 30 schools plus "one school for girls in Granada"; the Department of the Occidente maintained 19 schools which submitted no enrollment figures; the Department of Nueva Segovia had 10 schools with 614 students; Matagalpa had one school. [138] Municipal officials visited the only school in Jinotega in 1853. Financed partly by the municipal government and partly by voluntary subscription, the school had been functioning for only seven months. The 95 students were learning reading and writing, and they were struggling with the alphabet when the local worthies arrived. They advised the "Sr. Preceptor to explain from time to time the rights and duties of a citizen" to his young charges.[139] In 1854, the traveler Carl Scherzer recorded a comparatively optimistic educational census. He believed that the entire country possessed 60 primary schools enrolling 2,800 students, one percent of the population. He mentioned five schools for girls.[140] Although Peter F. Stout visited only one primary school in Masaya in 1859, with "about sixty boys and girls busily engaged in poring over their books," he concluded, "Education is at a low ebb."[141]

That judgment embraced university education too. The library of the University of León housed 1,500 volumes; the University of Granada included no library.[142] Although the two universities poorly served the needs of about two hundred students, they absorbed the lion's share of the educational budget.[143] Such disproportion was unique neither to Nicaragua nor to the nineteenth century. While the full significance of the imbalance may be complex, the expenditure exemplified the attention bestowed on the education of the elite, those most likely to attend the university, to the neglect of a majority unserved because of the paucity of primary schools. Nor did the money spent on the few benefit the nation, since the education provided no instruction in subjects that might encourage local economic development, such as sciences, mineralogy, mathematics, agriculture, or engineering.

The critics suggested changes. Distraught that his Granada, a city of 13,000, supported only two primary schools, that virtually no instruction for females existed, and that instruction was more theoretical than practical, Pedro Francisco de la Rocha submitted a thoughtful plan for the reform of public education in 1850. He recommended more primary schools, better equipment and support for the schools, higher pay for the teachers, a Normal School to prepare the teachers better, greater access to education for girls, and fees for university instruction in law, philosophy, and Latin but none for instruction in design, mathematics, Spanish, and English. Señor de la Rocha understood that Nicaragua needed a different type of education if it was to engage in world commerce, avoid dependency, and develop economically:

> It is necessary to give a new direction to our education in order to bring it up to the level of our present needs and potential and to meet the challenges of our contacts and relations with foreigners as we integrate more and more into the commerce of the New World with the Old. It is not enough just to have a wondrously fertile country and sit back with our arms crossed expecting happiness. . . . The peoples of the North Atlantic demand from us the rich

products that the cultivation of the fertile soil of our country can provide. Constantly ships arrive at our shores loaded with industrial products in exchange for our products. It is impossible for us to remain at our present social and economic level. If we do not cultivate our fields and exploit our mines, foreigners will do it for us. Working the soil favors the nation just as it does the individual. If we do not cultivate it, we will lose it. Civilization and industry dominate the world in which we live. Lazy and ignorant people only earn the shame and scorn of civilized nations. Work and more work and always work are the law of progress. Furthermore, work is the admirable instrument of social harmony because all interests converge nowadays in the prosperity of industry and commerce. Work is the fountain and legitimization of both public and private fortune. . . . And what is more, work is the means of establishing political stability and public tranquility. [144]

The author ranged far in his plan, but the focal point of his recommendations and of the nation's hopes was a useful education. An educated people would be a working people; a working people would be prosperous, protective of their nation and able to develop it. A strong sense of nationalism and a sensitivity to the international pressures bearing down on Nicaragua characterized these ideas.

The increased turmoil of the 1850s prevented the enactment of any of those recommendations. Yet at the end of the decade, the Minister of Development, Education, and Public Credit returned to them. He advocated a new educational system which placed emphasis on primary education rather than the university, urged an increase in the number of schools, and proposed a Normal School. The Minister ordered that university students pay a tuition and concluded sternly, "This nation needs more citizens, not inhabitants; it needs artisans, merchants, craftsmen, engineers, and mechanics, not more lawyers, physicians, and intellectuals."[145] For the course upon which the elites had embarked after 1857, he was correct.

Despite the overwhelming problems eroding even the best efforts to promote and provide education, intellectuals did exist, and their numbers increased. Pedro Francisco de la Rocha affirmed in 1850, "Intellectual life is not lacking in our country. In fact, a notable progress in intellectual activity has occurred."[146] The urban setting encouraged that process in which people think about themselves and conceptualize their relationship to a larger environment, past, present, and future. Within that setting, the intellectuals performed functions and pursued activities vital for the realization of the elites' vision for the future.

Based on biographical data available for twenty-two men, a shadowy profile can be sketched of the intellectual.[147] Most of them enjoyed access to the universities, although a few were autodidacts. They were a part of or formed a close association with the creole elites. All lived in the cities, not surprisingly spending most of their time in León or Granada. Eight were born in León; six in Granada; three in Masaya; and one each in Segovia, Managua, Potosí, Guatemala City, and Seville, Spain. Twelve studied at the University of León; six at the University of Granada; and five at the University of San Carlos, Guatemala. Some of those intellectuals studied at more than one university. Buenaventura Selva began his studies at León but received his law degree from Granada. José Benito Rosales studied law in León but his professional academic association was with Granada, where he taught law and served as rector of the university. Pedro Francisco de la Rocha took his degree in medicine at León and in law at Granada. Fifteen studied law, and three earned degrees in both law and medicine. One earned a degree in mathematics and surveying. Those men played multiple roles in their society. They wove their intellectual pursuits into busy daily lives. They engaged in ranching, agriculture, business, commerce, journalism, law, the military, the priesthood, education, diplomacy, and politics. Their many and varied activities afforded little time for theoretical speculation. Some of the most thoughtful insights into contemporary social, economic, and political realities emerged from the pens of Pedro Francisco de la Rocha, *Revista Política sobre la Historia de la Revolución de Nicaragua en Defensa de la Administración del Ex-Director Don José León Sandoval*; Jesús de la Rocha, *Informe Presentado por el Ministro Interino de Relaciones Interiores y Exteriores a las Cámaras Legislativas de Nicaragua*, and S.C., "Estado de los Pueblos al Establecerse la República Democrática."[148]

The evidence at hand suggests a highly politicized intelligentsia. In a tradition that was becoming well established throughout Latin America, the intellectuals were social and political activists. Many directly participated in the governing process. In fact, twenty of the twenty-two intellectuals participated actively in politics at the municipal, departmental, and national levels. They were mayors, prefects, deputies, senators, ministers, and supreme directors.

The intellectuals lived in either León or Granada, where political action was most likely to occur. They shared an urban perspective and to the extent possible imposed it on the nation. As a group, the Nicaraguan intellectuals favored a modern state shaped by the examples of Europe and the United States, an export-oriented economy, a canal across Nicaragua, and progress, again a slippery concept related to what was perceived to be happening in the North Atlantic nations. In their minds, the shape of the future—progress and Europeanization—depended on the country's ability to export agricultural products and in other ways to exploit the natural wealth and resources. On this point, they made common cause with those rural landowners who were eager to export.

The intellectuals discussed the nation-building process. Those discussions reflected their urban orientation and their European self-identity. They thought of themselves essentially as Europeans transplanted to the New World. Having identified with the European heritage and orientation, they determined to convert the rural population to new ways rather than to valorize its folk heritage. They consciously fostered patriotic feeling, although much of it represented the regionalism of the city-states and only some of it, particularly after 1855, reflected an incipient nationalism, one rooted in European preferences and urban vision. Those characteristics assumed significance because much of the population remained rural or rural- and folk-oriented. Rural, folk, and, for that matter, traditional patriarchal orientations challenged an emerging urban vision of modernity and the intellectuals' perception of the goals of nationalism. They delayed the creation of a modern state.[149] As the urban intellectuals gained confidence and influence during the last half of the nineteenth-century, they provided a seemingly convincing rationale for the destruction of folk societies.

Prior to 1858, the concerns of the intellectuals found expression within the two universities; the political discussions of the tertulias; sermons, lectures, and speeches; and in the press, both the official newspapers and those ubiquitous broadsides. The printing press arrived late, in 1829. Granada boasted of the first one, the Imprenta del Gobierno; the Imprenta del Estado began to operate in León in 1833. Soon thereafter, Masaya, Managua, and Rivas had type shops and presses.[150] The first newspaper, *Gaceta de Nicaragua*, is reputed to have appeared in August 1830, possibly only one issue; the second, *La Opinión Pública*, in 1833.[151] Those newspapers, and others published in 1837 and 1838, were of small size and few pages, rough pioneers printing largely government decrees and laws. After 1840 the newspapers improved in quality and quantity, inserting essays, editorials, and verse among the official decrees.

At the same time, the elite took to publishing broadsides to disseminate some message, frequently, but not always, political. Often the urbanites awoke to find the broadsides plastered on street walls or slipped under their doors. Because some verged on gossip or libel and others were frankly humorous, they commanded a careful reading and considerable commentary. The published "Funeral Orations" of members of patriarchal families contained biographical data and splendid insights into family and social life. The first "book" published in Nicaragua, *Breve y Sencilla Narración del Viaje que Hizo a Visitar los Santos Lugares de Jerúsalen el P. José M. Guzmán, Americano* (A Brief and Simple Narration of the Journey that Father José M. Guzmán, an American, Made to the Holy Places of Jerusalem) bore the date 1838 and numbered forty-seven pages. The first important book was Pedro Francisco de la Rocha's *Revista Política sobre la Historia de la Revolución de Nicaragua en Defensa de la Administración del Ex-Director Don José León Sandoval* (1847), judged by Jorge Eduardo Arellano to be the first history of Nicaragua written by a Nicaraguan.[152]

Libraries were uncommon. The University of León boasted of one, possibly the largest. Miguel Larreynage deposited his private library of about 3,000 volumes in the university before he left Central America for Spain in 1818.[153] Little information on private libraries exists.[154] Anselmo H. Rivas (1826-1904), one of the major nineteenth-century intellectuals and largely self-taught, enjoyed access to such libraries, particularly those of Pedro Chamorro and Pedro Rouhaud in Granada.[155] A foreign visitor inspecting the library of a Dr. Rivas in Managua in 1850 commented, "He was a young man, educated in Guatemala, which he termed the Paris of Central America, and his library was well supplied with books in the German, French, Spanish, and Latin languages."[156]

European and Latin American books made their way into Nicaragua, but their route from publisher to reader has not been explored. Dionisio de la Quadra demonstrated in the early decades of the century how one determined bibliophile obtained books. He kept funds in Havana to pay for the ones he wanted.[157]

The reading habits of the nineteenth-century Nicaraguan elites are somewhat clearer. In 1803, Tomás Ruiz opened the doors of the reinvigorated Seminario Conciliar de León to the Enlightenment by including Condillac in his logic course.[158] A few years later, studies in the Seminario introduced the young Rafael Francisco Osejo to the ideas of the Enlightenment. In the philosophy course given by Ruiz, he read Locke, Rousseau, and Montesquieu, whose ideas Chester Zelaya has traced in the later writings of Osejo.[159]

The University of León, officially inaugurated in 1816, also diffused the ideas of the Enlightenment. In book and lecture, the ideas of Bacon, Pierre Gassendi, Descartes, Boyle, Locke, and Benito Jerónimo Feijóo, long neglected, ignored, or proscribed in Nicaragua, as well as the ideas of Buffon, Raynal, Condillac, José de Cadalso, Luís Antonio Verney, Lavoisier, Voltaire, Rousseau, Montesquieu, Diderot, Laplace, and others closely associated with the eighteenth-century Enlightenment, made their entrance into the university.[160] It would seem that the sun of the European Enlightenment shone brightly in Nicaragua.

Its rays obviously illuminated Pedro Francisco de la Rocha. In his *Revista Política* he quoted from such luminaries of the Enlightenment as Montesquieu and Emmerich von Vattel as well as later ones, Benjamin Constant de Rebecque, Mme. de Stael, Francisco Martínez de la Rosa, Louis Adolphe Thiers, Francois Pierre Guillaume Guizot, José María Luís Mora, Louis Blanc, and others. De la Rocha's quotations point out that savant's reading preferences.[161] More or less at the same time, the mid-1840s, Jerónimo Pérez frequented the house of Pío Bolaños in Granada. The two read rather conventional religious books from his library and discussed them. Pérez observed that family members pressured Don Pío to buy novels for them to read, and that several of the periodicals to which the older gentleman subscribed contained serialized novels.[162] Referring specifically to the preferences of Anselmo H. Rivas, Carlos Cuadro Pasos generalized about the reading habits of Nicaraguans at mid-century. They enjoyed French writers, particularly René de Chateaubriand and Victor Hugo.[163] Squier corroborated that observation. On the sugar plantation San Gerónimo near El Viejo in 1849 he encountered the owner "swinging in a hammock, suspended in the corridor on the shaded side of the building and engaged in reading a Spanish translation of [Eugene] Sue's *Mysteries of Paris* [first published in Paris in 1842-43]!"[164] The young man in a hammock on his hacienda, leisurely exploring French "mysteries," personified an elite increasingly absorbed by Europe, increasingly convinced that Europe provided the model they hoped to emulate.

In significant respects, both the form of education and the behavior of the intellectuals augmented rather than assuaged social fragmentation during the age of anarchy. The government failed to use the powerful tool of education to instill and to shape nationality and nationalism. It bent to local pressures, creating two universities, thus strengthening the concept of the city-states. The intellectuals drank from the well springs of

European thought and shared the economic dream of international trade and transit. Those very commonalities cut them off from the folk and the popular roots of potential Nicaraguan nationality. Further, they tended to use their intellectual talents in favor of the city-states, on which they lavished a loyalty that impoverished their potential to promote nationalism.

The Limits of Patriarchy

The patriarchate played a key role during the age of anarchy. It may well have been the most effective institution within the nation, sharing that distinction with the robust Indian communities. The patriarchs eventually achieved political domination over those communities, but failed to prosper economically, at least to the extent their tantalizing vision promised.

The possibility of fulfilling patriarchal hopes for international commerce and domestic prosperity dimmed as the clouds of anarchy overshadowed Nicaragua. To the extent that the patriarchs themselves looked outward, beyond the confines of their estates and the boundaries of their nation to an inviting world market, they required changes in their own economic patterns and in the structures, institutions, and social habits of their new country. To enter that beckoning capitalist marketplace, they required, among other things, peace, order, banks, capital, transportation, labor, and technology. To deal with the strong, well-defined, and aggressive nations of the North Atlantic, they needed a realistic sense of proportion, purpose, and the possible. To transform Nicaragua into a bustling highway of world commerce, they required all those advantages in addition to a high degree of international sophistication in order to deal with Great Britain, the United States, and other major powers of the period whose interests in such a highway were intense and, even more worrisome, hegemonic. Was a small, impoverished, powerless, illiterate, divided, and politically naive nation ready to deal with those capitalist nations on their terms? The painfully obvious answer was no.

If anything, Nicaragua's situation at mid-century was less propitious than on the eve of independence. Anarchy reigned. Production and trade alternated between stagnation and decline. The Nicaraguans lost whatever protection Spain had afforded them. Their own naivete exposed them to international scoundrels and aggressions. Nonetheless, in an address to the legislators in 1849, Supreme Director Norberto Ramírez reminded his listeners yet one more time of the need to take advantage of

Nicaragua's fertile lands and natural resources. He appealed to them to enact measures to substitute real prosperity for elusive vision.[165] They applauded but did not, or could not, heed his words. Time had run out. Other nations had discovered Nicaragua and appreciated its resources and potential. By 1849 they already had begun to take advantage of the perceived benefits Nicaragua offered. A startling transformation occurred. No longer the promoters of a vision, the Nicaraguans fell victims of it.

Clearly, the major failure of the patriarchs had been their inability to come to a political consensus. That lack of agreement delayed the consolidation of the nation-state. The delay frustrated their economic goals, just as it facilitated foreign penetration. For despite bitter geographical rivalries and some discord over political philosophy, members of the elite professed a rather uniform concept of "national interests" because they identified—or confused—their own interests with those of the nation. They wanted to increase trade, to construct the interoceanic route, to achieve security for the nation, and to govern. They were simply unable to resolve who would govern and how.

The patriarchs rarely considered the interests of the humbler classes, and dismissed the "shoeless" masses as barbaric. Those interests existed, however, and differed from the interests of the patriarchs. Whatever the *real* national interests were or might be, they could not be meaningfully discussed and certainly not implemented until a large proportion of the population achieved greater homogeneity. This did not happen in the nineteenth century; the struggle to create such homogeneity and the resistance to it became a major theme in Nicaragua's twentieth-century history.

Frustrated, probably even frightened, the Nicaraguan elites at mid-century looked with envy on the experiences of the Costa Ricans and Guatemalans. In both of those Central American nations, caudillos—Rafael Carrera in Guatemala and Braulio Carrillo in Costa Rica—had stepped forward to exert firm political control. The caudillos overcame the political differences, geographical rivalries, and class separations which also bedeviled Nicaragua.[166]

In an otherwise caustic series of essays published in the *Registro Oficial* in 1847, S.C. praised the contributions of Carrillo and Carrera.[167] According to the author, the two caudillos had this in common: overcoming political anarchy, they imposed order and unity. Faced with political chaos and geographical rivalries not dissimilar to those that tormented Nicaragua, Carrillo announced, "We will suffocate the shouts of passion in order to hear in silence the voice of justice and public accord."[168] He did suffocate them. One widely read Costa Rican historian, Carlos Monge Alfora, characterized Carrillo as the "incarnation of the stern patriarch."[169] Both Carrillo and Carrera governed as political patriarchs. Although both encouraged coffee culture, they had very different land ownership policies, in view of their radically different populations. Carrera strengthened the Indian communal ownership of land; Carrillo divested the municipalities of their communal land to distribute it to individuals, a trend that would characterize Central America after the mid-1870s. After visiting Carrillo, John L. Stephens praised him and concluded, "In that country the alternative is a strong government or none at all."[170] In his newspaper articles S.C. concurred, longing for a "stern patriarch" to put Nicaragua's house in order. None appeared until 1857.

Although the Constitution of 1838 enshrined the patriarchs, their disunity brought about a failure of government. Yet for whatever reason—perhaps the constitution or the political system successfully prevented it, perhaps no one possessed the ability—no strongman emerged to dominate politics sufficiently to unite and to govern the nation. At best, the supreme director was a kind of "first" among his peers.

If the Nicaraguan patriarchs had failed to impose political order and to consolidate the nation-state, they likewise failed to make the nation hum economically. Much of that failure derived from their inability to regulate labor. After independence, they manumitted the few Black slaves and relaxed the colonial regulations of Indian labor without making other arrangements to control labor in a country in which the population was scant and the available land seemingly limitless. To export, to dominate the countryside, the elites needed a means of enticing or coercing labor. They did not have it, nor did they achieve it.

Because the rural population preferred to work its own lands, the plantations, haciendas, and ranches suffered a chronic labor shortage. Stephens commented on the resulting low plantation productivity around León in 1840.[171] Squier noted that landowners lacked "enforceable labor contracts" to regiment the Indians for production.[172] Frederick Boyle lamented in the mid-1860s, "Difficulty of obtaining labor is the bar to all success [on the plantations]."[173] The foreign travel literature of the period abounds with comments on the low productivity and abandonment of the rural estates because of the lack or shortage of labor. The foreigners merely repeated the conclusions of the locals. When the government asked landowners in 1860 to comment on the reasons agriculture remained underdeveloped, Joaquín Elizondo of Rivas replied, "Agrarian capitalists need a good agricultural law to regulate contracts with workers and agrarian judges with the means to enforce such contracts."[174]

Control of labor would require control of land, for so long as land remained open to squatting the rural inhabitants gravitated toward it. They preferred to plant, tend, and harvest their own corn and beans rather than to work for wages or for a share of the crop on the lands of others. That situation was by no means peculiar to Nicaragua. In Brazil, too, during the same period, the rural poor preferred to squat on land and work it for themselves. The Brazilian landowner had met the challenge with the importation of African slaves before 1850, but after the closing of that trade, he faced a new reality in recruiting labor that necessitated a firmer dominion over the land.[175] The Nicaraguan patriarchs lived the worst nightmare of the landowning class: a failure to recruit labor to turn the land into wealth. Labor shortages—and they increased after independence, when the government abolished the tributes once borne by Indians—accounted for declining or stagnant exports as much as anarchy did.

Significantly, an ideological contradiction existed between traditional patriarchy and its economic vision. The patriarchy rested on a type of patrimonialism of pre- or neocapitalistic origin, while the materialization of the vision presumed and required modern capitalism. José Coronel Urtecho pointed to the prevalence of economic contradictions in the early national period, "Among us appeared what you might term a local form of family capitalism, that is a Latin American variety of capitalism, not entirely devoid of feudal antecedents or of the colonial mentality and of course closely linked to family needs, goals, and considerations."[176] As the patriarchs set out to turn their vision into a reality after 1858, they planted more than coffee trees. They also propagated the seeds of their own destruction. The patriarchate they historically experienced and the capitalism they pursued clashed.

The patriarchy managed to hold on to power during the transition from anarchy to order. It put down popular rebellion and eventually turned back foreign interventions, both impressive achievements. At the same time, the historical record reveals its limitations. An inability to achieve articulated goals further underscores them. From the patriarchs' own point of view, they failed. Greater power eluded them. They did not consolidate the nation-state. Tomás Martínez, a marginal figure to the patriarchate, came closer to achieving that goal after 1858 on the political ruins created by the patriarchs. Prosperity also eluded them. Nicaragua never became a global commercial emporium.

The patriarchs constituted only a tiny, albeit very significant, percentage of the population. What about the humble majority? While anarchy inflicted undeniable hardships on the poor, they might have drawn more advantages from the inefficient patriarchal system than they could hope to wrest from a strong, modern, capitalistic nation-state dependent on agrarian exports. The following chapter explores that possibility.

· III ·

Folk: the Popular
Nature of Society

An Attitude

Whirling around the stage to the music of drums, flutes, and whistles, Governor Tastuanes pauses to lament to the Chief Constable, "It is a great shame that we have no golden table, no embroidered tablecloth, no golden inkstand, no pen of gold, no golden blotter, not even white paper, and no similar suitable items for a session of our Noble Government." Clearly, Nicaragua is too poor. As one immediate if temporary solution to the budget crisis, the two authorities resolve to tax the Indian Güegüence. The governor orders his immediate appearance. So begins the lively, amusing, and popular dance-drama *Baile del Güegüence o Macho-Ratón*, a unique folk document for the study of Latin America, comparable only to the dance-dramas *Rabinal Achí* of Guatemala and the *Ollantay* of Peru.[1]

With its origins lost sometime in the sixteenth or seventeenth century, the *Güegüence* generously mixes Spanish and Indian cultures, just as it fuses the Spanish and Náhuatl languages into a unique patois.[2] Most authorities speculate that a mestizo might have written the dance-drama.[3] Nonetheless, the content reflects the manners, humor, and world view of the Indians. The *Baile del Güegüence* retained its popularity during the nineteenth century and seems to have been performed throughout the twentieth as well.[4] One of its dances, the perennially favorite Dance of the Macho-Ratón (the little mule), remains a staple of any self-respecting Nicaraguan folk-dance troupe.[5]

As a significant means of nonverbal communication, dance plays an important role, particularly in nonliterate societies. Dance can educate; it expresses popular feelings and transmits sentiments; it offers an emotional release from restraint and inhibition. It can lift ordinary people from their daily routines, conferring on them an extraordinary experience. While dance can reaffirm social behavior and tradition, it can also challenge them. It provides a means of public expression of criticism that ordinary people might reserve for private conversations, if they verbalize it at all. For whatever reason, dance often gets away with criticism that authorities might censor in other media. Drawing people together in solidarity, the dance spectacle is capable of arousing the consciousness of the participant and the beholder.[6] It contributes to the formation and strengthening of what Emile Durkheim called the "collective conscience." The music accompanying dances also carries a message of meaning and most certainly of emotion.

While the emotional impact of the dance is relatively easy to understand, the message it imparts may need to be decoded to the outsider. The accompanying dialogue simplifies that task, and significantly expands the message of dance and music. Although the interpretations of that message vary, they must all take into account two basic factors. First, this particular dance-drama retained its popularity for ordinary people over the course of several centuries. Second, it relates historical and social realities as perceived and appreciated by them. Thus it constitutes an important source for the study of the history of collective perception and psychology.[7]

The theme is a universal one, the interplay of authority and resistance. It takes place in a Pacific coastal region of Nicaragua. The governor, constable, secretary, and registrar in the cast obviously represent authority. Güegüence personifies resistance. The protagonists are clearly identifiable: the rulers, the Spaniards and their New World descendants the creoles, and the ruled, the Indians and the ladinos. Two cultures clash. To Indian and ladino audiences, the plot emphasized "us" and "them." They immediately recognized the situation and enjoyed, doubtless identifying with, the many ploys of the underdog to thwart authority, avoid taxes, and ridicule regulations. In the end the wily old fellow kept authority at bay and even used it to gain his own ends. Thus the dance-drama ritualized collective social hope and reaffirmed popular thought.

The lively music, resplendent costumes, skillful dancing, and hilarious dialogue complemented each other, heightening the theatrical/political experience. Even in English translation, the dialogue flows mirthfully as this staccato example between the constable and Güegüence illustrates:

Constable

Ha, Güegüence, ya estamos en el paraje.	Ha, Güegüence! Here we are at the place.

	Güegüence
Ya estamos con coraje.	Here we are, with heart of grace.
	Constable
En el paraje.	At the place.
	Güegüence
En el obraje.	To work apace.
	Constable
En el paraje.	At the place.
	Güegüence
En el paraje.	At the place. [8]

As much as the madcap patter evokes laughter, Alberto Ordóñez Argüello claims that the farce is even more evident in the dance. [9] At any rate the spectacle was great fun as it drew on a wide variety of standard dramatic devices of humor.

But mirth was secondary to message. In ritual reiteration of sentiment, Güegüence challenges authority and ridicules European customs. Participation in and attendance at the dance-drama must have solidified sentiments of disdain of foreign authority, that is, the Spaniards and later the creoles. Community laughter and enjoyment bespoke an approval of Güegüence's challenges and triumphs, an approval of passive resistance. Clearly Güegüence was more clever than the authorities, his cleverness an affirmation of folk opinion and communal memory. [10]

During the course of the dance-drama, the authorities make a series of demands—recognition, respect, pleasure, and taxes—on Güegüence. He responds by drawing on traditional devices of Indian evasion and humor: feigns deafness, pretends to be ignorant, misunderstands words, assigns double meanings to words. Such faulty communication—such passive resistance—always evoked great glee from audiences, which enjoyed watching Güegüence poke fun at, outwit, and ridicule the authority figures. They identified with the old man's efforts to avoid exploitation. Perhaps they drew from this popular dance-drama a confirmation of their own passive resistance. After all, they too declined to work on the plantations of the patriarchal elites. The men hid or fled to avoid military conscription. They avoided taxes whenever and however they could. On many levels, they could relate to the desire of Güegüence to be left alone.

The dance-drama concludes on a realistic note, a kind of accommodation between authority and resistance. Güegüence renders some respect; he cannot avoid paying some tribute. More significantly, a marriage is arranged between Suchi-Malinche, the daughter of the Governor, and Don Forcico, the son of Güegüence. Obviously it represents the union of two peoples, two cultures. Through that accommodation, the pattern of the future emerges. Still, the union and the accommodation do not prevent Güegüence from reminiscing about the "good old days:" "In my time, when I was a lad, in ancient times. . . . Let me remember past times. With such memories, I console myself. Ah, my sons, where do we go from here? Backwards or forwards?" Amid the laughter generated by the farce, a thoughtful note sounds: change has occurred, "ancient times" are finished. Güegüence wonders whether or not the change is for the better. For audiences submerged in nineteenth-century political anarchy, the question hung ominously in the air: "Where do we go from here?"

Symbolism saturates this dance-drama. Of all the dances, why was— and is—the Dance of the Macho-Ratón unquestionably the most popular, the most remembered, and the most repeated? One explanation would focus on identification of the viewer with the Macho-Ratón. Obviously the Macho-Ratón symbolized something special to the audiences. After all, the dance-drama bore two titles: the Güegüence OR the Macho-Ratón. Did not the title therefore equate Güegüence with the "small mule"? Indians always have placed great value on animal symbolism and representation. Much of their religion and mythology, many of their tales and jokes involved animals and animal spirits. Humans took animal forms and vice versa. If Güegüence could have an animal counterpart, perhaps it was the small, sturdy, reliable, and hard-working Macho-Ratón. Hence the Dance of the Macho-Ratón paid tribute to the clever Güegüence. If the audience identified with Güegüence, they also identified with the Macho-Ratón. The two merged into one in accordance with Indian logic. Whatever interpretation one might place on that identification, the dance at the end of the piece was the highlight, a grand finale that came to symbolize the entire drama.

The richness of the *Baile del Güegüence* lies partly in psychological interplay between actor-dancers and the audience. The entertainment reflected popular sentiments. People identified with the situations, with Güegüence, and with Macho-Ratón.[11] The play is also a satire, a parody, and a metaphor. It enjoyed far too much success among ordinary people in the nineteenth century to be considered exclusively as an amusement or a curiosity.[12]

The vast literature on the *Baile* reveals the many interpretations that can be assigned this dance-drama. Yet not until the mid-1960s did much attention focus on the political and economic messages encoded in it. They, too, merit study. In 1966, Alejandro Dávila Bolaños wrote of its profoundly political and revolutionary implications. In 1971 Gladis Miranda called it "the first literary protest in Hispanic America against the oppressive and unjust governing structure."[13]

Such interpretations suggest to the non-Indian population the complexities of meaning that folklore can convey.

The *Baile del Güegüence* was but one dance or dance-drama in the Indian repertoire. Others, too, spoke to historical themes. Popular in the nineteenth century, according to Daniel G. Brinton, was the *Baile de los Cinco Pares de Francia* (Dance of the Five French Couples), which, despite its unusual name, constituted one variant of the ubiquitous Dance of the Moors and the Christians.[14] Likewise, the folk drama *Original del Jigante* (The Original Story of the Giant), a variant of the Biblical David and Goliath story, involved in this Nicaraguan rendition the clash of the Moors and the Christians.[15] The conquest of the infidel Moors by the European Christians told a tale of violence the Indian mind identified with the Spanish invasion and conquest of the early sixteenth century.

The violence, trauma, and disastrous impact of the conquest preoccupied the Indians throughout the hemisphere and across time. The Dance of the Moors and the Christians—the Dance of the Conquest, directly germane to the history of the New World, but seemingly not danced in Nicaragua—was (and is) performed from Mexico to Peru. Bishop Bartolomé de las Casas concluded in the sixteenth century that these dances relating to conquest and the songs accompanying them kept alive a historic memory among the Indians. They related "the coming of the Christians, the arrival of these last and how they invaded their [Indian] lands with violence."[16] Three centuries later, in 1856, Father José Antonio Urrutia, a priest in the predominantly Indian town of Jutiapa, Guatemala, reflected on the continuity of those dances and their impact: "In most of the Indian towns the custom is still general of preserving a knowledge of great events in their history by means of representations, called *bailes*, which are, in fact, dances in the public squares, on the days or evenings of great solemnities. It is most interesting for one who understands something of the language to participate in those *bailes*, as he can thereby obtain some knowledge of the most remote traditions and events in the history of the Indians."[17] Studying those same dance-dramas in the twentieth century, Nathan Wachtel marvelled at how the arrival of the Spaniards and the conquest lived on in native folklore:

"These traditional folk dramas make one appreciate to what extent collective memory perpetuates and passes on events of the past."[18] While he questioned the historical accuracy of those dramatic presentations, Wachtel concluded that they preserved for the Indians a memory of their heroic resistance to the outsider. From the tribute those representations paid to the Indian fighters, the viewer drew inspiration and maintained a link with the past.[19] In Nicaragua, the Dance of the Five French Couples preserved the memory of the violence of conquest and strengthened solidarity within the Indian community. The sobriety of the Five French Couples contrasts markedly with the gaiety of the Güegüence.

Foreign travelers to Nicaragua at mid-nineteenth century, such as E. G. Squier and Julius Froebel, frequently mentioned the dances they witnessed. Froebel recounted his experience in Telica, near León, in 1850. Passing the night in that Indian village, he watched a dance-drama entitled *El Juramento ante Dios* (The Oath before God).[20] The plot centered on the relations between a Moorish and a Christian king, who were neighbors. In one of their frequent wars, the Moor captures the Christian, befriends him, and signs a treaty of friendship and peace with him. Then the Moor sets the Christian free. Later, treacherously, the Christian king attacks the Moors and again falls prisoner. Arguing that virtue without true faith is worthless, the captive converts the Moorish king to Christianity amid joyous singing and dancing, all accompanied by marimba music. Throughout the Americas, the Moor—the non-Spaniard—came to represent the Indian. The Indian audiences did not miss the symbolism. In *El Juramento*, the non-Christian, which is to say the non-Spaniard, represents virtue as well as strength. This complex dance-drama rationalizes Christianization, while subtly proclaiming the superiority of the Moor, that is the Indian. The Indian audiences could extract from the plot a symbolic account of their own history.

Ritualized dance enjoyed great popularity among the ordinary inhabitants of nineteenth-century Nicaragua. Juan M. Mendoza remembered eleven different dances performed annually in his village of Diriamba during the nineteenth century, among them "el Machorratón."[21] The periodic repetition of dance-dramas satisfied the participants and observers by giving vent to feelings of repressed hostility and by reinforcing popular interpretations of the past.[22] Further, the dances contributed to the strengthening of the "mestizo" and "communal" Nicaraguan culture that, according to José Coronel Urtecho, evolved as the result of a long colonial past.[23]

Popular tales reinforced the attitude created by the dance-dramas. Circulated widely by word of mouth, they were a form of popular entertainment. Skillful story tellers, the Indians wove into those tales their pride, intelligence, and insight. They treated the topics which most concerned them with a humor honed into a razor-sharp instrument of ridicule and pride.[24] One popular kind of story focused on the Indian's ability to get the best of the European, the infinite variations on the plot of Güegüence. From that theme arose an entire oral canon that amused and delighted the listener before and during the nineteenth century.[25]

In his travels around Nicaragua in 1850–51, Julius Froebel stopped for shelter one night at an Indian hut in the vicinity of León. There he witnessed among the Indians an animated story-telling session:

> Before going to bed, the company, sitting in front of the door of the house, amused themselves by telling stories, the obligation to contribute by this means to the general entertainment of the company passing around the circle. I have observed the same pastime amongst the herdsmen and muleteers of Mexico. In the present case the stories were all of one stamp. An Indian has a pretty wife, whom the priest tries to seduce. But the Indian is too sharp for the priest, and the latter is caught in a trap. *Otro Indio*—another Indian [story]!—was the call inviting the next in the circle to come forward with his narrative.[26]

Exactly like Güegüence, the Indians in those stories outwitted the European much to the satisfaction of the listeners.

The type of tales that enjoyed such popularity fell under the general rubric of "El Indio y el Chapetón" [The Indian and the Spanish-born Resident]. One way or another, these tales repeated the idea that the Indian was cleverer than the Spaniard.[27] Many of those stories pitted the Indian against a priest, a doctor, or a bureaucrat, often the mayor.[28] How he outsmarted the *chapetón* was what attracted and amused the listener. Apparently this type of tale can be found in the oral literature of most Indians of the Western Hemisphere.[29]

In one of the most intriguing Nicaraguan tales, the Indian takes on not just a local official who has been harassing him but the king himself! Appropriately entitled "The King and the Indian," the story unfolds in this fashion:

> One day as an Indian was leaving his village, the Spanish mayor called to him, "Where are you going, Indian?"
> "I'm off to the city on some errands."

"What are you going to do, steal chickens?" said the mayor with a laugh.

The remark offended the Indian but he didn't let his face show it. He thought to himself, "The mayor is always putting us down. Well, I think I'll teach him a good lesson."

"Well, Mr. Mayor," the Indian replied, "I'm going to visit my friend the King. I'm going to have lunch with him."

"What the devil! You're not going to talk with the King, much less have lunch with him."

The Indian answered, "I bet my mule against your horse that I am going to have lunch with the King." The mayor owned a handsome horse, a Peruvian steed worth more than five thousand pesos, while the Indian had an old, broken-down mule that wouldn't even serve as a meal for a buzzard. The mayor responded, "With great pleasure I accept your bet. I'm going to accompany you to see if you have lunch with the King."

The two set out together and upon arriving at the palace one of the soldiers stopped them and asked, "What do you want, Indian?"

Very humbly the Indian replied, "Well, I only wanted to visit the King in order to ask him a little question."

The guard answered brusquely, "The King has no time to talk with the likes of you. Ask me the question."

The Indian said, "I only wanted to ask the King if a piece of gold about the size of my fist would have much value."

His eyes wide, the guard replied, "OK, hang on just a second." He ran to get the captain of the guard.

The captain asked, "What do you want, Indian?"

With great humility he replied again, "Well, I only wanted to visit the King in order to ask him a little question. I only wanted to ask him if a piece of gold about the size of my fist would have much value." At that point the Indian raised a calloused fist scarred by cuts and bruises.

The captain said, "Hang on just a second, Indian." He entered the palace. Immediately he returned on the run and said, "Look, Indian, by pure chance, the King isn't busy right now and he can talk with you. Enter."

Accompanied by the mayor, the Indian entered the palace, and the King embraced him warmly, saying, "How are you, my little Indian? How is your wife? And how is the corn crop? Are the kids well?"

He began chatting with him amiably. After a short time, the King said, "Look, my friend, it is time for lunch. Stay here and have lunch with me."

The Indian replied, "Oh, Your Majesty, I am very sorry, but I have many errands to run while I am here in the city."

The King, somewhat impatiently, said, "No, my dear man, stay here with me. I insist. You can't refuse the invitation of your King!" To which the Indian responded, "Well, if Your Majesty insists, then I can't refuse." And he and the mayor sat down at the King's table.

Needless to say, the mayor was downcast and sad. In his mind he bid fare-well to his handsome Peruvian steed and said to himself, "Hmmm, I want to see how the Indian gets out of this mess. I'm certain he hasn't a grain of gold. He's got himself into trouble now."

The servants brought them an exquisite banquet with three kinds of meats, four kinds of fruit, three varieties of wine, and they all ate joyfully except the mayor who was so upset that he couldn't swallow a bite. After the banquet, the King offered the Indian a glass of cognac and one of those fat cigars he enjoyed smoking. Afterwards, the King said to the Indian, "Well, my friend, they told me that you wanted to ask me something. What is your question?"

The Indian said, "I only wanted to ask Your Majesty what a piece of gold the size of my fist would be worth?"

The King answered, "That is difficult to answer because much depends on the quality of the gold. But, tell me, my friend, where did you find this piece of gold the size of your fist?"

The Indian replied, "Well, in reality I haven't found it yet. But just in case I might find such a piece, I wanted to know how much it might be worth."

The King became furious and shouted to the mayor, "Why have you brought this country bumpkin here to waste my time?" The King added to an official at his side, "Throw this mayor in jail. I'm going to teach him that he can't fool with me."

And the Indian left to return to his quiet little village.[30]

This delightful tale arouses interest, sustains suspense, and displays a good sense of humor. Indeed, it provokes laughter. The Indian satirizes the lust for gold and condescension toward the Indians. He outsmarts the mayor, the king, and the system. After eating a fine meal, causing tur-moil in the palace, winning the mayor's horse, and having the satisfaction of seeing His Honor incarcerated, the Indian quietly returns home a victor.

Alongside the longer tales, snappy Indian-chapetón anecdotes circu-lated widely. They served the same purpose as the tales. The chapetón asked, "Where does this road go?" The Indian replied, "The road goes nowhere. It is the traveler who goes to and fro on the road."[31] As might be imagined, many of these anecdotes and stories rely on a play on words and double meanings, making most of them difficult to translate.

Variants of the Indian-chapetón stories circulated throughout much of Central America. Some evidence exists that the patriarchs knew, repeated, and used the stories. One example illustrated how they moved across both geographic and cultural boundaries. A Spanish traveler in the

Guatemalan highlands asked an Indian who was better, the priest or the mayor. "The two are the worst," replied the Indian. Applying that Guatemalan anecdote to the two political parties of Nicaragua in 1851, a Salvadoran broadside concluded neither one was any good and both "were the worst."[32]

The stories and dances were not novelties of the nineteenth century. They did not appear suddenly with the advent of independence in 1821 or disappear when anarchy was vanquished in 1857. With roots deep in the colonial past, they flourished throughout the nineteenth century. The attitudes they reflected and shaped seemed to have strengthened after the collapse of Spanish rule and throughout the 1821–1857 period. The sudden absence of the crown's authority and protection, tenuous and problematic as they might have been in that distant corner of the king's realm, actually buttressed the social and economic position of the Indians so long as the patriarchal elites failed to govern effectively. During the anarchic hiatus, work requirements and tax collections diminished, giving Indians greater freedom. An absence of enforceable demands in a very real sense liberated the Indians. The status of the mestizo also improved. At least as far as the Indians were concerned, such situations tightened communal bonds and enhanced folk attitudes.

An argument can be mounted convincingly that during the age of anarchy the folk community enjoyed its greatest strength since the conquest. It counterbalanced the other powerful institution of the period, the patriarchal and family structure of the elites. The patriarchate and its antithesis the folk community coexisted. Indeed, patriarchal characteristics pervaded the Indian social structure: respect, homage, and duty to elders remained a fixed moral value. Both the patriarchate and the folk community exercised considerable power; each provided continuity and a measure of stability for the creoles on the one side and the Indians on the other.

Both institutions excluded many of the numerous mestizos, whose position grew highly complex. To some extent, they shared both cultures. In accordance with myriad social and economic considerations and realities, ladino individuals occupied a wide social spectrum, some identifying more with Indian life styles, others enthusiastically embracing European models. The ladinos who inclined more to the Indian side—probably those living away from the immediate influences of either León or Granada—shared the attitudes expressed and propagated by the Indian stories and dances.

The stories and dances provide a peek into the Indian mind, a furtive exposure to the thoughts and attitudes of approximately half the population of Nicaragua. Most of them lived apart from the European and Europeanized segment of the population. During this period, their communities, the folk societies, flourished. It was their final flowering.

A Community

The *Baile del Güegüence* and the stories of the Indian and the chapetón reflected the reality of a socially divided society. On the one side stood the creoles. The Indians occupied the opposite side of the social spectrum. The estimates of the percentage of the population which was Indian during the first half of the nineteenth century varied. The nineteenth-century evidence concerning racial and ethnic compositions of the population reflected the individual observer's impression, perhaps his preconception of the society. None estimated the Indian population to be lower than Frederick Boyle did in the 1860s, two-fifths of the population.[33] Many thought it larger. The usually reliable E. G. Squier started at mid-century, "The Indians of Nicaragua . . . predominate in the country."[34] Twenty years later, the equally reliable Paul Levy agreed. He concluded that the Indians were *el pueblo* (the people).[35] At the same time, the ladino or mestizo population, large and growing, became the dominant group before the end of the century. The economic and political roles of the mestizos in Nicaraguan society increased impressively over the course of the nineteenth century. Unaccommodated, at least officially, by Spanish institutions, the ladinos benefited by independence, which psychologically and socially liberated them.

Strained relations existed between the mestizos and both the patriarchs and Indians. Many ladinos sought social and economic improvement; a few obtained it. Most earned very modest incomes, and their status differed little from that of the Indian.[36] Nonetheless hostility often characterized their relations. The Indians had their pride, feeling "themselves to be quite equal in intelligence with the mestizo population, and superior to them in civilization."[37] For their part, the ladinos looked upon the Indians as a conquered race to be exploited in every possible way.[38]

Considerations of the Indian populations, their contributions, and participation in national life followed geographical and historical criteria. The Central highlands formed a physical division. East of the highlands, on the Atlantic coast, the Indians bore some relationship to the Chibcha linguistic family of northern South America. They had greater contacts with the English, European pirates, and Blacks than with the Spaniards. In the mid-seventeenth century, an African slave ship floundered near Cabo de Gracias a Dios. The African survivors mixed with the local Indians. Later, Jamaican Blacks arrived to work in English economic enclaves, and they too contributed to the Black-Indian miscegenation, a *zambo* population known as the Mosquito Indians. None of those peoples had experienced the Spanish colonial past, although, for other reasons, the patriarchal family structure characterized their societies. The English language and Protestantism had more impact on their evolving culture than Spanish and Roman Catholicism. At mid-century, the population of this vast area probably did not exceed 30,000. The Afro-Caribbean influence predominated, including their diet of fish, turtles, root crops such as manioc, plantains, and pineapples. The inhabitants lived quiet lives, undisturbed by the anarchy rocking the Pacific coastal region. They would not play a significant role in Nicaraguan national life until the late nineteenth century.

The more numerous Indians west of the highlands, on the Pacific coast, demonstrated linguistic and cultural affinities with Mesoamerican societies to the North. They fished, raised turkeys and dogs for food, grew maize, beans, chili peppers, avocados, and cacao, and cultivated cotton. They fell under Spanish rule. Spanish eventually replaced the Indian languages, which, however, lived on in the geographical nomenclature and, for that matter, as the names for whatever the Spanish had encountered new to them. At least nominally, the Indians converted to Roman Catholicism. These Indians played a role, willingly or not, in the evolving Nicaraguan nation during the nineteenth century, more perhaps in its social and economic life than in its politics. The crops, the preparation of food, the meals, the drinks made from maize and chocolate, the ordinary architecture, the ubiquitous hammock, the melody of the marimba, indeed the daily rhythm of life reflected the Indians' presence and influence. The Indian population tended to be a very young one. One authority estimated that rarely did an Indian live beyond the fortieth birthday.[39]

The Indians maintained as much social distance as possible from the creoles and the mestizos. They preferred to live within their own communities and shunned outsiders. At León and Granada, the major concentrations of creoles and mestizos, the Indians lived in their own parallel and detached communities, Subtiava and Jalteva, under their own governments of Indian officials. In other towns, a small number of

Figure 3. Church. The Indians designed and built this massive, fortresslike structure in Subtiava, between 1700 and 1705. This church and the plaza on which it fronts have since served as the focal point for the Indian community around León. Source: collection of the author.

creoles, a larger number of mestizos, and many Indians lived under one municipal government but not necessarily in integrated neighborhoods. Because of their numbers, the Indians left a characteristic impress on such towns. Thomas Belt observed in one such community. "Doubtless much European blood runs in the veins of the inhabitants of Jinotega, but their whole manner of living, they follow the Indian ways."[40]

Domestic architecture and its accompanying daily life-style indicated the continuity of the Indian culture. The nearly uniform *rancho* with its origins in the pre-Columbian period represented simplicity, functionalism, and harmony with nature. The rectangle usually measured something like 15 by 20 feet; the walls of the rancho were built of posts and cane or maize stocks; woven grass made the roofs impermeable to water but they had to be changed every year or two. In the informal custom of exchange labor, relatives, neighbors, and friends joined together to construct the rancho for the person needing a house, usually a young man recently wed or about to marry.[41] It had two parts: a sleeping room and a kitchen which also served as living room, dining room, and workshop. The rancho contained little furniture, perhaps some chairs or tree trunks or stones that served the same purpose; perhaps a simple bed of skins stretched on a frame. The *solar*, the land around the rancho, might contain a small, walled but roofless washing area. The inhabitants defecated and urinated in the open yards, which also contained gardens, fruit trees, and animals. Those who lived away from rivers and lakes drew water from a well, often belonging to the community rather than a single family. Much of the mestizo population adopted the rancho dwelling.

With scant concern for nation-building, the Indians pledged loyalty to their local community. They hoped to distance themselves from the civil strife and labor demands of the patriarchs. They opted for agrarian self-sufficiency, a local economy, community harmony, and a life regulated by local customs. Much of that community life ran in pre-Columbian patterns. Paul Levy concluded that the Indians of Nicaragua lived apart from the rest of society but neither as separated as their counterparts in Mex-

Figure 4. Indian Dwellings. This scene, photographed in either 1899 or 1900, is typical of the domestic architecture and village street of the entire nineteenth century. The Indian construction of the house at the left well represents a style and technology preceding the Spanish conquest of Nicaragua. Photograph source: Library of Congress, Prints and Photographs Division, Archambault collection.

ico and Guatemala nor as integrated as in El Salvador and Costa Rica.[42] Because of a preference to live together in groups, they dwelled in towns and villages, just as they had done in the pre-Columbian past. They walked out to the fields they worked. Squier described the rural/urban nature of the predominately Indian towns of Potosí and Obraje as "a curious compound of city and country, plazas and plantations."[43]

Foreign travelers visited and commented on the Indian communities. In the early 1820s, Orlando Roberts passed through the Indian town of Pueblo Nuevo, where he met the *alcalde*, an Indian bearing his "badge of office, a handsome silver-headed cane." The town consisted of about a hundred "mud houses" and a church, but Roberts saw no priest. He noted the strategic location on the road from Lake Nicaragua to León and the "rich land, bearing heavy crops of Indian corn, and cocoa."[44]

E. G. Squier tended to be florid in his descriptions of Indian villages. Journeying from Granada to Managua, a heavily populated region, he passed through Nindiri, which, in a moment of poetic fancy—not at all unusual for the American diplomat—he compared it to "some dreamy Arcadia":

> This little Indian village far surpassed, in point of picturesque beauty, any-thing we had yet seen. Oranges, plantains, *maranons, jocotes, nísperos,* mamays, and tall palms, with their variously-colored fruits blushing brown or golden among the leaves, and here and there a low calabash tree, with its green globes strung on every limb, all clustering together, literally embow-ered the cane huts of the simple-minded and industrious inhabitants. Indian women, naked to the waist, sat beneath the trees spinning snow-white cot-ton or the fibre of the *pita* (agave), while their noisy, naked little ones tum-bled joyously about on the smoothly-beaten ground.[45]

Despite the poetry, Squier realistically understood at mid-century that those "idyllic" days were numbered: "We were there in an auspicious period: those days of primitive simplicity are passing away, if, indeed, they are not already past."[46] Julius Froebel, who visited Nindiri at about the same time, corroborated the beauty. If anything, he waxed more even poetic than Squier, calling the "large Indian village" one of "the most charming scenes I have ever seen."[47] "The whole town resembled a care-fully kept botanical garden," in the judgment of Jacob Stillman, who like his compatriots fell under the charm of Nindiri. He praised the villagers largely because they retained, to use his words, "all their primitive customs."[48]

Squier also described the Indian town of Obraje when he visited it at mid-century: "It was a large, straggling town, a town of gardens, and, judging from the accounts of the chroniclers, built very much after the plan of the aboriginal towns, before the Conquest."[49] At about the same time, Froebel made this observation about Jinotepet, a town of 4,650 inhabitants twenty miles southwest of Granada: "The inhabitants of the village, who are almost exclusively Indians, are a very industrious race. They are the principal sugar growers in Nicaragua, and all around, during my visit, I heard the rattling noise of their *trapiches*, or primitive sugar-mills, turned by mules. The cultivation of the coffee, too, has been introduced at Jinotepet. . . . A considerable stock of cattle is kept on some farms of this neighborhood."[50] Froebel also mentioned that the Indians sold cheese and cattle hides.

Doubtless one of the most important of the Indian communities from the point of view of size, location, agrarian production, and crafts was Masaya. In 1865, Frederick Boyle had this impression of it:

> Masaya is said to have eighteen-thousand inhabitants . . . . Nine-tenths are Indians of pure blood, and still live, if not in the identical huts of their fore-fathers, at least in buildings precisely similar. The walls consist of an open framework of bamboos, which allows air to pass freely, while a heavy roof of palm thatch excludes the sun. In all cases the huts stand in a swept yard, planted with *coyol* palms and flowering shrubs. Each family thus occupies a great deal of ground, far behind the yard extends a grove of orange trees or *jicaras*: some huts of a single room will monopolize an acre of land. [51]

Froebel visited the busy market early one morning. The variety of goods for sale impressed him. [52]

None of the predominantely or exclusively Indian communities described above existed in total isolation. Roads passed through them, links to León or Granada. If no Roman Catholic priest lived in the community, at least one paid a periodic visit. Itinerant merchants arrived to peddle their wares. Even foreign travelers, like Roberts, Squier, Froebel, or Boyle visited them. If governmental officials were not in immediate evidence, they appeared when something was needed: taxes, workers for the roads, soldiers for the army. The folk community increasingly had to adjust the interplay between "folkways" and "stateways," to use the concepts of Robert Redfield. [53] Inexorably those communities were being drawn into the emerging nation.

The folk societies and cultures of Nicaragua during the nineteenth century shared certain classic characteristics with such societies and cultures throughout Latin America. In Nicaragua however, the fragility of the state during the first half-century of independence deprived it of the strength to challenge the folk societies. The anarchy prior to 1858 preserved and strengthened them at a time when nation-building and modernization undermined their strength and cohesion elsewhere in Latin America. Perhaps unconsciously, Squier recorded a symbol of quiet success of the folk amid the havoc wrought by the patriarchs. Observing the destruction of León during the civil wars, he commented, "Entire streets, now almost deserted, are lined with the remains of large and beautiful edifices, destroyed in the civil wars. Within their abandoned courts stand rude cane huts—as if in mockery of their former state."[54] Anarchy weakened the Europeanized foundation of the state; the folk triumphed.

As far as possible, the attention of the folk focused on themselves. Ordinary people came together as a community in a collective effort to achieve and maintain well-being, or even more simply, just to survive. Its members shared a common way of life, a similar world view, and the same attitudes, in short a folk culture.[55] Folk societies always possessed a folk culture. This culture more pervasive and elusive than its place of origin, could and did exist outside of the folk society.[56]

Within broad parameters, community life drew on preconquest life patterns modified by the long Spanish colonial experiences. Spain imposed a language, a religion, work requirements, and taxes. Yet because Nicaragua remained peripheral in the vast imperial scheme, those impositions rested lightly. Until the last quarter of the nineteenth century, Nicaragua contained many small, nonliterate, homogeneous, and rural folk societies. They fit in the space between the isolated farms and the commercial plantations on the one hand and the heterogeneous cities on the other. Close relationships between family members, kin, friends, and neighbors bound the folk society together. So did their common belief system. The folk shared the same traditions, a pragmatic distillation of Indian and European contributions—and on the Pacific coast of African as well. Change occurred slowly, and when it did it was well mediated. For example, the Indians of the Pacific coast had found it necessary, desirable, and useful to abandon their own languages and speak Spanish. By the mid-nineteenth century, a frustrated Carl Scherzer, among others, vainly sought Indians who could speak one of those languages.[57] In contrast, well into the nineteenth century the Indians manifested a certain duality in their religious practices.

They professed the religion of the conqueror. Roman Catholicism served the Spanish empire well. It bridged cultural differences between the European patriarchs who governed and the Indian folk who served. It infused some degree of Europeanization into the folk community. Yet the foreign travelers insisted they glimpsed among the Indians some reminders that the old gods had not been completely forgotten. The Indian population on the Island of Ometepe in Lake Nicaragua practiced their "idolatry," according to Squier, until well into the nineteenth century.[58] Stillman commented on the presence of an ancient stone god near the principal church in Managua in 1850.[59] Squier reported that Indians left "offerings" to *piedras antiguas*, ancient carved figures, on certain street corners in Granada.[60] Boyle spoke of those same *piedras*, when he visited Granada a decade and a half later:

> The descendants of the sculptors, fervent Christians though they be, can still find room in their hearts for other worship besides the Virgin and the very ugly saints provided for them—and the old gods came in for a share more than equal in times of trouble. A gentleman in Granada, whose house is near a broken idol with a wide mouth called "La Boca," which stands at the corner of a street, told me that when a revolution is imminent, and during its progress, the gaping mouth of this statue is every morning crammed with flowers, which the watchful priests remove at daylight.[61]

Still, no one seemed bold enough to remove the statues from their prominent locations on major street corners of that important commercial city and oft-times national capital.

Customs in places far less Europeanized than Granada further suggested religious syncretism among the folk. On a Sunday morning as Thomas Belt passed through Totogalpa, an Indian town just south of Ocotal, he witnessed a ceremony which appeared to combine Roman Catholic elements with preconquest celebrations. In the plaza before the church, three men, one playing a whistle and two beating drums, accompanied the ringing of the bells in the tower of the church, for which there was no priest. A procession of town authorities with their official staffs of office exited from the church carrying or escorting a table laden with silver and brass religious ornaments. They paraded around the plaza before seating themselves in front of one of the houses on the plaza. Each received a gigantic bowl filled with *chicha*, the Indian corn alcohol. As they solemnly drank, Belt recalled the sixteenth-century descriptions of Nicaragua written by Pascual de Andagaya, relating how chicha accompanied the religious ceremonies among the Indians. On that particular occasion, the drinking accompanied the ceremonial washing of the religious objects from the church. Meanwhile, women decorated the interior of the church with wreaths of flowers they had woven, "another beautiful trait of the old Indians that their descendants had not lost."[62] The Indian sense of decoration appeared in a "unique little church" Squier visited in "the little Indian town of Brita." The local inhabitants had painted the church "after the Indian fashion, with all the colors of the rainbow—here a row of urns, there a line of flowers, curiously festooned, and the whole altogether more resembling the flaming front of a wooden clock from Yankeeland, than anything else under heaven."[63]

On one May 15, Belt observed an annual festivity in Condego in the municipality of Estelí. On the evening preceding the festivity, the Indian inhabitants planted in the plaza in front of the church fully grown plants of maize, rice, beans, and other vegetables they produced. They also brought in wild animals and birds captured for the occasion. Belt speculated, "The custom of planting the square with vegetables, and bringing together all the wild animals that can be collected, is doubtless an Indian one. The ancient Nicaraguans are said to have worshipped maize and beans, but the service may not have had more significance than our own harvest feasts."[64]

The syncretism evident in religion carried over in many aspects of society. It testified that while the Indians might have lived somewhat isolated from and parallel to the Europeanized society and culture, they were in the end influenced by the major European institutions. The politically chaotic circumstances and the small number of creoles probably minimized such influence, but nonetheless the process of syncretism, mediation, and adaptation continued.

Certainly there were periods and places where the folk societies dominated with minimal incursions from priests and politicians. These communities then held the outsiders at bay, preserving most or much of their own culture. George Byam observed such communities during his rural residency, 1839–40.[65] Ometepe was such a place. The Indians refused to allow outsiders to own land or even to reside on the island. Isolated folk communities characterized much of the Atlantic portion of Nicaragua. Benjamin I. Teplitz reported positively on their functioning for the benefit of their inhabitants.[66] Another major imbalance between the folk society and the patriarchs, then, was that the folk preferred minimal outside contacts, while the patriarchs depended on constant contact with the folk, primarily for labor but also for crops, crafts, taxes, and services, not the least of which was in the military. The divergence of interests contained the seeds of conflict.

The Indians' loyalty to their community remained steadfast, reinforced by the informal education that inculcated particular values into the new generations. A formal education imposed by the state did not exist. The folk societies through example taught children about their relationship to the group and the moral behavior honored by the community. Parents taught their children their skills, crafts, and duties. A shared moral order—as contrasted with the more technical and institutional order of the state—contributed significantly to the community bond. It facilitated the resolution of disputes and problems. The individual's status within the society was fixed at birth. Age, sex, and occupation determined the individual's rights and obligations.

Their life patterns emphasized an elementary equality.[67] Pierre Clastres posited a thoughtful conclusion about Indian society in the New World: "The chief is there to serve society; it is society as such—the real locus of power—that exercises its authority over the chief."[68] However simple the folk society might have appeared to the outsider, it incorporated a complex relationship between the individual and the group. Both served each other. Both drew strength from each other. Each placed restrictions on the other. While the balance was delicate, the folk societies seemingly succeeded in maintaining it.

As a human society, the folk community doubtless fostered negative characteristics as well. No documentation by insiders about pre-1858 Nicaraguan folk societies has been discovered. Later, Latin American novelists wrote about the village, the small town, and the enclosed, self-contained community, but the perceptions of those outsiders varied widely. Ignacio Manuel Altamirano projected the Mexican village as an ideal of community spirit and patriarchal wisdom in his *Christmas in the Mountains* (1871). His compatriot Agustín Yáñez depicted quite a different scene in his *The Edge of the Storm* (1947), one in which frustration, repression, and ignorance gripped the inhabitants of a small, isolated town at the opening of the twentieth century.

Whatever the drawbacks of the folk society, much of its harmony rested on the distribution of its resources. Every member of the society enjoyed access to these, the most important of which was land. The folk society was rooted in the land, which, in the last analysis, integrated and fortified the people.

"The Right to Live"

A small population and abundant arable land characterized nineteenth-century Nicaragua. Only a small fraction of that land fell under cultivation. Even claims to land covered only a minor part of the total. In contrast to most other newly emergent nations of Latin America, the Church owned little land here. Estimates of the amount owned by the government of Nicaragua ranged as high as 80 percent.[69] Squier calculated the potential to increase rural production as optimal because "the forests are easily removed, and genial nature yields rich harvests to the husbandman."[70] Those mid-century conclusions echoed what the merchants and land-owners of Rivas had boasted a half-century earlier.[71]

Together, the large estates, small farms, and communal landholdings harvested the major crops, which they sold locally, regionally and internationally: indigo, cotton, tobacco, rice, maize, beans, sugar, and cacao. At mid-century, coffee, destined to dominate the economy by the end of the century, had been introduced. Wheat and other grains requiring a temperate climate grew in the highlands of Nueva Segovia. A cornucopia of vegetables and fruits, many of them at that time unknown outside the tropics, provided food for the population.

In preconquest societies, the Indians enjoyed access to and use of the land.[72] Some authorities claim their agricultural system "corresponded to communal production."[73] Others, it should be noted, have argued that those Indians practiced a restricted form of private ownership of land. Germán Romero Vargas seems to have opted for community ownership of land but individual ownership of the product.[74] The community "owned" (decidedly a word with strong European meaning so perhaps "exercised control over" might come a little closer to Indian concepts) the land; the individual enjoyed access to its use. The distinction between "ownership of" and "access to" land is significant. No debate exists over the historical reality that Indians had access to the use of land. Custom proscribed misuse of the land or the monopolization of more than could be properly used.[75] Thus, while the Indians were not owners of land in any European sense of possessing a title, they could justly lay claim to what they planted, grew, and harvested on it.[76]

After adjusting to the Spanish colonial institutions, the Indians continued to have access to land, although they had to meet labor—the *enco-mienda* and *repartimiento*—and tax demands. The community continued to hold the lands, parceling part of them out to families for their use. The size of the family plot depended on the amount of land the community owned and the number of families that composed it. No Indian could give away, sell, or mortgage that inalienable community land.

Custom buttressed by royal grants conferred inalienability upon the lands held and administered by the communities, often designated *pueblos*. Spanish law protected Indian communal lands.[77] Colonial laws and customs drew at least partly upon Spain's own Iberian experience with the "nucleated form of settlement" with its "open field pattern" and tendency toward "some sort of communal ownership or regulation of the agricultural resources."[78] A document from the end of the eighteenth century described the rural structures of northwestern Nicaragua in which individuals farmed lands that formed a part of a larger community:

> One of the principal causes of the abundance characteristic of these peoples is the well-proportioned distribution of the land in Nicaragua, in contrast to almost all the rest of the Americas. Each inhabitant, particularly in Chinandega, has his own land and together with the members of his family they cultivate corn and cotton. They grow enough for their own consumption and do not have to hire any outside workers. Despite their groves of plantains and cacao, the large estate owners enjoy few advantages over these peasants because hired workers drain away their profits. Hired workers are few in number because almost everyone has access to his own land to farm.[79]

The political changes wrought by independence, incorporation into the Mexican Empire, and participation in the federation of the United Provinces of Central America did not alter land patterns and practices. Ready access to land continued to characterize the Indians' and the mestizos' rural reality.

While individual Indians might have looked poor to the outsider, their communities often were prosperous. The communities enjoyed three sources of income: rents from some of the lands; the sale of products from community lands worked by community labor, from the community cornfields for example, whose profits were guarded in the *cajas de comunidad* (community strong boxes); and the cattle which belonged to the local *cofradías* (religious brotherhoods) and could be sold to benefit the brotherhood and its projects.[80]

The distinctive land systems of Indian communities paralleled the private ownership of land introduced by the Spaniards. Obviously the two systems of land ownership and use differed. On the one hand, the Indians produced primarily for themselves and for local markets. Agriculture was not a venture for profit but rather a way of life conferring both satisfaction and sustenance. On the other hand, the patriarchs became increasingly interested in export agriculture, crops destined for distant foreign markets, production for profit. Eventually the two systems clashed, when the patriarchs sought to expand their landholdings and to coerce labor. Already in the eighteenth century, Germán Romero Vargas concluded, the Indians "had to defend their land tenaciously."[81] Thus despite an abundance of land, large landowners displayed an early propensity to encroach upon the fertile fields of smaller neighbors, particularly in the populated belt from Chinandega to Rivas. Landless ladinos also encroached.

The early laws and constitutions, first of the state and then of the republic, protected both land systems. Article 36 of the 1826 Constitution of the State of Nicaragua guaranteed the property ownership of individuals and communities. The State Legislative Assembly of Nicaragua reconfirmed the legality of communal lands on July 13, 1832.[82] The first article of the decree recognized "*tierras comunales* or *ejidos* in all the towns [*pueblos*] of the State." *Tierras comunales* implied municipally owned lands, rented out at a nominal fee to the inhabitants of the *pueblo*. *Ejidos* could signify landholding communities or, possibly, lands used by the entire community together, as for grazing cattle. Confusion exists whether these two corporations were in fact separate, or were *always* separate, or were synonymous in nineteenth-century Nicaragua. Clarification of the confusion awaits further research. Neither ambiguous nor contradictory was the reality of access to land. In the most populated region of Nicaragua from León southeast through Rivas, ordinary people enjoyed access through the communal lands of the towns. In the less populated regions outside that band, people simply squatted and claimed a right to work the land, usually respected during the period of anarchy when export agriculture stagnated and the patriarchs could not control labor.[83]

The legislative decree of 1832 required setting aside separate areas of the communal lands for planting crops and grazing animals. It stipulated the size of lands allotted to the pueblo according to the population and the amount to which each peasant was entitled. Failure to work the land meant forfeiture of access. Full exploitation of an allotment entitled the peasant to rent more. The rental fees provided income for the pueblo.[84]

After Nicaragua withdrew from the Central American federation in 1838, its new constitution, promulgated the same year, guaranteed in Article 41 the property of communities as well as of individuals. Thus law and practice in the newly independent Nicaragua recognized a fundamental principle from the Indian and colonial pasts and from experience during the Central American federation: access to land, signifying the availability of food or, as Squier imaginatively phrased it, "the right to live."[85]

The legal concern with land ownership and use expressed in the constitutions of 1826 and 1838 and the decree of 1832 increasingly preoccupied the patriarchs in the 1840s. They became obsessed with that vital subject in the following decade. By then, both Liberals and Conservatives manifested a nonpartisan determination to regulate the land, to standardize landowning, and, eventually, to restrict communal landowning.[86] The multiplication of laws, restrictions, and requirements favored the literate and those conversant with the increasingly Europeanized bureaucracy administering them. In short, it favored the patriarchs at the expense of the folk.

Constituent assemblies provided one insight into changing official attitudes toward communal lands. The written but unadopted Conservative constitutions of 1848 and 1854 provided no guarantees to communal lands. The bipartisan Constitution of 1858 did not mention them.[87] Article 78 spoke only of "the inviolability of property." The constitutional concern with communal lands shifted from affirmation in 1826 to silence in 1858, a significant and ominous legal change for the majority of the Nicaraguans, a harbinger of future problems and woe for the folk.

Not surprisingly, the laws and decrees concerning land ownership and use reflected the constitutional trends. While some of the rural laws did not directly affect the communal landholdings, all strengthened the individual landowner. A law of January 28, 1852, facilitated the sale of vacant lands "for the benefit of the public treasury, credit, and progress." A very ominous law of October 22 of the same year required the immediate surveying of all lands. In the process, the government hoped to ascertain the extent of the *tierras comunales*. While such laws sounded reasonable, they actually favored those who knew the law and could hire surveyors. Such laws throughout Latin America always rang up the curtain on the drama of the expansion of the large estates. Nicaragua proved to be no exception. The government announced in 1853 its intention to regulate the communal lands but did not specify how.[88] It wanted to "distribute land by selling vacant land and adjusting the communal lands."[89] Civil war and then the National War postponed such regulations and adjustments.

With the return of peace the government vigorously directed its attention to the communal lands. On March 30, 1858, it issued regulations for settlement on lands. A year later, on March 29, 1859, it promulgated the law for "the division and alienation" of communal lands. It limited their size and made portions of them available for purchase and private ownership. A regulation of April 8 announced that anyone who had settled on a *solar*, residential property, within the communal lands for four years could claim title to that land. Further laws facilitated the acquisition of vacant lands (July 19, 1861) and strengthened the authority of the agrarian judges (February 18, 1862), particularly empowering them to enforce labor contracts. [90] The unmistakable trend of assault on communal lands accelerated throughout the rest of the nineteenth century. In 1900 and 1916, the National Archives of Nicaragua published an *Indice de los Documentos que Comprende la Sección de Tierras y que Existen en Depósito en el Archivo Nacional* (An Index to the documents in the Land Section of the National Archives). [91] The government sponsorship of the project suggested the importance authorities placed on land questions and the settlement of them. In the first and even more in the second volume, the overwhelming majority of land cases bore a post–1860 date. Part of the explanation can be ascribed to improper care of older documents and their loss or destruction during the age of anarchy. Part was due to the new importance land acquired with the rise of coffee production and export. While most of the cases concern rather standard acquisitions of land or legalization of title, the researcher will also encounter more ominous entries. For example, on May 31, 1878, Señora Jerónima Morales made claim to a plot of land in the *terreno ejidal* of Laguna de Apoya. [92] Similarly, on September 19, 1884, the municipality of Posoltega sold a part of its community lands to Dr. Bernabé Portocarrero. [93] In short, the brief entries record erosion of the community land holdings after 1858. In the meantime, their days numbered, the communal lands flourished during the age of anarchy, providing a satisfactory standard of living for their inhabitants.

A harsh reality confronted the Indians. Since the conquest, they had to guard constantly against land seizures and encroachments. These attempts increased after independence, heightening tensions between the Indian communities—and also the mestizo peasant—and the patriarchal landowners. [94] Outsiders frequently trespassed, encroached upon, and squatted on communal lands. In other cases, the community rented lands to outsiders but failed to collect the rent. As time passed, the original renter laid claim to the land based on use and occupation. Legal complications arose and apparently multiplied.[95]

The abolition of the colonial labor and tax laws after the declaration of independence from Spain partially explained the vigor of the rural folk societies in the early national period.[96] Political anarchy was also instrumental in allowing the folk societies to turn inward, to focus on themselves and their land rather than on broader issues which could be construed vaguely as national. To the extent possible they withdrew from contacts with the creoles. The land permitted them to feed themselves and they maintained a high degree of self-sufficiency. Those conditions continued as significant characteristics of the Nicaraguan countryside until the last quarter of the nineteenth century.[97]

Foreign travel accounts offer valuable insights into the economic structure and functioning of the folk societies. In 1850 Squier described the municipal landowning system, in this case for a city inhabited exclusively by Indians: "The municipality of Subtiava, in common with barrios of some of the towns, holds lands, as I have said, in virtue of royal grants, in its corporate capacity. These lands are inalienable, and are leased to the inhabitants at low and almost nominal rates. Each citizen is entitled to a sufficient quantity to enable him to support himself and his family; for which he pays from four trials (half a dollar) to two dollars a year. This practice seems to have been of aboriginal institution."[98]

Thomas Belt took note of communal lands in Nueva Segovia around 1870: "None of the lands around here were enclosed—all seemed to be common property; and every family had a few cows and two or three brood mares. A little maize was grown."[99]

As travelers ventured farther from the areas of population concentration, they encountered farming families squatting on and claiming the land. Although a high degree of cooperation existed among the frontier farmers, they were not, or need not have been, members of a folk society. George Byam lived among them in Nueva Segovia in 1840 and he remembered,

> "Remote from cities," they lead a rather uncertain precarious life, but, with a little hard work for a short time in the year, they can assure subsistence to their families. An acre of forest land, cleared, burnt, and fenced, is sure to produce an abundant crop of maize; and if a few join together in felling and fencing . . . the work is better and quicker done, and produce divided. The ground may last for three years, when another piece is cleared in the same

way. Every rancho has its fowls, and often wild turkeys. The man, after he has sowed, has all his time to himself; he mostly possesses a tame cow or two to find him in milk, curds, and a coarse cheese; they feed in the forest and cost him nothing; he fishes in the river, now and then kills a deer, traps a rabbit, and is always on the look out for iguanas and their eggs; brings home sometimes a wild pig; he very often possesses a young horse or mule, that he breaks for the journey he makes once or twice a year to some large town, where he sells it; he looks after his own horse or two that he rides about on, hunts bees, and preserves the wax, using the honey at home; and when the day comes for him to go to the town, he leads his colt and takes his wax there, where he sells them both, the later to make tapers for the Virgin Mary and saints, and returns home with a flare-up piece of chintz for his wife and daughters, a piece of strong linen for his Sunday white trousers and shirt; and is altogether . . . superior to the townspeople, both physically and morally. [100]

In other passages of his book, Byam recounts some of the cooperative tasks of those largely self-sufficient frontier farmers. They practiced "exchange labor," a custom already discussed in the building of ranchos.

Thirty years later, Thomas Belt passed through approximately the same region and left his own impressions of life of the edge of the forest:

On the top of a rocky range we stayed at a small house for breakfast, and they made us ready some tortillas. As usual, there seemed to be three or four families all living together, and there were a great number of children. The men were two miles away at a clearing on the edge of the forest, looking after "milpas," or maize patches. The house, though small, was cleaner and tidier than the others we had seen, and in furniture could boast of a table and a few chairs, which showed we had chanced to fall on the habitation of one of the well-to-do class. The ceiling of the room we were in was made of bamboo-rods, above which maize was stored. The women were good-looking, and appeared to be of nearly pure Spanish descent; which perhaps accounted for the chairs and table, and also for the absence of any attempt at gardening around the house—for the Indian eschews furniture, but is nearly always a gardener. We finished our homely breakfast and set off again, cross-ing some more rocky ranges, and passing several Indian huts with orange trees growing around them. [101]

Such observations confirm the self-sufficiency of the peasants and the availability of land. Paul Levy, who resided in Nicaragua at the same time as Belt, also detailed the ease by which any person could claim, take pos-session, and obtain title to the land. [102] Those observations applied to vast regions outside the population belt along the Pacific coast.

Attached to their own land, the peasants refused to work for others. It was an old story.[103] By all accounts, they worked hard for themselves. Witnesses testified to their industry. Not at all uncommon was this observation from Squier: "It was just daybreak when we rode through the suburb of Guadalupe, but already the Indians were yoking their oxen and preparing for their day's work."[104]

Most of those farmers and communities produced a small surplus to trade in local markets for items they could not or did not produce. However, in those nonmaterialistic folk societies, economic decisions took second place to social considerations. Community obligations, traditions, and moral dictates, not economic forces, governed transactions. The concept of accumulating individual wealth was alien. Folk societies and local markets remained relatively free from national and international economic demands and fluctuations.[105]

In Nicaragua's period of anarchy, one economic consideration weighed heavily on both plebe and patrician: the fear of confiscation of goods.[106] Armies roamed the countryside in search of food and livestock. All armies took what they wanted; perhaps a few vaguely promised a payment the owner never expected to receive. John L. Stephens provides an insight into the panic these confiscations caused. He was in León in 1840 when the army issued a call for mules: "the two [servants] returned in great haste with the intelligence that piquets were scouring the city for men and mules, having entered the yard of a padre nearby and taken three of his animals. The lady of the house ordered all the doors to be locked and the keys brought to her; an hour before dark we were all shut in and my poor mules had to go without water."[107] More than a decade and a half later, in southwestern Nicaragua, Private David Deaderick III of William Walker's Mounted Rangers participated in more than one raiding party to round up mules and horses from Nicaraguans careless enough to leave them exposed.[108] Any considerations of economic performance during that period of Nicaraguan history must take into account hungry armies, government requisitions, and forced enlistments, all of which inhibited the production of surpluses for peasants and patriarchs alike.

The level of satisfaction within the folk societies or for the solitary farmers is very difficult to establish. They left no written record. But when they experienced a threat to their life-style, they reacted to protect it—an impulse that suggests some level of satisfaction with the course of their lives. The attitude expressed in the dance-drama *El Güegüence* and the Indian and the chapetón genre of stories also affirmed preferences favoring the folk society.

Although the recorded observations of outsiders are useful, they are not, after all, the voice of the folk. In the late 1840s, Alexander von Buelow concluded that because of abundant land, plentiful food, and a benign climate, the population in general lived well: "The half-naked Indian lives as happily and carefree as the rich Spanish creole." No beggars could be found in Nicaragua, he emphasized.[109] In the "mestizo village" of San Rafael near Matagalpa the eighty-year-old Miguel Lansas, the only creole inhabitant, confided to Carl Scherzer in 1854 that with the removal of the injustices of the Spanish colonial past, the quality of life of the Indians had improved.[110] Belt concluded, "Those communities are the happiest and the best-governed who retain most of their old customs and habits."[111] Juan F. de la Rocha provided a modest assessment of his own society in 1865, noting, "The misery of nakedness and rags afflicts no one."[112]

The degree to which the folk societies participated in the wider national life varied. None escaped such participation entirely. The major links with the national government and economy were three: the peasants' need or demand for certain items they did not produce, the government's recruitment of soldiers and imposition of taxes and laws, and the plantation owners' demands for labor.

Nicaragua suffered an acute labor shortage. With easy access to land, most Nicaraguans preferred to work for themselves or within the communal framework. The incessant wars exacerbated the chronic shortage. León and Granada pressed the males into their armies. In turn, the men fled to escape, military service. Word that "recruiters" roamed the vicinity sent men scurrying into the hills and woods.[113] Their flight not only deprived the generals of troops, but also reduced the numbers available to work the land. "As usual in Central American wars, all the men ran away to the forest, leaving the women to take care of the houses. . . . There was not one laboring man in Chinandega," Robert Dunlop reported in 1844.[114] The labor shortage was national, not regional. If anything, San Juan del Norte experienced greater difficulties than the more populous west coast.[115] During the brief interludes of peace and when the folk did sell their labor, they earned wages higher than customary in Latin America. Even in the modest market economy of nineteenth-century Nicaragua the two realities of plentiful land and scarce labor dictated that wages would be comparatively high. Belt always searching for men to work the mines he managed, concluded, "There is plenty of work for all who are willing or obliged to labor; so the healthy and strong amongst the poorer classes lead an easy and pleasant life."[116]

In the late 1850s, investigating why agriculture had not developed its potential, the government requested the opinions of the mayors throughout the country. Joaquín Elizondo, a leading landowner in Rivas responded, blaming the poor performance on the lack of laborers. The landowner succeeded in hiring few workers and those he employed worked "just enough to earn a meager amount, but that small amount seems sufficient to satisfy their simple needs." The brutal truth of the matter, Elizondo complained, was: "Our workers, without the respect for wealth that characterizes civilization, without that noble aspiration to improve their lot, refuse to work on the estates."[117] His statement reveals an apparently unbridgeable cultural chasm yawning between the would-be capitalist and the folk. Neither side understood the aspirations of the other. The frustrations of Elizondo with the labor market echoed a common sentiment among his class.[118] Abandoned or unused plantations also testified to the effects of the labor shortage.[119]

Contrary to the experience of their counterparts in much of the rest of Latin America, the Nicaraguan elites failed to create a viable labor system prior to 1858 to serve their needs and goals. With some knowledge of the Caribbean and Latin America, Squier was astonished to find that "The system of peonage (slavery under a less repugnant name) is here [Nicaragua] unknown."[120] Although Levy resided in a Nicaragua that was witnessing extensive change by 1870, he, too, concluded, "Peonage such as it is known in Mexico and other parts of Spanish America does not exist in Nicaragua."[121] He pointed out that the Nicaraguan worker enjoyed low living expenses and relatively high salaries, a situation which he labeled a "phenomenon."[122]

The patriarchs failed to understand the reasons for the labor shortage. They hurled charges of "laziness" at the peasants because they could not recruit them for their estates. The *Correo del Istmo de Nicaragua* carried a long editorial in 1849 entitled simply "Laziness," one of the cardinal sins to which it attributed all the ills besetting Nicaragua, especially underdevelopment, poverty, and corruption.[123] It seemed that, the poor, the humble, the peasant, the Indian bore the blame for the social and economic problems troubling the elites. If only they would work for the patriarchs, prosperity would ensue. The supreme director made an effort to coerce 'the lazy' to work in 1843, decreeing a vagrancy law. The decree, stating that "laziness was the origin of all vices and crimes," threatened the "unemployed" with punishment and work.[124] Actually such a decree was far ahead of its times for Nicaragua. Anarchy prevented enforcement. In due time, however, law books bulged with such decrees. After 1858, the government seriously set about to coerce labor.

The workers rather than the landowners controlled the labor market, an unusual circumstance in Latin America. It frustrated the landowners and created tensions between the two groups. Part of the explanation for the advantages enjoyed by labor lay in the small population and large tracts of vacant land, but such a situation characterized much of Latin America. It most certainly characterized nineteenth-century Brazil. The landowners there, however, felt few compunctions about maintaining an extensive African slave system throughout most of the century to fulfill part of their labor needs. After 1850, they increasingly controlled labor by restricting access to land, a method also widely used by their counterparts in much of Spanish-speaking Latin America. The landowners' inability to control labor in Nicaragua was primarily the result of the "institutionalized anarchy," the failure of the patriarchal elites to reach a consensus of rule. The lack of labor control paralleled, not surprisingly, a lack of social and political control as well.

The disorder, thwarting the efforts of the elites to turn their rich lands into profits, clearly carried benefits for the folk. In his innovative study of nineteenth-century Mexico, *Disorder and Progress*, Paul J. Vanderwood mused, "Order and disorder are created by humans to serve their needs and ambitions. Order serves one group and disorder another. . . . People also use order or disorder, or both, to protect their interests."[125] Patriarchal struggles relieved the folk of the demands and pressure of an export economy. Institutionalized anarchy spawned a type of rustic Enlightenment in which the humble enjoyed an unusual degree of liberty and freedom to pursue their own life-styles. It protected their lands and labor by diverting the attention and energy of the patriarchal elite from the corn fields to the battlefields. The disorder certainly inflicted hardships on everyone, but throughout that period the folk maintained, perhaps even strengthened, their society and culture. To a degree that would be unknown after 1858, they were left alone. Relating the stories of the Indian and the chapetón, participating as spectator or actor in the *Baile del Güegüence*, confirmed for them their attitude favoring such separation.

Distance and Deference

In a generalization about Indian societies in Latin America, the French anthropologist Pierre Clastres speculated, "It might be said . . . that the history of peoples without history is the history of their struggle against the State."[126] His generalization applies to Nicaragua during the nineteenth century. The Indians struggled actively and passively against coercion by the amorphous state and its feuding ruling class. They wanted to be left alone; the Europeanized Nicaraguans refused to leave them alone. The conflicting desires motivated psychological drama when they did not incite violence.

Rivalry between León and Granada facilitated the passive struggle of the folk. Maintaining a local loyalty, the Indians and to a lesser degree the mestizos withdrew into their folk societies. They stood apart from the patriarchs. For all practical purposes, they exercised autonomy in routine daily matters, not only from the ambulatory capital but from each other as well. *The Eco Popular* of Granada correctly concluded that ordinary people, preferring to work for themselves and care for their families, turned their backs on the national government.[127] Another newspaper lamented their "indolence" and "indifference," blaming their lack of involvement for part of the problems bedeviling Nicaragua.[128]

With access to land, the folk controlled their agrarian production and labor. To the degree that they controlled labor, they influenced the production or lack of it on the haciendas, plantations, and ranches. Only with reluctance, under coercion, or temporarily did they work on the big estates. They fled from impressment as foot soldiers in the army, another significant manifestation of withdrawal. Without the effective cooperation of the folk (and without adequate means of coercion), the patriarchs could not realize their economic vision of exploiting Nicaragua's wealth and geographic location. Given the disunity of the patriarchs and the withdrawal of the folk, the conditions were less than propitious for the creation of a nation-state.[129]

Ample experience from the conquest through the long colonial administration had taught first the Indians and then the folk in general the wisdom of maintaining both distance from and a certain deference toward government officials. A prudent balance of the two benefited the folk, guaranteeing them the maximum freedom possible. No group better illustrated the desire to be left alone than the Indians of Ometepe Island in Lake Nicaragua. Geography facilitated their isolation. They discouraged visits from all outsiders but most particularly from "foreigners" (that is, non-Indians). Even as late as the mid-1850s, less than 10 percent of the island's population was mestizo.

The state required deference and the folk rendered it when they had to. They paid taxes; they obeyed laws; and, when unavoidable, they provided labor and troops. But as *El Güegüence* revealed, passive resistance came in many guises while a person still maintained the illusion of deference, no matter how thin. Demands could be skirted, misunderstood, acknowledged but not fulfilled, or modified. *El Güegüence* showed how resourcefulness and determination gave birth to compromise, at least a partial victory for the folk.

The distance and deference frustrated the great fathers when it did not exasperate them. Although the *Correo del Istmo de Nicaragua* once commented, "Above all, the mass of people are good"[130]; usually, however, after applying their own values and goals in judgment of the folk, the elite found them to be deficient. Lazy, obstinate, barbarous, backward, uncivilized, turbulent, improvident, immoral were but a few of the charges.[131] Felipe Sáenz, Prefect of the Department of Meridional, concluded that "the people were unprepared for civilization, lacking propriety, public spirit, and respect."[132] In a not unusual rationalization, the *Mentor Nicaragüense* exculpated the "educated men . . . virtuous fathers of family . . . honest landowners" for any social problems in anarchic Nicaragua to point the finger of accusation at "ambitious vagabonds and idlers," a catchall that included the masses, in this case particularly the ladinos.[133] Bishop Viteri y Ungo likewise held his flock in low esteem. While he found the people "docile," he also characterized them as "immoral and indolent." They lacked discipline. Only "religious fear" and "bullets" controlled them.[134]

Some of the patriarchs looked to gentler remedies. Subscribing to the tenets of the Enlightenment, they put their trust in education as the best means to civilize the masses. In this sense, education was a code word. It signified the substitution of European values for folk culture. The elites throughout the Americas clung to their determination to make Europeans out of the Indians.[135] Expressing a general consensus, Supreme Director Fruto Chamorro opined that the Indians were the most backward group within the population and would be the most difficult to change. Only time, education, and the good example of civilization would budge them. A radical or sudden campaign to do so would inevitably provoke disturbances. "Prudence counsels that for the Indians there be exceptional institutions, suitable for their customs and character."[136] Furtively the elite, and most particularly the Conservatives, cast an admiring eye toward President Rafael Carrera of Guatemala in approval of his ability to "control" the Indians.[137]

Discussions always returned to education. Neither laws nor coercions had drawn the folk into national life or made useful citizens of them according to the judgments and criteria of the elites. "It is necessary to change the customs and ideas of the people. . . . It is necessary to teach the people and to create a new society dedicated to work. . . . Only by educating the masses can this new society come about. . . . Public education is the goal toward which the government should direct all its efforts."[138] Yet during the age of anarchy, the patriarchs never put their ideas to a test. The few schools existed in the larger towns, serving ladinos and creoles already disposed toward the Europeanization of society.

Clearly the elites did not value the work the folk did for themselves on their own lands. Scant mention was made of it despite the viability and importance of the peasant economy. The dearth of laborers for the plantations did preoccupy the elites; illogically, they believed that education would convince the folk to neglect their own fields to labor in those of others.

Outside observers—the foreign travelers and visitors—differed from the patriarchs in their assessments of the folk. They judged them, particularly the Indians, as the hardest workers and most honest people in the society. Scoffing at the repeated charges of the Indians' laziness, Froebel considered them the most industrious, useful, and respectable part of the population.[139] Squier concurred and added that without their agriculture the markets would be empty.[140] He indignantly refuted the negative image of the Indian as widely but wrongly held.[141] Belt, who hired and supervised Indian workers in British-owned mines, likewise praised them: "The Indian is industrious by nature, and works steadily and well for himself. . . . As freemen, regularly though poorly paid and kindly treated, the Indians work well and laboriously in the mines."[142] As late as 1870, Levy testified that the Indians provided the labor, the food, and the artisan products for the nation. Although they were people of tradition and custom, often employing out-of-date techniques, in his opinion they alone "produced, worked," and thereby constituted "the most important segment of society."[143]

The foreigners criticized the elites just as regularly as they praised the Indians and folk, whom they found morally superior to the elites.[144] While the folk tried to live and work in peace, the upper class fomented turmoil.

From that class came the political agitators, the trouble makers, and the "revolutionists."[145] The folk lived together harmoniously, while the descendants of the Europeans bickered, argued, and fought. Their endless quarrels agitated the entire society.[146] Belt observed that the Indians governed themselves better than the non-Indians did.[147]

The contrasts between the folk and the Europeanized communities frequently prompted the travelers to philosophize. Why had the Europeans failed to create a viable society in Nicaragua? Why did the Indian appear as superior to the Europeanized sector of the population? Why did society depend on the folk communities for production? The troublesome question came up, whether European intrusion into Nicaragua had brought more evil than good. Belt, an engineer with unusual sensitivity to his environment, concluded: "Probably nowhere but in tropical America can it be said that the introduction of European civilization has caused a retrogression; and that those communities are the happiest and the best governed who retain most of their old customs and habits. Yet there it is so. The civilization that Cortéz overthrew was more suitable for the Indians than that which has supplanted it."[148] It was a remarkable conclusion, all the more so in the nineteenth century, when the North Atlantic countries felt they carried the cloak of civilization to clothe the grateful natives wherever they might be. Thomas Belt shared few of the convictions of his more famous compatriot Rudyard Kipling.

Like Belt, some other foreign residents or travelers showed a remarkable sensitivity to the tragedies of a Nicaragua ravaged by anarchy, civil war, and foreign intervention. They raised issues the local patriarchs never entertained. Frederick Boyle might well have asked the most emotional and controversial questions:

> Which is the savage? and which of these two shall so be called, the Spaniard or the Indian? The latter made his land to blossom like a garden; the former restored it to the wilderness. The latter built his house of wood and cane, and the former after three hundred years, is of the opinion that he was wise in so doing. The latter lived in order and comfort, and if he went to war, it seems to have been quite in a friendly way. By this time he might have boasted a set and stately civilization, to last as long as the mountains or the sea, like the Quiches and the Mayas. Look at him now! Which was the savage, the Spaniard or the Indian?[149]

Obviously the English professed no love for the Spaniard, and that hoary prejudice might have framed the question and predicted the response. Still, a compelling logic lies at least in the asking of the question. Perhaps some romanticism might have colored the answer, although the boundary between romanticism and realism can be porous. The foreigners provide a relatively consistent insight into Nicaragua, one, at least in this case, that contrasts markedly with that of the local elite.

While deference and distance of the folk often frustrated the elite, neither constituted a direct threat. On occasion, however, the folk felt provoked. They reacted. They rebelled. In the patriarchal society the rebellious child must be punished.

Resistance and Rebellion

To forge a nation-state, Nicaraguan political leaders sooner or later would have to address the withdrawal of the folk from national life and their cultural and economic self-sufficiency. Withdrawal and independence stood in the way of the unified, modern Nicaragua most national leaders envisioned. From their vantage points in León and Granada, they sought to shape the country in accordance with their vision of a people prospering through export of their abundant natural resources and exploitation of their potential as the crossroads of world commerce, and adopting European ideas and life-styles. Frequent discussions in governmental documents and newspapers suggested that by the 1850s the patriarchal leadership considered education as a primary step toward the creation of the nation-state. Such a Europeanized education theoretically would infuse the ideology of the elite into the masses. It would break down the self-imposed isolation of the people and involve them in the creation and activities of the nation-state. The folk would share a vision with the patriarchs. Such was the ideal. Its advocates faced a formidable challenge from villages that had complex temporal-spacial-structural differences from León and Granada, and inhabitants who were suspicious about the nature of the nation-state to be created and the Europeanized education to promote it. The folk preferred to mediate change themselves rather than have it imposed on them.

The observation that "The lower orders [in Nicaragua] take but little interest in the revolutions, or in politics" was correct so long as the folk did not perceive their interests to be at stake.[150] When they did, passive resistance became active and often violent, "their struggle against the State," to refer again to the ideas of Pierre Clastres. That readiness to defend their interests antedated the nineteenth century.

Historically, the folk had resorted to struggle to protect their life styles and their perceived interests. Throughout the long colonial period, Indian uprisings occurred whenever the Spaniards or their descendants pressed too abruptly or too heavily.[151] When mestizo life styles replicated, or nearly duplicated those of the Indians, the mestizos joined in the resistance.

Rebellions in the nineteenth century were rooted in colonial experience. During the latter part of 1811 and the early months of 1812, they erupted in Subtiava, León, Jalteva, Granada, Masaya, Monimbo and Rivas. Troops stationed at San Carlos, whose ranks consisted mainly of Indians from Chontales and Matagalpa, mutinied, held captive their officers (mainly Spaniards), and made demands similar to those heard elsewhere. The Indians protested the oppressive tax and work requirements of the chapetones.

Such specific complaints reflected deeper dissatisfactions. The rebellions took place within a vast imperial framework. Madrid's efforts to reform its empire during the eighteenth century to make it more efficient and manageable aroused more criticism than praise from the Latin Americans, who interpreted the changes as more imperial intrusion just at the time they wanted less. A prolonged economic depression also agitated the Americas. The Indians understood, as did other segments of society, that imperial policies had not always served their best interests. While broader issues are more difficult to assess, the tax and labor requirements were the immediate and compelling causes for insurrection in 1811 and 1812. The royal government dispatched troops from Honduras, El Salvador, and Costa Rica to repress the rebellions that had defeated local authorities.

The declaration of Central American independence did not immediately quell popular discontent. In June and again in August of 1822, the Indians of Subtiava and students of León joined together to oppose annexation to the Mexican Empire. A popular rebellion took place in Granada in October of 1822 and again the following January. Sporadic popular revolts continued through 1825.[152]

In contrast to the feuding patriarchal elites, Indians and mestizos alike experienced a period of relative tranquility in the years between the mid–1820s and the mid–1840s. During those decades, the Indians enjoyed freedom from previous taxes and work requirements as well as ready access to land. Despite, or more likely because, of the anarchy shaking Nicaragua, they had gained an opportunity to withdraw into their own folk societies. They returned to their preconquest position as subsistence agrarian producers.[153]

In the mid–1840s, political changes occurred in Nicaragua which disturbed the rural folk. Intrusions into their communal life increased. After two decades of withdrawal, the Indians and folk reacted violently. The capture, damage, and humiliation of León in 1845 by the Salvadoran-Honduran troops under General Francisco Malespín allied with the forces of Granada ended the Liberal control of the national government and brought the Conservatives of Granada to power under Supreme Director José León Sandoval. The folk perceived that two of the Conservatives' policies, an aguardiente law in 1845 and a constitutional revision in 1848, threatened them. Anxiety characterized the local communities. Feeling threatened, they reacted by challenging the new direction in which the central government moved. Their reaction constituted the major internal challenge to the patriarchs during the nineteenth century.

In 1845, Minister of the Treasury Fruto Chamorro wrote and enforced a law to regulate the manufacture and sale of the popular and ubiquitous aguardiente and to enforce the collection of taxes on it. He used the law as one means to exert moral control. People drank too much. If properly enforced, the law would limit consumption and also provide funds for an always barren treasury. The minister vigorously collected the tax. Revenues rose. By 1852, the tax provided more income than any other source, well over one-third of total government revenue or $109,161 pesos for a budget of $296,373. Tariffs ranked as the second source of income, $75,309.[154]

To collect the tax, the government strengthened supervision over production and sale. It authorized a few regional monopolies, closing the small stills and hunting down moonshiners. The impact fell heavily on the lower classes. It drove the small dealers, those ubiquitous home brewers and distributors, many of them women, out of business, while increasing the business and profits of the monopolists.[155] Control, monopoly, and taxes raised the price of a drink, while at the same time depriving many of their incomes. The folk protested government interference in their business and pleasure.[156]

Popular wrath over the aguardiente monopoly led to rebellion and the violent deaths of at least two sugar plantation owners, who were also political figures. Both cases indicated that Conservatives seemed to profit from the aguardiente law promulgated by a Conservative government. They also suggest a type of class conflict pitting the small against the large producers favored by monopoly. Senator Bernardo Venerio, for example, received a four-year monopoly in 1845 to supply aguardiente to León. On March 18, 1846, Bernabé Somoza leading a group of thirty men invaded the senator's principal sugar plantation and killed him. They shot other landowners and then proceeded to Chinandega where they killed three leading merchants.[157] In a popular uprising on June 3, 1849, the people around Rivas rushed onto the plantation of Rafael Lebrón and in the ensuing fight wounded him. He later died. The people disliked Lebrón. They remembered him as a stern prefect of the department who rigidly enforced the aguardiente monopoly.[158] Always on the look out for illegal stills, he energetically tracked down smugglers.[159] Lebrón also served as a deputy in the Constituent Assembly in 1847–1848.

The discussions in the Constituent Assembly and the constitution it produced in 1848 further agitated the public. Bitter debates erupted in the assembly over the changes advocated by the Conservatives, who wanted to invest the supreme director with greater powers to enable him to stem anarchy and strengthen order.[160] Failure of the delegates to guarantee the communal land provided yet another source of apprehension and discontent. In general, the discussions highlighted the reality that at mid-century, despite tremendous problems and differences among themselves, the elites were moving slowly but unmistakably toward the creation of a stronger government. By controlling land distribution and ownership, they would also create the labor pool for their estates that was essential to increase their plantation productivity. It was also necessary to limit the independence of the folk communities if they were to establish a nation-state. However, such moves threatened popular interests. The Liberals circulated warnings of the troubles the newly proposed constitution would create. The folk responded with more outbursts of rebellion, adding to the unrest already caused by the aguardiente law. Party rivalries, intensified by the capture of León in 1845, the election of the first Conservative supreme director the same year, and the debates in the Constituent Assembly, further fanned the flames of unrest. In their defense of folk interests, the Nicaraguan Liberals played an unusual role in nineteenth-century Latin American history: generally in the hemisphere, the Conservatives tended to favor or to tolerate the folk systems, while the Liberals hastened to change them.

Popular rebellion during the last half of the decade of the 1840s bespoke a new, social dimension of pervasive anarchy. Since the period of the Spanish conquest in the sixteenth century, Nicaragua had not witnessed popular struggles of the intensity of those during the 1845–1849 period. For the previous two decades, the folk had tried to ignore the party strife and the rivalries between Granada and León. To a large degree they succeeded, but the efforts to strengthen the central government and the intrusion of that government into affairs of immediate concern to the folk community aroused genuine popular anger. Nicaragua's struggles in the 1840s were no longer exclusively among the patriarchs seeking power but were expanding to include folk revolts against the patriarchy

Indian revolts flared in Matagalpa by mid–1845 and spread across the north to Jinotega, Metapa, San Isidro, La Concordia, Somoto, Totogalpa, Palacaguina, and elsewhere. The rebels defied government forces for much of the remainder of the decade. The government accused the Indians of all kinds of crimes and violence against the lives and property "of their innocent neighbors who are known as ladinos."[161] It labeled those Indians "indomitable" and blamed the rebellions on its past "leniency" toward them. Officials complained: "Three or four large rallies were held to prepare the attacks on the city [Matagalpa]. Several men were freed in León and Jinotega and they led the mobs. The Government cannot be everywhere at once and it trusts its subordinates, but some of them for reasons of compassion, and others through insubordination, aided and abetted those costly rebellions."[162] Under the leadership of Apolinar Gómez and N. Vargas, an armed band seized the little town of Totogalpa in northwestern Nicaragua in May 1846. They executed the mayor, Policarpo López, and other leading citizens. When they withdrew, they carried off six others to a fate unknown.

The rebellions did more than challenge the government. They also revealed old and deep antagonisms between Indians and ladinos, particularly those mestizos who, shunning their Indian past, emphasized their European heritage and in some cases were more determined Europeanizers than the creoles themselves. Pedro Francisco de la Rocha, a vocal Conservative advocate of the imposition of rigid order, characterized the tumult in Nueva Segovia and Matagalpa as a continuation of a "war to the death between ladinos and Indians," but he also acknowledged that the Indians possessed "an implacable hatred of all authority and social order."[163] The rebellions of 1845–1847 heavily damaged Matagalpa, and nervous landowners found it prudent to move to León, temporarily abandoning their lands.[164]

The Indians on Ometepe Island reacted violently to threats to their lands from outsiders. They murdered the family of a German-American named Woeniger who tried to establish a cotton plantation there in the mid–1840s; they burned his house down; they attacked him physically;

and eventually they drove him off the island. As late as the mid–1860s, outsiders found it difficult to arrange transportation for the short trip from Granada to the island.[165] The inhabitants jealously guarded their isolation and way of life.

The ladinos also rebelled. The aguardiente laws particularly agitated them. Plots, rumors of plots, clandestine meetings, and denunciations surfaced in Chinandega, León, Granada, and Managua. On June 15, 1845, about seventy men stormed through the streets of Managua, exchanging shots with the police. A week later, José María Valle, known as El Chelón, led eighty men in an attack on Chinandega. The government declared martial law in that region.[166] Attacks on haciendas and plantations struck terror among the patriarchs. In early 1846, the murders of Tomás Paíz on his hacienda near Nagarote and then of Venerio and others near El Viejo enacted their worst nightmares. During the night of February 5, 1847, ladinos attacked Nindiri and Masaya. They sacked the house of the mayor of Nindiri, Agustín Peralta, and the local aguardiente merchant. "They drank all the aguardiente they could hold and broke the containers where the rest was stored." In Masaya, they freed and armed all the prisoners in jail. The government accused local inhabitants of aiding "murderers, thieves, and bandits."[167] The plebes had "besmirched the honor" and "profaned the domestic hearth" of the patriarchs, in the judgment of Pedro Francisco de la Rocha.[168]

By 1848, the focus of popular rebellion shifted to the populous southwestern region, still fueled by the aguardiente laws and perceived threats of access to land. Discontent seethed in Granada and particularly in the adjacent Indian town of Jalteva. Fearful the Conservatives would take away their ancient rights to land, the local Indians crowned Miguel Cisneros their king to lead them in its protection. Cisneros urged the Indians to tear down fences erected by several large landowners of Granada, which the Indians claimed encroached on communal lands.[169] Although the army succeeded in protecting those fences, the Indians of Jalteva agitated for more than a year before the troops quieted them in 1849.[170] Disputes over fences erupted frequently, not just in mid-nineteenth-century Nicaragua but throughout the Western Hemisphere. Most often, those disputes pitted ordinary people who had worked the land against landowners in the process of expanding their estates or claiming new ones.

Rebels attacked haciendas in southwestern Nicaragua. At least two prominent Conservatives died during the sporadic but prolonged fighting, the former prefect of the department of Meridional, Rafael Lebrón (already mentioned), and the military commander of the same department, Captain Fermín Martínez. On December 3, 1848, agitated by fears of the newly proposed constitution, crowds gathered in Rivas and marched through the streets to attack the houses of leading Conservatives, including those of Antonio Mayrena, Patricio Rivas, and Felipe Sáenz. The Conservative patriarchs fled with their families, some to safer locations within Nicaragua, others to Costa Rica.

From Costa Rica, Felipe Sáenz penned a long account of the terror and indignation he and his family suffered. He charged that a "fanatical mob" broke into his house, destroyed property, injured members of his family, and forced them to flee the city. As a patriarch, Sáenz suffered the agonies of humiliation. Subordinates invaded his kingdom—the home—and harmed its most sacred icons: his mother, wife, daughters, and nieces, the women under his protection. Such actions marked the most grievous offenses in the patriarchal code, an attack on the women under the patriarch's protection and his inability to defend them from harm. Lamenting the disorder disturbing Nicaragua, Señor Sáenz identified the political motives of the "mob." The people shouted, "Death to the deputies [of the Constituent Assembly] and to the new constitution!" Sáenz compared them to the contemporary "French rabble." In his eyes, they behaved like the followers of Louis Blanc, attacking the very foundation of society, private property. Their disdain of the property of others sprang from the influence of communism, a term he employed on three occasions. Their actions foretold what would happen if men without property made decisions.[171] Sáenz's account of the events in Rivas bears ample testimony to the terror the elites felt in the midst of a popular uprising. Even accepting his probable exaggerations and known prejudices, his statements testify to the wide political and ideological differences between the fathers and the folk. The fathers desperately sought to impose order, while the folk saw the triumph of their goals resulting from the disorder they created.

Even as Sáenz prepared his report in Costa Rica, disorder mounted in Nicaragua. On April 16, 1849, the soldiers in the León barracks mutinied, while discontented mobs attacked soldiers stationed in Nandaime and Rivas. The *Correo del Istmo de Nicaragua* reported, "The rebels race through the haciendas creating havoc and leaving a trail of ruins."[172] In Rivas, they burned the house of José Laureano Pineda, lawyer, politician, deputy to the Constituent Assembly of 1848, and future supreme director. The flames devoured the twelve fat manuscript volumes of the national laws he had been compiling.

Nicaragua's anarchy reached an apogee in the last half of the 1840s. Granada battled León; the Conservatives struggled with the Liberals; the Indians fought the mestizos; and the folk challenged the patriarchs. Caste, class, economic, and political struggles tore society apart. "An entirely new situation of political pathology" characterized Nicaragua, in the judgment of Isidro Urtecho. He claimed that the "sudden uprising of the masses, an outburst of the suburbs against the center of the city" occurred "without any ostensible reason."[173] Pedro F. de la Rocha lamented, "The very principles of basic social order were not present."[174] The patriarchs appeared to have little or no understanding of the motives of the folk. But fear shook them.

In the increasingly complex situation, "official" anarchy gave rise to "popular" anarchy.[175] The state lost its monopoly of violence. The folk exercised violence for their own benefit or protection. Others employed it with impunity for their own objectives. As government power diminished, laws became even more impotent. Neither judges nor witnesses dared to prosecute those accused of crimes because they feared revenge.[176] Murder was commonplace. Robert Glasgow Dunlop observed in the mid–1840s, "Assassination is now so common in the state of Nicaragua, that it is little thought of, and is almost never punished by the authorities." However, relatives often avenged such deaths.[177] The Conservatives believed that the Constitution of 1838 facilitated anarchy, even making it inevitable.[178] Their efforts to write a substitute constitution certainly encouraged strife. Such conditions emboldened the bandit, and, not surprisingly, banditry increased in the 1840s.

Banditry was one way of getting ahead in violent times. Through robbery and murder the bandit enriched himself and enhanced his reputation. Perhaps many or most bandits were men who simply seized the advantage of the lack of authority in a disintegrating society for lack of more conventional means to benefit themselves. The flourishing bandits of Nicaragua preyed on road traffic. Security outside the towns could not be guaranteed. Banditry further contributed to stagnation of commerce. Whatever commerce continued during the final half of the 1840s, it proceeded to its destination in armed convoys. Travelers found no safe roads.[179]

Other men may have followed a life-style characterized by those in authority as banditry in order to protest some injustice, to right a perceived wrong, or to seek political revenge. Since most often the rich and powerful suffered the effects of banditry, the poor conceivably could detect in some situations, otherwise characterized as banditry, social justice or even liberation. As in other parts of nineteenth-century Latin America, a rise in banditry and the challenge to patriarchy coincided in Nicaragua. In a study of Peruvian banditry, Enrique López Albujar characterized it as "a protest, a rebellion, a deviation, or a simple means of subsistence."[180] Such generalities seem applicable to Nicaragua. Speaking of Mexican bandits and the havoc they created in nineteenth-century Mexico, Paul J. Vanderwood mused, "Sometimes they create disorder to preserve a kind of order."[181] To the extent that disorder preserved the folk communities from patriarchal intrusion and thwarted the implementation of the aguardiente laws—in the wider sense, the imposition of unpopular national laws on the local community—the rise of banditry served the folk as a useful means of keeping outside authority at bay and thus preserving their own communal order. It also must be emphasized how slippery and subjective the term banditry could be. The Nicaraguan governments routinely labeled anyone opposed to them a "bandit."

In Nicaragua of the 1840s, the boundary line between banditry and rebellion remained murky. What the individual might nobly conceive to be an act of defiance or rebellion, the government might summarily dismiss as an act of banditry. Who was correct? Bernabé Somoza (1815–1849) provided an excellent example of how the "outlaw" or "bandit," terms employed by the government, became a revolutionary caudillo in the eyes of his admirers and followers. Possibly the term "revolutionary" signified at that time the overthrow of the patriarchal government of the city-states in favor of ladino and Indian interests, if, indeed, their interests could be reconciled. Perhaps, technically, Somoza was both "bandit" and "revolutionary," evolving from outlaw to revolutionary within the political environment of anarchic Nicaragua. Somoza certainly would be neither the first nor the last in Latin America to trod that evolutionary path. Francisco (Pancho) Villa of Mexico is another and much better known example of the "bandit" turned "revolutionary." Likewise, in the case of Somoza personal honor became wrapped up with national destiny.[182]

In Jinotepe, one Fernando Somoza lived modestly with his family. He owned a small farm and served the community as a *curandero*, prescribing herbs and dispensing medical advice. He developed a rivalry with Leandro Matus, also a modest landowner and curandero. They competed for the local medical practice, a competition with definite political implications. The Somozas wore the badge of Liberalism; the Matuses waved the banner of Conservatism. After Matus became mayor, he tried to arrest

Francisco Somoza, and young Bernabé came to the aid of his brother. In a duel, he wounded Matus, who then pressed criminal charges. The entire Somoza family fled to El Salvador, where they strengthened their ties with the Liberal Party and fought in various Liberal armies. Later, they helped to defend León against the Salvadorans and Granadans. Still pursued by the charges brought against him by Matus, Bernabé Somoza decided to go to court to settle the matter and clear his name. The government, then in the hands of the Conservatives, appreciated neither his fight with Matus nor his defense of León. Finding him guilty as charged, the judge sentenced him to imprisonment in the Castillo. The judgment embittered Somoza. He argued that he intervened to save his brother from certain death at the hands of Matus. He saw collusion among the accuser, the court, and the Conservative government in power. He vowed vengeance on them and the city of Granada.

At that time, the popular and feared José María Valle (El Chelón), had been captured as a bandit and confined to prison in San Juan del Norte. Somoza and Valle, both of acknowledged Liberal allegiance, communicated through messengers, coordinated their escapes, and fled to El Salvador where they plotted vengeance against the Conservatives. They linked personal honor with political hatred. They spoke boldly of returning the political power of Nicaragua to the Liberals of León.[183] By all accounts, the two understood the goals of the Liberal parties of Nicaragua and El Salvador and the European ideas from which those goals sprang.[184]

At the head of an armed force invading Nicaragua in July 1845, they briefly seized El Viejo and Chinandega.[185] They split their forces at León. Somoza marched to Managua. He won and held the town long enough to kill his enemy Leandro Matus in combat, combining familial vengeance with party and patriotic achievement. At León, General José Trinidad Muñoz defeated El Chelón, who then retreated to Managua just as Somoza withdrew. Together they rushed to recapture it, failed, and returned to El Salvador. The fires of rebellion flamed in northwestern Nicaragua, but General Muñoz successfully, if temporarily, extinguished them.

A century later, a Nicaraguan history text summarized the significance of the events unfolding in 1845 in this manner: "Society was divided into two classes. The capitalist class favored order and the improvement of public administration. The other class, the disinherited, led by outlaws, tended toward disorder and the destruction of the country."[186] Despite the passage of so much time, the sentiments expressed in the text reflected those of Muñoz, the government, and the patriarchs of the mid-nineteenth century. They also reflected the trends and concepts of traditional Nicaraguan historiography. Nicaraguan historians of the nineteenth century and much of the twentieth tended to ascribe to the past a uniformity more harmonious with the patriarchal or class vision than with the totality of experience. Liberal and Conservative historians may have differed on ideological or geographical (León or Granada) merits, but they united on the issue of popular rebellion to condemn it.

Popular opposition to the aguardiente laws imposed by the Conservatives in 1845 and the constitution proposed by them in 1848 might at first glance imply that the Liberals made common cause with the folk, against Conservative governance. Events contradicted that seemingly logical alliance. The Liberals appreciated the importance of the liquor revenue. They were also in the process of rethinking their attitudes toward communal landownership. At the zenith of the popular challenge to tax powers and apprehensions over the proposed constitutional redefinition of land policies, the Liberals apparently felt more comfortable with the Conservatives, their fellow patriarchs, against the folk. The popular appeal of the flamboyant Bernabé Somoza sealed the Liberal-Conservative alliance.

In March 1846, Somoza reentered Nicaragua and briefly held Chinandega, where he executed four men in revenge for the government mistreatment of his followers the preceding year. Under attack from government forces, he withdrew from Chinandega but remained active in contraband and "banditry" until the rebels in the southwest called him to Rivas in 1849 to be their leader.

His arrival in the Departamento Meridional coincided with uprisings in Granada and Nandaime, further unnerving the patriarchs.[187] Somoza never forgot his personal vendettas, another cause for concern among the ruling fathers of Granada. They remembered that after the court sentenced him in 1845 he swore to burn Granada.[188] Nor had Somoza forgotten the Matus clan. He assaulted Jinotepe on June 6, 1849, and went directly to the house of Benigno Matus, a relative of Leandro. He took Benigno, his brother, and his nephew prisoner, threatened to execute them, and finally ransomed them for two thousand pesos.[189] The patriarchs paled. The man was doubly dangerous: as an individual pursuing his vengeance and as a leader capable of unifying the folk. From the popular point of view, he appeared as a new Güegüence getting the best of the authorities.

Legend has made of Bernabé Somoza both a devil and a hero. A handsome man, who played a beguiling guitar, he reputedly won more than his share of feminine hearts. Squier depicted him as cavalier, gallant, generous, dashing, attractive, and winsome. He rode well and fought furiously.[190] Indeed, those adjectives and this type of description circulated widely among Nicaraguans: "Standing beside the mast was a tall, graceful man, with a feather in hat, a red Spanish cloak hanging over one shoulder, a brace of naked pistols stuck in his belt, and a drawn sword in his hand."[191] That dashing figure was Bernabé Somoza. Such nineteenth-century prose predated a thousand romantic, film-script descriptions of swashbucklers in the Caribbean. It was also a contributory ingredient to the making of the "bandit-hero" image.

Some of the patriarchs feared that Somoza would win the confidence of the Indians and unite them. He embodied a compelling leadership mystique. In their separate communities, the folk lacked a wider leadership which could draw on the scattered communities, unify them into a cause, and confront the patriarchs en masse. The possible emergence of such a leader was an ever present danger to the patriarchs, hence Somoza's appearance in and around turbulent Rivas in 1849 electrified them, Liberal and Conservative alike. So upset were they that they suspended their institutionalized quarrels to ally against the threat he seemed to pose against their continued authority. Previously nothing or no one had welded the two parties into such unity

The government had already issued an order to seize firearms from citizens, forbid illegal gatherings, and to take "the most efficient and energetic measures to save the people from the horrors of anarchy."[192] General José Trinidad Muñoz, the pillar of the Liberal Party in León, and Lt. Colonel Fruto Chamorro, who personified the Conservative Party in Granada, brought their joint firepower to bear on Somoza. The *Boletín Oficial* praised the bipartisan support of the "cause of humanity."[193] For a brief period, a real class war raged.

The official press fired a ceaseless barrage of pejoratives against Somoza: "barbarian," "cannibal," "savage," "bandit," "madman," and "brigand."[194] The only political allegiance he recognized, the *Boletín Oficial* raged, was to the party of "vandalism."[195] It accused him of burning haciendas and killing at least one patriarch.[196] General Muñoz compiled a list of grisly deeds he ascribed to Somoza: "I have trustworthy news from Rivas, and I know that Somoza is still in that city committing excesses. He shot all the wounded; he robbed the churches of everything they contained; he set fire to city; he dug up the corpse of Lt. Col. Martínez and paraded it through the streets. In short, this barbarian carried out thousands of atrocities."[197] Minister Gregorio Díaz reported a similar sensational account, adding the victimization of the aged and crimes "against the honesty of the fair sex."[198] The facts do not seem to corroborate the extremes of those statements. At any rate, the behavior of Somoza did not seem much different from other leaders or armies, the Conservatives or the Liberals. The ruins of twice-sacked León amply testified, for example, to the brutalities of Nicaraguan warfare. What doubtless intensified the heat of rhetoric in this case was the popular dimension of this war, its potential threat to all patriarchs. The sporadic rebellions had lacked a charismatic figure to unify them and thereby to intensify their impact and threaten the domination of the two city-states. If the populist language and the dashing figure of Bernabé Somoza succeeded in coalescing discontent, the elites would confront a formidable foe.[199] They feared a unified and popular agrarian movement.[200]

The patriarchs persuaded themselves that nothing less than Western civilization was at stake. They cast the popular phase of anarchy within the increasingly familiar mold of "civilization versus barbarism." While depicting the rebels as barbarian, the Boletín Oficial emphasized to its readers that the government defended "humanity, religion, and fatherland . . . liberty and independence."[201] The army marched against the rustic rebels "to save society."[202] General Muñoz affirmed, "The social order is being attacked. Bands of bloody destroyers menace our most cherish interests."[203] A broadside printed in Rivas in 1849 cried that "barbarians" were attacking "civilization and private property."[204] On behalf of the aggrieved patriarchs of Rivas, Felipe Sáenz summarized the significance of the popular resistance and the government reaction: "Power rests in the hands of the barbarian who has declared war on civilization. . . . The cause I defend is the civilization of the nineteenth century against the barbarism of the thirteenth."[205] Coincidence or not, Sáenz repeated in his Costa Rican exile in remarkably similar language what the famous Argentine exile Domingo Faustino Sarmiento had written in Chile in 1845 about Argentina: "Two distinct forms of civilization meet upon a common ground in the Argentine Republic: one, still in its infancy, which, ignorant of that so far above it, goes on repeating the crude efforts of the Middle Ages; the other, disregarding what lies at its feet, while it strives to realize in itself the latest results of European civilization; the nineteenth and twelfth centuries dwell together—one inside the cities, the other without them."[206] Sarmiento identified the popular Argentine provincial caudillo Juan Facundo Quiroga and his rural followers with barbarism. Sáenz applied such an identity to the Nicaraguan folk. Both writers witnessed the same struggle; both shared the same fears; both denigrated local culture; both advocated the Europeanization of America. In every country in nineteenth-century Latin America, at one time or another, the elites cried out that the barbarian masses clamored at the gates of their civilization. Such a cry conferred license to any form of defense and ultimately of repression.

Succeeding generations of Nicaraguan historians took up the cry of imperiled civilization. Anselmo H. Rivas (1826–1904) well represented that historiographical trend. He judged the disorders of the last half of the 1840s as "bloody and destructive struggle of civilization versus barbarism."[207]

The Nicaraguan elites feared rural unrest for it threatened their economic foundation. But so long as they themselves promoted and perpetuated it, they felt they could control it. A populist leader unifying the rural population to challenge the patriarchs raised the curtain on quite a different drama, and one that panicked them. They associated Somoza with threats and actions against the plantations, patriarchs, and privilege. That panic explained why in 1849 they forged a unique, if brief, unity.[208] Together Muñoz and Chamorro defeated the popular forces by mid–1849. They tried, condemned to death, and on July 17, 1849, executed Bernabé Somoza and his principal lieutenants: Juan Lugo, Camilo Mayorga, Apolinar Marenco, and Estéban Bendaña.[209]

As the army gained the upper hand in the struggle with Somoza, the government announced with apparent relief and great satisfaction the end of violence against property and the triumph of civilization. It had vindicated the patriarchal belief that "Property is the base and root of society."[210] The government emphatically, if somewhat enigmatically, added that all "outrages against our brothers the North Americans" had been terminated.[211] Doubtless the government hoped that such an affirmation would catch the eye of the newly arrived U.S. Minister Ephraim George Squier, with whom the authorities wanted to sign appropriate treaties to reverse English aggression and to promote the transit route.

The following year, Minister of Internal and External Relations Sebastián Salinas informed the nation that peace, "the first of all blessings," reigned throughout the nation. Prefects had been appointed and were functioning in all five territorial departments: Occidente, Oriente, Meridional, Matagalpa, and Segovia. The economy demonstrated signs of modest recovery. Spain extended diplomatic recognition to its former colony, and the United States offered help to counter British incursions and to expedite a transit route.[212]

The patriarchs breathed a collective sigh of relief. They had defeated a popular threat; they had turned back barbarism. They remained in power, their property safe. They were free to impose their agenda. They were also free to resume party squabbles. Their triumph terminated for nearly three-quarters of a century any serious challenge to their dominance. Their victory, in the long run, consecrated export over subsistence agriculture.

In truth, more than one threat had united the elites by 1849. Bernabé Somoza and popular rebellions constituted a major internal threat. Aggressive foreigners proved to be equally menacing. Imperial England pushed its claims to a protectorate over the Mosquito Coast in the 1840s and seized San Juan del Norte in 1848. London threatened the pathetically weak and divided Nicaragua with territorial dismemberment and exclusion from the Caribbean coast. The elites agreed that their vision of the future required the Caribbean resources and ports, and they jointly voiced their protests to Her Britannic Majesty. At exactly the same time, a splendid opportunity seemed at hand to build the oft-discussed and much desired trans-Nicaraguan transportation route. The incorporation of California into the United States after the defeat of Mexico in 1848 and the discovery of rich deposits of gold there the same year focused attention on Central American routes to speed up travel from the East to West coast of the United States. Nicaragua offered an appealing water-land route to expedite the migration to California, a route that would not only help to unite the two coasts of the United States but those of Nicaragua as well. Already in 1849, a few North Americans made their way across the isthmus to California. New opportunities tempted the patriarchs who hoped the moribund Nicaraguan economy would respond to those welcome stimuli. In those extraordinary circumstances, their first order of business was to impose peace on the countryside. By mid–1849 they had accomplished that goal. Accordingly, the government turned its attention to foreign threats and opportunities.

Fatherland: Foreign Intervention and the Incipient Nation-State

The Threat

After defeating the folk rebellions in mid–1849, the patriarchs turned their attention to the outside world. On the international horizon, dark clouds of threat alternated with bright rays of sunny promise. Despite this uncertain prospect, the patriarchs reiterated their vision of the future: the time had arrived for Nicaragua to play its transcendental role as the bridge between the two oceans, the highway of global commerce. Echoing a history of hope, the *Gaceta del Gobierno* discussed the desire for a transisthmian canal and asked rhetorically, "Where is the person of human emotions, the patriot, the wise man who does not want to see this productive project carried out? Is there a Nicaraguan so hostile to his own country that he cannot feel deep emotions when he contemplates the success of a project that will assure the well-being and happiness of future generations?"[1] No doubt about it, Minister Gregorio Díaz assured his compatriots, such a canal guaranteed the future greatness of Nicaragua.[2] An impressive confluence of international events indicated that indeed the moment had arrived to realize an old and elusive dream.

Since its conquest and exploration in the sixteenth century, Nicaragua had attracted attention as the logical link between the Atlantic and Pacific oceans. A waterway composed of the San Juan River and Lake Nicaragua penetrated from the Atlantic to within ten or twelve miles of the Pacific. That short span of terrain was relatively flat. A spectacular rise in world commerce in the nineteenth century intensified the need for and discussion of a canal. Central America barely had declared its independence when the English firm of Barclay and Company began to explore the possibilities of a trans-Nicaraguan water route. A Dutch group obtained a canal concession in Nicaragua in 1830. Repeating the evaluation of a

French study from the end of the eighteenth century, Alphonse Dumaytray and Pedro Rouhaud published a pamphlet in Paris in 1833 to emphasize the impressive natural wealth of Nicaragua, foremost of which was its geographic position as the logical site for an interoceanic canal.[3] At the behest of the federal government of Central America, John Baily, an English naval officer, surveyed a canal route across Nicaragua in 1837–38, which the American diplomat John L. Stephens verified, partially in situ, in 1840.[4] He represented Washington's consistent interest in a transisthmian route. As early as 1826, the U.S. Congress spoke of constructing a canal in Central America. The Senate urged the president in 1835 to sign a treaty with Central America to facilitate it.[5] It raised the issue again in 1839 and 1846. The Guatemalan Alejandro Marure published in 1845 a history of the consistent and mounting international interest in building a canal.[6]

Nicaragua received a bonanza of publicity from an unexpected source in 1846, the pen of Napoleon Louis Bonaparte, the future Emperor Napoleon III. The prospect of a canal across Nicaragua fired his imagination to write the *Canal of Nicaragua: or a Project to Connect the Atlantic and Pacific Oceans by Means of a Canal.* His enthusiastic conclusions measured the heat of that fire:

> As Constantinople is the centre of the ancient world, so is the town of León, or rather Masaya, the centre of the new; and if the tongue of land which separates its two lakes from the Pacific Ocean were cut through, she would command, by her central position, the entire coast of North and South America. Like Constantinople, Masaya is situated between two extensive natural harbours, capable of giving shelter to the largest fleets, safe from attack. The state of Nicaragua can become, better than Constantinople, the necessary route for the great commerce of the world.[7]

The Nicaraguans believed him. He shared their vision. So, too, did many of the maritime nations of the North Atlantic.

As a consequence of that belief, two expanding metropolises, one old, London, and one new, Washington, met on the small stage of Nicaragua during the mid-nineteenth century. At that moment, England's power in the Caribbean was at its height. The United States resolved to check and then to reverse it. Its success heralded its future domination of the region. Divided Nicaragua remained as much a prey to the new metropolis and its commercial and strategic priorities as it had to the old, and in some situations, sadly, became a spectator to its own history. Nicaragua was learning that its unique geography could be both a potential resource and a real threat. One newspaper editorial observed with foresight that Nicaragua's geography invited foreign intervention: "The waterway across the Isthmus of Nicaragua is the apple in our Eden. It will be our curse."[8] That eerie prediction hung ominously over Nicaragua.

External rivalries disturbed the fledgling nation. A failure to consolidate its independence, an inability to create a viable government, a small divided population, and an empty treasury weakened it as two powerful nations expanded into its territory. Fruto Chamorro worried, "The essentially ruinous internal wars serve to lead the people to foreign domination and to place them under the control of others who have no respect for them."[9] Reality more than justified Chamorro's concerns. Without peace, order, unity, and stable institutions, Nicaraguans opened their territory to foreigners with the hope– unfounded as it turned out–that their presence somehow would benefit the nation. Some evidence suggests that the Conservatives more than the Liberals favored a transit route across Nicaragua. They felt that Granada in particular would benefit economically from the route and the stimulation it would give commerce.[10] The government's decisions gave preference to material progress over political order. Such decisions further opened the door to foreign intrusions. The foreigners gleefully entered.

With claims to the Atlantic coast of Nicaragua since the seventeenth century, the British eagerly sought to control any transisthmian trade route, a logical complement to their growing global empire and lively international commerce. They intensified their efforts to dominate Central America after it separated from Spain. Granada continued to use the Lake Nicaragua-San Juan River water route for its import-export trade, but only token military garrisons were posted at San Juan del Norte and San Carlos. In 1824 a small detachment of Englishmen and Mosquitos briefly seized San Juan del Norte, claiming it to be a part of the Mosquito Kingdom. The primary goal of the astute English consul-general in the isthmus, Frederick Chatfield, during the seventeen years he served there, 1834–1851, was to secure trade, territory, and influence for Great Britain, while first weakening the Central American federation and then widening the divisions among the five republics into which it disintegrated.[11] During those years, the British presence in the Caribbean extended from the Bahamas to Trinidad, with the fulcrum of power located in Jamaica. The Union Jack flag was firmly planted in British Guiana on the northern coast of South America; London laid claims to the coast of Central America from Guatemala into Costa Rica. One hostile pamphlet accused Great Britain of using its "African subjects" to create a "black empire" of influence in the Caribbean.[12] In 1836 British activity accelerated in Nicaragua. The English began to exploit on a larger scale the rich stands of timber. Their vigorous activity alarmed one prominent resident of Granada: "They want to dispossess us of our north coast and adjacent islands and the will do it if it pleases them."[13]

To the Caribbean shores of Nicaragua, the British over the course of nearly two centuries introduced Black slaves and workers from the islands to join the small Indian populations in collecting raw materials for export. English, or a Caribbean variation thereof, became the principal language, and the Church of England dominated the religious life of the inhabitants until missionaries of the Moravian Church arrived in 1848 to spread their own Protestant faith. The English-speaking, Protestant, zambo population of Nicaragua's east coast contrasted sharply with the Spanish-speaking, Roman Catholic, increasingly ladino population of the west coast, adding a dramatic cultural division to the already significant challenges to nation-building.

As accelerating international trade heightened interest in the much discussed transisthmian route, London grew ever more mindful of the continental expansion of the United States with its burgeoning trade and expressed its own interest in a Central American canal. Without warning, Great Britain increased its claims along the Caribbean coast in 1841. Superintendent Alexander MacDonald arrived at San Juan aboard a British warship accompanied by King Robert I of the Mosquitos. Britain had imposed a European-style monarchy on the Mosquitos, which had nothing to do with their customs or history. Yet for decades the British encouraged the charade of a Black, Caribbean monarchy, the pliant tool to impose a protectorate over the region. In this particular case, MacDonald used the king to extend the boundaries of the protectorate to include the mouth of the San Juan River and, of course, the port of San Juan del Norte. The action threatened to restrict Granada as well as Nicaragua to the Pacific Ocean.[14] When the Nicaraguan commander of the port protested, MacDonald arrested, humiliated, and expelled him. Meanwhile, subjects of Her Britannic Majesty had organized in 1840 the British Central American Land Company, one of several efforts to colonize the Mosquito region. While none of the projected colonization schemes ever worked, the very talk of them unnerved Nicaraguan officials.

The seizure of San Juan del Norte ignited Nicaraguan nationalism, at least among those patriarchs faithful to the economic vision. It also persuaded the leadership to favor policies to reunify Central America as the most effective means to counter foreign aggression. In 1842, 1845, 1847, and again in 1849, Nicaragua energized efforts to recreate some degree of Central American unity. Little resulted from those efforts. The government also resolved to establish diplomatic missions abroad to protect Nicaraguan interests better.[15] The process was slow. In 1850 Spain recognized Nicaragua and signed a treaty of peace and friendship. The following year the government dispatched the skillful José de Marcoleta to Washington as Envoy Extraordinary and Minister Plenipotentiary. By 1853 Nicaragua enjoyed diplomatic or consular relations with Great Britain, Belgium, France, Spain, the German States, Sardinia, the United States, Mexico, Peru, Chile, and the four other Central American states.

Britain's shadowy claims to the Mosquito Coast deeply disturbed the enfeebled Nicaraguan governments. When the popular rebellions absorbed the government's attention, Britain made its most serious move to incorporate San Juan del Norte into Mosquitia. By 1844 London was referring to the Mosquito Kingdom as a "protectorate." In 1847 it proclaimed that protectorate included the mouth of the San Juan River, a claim to which the Nicaraguan government reacted at once. The minister in charge of foreign affairs termed it "the most delicate, important, and transcendental matter before Nicaragua: a question of our territorial integrity and sovereignty."[16] On January 1, 1848, the British seized the port of San Juan del Norte, drove Nicaraguan officials out, raised the Mosquito flag, and changed the port's name to Greytown in honor of Sir Charles Grey, Governor of Jamaica. General José Trinidad Muñoz immediately went downriver with sufficient forces to reclaim the port. The British reacted at once to recapture the strategic site. Then they ascended the river to seize both Castillo and San Carlos, where they forced the Nicaraguan government to recognize the Mosquito occupation—but not the ownership—of San Juan del Norte before agreeing to withdraw from Nicaragua. The Nicaraguans complained bitterly that "England had usurped the most interesting and valuable part of our territory." Indeed, the seizure of the port in 1848 reduced Atlantic customs revenues that year by at least US$30,000.[17] The *Correo del Istmo de Nicaragua* called upon the Liberal and Conservative parties to resolve their differences, "whose origin is perhaps some ridiculous passion," in the face of foreign aggression, so that a united Nicaragua could confront these threats to its sovereignty.[18]

The foreign incursions after 1841 clearly demonstrated that bitter internal political divisions facilitated interventions. That combination of internal conflicts and external interventions became a tragic leitmotif in Nicaraguan history. Within their larger imperial scheme, the British regarded the control of the San Juan River as but one goal. At the same time, they moved to position themselves favorably to control other possible canal routes across the isthmus. They acquired Roatán Island in the Gulf of Honduras and temporarily seized Tigre Island in the Bay of Fonseca. However, British imperialism failed to keep ahead of American expansionism.

By 1848 potent forces were in motion that would affect both Nicaragua and Great Britain. The arrival in Nicaraguan waters of the steamship, that impressive symbol of modernity and technology, assured an end to Nicaragua's somnolent isolation just as it indicated a challenge to the monopoly Great Britain exercised over the Atlantic coast of Central America. For the first time direct, scheduled steamship service operated to and from Nicaragua, sustaining contact with the wider world beyond and focusing attention to a greater degree than before on the country's geographical advantages. In April 1847, the U.S. Congress awarded the United States Mail Steamship Company a contract to transport mail to the ports on the Atlantic side of the Central American isthmus; seven months later the Pacific Mail Steamship Company received a similar contract for the western side. The following year the English themselves inaugurated direct steamship service between Southampton and San Juan del Norte.

Another historic force exploded even more dramatically on the North American continent: the territorial expansion of the United States to the drumbeat of Manifest Destiny. In 1848 the United States wrested California from Mexico. The new territory sparkled with gold, luring the Yankees westward to the El Dorado of the Pacific shores.

The incorporation of California within the United States and the simultaneous discovery of gold in that new territory thrust Nicaragua into new geographic, commercial and historical roles. The patriarchs understood more clearly than ever that political order—and, later, the new "political institutions" Fruto Chamorro called for—were needed to take advantage of the new opportunities. [19] The new opportunities in due course created a "perceptual revolution" favorable to the introduction of modern capitalism into Nicaragua and the consequent changes in production with a greater emphasis on exports. That perception of a capitalist and modernized society melded with the old vision to guide the patriarchs through the 1850s and far beyond.[20]

The triumph of Manifest Destiny on the North American continent carried General Zachary Taylor into the White House in the presidential elections of 1848. The following year, when President Taylor advocated immediate statehood for California, more than 80,000 Americans already had arrived there, over a third of them via either Cape Horn, a long, rough all-water route around the Southern tip of South America, or via Panama. The march to the west coast had begun, and Taylor determined to accelerate it.

That determination solidified hitherto vague U.S. policies toward Central America, where Panama and Nicaragua offered relatively safe and swift routes from the east coast of the United States to the distant but increasingly important west coast. Congress insisted on the immediate integration of the newly acquired Pacific coast with the Atlantic one:

> The recent acquisition of California and the recognition and establishment of the right of the United States to the Oregon territory render exceedingly important the question as to the best mode of communication with those immense possessions. . . . The means of an easy and rapid communication between the two oceans has heretofore been a subject of great interest to the United States in common with all civilized nations. It has now become a matter of utmost practical importance, and the duty and necessity of uniting the remote and extended possessions of the country, is most obvious and undeniable.[21]

Railroads and a canal across Central America emerged as items of priority. Domestic and foreign policies of the United States melded into one.

President Taylor appointed a Secretary of State, John Clayton, who was in tune with and prepared to direct the energies of Manifest Destiny. Events and personalities in the United States thus came together to formulate an active, well-defined policy toward Central America in the place of a previously more passive one. Clayton scorned any British claims to Mosquitia and pressed London to abolish its protectorate and pretenses. He hoped to avoid conflict by advocating a policy of open access to canal routes upon the basis of equality, a policy whereby the new and junior power successfully checked the veteran.

At that moment in the mid-nineteenth century, the attention of three nations converged on the lush tropical banks of the San Juan River. Great Britain maneuvered to strengthen its control over the Mosquito protectorate, to gain control of the potentially valuable trans-Nicaragua trade route, and to check the expansion of U.S. hegemony over Central America. The United States also hoped to control the trade route, thereby restricting British influence while expanding its own. Nicaragua, the least unified and most anarchic nation of the isthmus, struggled to prevent further intervention, to restore its authority over the Atlantic coast, and to exercise some jurisdiction over any future canal or trade route across its territory. Control of San Juan del Norte determined which nation could carry out its policy successfully.

The port at the entrance to the San Juan River had been Granada's gateway to the North Atlantic. Starting in 1849, it also served as the Atlantic terminal for the interoceanic transportation route stretching across Nicaragua. The port illustrated two harsh realities for Nicaragua: its insubstantiality and the dominance of foreigners.

The port, a collection of thatched bamboo huts and a few simple clapboard structures with a population of 129 in 1848, hardly looked like the place where empires would collide.[22] By 1850 a transient population of international rowdies dominated the port, and the flag of Mosquitia fluttering over it only encouraged their excesses. Charles Parke, who spent several days there in November of that year, described the strategic port in this way:

> Graytown or San Juan is the poorest kind of town on a flat beach. The harbor is poor. Vessels cannot approach within 1/4 mile of shore. This place seems to be governed by a set of Negro officers under the protection of a British Man of War, which is now anchored outside. . . . The houses are built of plank and bamboo. The inhabitants are mostly a mixture of Negro and Indian with a slight dip of Spanish, the wooly head predominating. There is very little work done here. Vegetables grow so luxuriantly, the natives are natural vegetarians. It takes work to produce animal food. These people prefer less meat and more rest. Young Negroes, huge Mastiff dogs, and turkey-buzzards seem to take possession of the streets. The buzzards are the principal scavengers. Lord only knows how many different smells there would be in town if it were not for the buzzards. They gather the filth from the streets, and in order to be near their work in the morning, roost on the housetops every night. There is a heavy fine against any one who kills a vulture. And I think it's correct. As he is the only truly industrious inhabitant of the city.
>
> The only amusement here is the "fandango." Some of our boys attend every night. The room or hall is about 60 feet in diameter with seats all around the outer circle. The dance is nothing more than a waltz round and round the circle until tired. Then you seat your "Dulcinea" and play the agreeable until rested when you engage in another waltz. The city or town

marshal is a big, burly Negro wearing "brass buttons." I understand he is appointed by the English government. I believe England pretends to protect this place and people, I know not why.

As in all civilized, Christianized, and highly cultivated countries, there is plenty of whisky here and is freely used at all important gatherings, especially the "fandango." Our American boys, especially Boston and New York boys, can easily be persuaded to take a drink with the dusky Señorita when away from home, in fact too polite to refuse her. This being the fact, almost every night the dance would break up in a row, leaving the Americans and the dusky females in possession of the Hall. Complaint was made to the commander of the English Man of War in the harbor as to the rowdy conduct of the foreigners. The boys managed to keep on the soft side of the marshal by "feeding and watering" him well. [23]

Parke's report revealed a rough, transient society in which authority was difficult to identify and easy to circumvent. The port boomed during the early 1850s. [24] The growing population only seemed to magnify the drinking, gambling, fighting and whoring beneath which political intrigue and economic greed seethed. The British were hard-pressed to maintain authority. Robert Walsh, passing through San Juan in May of 1852, reported, "The flag of the Mosquito King is still flying here, but that is the only evidence of his sovereignty. The control of the town is in the hands of foreign residents, principally Americans."[25] They scoffed at Mosquito and Nicaraguan claims of sovereignty.

In the pinch of pressures exerted by the North Atlantic giants at mid-century, little Nicaragua took recourse in an old strategy to escape the crushing embrace of the two. It played one off against the other. The Peruvian diplomat Felipe Barriga Alvarez, serving as his nation's chargé d'affaires in León in 1850, witnessed the international drama at close range. He informed the Peruvian Minister of Foreign Affairs, "After the efforts of England to seize the Río San Juan, the Government of Nicaragua skillfully sought out the United States as a balance to that powerful enemy and to alleviate the danger." While signing a canal treaty with a U.S. company did not guarantee Nicaragua's independence, it saved the country at the time, according to Barriga Alvarez:

> If you examine the special circumstances of Nicaragua, you will see that it was the only means of salvation it had. Nicaragua with its ports on both the Pacific and Atlantic oceans, with its level land that even now is traversed by carriages, with its lakes and rivers, seems to be expressly destined by God to satisfy that need expressed for so long by the world: a route to link the

*Figure 5.*San Juan del Norte. This is a somewhat idyllic representation of the port at mid-nineteenth century. Sailing ships, river boats, and at least one steamship suggest considerable transit traffic. Lithograph source: *Meyer's Universum, oder, Abbildung und Beschreibung des Sehenswerthesten und Merkwurdigsten der Natur und Kunst auf der ganzen Erde* (Hildburghausen: Druck und Verlag vom Bibliographischen Institut, 1848–1852).

oceans, to connect Europe and Asia through the Americas. Underpopulated and impoverished, Nicaragua will not be able to build a canal and she could disappear as a nation when by force or cunning a powerful nation wants to undertake the construction. For a long time England wanted to be that nation. The present government of Nicaragua has understood the true situation of the country. Not being able to free itself totally from foreign intervention, it has thwarted the nation most hostile to its existence in favor of another that respects its nationality and will help it recover the usurped territory [Mosquitia]. [26]

In a very real sense, Nicaragua's choice turned out to be a choice between submission to one Atlantic power or another. Until that moment it had suffered no distress from Washington whereas London had bullied, humiliated, and raped it. Understandably, Nicaragua favored the United States. In that choice, it enjoyed some modest success. In the long run, it succeeded in maintaining its territorial integrity on the Atlantic coast, something that Guatemala, for example, failed to do. In the short run—for good or for bad—it hosted a transcontinental transportation route. Quite unbeknown to the actors in the intense tropical drama, the power of Great Britain in Nicaragua had reached its maximum in 1848.

The year 1849 vibrates with historical significance for Nicaragua. In March the Gordon expedition, the first organized group of Americans traveling to California, arrived to cross Nicaragua from San Juan del Norte to Realejo. Minister Ephraim George Squier, arrived in June, the first U.S. diplomat accredited to Nicaragua. In September, Joseph L. White signed a canal and transportation agreement with the government of Nicaragua. The Yanks had landed. The United States presence was unmistakable. For the moment, the Nicaraguans cheered them, a welcome that did not go unnoticed by the English. [27]

To respond to the siren call of California required a long and dangerous trek across the plains and through the Rocky Mountains. Some experimented with alternative routes in the hope of finding more comfort, speed, and safety. One of the most satisfactory crossings was through Panama, which over the centuries had served as the traditional link between the Atlantic and Pacific oceans. On the map Nicaragua looked closer, thus the distance shorter; and the San Juan River combined with Lake Nicaragua seemed to reduce the land crossing to a minimum. Guided by such considerations, the entrepreneur George Gordon organized a party of 136 men to try it. They sailed from New York harbor for San Juan del Norte on February 20, 1849. They arrived at San Juan on March 19, and on April 4 embarked on their river adventure. It took three weeks to reach San Carlos, the garrison that marked the union of the river and lake. When the hardy travelers arrived at Granada on the opposite side of the lake "upwards of five hundred of the citizens of Granada assembled on the beach to receive and welcome [them] with enthusiastic shouts." Unable to get a ship out of Realejo until July 20, they did not arrive in San Francisco until October 5. Their journey had lasted more than seven months![28]

Transportation and accommodations for the large group taxed all the Nicaraguan facilities at that time. The small army of adventurers needed lodging and food, as well as liquor and women. Yet the novelty of their presence created but a ripple in the Nicaraguan pond when compared to the monumental splash of the arrival of Minister Squier on June 22, 1849.

His arrival coincided with the defeat of the popular rebellions. It also coincided with the patriarchs' fear of the loss to Great Britain of San Juan del Norte and the commercial route to the Atlantic upon which so much of their vision focused. In a rare demonstration of unity, Liberal and Conservative patriarchs embraced the new American diplomat as a possible savior. No ceremony could be too exaggerated to communicate their hopes and expectations. They overwhelmed the young Squier, who was only twenty-eight as he began his historical mission.

Squier trooped in a triumphal procession through Granada, villages, and towns, and finally into León, seat of the government. An extraordinary issue of the *Boletín Oficial* proclaimed the arrival of the American minister into the capital: "Today is the magnificent day of the greatest hope of Nicaragua." It saluted the close relations uniting the two countries and confessed that Nicaragua recognized the northern republic "as the natural protector of the continent and most particularly of countries like Nicaragua which identify their security with that respected republic." The government dispatched a large and colorful reception party to meet the American as he approached León. Bishop Jorge de Viteri led the distinguished committee composed of the prefect of the Department of the Occidente, the highest ranking military officers and clerics, and the most worthy citizens. The paper reported that the minister "distinguished himself by his friendliness, his republican character, and his ardent wish for the happiness of Nicaragua." Lively band music, the discharge of cannons, and the ringing of the cathedral bells announced Squier's entrance into León. The crowd observed "with singular satisfaction" that one of Nicaragua's most honored officers, Lt. Col. Laureano Zelaya, rode at Squier's side "carrying the victorious flag of the United States." That gesture "symbolized the sincere friendship between the two peoples." The newspaper concluded, "We boldly predict the most successful results from this diplomatic mission."[29] A much later account by the Nicaraguan historian A. H. Rivas praised Squier and noted that "he personally won the affection of the Nicaraguans."[30]

Squier himself narrated the events no less euphorically. The encounter with the welcoming committee "a hundred or two in number" thrilled him: "First came the Bishop in purple robes, splendidly mounted, flanked by a group of priests, and followed by a train of officers, in uniforms absolutely dazzling in the noon-day sun!" Bishop de Viteri y Ungo impressed Squier as "informed, courteous, and affable, with manners which would have graced the proudest courts of Europe." The bishop confided to Squier as they conversed in Spanish on the approach to León, "We want only an infusion of your people to make this broad land an Eden of beauty, and the garden of the world." Those words of trust mixed with hope revealed sentiments often expressed before and after by members of the elite. Squier remembered the incident of the flag in these words, "A dashing young officer rode up to me, as I approached, and begged to be permitted 'to carry the glorious flag of El Norte,' which request was, of course, graciously acceded to."

The reception of the capital awed the minister. After passing through the Indian suburb of Guadalupe, the party took "a broad, graded way, paved with stones" that led to the main plaza:

> I had merely time to observe that the streets were in gala dress, when the thunder of cannon, and the sudden pealing of the bells of the churches, above which those of the cathedral rose full and distinct, proclaimed our arrival. "Vivan los Estados Unidos del Norte!" exclaimed the officer who bore my flag, as he dashed at full speed to the head of the column. The whole party caught the spirit, and echoed the "viva," and the Bishop himself waved his hand and cried "Adelantamos!" On! I remember but little more, except a confused sound of trampling horses, shouting people, the ringing of bells, the thunder of cannon, and cloud of dust, until we rode into the great plaza. Here the entire garrison was drawn up, who presented arms and cheered for the United States as we entered. The band struck up a martial air, and the ladies of the metropolis waved their handkerchiefs to us from the balconies of the House of the Government . . . .

> High Mass had been said the day before in the church of La[s] Mercedes for our safe arrival, and now a Te Deum was chanted in the cathedral in acknowledgment of the protection which Heaven had vouchsafed us. In the evening fireworks were let off in the Plaza, and we were serenaded by the band attached to the garrison, which, to our surprise, we found almost as effective as any that we had ever heard. [31]

A few days after his regal welcome to the capital, Minister Squier officially presented his credentials to Supreme Director Norberto Ramírez in an impressive ceremony. The North American sensed the significance of the occasion for the Nicaraguans, tired as they were of internal wars and external pressures and longing for peace, order, and stability. Their hopes for support and friendship from the United States seemed to infuse "new energy" into them. Those hopes humbled, almost unnerved, the unflappable Squier. [32]

Following international diplomatic practice, the minister handed his credentials to the chief-of-state and offered the usual platitudes. Nonetheless, his remarks touched upon several topics of supreme interest to the Nicaraguans:

> It shall be my aim, Sir, in my official and personal intercourse with the Government and people of this State, not only to confirm the present harmony and good correspondence which exist between the two Republics, but to

create new ties of friendship, and to promote a closer and more intimate relationship between them. . . . While we would cultivate friendly intercourse, and promote trade and commerce with all the world, and invite to our shores and to the enjoyment of our institutions the people of all nations, we should proclaim, in language distinct and firm, that the American continent belongs to Americans, and is sacred to Republican Freedom. We should also let it be understood, that if foreign powers encroach upon the territories or invade the rights of any one of the American States, they inflict an injury upon all, which it is alike the duty and determination of all to see redressed. . . . I have been deeply impressed with the capabilities of the country, and vastness of its internal resources. I have seen, also, with pleasure, the many evidences of industry and civilization which exist within your borders, and I have been led to indulge the belief that the time is not far distant, when the commerce of two hemispheres shall find within your territories an easy passage from sea to sea. It is one of the objects of my mission to assist in an enterprise so important to the whole world—an enterprise, the successful prosecution of which must enable this country to attain a degree of prosperity second to that of no other on the globe. With your cordial co-operation (of which I am well assured), and of that of the citizens of this Republic, I hope soon to have it in my power to announce to my Government, that the initiatives to this grand and glorious enterprise have already been taken. . . . That the new relations which are this day opened between this Republic and my own, may result in lasting benefit to both, is, Sir, my sincere prayer, and to this end I shall direct my most earnest endeavors. [33]

The pledge of closer ties, the denunciation of European intervention, and the encouragement of a transisthmian route confected a verbal feast that the assembled crowd hungrily devoured.

Obviously Supreme Director Ramírez enjoyed the rhetorical repast. No less emotional than the North American minister, he replied:

The satisfaction which I experience in having the honor of receiving, for the first time, a representative of the Republic of North America, is only equalled by the aspirations and high hopes which that event inspires. The gratitude with which your words have animated me, the extraordinary intervention of your Government under the circumstances with which Nicaragua is surrounded, impose on me the pleasing duty of returning thanks to Divine Providence for its benefits. . . . I now see all the elements of a happy future brought before us; there is good faith in the Government with which I am connected; the friendliest feelings towards North America pervade every Nicaraguan heart; and we have the assurances of the sympathy and support of the American Government. We have consequently all things which can be desired to make available the advantages with which Heaven has surrounded us. Our State, considering its geographical position, ought to be the most prosperous in Spanish America; but our experience at the time of our separation from Spain—our limited resources, and the civil commotions that have intervened, have retarded the happy day which is now drawing upon us. . . . I entertain no doubts that we shall succeed in establishing the most intimate relations between the two Republics, and in opening the way to the consummation of that most glorious enterprise which it has reserved for the successors of the immortal Washington to undertake and perfect. I shall have the greatest pleasure in being able to contribute my humble share towards this result, and to the consequent happiness of Nicaragua. I thank you, Sir, and through you, your Government, for its proffered cooperation in so glorious an enterprise.[34]

In the hush of the diplomatic ceremony as the supreme director concluded his remarks, a spontaneous emotional outburst startled Squier and highlighted the significance of the event.

A young military officer, Col. Francisco Díaz Zapata, suddenly pushed his way to the front of the room of dignitaries. Motioning to the intertwined flags of the United States and Nicaragua above the chair of the supreme director, he impassionately recited a poetic salute to the American banner:

> Sign of power and grandeur!
> Illustrious example of virtue and glory!
> I contemplate you on high;
> And from that contemplation I feel
> That with my Fatherland you will make history.
> Those beautiful stripes,
> And that joyous arrangement of your stars,
> When wafted by the winds
> Wave and flutter majestically,
> Even more beautifully than shining heavenly lights;
> The flagstaff strong and noble,
> Completes the picture of solid strength.
> No longer must Nicaragua
> Submit to sad misfortune.
> Your flag reveals to me what you will do
> In all your splendor and power.
> Beneath your shadow still breathes
> The Great American Hero,
> Whom memory deifies as
> The glorious George Washington.

Beneath your shadow, arises sovereign
The power of law;
And knowledge and happiness grow
With prodigious vigor,
To weigh upon the sway of Kings.
And the Heroes of the Americas exalt
Your sacred memory,
Your tombs, your blood of warriors,
And the triumph of your sword,
Beneath the sweet brilliance of your radiance.
All under our rule prospers,
Illustrious and marvelous flag.
Filled with enthusiasm, I salute you;
And swollen with pleasure and hope,
My heart beats within my breast
With such ceaseless intensity
That my impassioned body can catch no breath.
The soft and gentle breeze,
The full sun with rays resplendent,
The air in all its purity,
The benevolent smile of the heavens,
And the soothing fragrance of the flowers,
All salute you with me.
We celebrate in the most fitting manner
Your arrival, friend,
To our suffering and distressed Fatherland.
Fill it with your honor and your grandeur
And force its adversary to bow his head. [35]

The poet's words of patriotism and hope rang through the silent chamber. Squier recorded the reaction of the crowd: "The effect was electrical, and the whole of the assemblage seemed to catch the spirit of the speaker, whose appearance, action, and language were those of the intensest emotion. They pressed eagerly forward, as if anxious to treasure every word which fell from his lips; and when he had concluded, forgetting all other consideration, their enthusiasm broke forth in loud and protracted 'vivas,' which were caught up and echoed by the people in the plaza, and the soldiers of the garrison."[36] Obviously that exposure to the emotional fires of nationalism—most unlikely to occur at any Washington ceremony—profoundly affected Squier.

The meaning of the poetic message was patent. United with Washington, Nicaragua could deflect the physical threats of the English and pass over the humiliations of the past to contemplate the goals of the future. The elusive vision seemed to be almost within Nicaragua's grasp. The *Boletín Oficial* echoed the sentiments, acknowledging the "natural" leadership of the United States and identifying with the principles and institutions that guided and governed it. The newspaper praised "the immortal [George] Washington," who would also serve to inspire Nicaragua.[37] The reception, the words of the supreme director, the spontaneous poetry, and the effusive newspaper report all complemented the mission entrusted to Squier by Secretary of State Clayton.

Clayton had instructed Squier to frustrate Britain's claims to a Mosquito protectorate and to San Juan del Norte; to help Americans acquire a contract to build a canal and to operate a transit company; and to guarantee "equal passage for all nations" through the canal or along the transit route. The minister drew up a treaty of friendship with the Nicaraguan government just as the representatives of a private U.S. company, not without Squier's approval, prepared a contract to build a canal, both of which the Nicaraguan legislature unanimously ratified in mid-September 1849.[38] Public opinion greeted the news of the ratification with the same high spirits it had welcomed Squier a few months earlier. In a note to Squier, Minister of Foreign Relations Sebastián Salinas graciously effused, "Your presence in Nicaragua has made reappear the national spirit, and raised the country from the chaos in which in has for so many years been plunged."[39] The minister's effusion mirrored the patriarchs' new confidence bolstered by their momentary unity, recent victory over the folk, and renewed hopes of realizing an old vision. The ruling class rode a cresting wave of confidence.

Lest anyone missed the significance of the Squier mission for Nicaragua, one newspaper published a parable whose meaning shone clearly in its simplicity. It read:

> There is a beautiful, rich, young lady, full of virtues and exposed to the eyes and actions of the men who court her. Some flirt with her, others love her, and still other attack her meanly. To whom should she give her heart: to him who flirts with her as a vain pastime; to him who attacks her with force, is a tyrant and consequently odious; or to him who loves her, even though he may flirt with others while ordering her around, proceeds in good faith, and wants a sincere union.
>
> Central America is the young lady. Many flirt with her. England attacks her, hoping to dominate her by force. It is the United States who loves her. The one she should favor is obvious.[40]

The courtship seemed ready for consummation.

Relations between Nicaragua and the United States reached a high point that has never been equaled since. Yet while Squier reflected on the success of his diplomatic mission, he recorded an ominous misgiving: "It is most earnestly to be desired that the hopes which [the treaty and contract] created may not, from the mistaken policy of Government, or the bad faith of companies, owing their very existence to Nicaraguan generosity, give place to despair and respect be changed into contempt, and friendship into hate."[41] Apparently he harbored some apprehensions about future relations, less on the part of the Nicaraguans than on the part of his compatriots.

Squier lent his prestige and wisdom to the negotiations between the United States entrepreneurs and the Nicaraguan government on matters pertaining to the canal and transit route. Business interests in both countries promoted the goal of an interoceanic canal and, until that challenging project could be undertaken and completed, a combined water and land transportation route. Their first objective was to move passengers. Travelers to and from California increased monthly, and capitalists like Commodore Cornelius Vanderbilt believed the shorter and healthier Nicaraguan route could compete successfully with the well established and lucrative Panamanian passage.

Aspiring Nicaraguan entrepreneurs were no less confident that the transportation route would increase demands for food and services. In their minds, Californian markets beckoned, a contemporary El Dorado to enrich Nicaragua.[42] Indeed, according to the British vice-consul, the Nicaraguans experienced a rise in demand for agrarian products from Panama, California, and the transit route.[43] However, hope more than statistics bolstered such claims. Nonetheless, the mere promise of a California market both revived and revised the old economic vision. While trade had once centered on North Atlantic markets, thus a boon to Granada and San Juan del Norte, it expanded in 1849 to embrace the new Pacific coast of the United States, bestowing unexpected benefits on León and Realejo. The common gains both city-states expected united them in support of the new project, a noteworthy contribution toward the eradication of anarchy.

A few local speculators foresaw increasing real estate values promoted by the canal. Lucien McLeanthan Wolcott noted in his diary while in Nicaragua in 1851, "Natives own all the land. They think their place will become a point of note. Some hold land high & are building rapidly. If the ship canal strikes this point, their anticipation will come true, & everyone is ardent in believing it will."[44] Nicaraguans also concluded that a transportation route in the hands of Americans would provide Washington's protection against further English intervention, not an insignificant consideration as they raged against British imperialism.

Vanderbilt's agent, Joseph L. White, experienced no difficulty in signing a contract with the government. The contract agreed upon on August 26, 1849, granted Vanderbilt's company exclusive rights to build a canal at its own expense and open to the vessels of all nations. The company was to pay Nicaragua US$10,000 upon signing the contract and US$10,000 each year until the canal was complete. The contract allowed the company twelve years in which to raise the capital and complete the project. It also enjoyed exclusive rights to construct railroads and carriage roads as well as to establish steamship routes on rivers and lakes. The company guaranteed Nicaragua a share of the profits from any transit line.

The company failed to raise the capital for the canal, blaming its failure on Lake Nicaragua. The lake, said the company, unable to accommodate vessels drawing more than thirty-six feet of water, would exclude the most important ships, those most in need of such a canal. The company prevailed on the Nicaraguan government to divide the contract and put everything concerning a land and water transportation route into separate charter. The Nicaraguans acquiesced. Fruto Chamorro, Mateo Mayoraga, and Joseph L. White signed an agreement on May 1, 1851, creating the Accessory Transit Company.[45]

As events moved swiftly, some Nicaraguans voiced doubts about their direction. Francisco Castellón, a major Liberal leader of the period, criticized the British actions at San Juan del Norte, while at the same time, May of 1850, he reacted with horror at the behavior of the North Americans passing through Realejo. The behavior of the travelers scandalized the authorities and citizens. "What can we expect from one group or the other?" he asked. "They will divide the spoils among themselves. Our national independence encounters multiple dangers at the present."[46] Toribio Tijerino Pomar was no less cautious. He concluded that a "hurried progress" based on foreign interests and companies endangered Nicaragua.[47]

The indifference of those foreign interests to Nicaraguan aspirations and sensitivities manifested itself quickly enough. The implications behind the Clayton-Bulwer Treaty of 1850 stunned the Nicaraguans. In it the United States and Great Britain agreed that neither would exercise exclusive power over any future canal on the isthmus or "dominion over Nicaragua, Costa Rica, the Mosquito coast, or any part of Central America." Washington felt satisfied that the treaty would check British expansion in a region ever more vital to its continental unity and security since it had become a two-ocean nation. While the Nicaraguans understood the treaty intended to reduce future British threats, they felt a deep disappointment that the two expansive powers could decide Nicaragua's future without even consulting them. In short, they had been left out. The initial euphoria of the Squier period evaporated. The stunned Nicaraguans were learning the harsh international realities for a small nation. The operations of the Accessory Transit Company would teach other unpleasant lessons. By 1852, if not before, disputes already raised tensions between Nicaragua and the company. [48]

Originally many Nicaraguans viewed the transit route as the logical materialization of the vision which placed their country at the hub of global commerce. Contrary to those high expectations, it increasingly became a foreign enclave over which Nicaraguans exercised little or no control. Even Nicaraguan participation in servicing the route remained minimal. Not only did the Nicaraguans draw little wealth from their most precious natural resource, but they also began to see it as an opening through which waves of immoral, violent, and haughty foreigners flooded their country. Those outsiders threatened its sovereignty.

The Gordon expedition in 1849 initiated the mass transportation of foreigners across Nicaragua, ascending the San Juan River, crossing Lake Nicaragua to Granada, and moving overland to Realejo. That route remained dominant for more than a year. More frequent steamship sailings and better organization of transportation through Nicaragua diminished transit time between New York and San Francisco in 1850. In November of that year, Charles Parke crossed Nicaragua in twelve days: six days by ox cart over the 144 miles between Realejo and Granada and another six days by boat along the 120 miles of waterway from Granada to San Juan del Norte. [49] Parke just missed the steamship at San Juan del Norte and waited about two weeks for the next one. Even so, his month in Nicaragua contrasted favorably with the four months the Gordon expedition had spent in Nicaragua the previous year.

The transit route soon made a logical shift from Realejo to San Juan del Sur, only twelve miles overland from the port Virgin Bay (La Virgen) on Lake Nicaragua, cutting 132 miles from the former land route. Slightly more that 200 miles separated San Juan del Sur from San Juan del Norte.

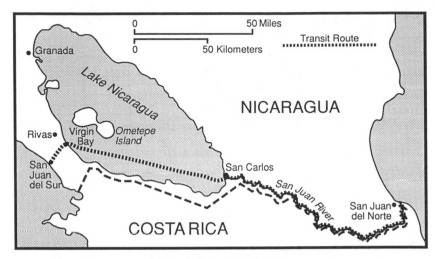

Transit Route, 1851–1857

On January 1, 1851, the first steamship crossed Lake Nicaragua, prompting Prefect Fermín Ferrer of the Department of the Oriente to rhapsodize, "Technology overcame the river's obstacles, and by some mysterious coincidence on this day the steamship *Director* arrived at these shores of our great Lake to announce to us that the happiness and good fortune of Nicaragua dates from this first day of the second half of the nineteenth century."[50] By late 1851, with very good luck in making connections, a traveler could transit Nicaragua in something just over twenty-four hours at the cost of US$40.00. The official Nicaraguan figures did assume perfect transportation connections, a reality unrealized for several years.

A proud and prosperous Cornelius Vanderbilt inaugurated his New York-San Francisco steamship service on July 14, 1851: ten days on the Atlantic from New York to San Juan del Norte, twenty days crossing the isthmus (including long waits), and fifteen on the Pacific from San Juan del Sur to San Francisco, a total of forty-five days. The return journey took twenty-nine days, thanks to better ship connections. By March of 1852, the company had two steamships on the Atlantic run, leaving New York on the fifth and twentieth of each month; and three on the Pacific route, leaving San Francisco on the first and fifteenth of each month; and five steamboats on the river and lake. The company boasted, "It is confidently anticipated that the trips through from New York to San Francisco will be performed regularly by this line in about 25 days." The steamships sailed nonstop from New York to San Juan del Norte, while on the Pacific route a

Table 10. Distance, Time, and Cost of Transiting Nicaragua, 1851.

Segment	Distance (miles)	Time (hours)	Cost (US$)
San Juan del Sur— Virgin Bay	12	4	5.00
Virgin Bay— San Carlos	70	6 (by steamship) 12-24 (by sailboat)	15.00 12.00
San Carlos—San Juan del Norte	125	14 (by steamship) 30 (by sailboat)	20.00 12.00
Totals	207	24 (steamship) 46-58 (sailboat)	40 (steamship) 27 (sailboat)

Source: Gaceta Oficial de Nicaragua. January 10, 1852.

regularly scheduled stop was made at Acapulco. Passages for the complete trip ranged from $180, steerage berth, to $320, "first class deck state room berth."[51] The Accessory Transit Company made significant improvements in its service by building wharves at Virgin Bay and San Juan del Sur and a macadamized road connecting the two. By the spring of 1855, steamers with dining and sleeping quarters plied Lake Nicaragua. In August 1853, the company set a record, 22 days and 3 hours, for the journey between San Francisco and New York. A year later, the time dropped to less than 21 days.

At first, transit time across Nicaragua depended largely on good luck in timing. Joseph Warren Wood disembarked in San Juan del Sur on October 17, 1852, and immediately rode by mule to Virgin Bay. He had to wait until the 22nd for the lake steamer, but once aboard, the rest of the trip went quickly. On the night of October 23, he boarded the steamship at San Juan del Norte for the voyage to New York. Apparently devoid of much curiosity, Wood confided little to his diary about Nicaragua.[52] In December of the same year, John Pratt Welsh made the same crossing in four days. While the pages of his diary contain little concerning his brief exposure to a Nicaraguan environment, he devoted several to the adventures of running aground while descending the San Juan River.[53] Transiting in the opposite direction, Alonzo Hubbard arrived at San Juan del Norte at 11:00 PM on March 14, 1852; boarded the river steamer on March 16; arrived at Virgin Bay on the 21st: and sailed from San Juan to San Francisco the following afternoon.[54]

In late 1854, James A. Clark traveled from his ocean steamship in the San Juan del Sur harbor to a similar vessel awaiting him at the port of San Juan del Norte in two days. His rapid and relatively comfortable trip fulfilled the promises of the Accessory Transit Company. Except for a few sentences describing El Castillo, Clark's brief account of the rapid crossing hardly mentioned Nicaragua. He transfered from a river to an ocean steamer without setting foot in San Juan del Norte.[55] The diary entries show that the route had become a significant part of a metropolitan transportation network, an enclave unintegrated into and increasingly unrelated to Nicaragua.

Only occasional travelers "discovered" Nicaragua in crossing the route. It captured their imaginations. Mentally they integrated the route within the context of a foreign nation—and one that appealed to them. Lucien McLeanthan Wolcott fell in love with Nicaragua, seeing it as a kind of lost paradise. "These people certainly are blessed. Providence or nature provides all their wants. Pigs, chickens, plantains, oranges, etc., grow all around them without the aid of labor. They have none of the cares or ills of life. Nothing to do but enjoy themselves and they do it." He liked the people, seemed to have met many, and apparently enjoyed at least one romance. "What I wish for most of all things is an acquaintance with the Spanish language. Could I converse freely with them I should be in a perfect Heaven on earth." His diary contains a long list of words and phrases in Spanish, testimony to efforts to learn the language. Surveying his novel surroundings, Wolcott sighed, "I hardly know myself awake or dreaming," as he proceeded onward to the reality of Ohio.[56] Charles Parke recorded his isthmian adventures with similar awe: "Our trip down through the State of Nicaragua from Realejo to this city [Granada], a distance of 144 miles, has been to me a very interesting one. This people have treated us very kindly from the start. Not one disagreeable incident from the time we left Realejo. This is an interesting country. We passed through beautiful forests and orange groves loaded down with the most delicious fruit—ripe on the trees and free to us. Also banana and pineapple plantations. The towering coconut tree is also seen."[57] He lost his young traveling companion from Baltimore. In Masaya, the Baltimorian met a beautiful eighteen-year-old and was "captivated by her charms. She has invited him to assist her in translating a public notice into English." He abandoned the journey to take up his new duties.[58]

By 1854, more than one thousand passengers a month crossed Nicaragua.[59] New York harbor registered 13,373 departures and 11,195 arrivals of trans-Nicaragua passengers for the period March 16, 1854, to

March 16, 1855.[60] The route well served the growth and importance of California, whose population jumped from 92,000 in 1850 to 380,000 in 1858. Soon the shorter and cheaper Nicaraguan route equaled that of Panama in importance. In 1851 only two out of every 15 persons transiting Central America did so through Nicaragua; one year later the figure rose to one out of every two.[61] By 1855 the transit line ran smoothly, comfortably, efficiently, and *profitably*. It cleared a million dollars a year.[62] The humming business seemed to excite the Nicaraguan entrepreneurs, who appreciated its potential more than they shared its profits.

The transit route exerted its greatest influence on the growth and activity of the two terminals, San Juan del Sur and San Juan del Norte. The population of the first grew from zero to over 1,500 in 1851. At the same time, the population of San Juan del Norte tripled to 3,000.[63] San Juan del Norte existed virtually as a city-state during the decade of the 1850s, with both British and North American warships standing off shore or within cruising range. Foreign residents controlled the port and surrounding countryside, keeping any Nicaraguans from holding office.[64] Nicaragua exercised virtually no sovereignty over its most important port.

After 1849 the population of San Juan del Norte displayed an international caste. Mrs. Henry Grant Foote, wife of the British consul in Greytown or San Juan (1852–53), recalled, "The inhabitants are principally Americans; but there is a sprinkling of Europeans, and the lower orders are nearly entirely composed of Nicaraguans, and Jamaica negroes." She attributed a special beauty to the spot which most other commentators seem to have overlooked. Food was scarce and hence expensive, and high prices soared higher with "the fortnightly influx of Californians."[65] High prices, an unhealthy climate, and lawlessness constituted the three characteristics of the port upon which visitors most frequently commented. U.S. Minister John Hill Wheeler conveyed his negative impressions in these words: "A large portion of this community is composed of men of the most lawless character; without any visible means of living; whose tastes and temper delight in scenes of tumult and crime and blood. Daily, at his place within my hearing, are outrages committed; and my repose is broken by their bacchanalian orgies making night hideous."[66] The British diplomats were no less sanguine in their characterization of the growing international population of the port, concluding that it represented "a very turbulent set of people, interspersed here and there, with some of the most violent characters on earth."[67]

The growth of those ports with their disproportionate numbers of for

eigners told a thought-provoking tale. To the disappointment of Nicaraguans, who accepted the Accessory Transit Company as a major step
toward the realization of their vision, it exerted a more negative than positive influence. The company functioned within the territory of Nicaragua,
yet somehow removed from it. Americans owned and ran the steamships:
they eventually owned the carriages, mules, and horses. Americans
owned and operated the hotels, restaurants, and taverns in San Juan del
Norte, Virgin Bay, and San Juan del Sur, those places where, after 1851,
the travelers spent their time and money.[68] Menial service jobs went to
the Nicaraguans; the profits went to the Americans; both trends characterized an enclave economy, then and later. The Nicaraguan patriarchs
watched North Americans getting rich on Nicaraguan soil by using Nicaraguan resources. True, Nicaraguans sold fruits, vegetables, and meats
to feed the hungry travelers, but even that new market sparked some
second thoughts. The ladino proprietor of the estate "Sweet Name of
Jesus" outside of Rivas, a town located near the transit route, complained
in late 1854 "how everything had changed since the Americans had come
into the country, and since the Transit Company had established themselves at Virgin Bay." Prices rose, the value of money depreciated, infla-
tion threatened. While the farmers earned more from the sale of products, the soaring wages of scarce labor offset profits. "The produce of
their land brought four-fold what it had done, but the wage of the
labourers had risen in equal proportion. A *real*, or about sixpence, a day
had been formerly the customary wages, and they were now four, or, in
the time of the cacao harvest, often much more."[69] The transit route complicated the economics of many large landowners by tempting away
already scarce labor with offers of higher wages. At least one observer
speculated that the working classes garnered the monetary benefits
accruing to Nicaragua from the route.[70]

Chronically short of money, the Nicaraguan government did not receive
from the Accessory Transit Company its share of the profits as stipulated
in the contract. The company claimed it earned no profits and kept its
account books in the United States far from curious Nicaraguan eyes. In
early 1854, Supreme Director Fruto Chamorro demanded payment,
threatening that his government would attach the company's local
assets.[71] He brought serious charges against the company and accused it
of "putting its hand into everything as if it were the absolute lord of the
land."[72] He lamented that the company's ships introduced every kind of
human riffraff into the country. Vagabonds filled the ports and wandered

the roads to the growing alarm of the Nicaraguans, who considered them to be dangerous men, disrespectful of women and local customs. Drink drove them to fighting and killing.

A tragic assault on Nicaragua inflamed public opinion against the company and the United States, the two perceived as one and the same by the Nicaraguans. As the company's steamboat *Routh* descended the San Juan River in May of 1854, it collided with a small Nicaraguan boat plying the river. Captain T. T. Smith argued abusively with Antonio Paladino, then aimed his gun and killed the Nicaraguan. Solon Borland, the U.S. minister to Nicaragua and on board the *Routh*, witnessed the event. At San Juan del Norte, when local official attempted to arrest Smith for murder, Borland intervened to prevent it. Later, in a public demonstration to protest the murder, a bottle thrown in the melee grazed Borland, slightly cutting his face. In response to that injury to the U.S. minister, President Franklin Pierce dispatched the warship *Cyane* to bombard the port.

Following the bombardment on July 13, 1854, sailors landed and burned the remaining buildings to the ground.[73] Doubtless, from the broadest perspective, the brutalities reflected the tensions among Great Britain, the United States, and Nicaragua over the status of San Juan del Norte. The Nicaraguans interpreted them otherwise. They saw them as an affront to Nicaraguan sovereignty, the strength of the powerful exerted on the weak. The event discomforted the other Central American governments as well. The *Gaceta de Guatemala* observed, "For a long time now, the hand of the United States has been stirring up trouble in Central America. Ever since the government of Nicaragua permitted an American company to establish a transit route across the country endless violations have occurred."[74] To the violent acts of individual U.S. citizens on Nicaraguan soil were added official acts of U.S. violence against Nicaragua. By mid–1854, Nicaraguans saw quite a different face of the United States from the one shown by Ephraim George Squier.

The transit route appeared more and more to Nicaraguans as a breach. The North American tide rose. Foreigners flowed in and across Nicaragua. The rhetoric accompanying the human flood sounded not only disrespectful to Nicaraguans and their government but threatening as well. The plans and actions of the North Americans worried the Nicaraguans. In the 1850s Colonel Henry L. Kinney, once active in detaching Texas from Mexico and attaching to to the United States, appeared in their midst. He claimed to hold an enormous territorial grant—something like 22,500,000 acres in eastern Nicaragua—from the Mosquito king for his

Central American Land and Mining Company. While helping to rebuild San Juan del Norte after American sailors burned it, Kinney maneuvered his own election as Civil and Military Governor of the City and Territory of San Juan del Norte, a title not conducive to helping the patriarchs sleep quietly in Granada. He spelled out his intentions to a Texan friend, "It requires but a few hundred Americans and particularly Texans to take control of all that country [Nicaragua]. I have grants of land, and enough to make a start upon safely and legally. I intend to make a suitable government, and the rest will follow."[75] The Nicaraguans did not recognize the validity of Mosquito king's generous grant and regarded the presence of Kinney and his followers as an invasion. Kinney found himself in the vortex of British-American-Nicaraguan rivalries, claiming a region already beclouded by international rivalries. Further, the Accessory Transit Company also opposed him as a possible threat to its best interests. Kinney displayed no talent to master the complex situation.

More than anything else, Kinney symbolized the fever pitch to which Manifest Destiny had risen in the United States, where the urge to expand throbbed. In this aggressive mood, Americans bluntly stated their ambitions, which, for many, included Nicaragua, as a logical link between east and west, a link which for that moment in history helped to unify the sprawling United States. John Hill Wheeler, the U.S. minister to Nicaragua, confided to his diary, "The country [Nicaragua] must be under American influence."[76] Such statements paled beside the rhetoric of his compatriots. Nicholas Carroll, traversing Nicaragua in 1855, wrote to the *Sacramento Daily Union* of its natural beauty and wealth and then added, "In only one thing has it been found deficient—in the mongrel races inhabiting it, that have devastated this paradise. Now there comes a new epoch—fresh, young, and energetic men of 'that race whose impress is everywhere and everywhere for good.' "[77] Ironically, nine days after writing the letter, Carroll died at age thirty-five in Nicaragua. Fresh, young, and energetic he might have been but not immune to tropical diseases. The *New York Times* extolled U.S. expansion into Nicaragua. It praised Col. Kinney as the harbinger of what Central America could expect. In the spirit of nineteenth-century racism, it rationalized the triumph of the north in anthropological terms:

> Central America is destined to occupy an influential position in the family of nations, if her advantages of location, climate, and soil are availed of by a race of "Northmen," who shall supplant the tainted, mongrel, and decaying race which now curses it so fearfully. The success of Col. Kinney and his friends

will settle our Mosquito question with Great Britain most effectively. . . . That the influence of the new Republic will speedily spread itself all over Nicaragua, and absorb the whole of that State with its inefficient Government, there can be little doubt; humanity will be the gainer by the event, and the commercial world will reap great benefit from the settlement of an enterprising, energetic people, and the establishment of a strong Government at a point where promptness and security in interoceanic communication is of primary importance.[78]

The highest officials in Washington never disguised their belief in the importance of the transit route, and hence of Nicaragua, to U.S. growth. President Franklin Pierce mused, "It would be difficult to suggest a single object of interest, external or internal, more important to the United States" than the communication and transportation routes between the east and west coasts. He deemed them vital "to national integrity and sovereignty."[79]

All those pronouncements of Manifest Destiny worried the increasingly disillusioned Nicaraguans. They increasingly felt the consequences of the psychological effects of Manifest Destiny not just through overt aggressions but also through myriad slights, insults, and condescensions, which relegated them to the status of second-class citizens in their own land.

U.S. diplomats on occasion reported the Nicaraguan resentments. Charge d'Affaires John Bozman Kerr in 1852 wrote to Secretary of State Daniel Webster about the hostilities of the government toward the Accessory Transit Company as well as the suspicions of the United States.[80] Later, Minister Solon Borland commented obliquely but revealingly on the emerging Nicaraguan nationalism, whose admixture of hostility resulted in part from foreign pressures and prejudices:

It is almost impossible to conceive, unless personally observant, of the nature and degree of jealousy, in regard to everything belonging to them, and of the suspiciousness, with which they watch everyone who approaches them, that characterize this people—and, in which characteristic, they are most faithfully represented by their government. These, no doubt, are in a great measure, peculiarities of this race (if, indeed, that be regarded as one race which is, really, an amalgamation of several)—ingrained, as it is,—with ignorance, superstition, and the spirit of isolation. As peculiarities, however, they have with as little doubt been greatly strengthened and sharpened by intercourse with those who, as they allege, with too much truth there is reason to believe, have habitually treated them with injustice. . . . Now, and for some time past, it [suspicion] has extended to every person having a white face and speaking the English language. . . . This [sensitivity] is exemplified in the cases of personal dispute which, sometimes, take place, between natives of the country and foreigners resident here or passing through. The ill feeling and resentment in such cases, are, on the part of these people, not limited to the individual parties to the dispute. The whole population, as far as they know of it, regard themselves aggrieved, and the government sympathizes with them . . . the obnoxious party being a foreigner, they blame and denounce all foreigners, who are of the same color and who speak the same language, especially if they be of the same country; while their government proves its sympathy, by sharpened suspicion and diminished friendship towards the corresponding foreign government.[81]

Borland thus confirmed the cooling attitude toward the United States. No Nicaraguan stepped forth after mid-century with a poetic salute to the Stars and Stripes.

A far more complex international situation than ever before confronted Nicaragua as it moved into the second half of the century. An enclave, the Accessory Transit Company infused much trouble but little wealth into Nicaragua. It attracted not just international attention: it facilitated foreign penetration. Nicaragua was losing control of its most important geographical asset. Adventurers descended on the country, and when in trouble those foreigners could rely on their governments to defend them regardless of outrageous conduct and cockeyed claims. Both Great Britain and the United States manifested expansive moods. Despite the wording of the Clayton-Bulwer Treaty, London showed no signs of withdrawing from the Mosquito territory. The two North Atlantic powers vied to control San Juan del Norte, which, at best, remained a kind of free and open port. Nicaragua exercised no authority there despite its importance to the national economy. The advocates of Manifest Destiny in the United States proclaimed the need to absorb Nicaragua. Even neighboring Costa Rica pushed to expand its boundaries to include the once Nicaraguan territory of Guanacaste, approximately 4,000 square miles. Nicaragua reeled under mounting international interference. Surprisingly, despite the very national disintegration they threatened, internal politics bumped along the customary rocky road of anarchy. With no peasant uprising to distract them, the patriarchs returned with alacrity to the arena of conflict between city-states. Distracted by mutual rancors, they neglected the menacing international changes. By the mid–1850s, however, internal and external events no longer could be isolated from each other.

The year 1854 opened amid rising international and internal tensions.

They inspired fearful expectations in "To the Year 1854 on the Night of December 31, 1853," which read in part:

> And you, 1854, what can you tell us?
> Is your news good or gloomy?
> Will your days be sad and mournful
> Or prosperous, happy, cheerful?
> But, oh woe!, when a four appears in any decade
> Then trouble surely infiltrates that year,
> As in 1814 when war erupted,
> Events that repeated themselves in 1824.
> Remember the turbulence of 1834,
> Whose desolate memories still haunt us,
> Just as does fateful 1844, with its fires,
> Its assaults, its deaths, and its disasters. [82]

The poet's somber reminders doubtless reflected the foreboding of many Nicaraguans, who viewed the exile of the Liberal leaders by Supreme Director Chamorro not as the end of an affair but rather as an overture.

More determined to pursue his goals than mindful of poetic portents, Chamorro convened the Constituent Assembly on January 22 of the fateful 1854. He set the agenda for its business. He requested that the delegates correct "the defective institutions" that "deformed" the state: "Defective and weak, the present organization of Nicaraguan society lacks the necessary elements to grow and strengthen itself. Its institutions do not speak to the nation's needs, peculiarities, and requirements." The nation required order. To achieve order necessitated the strengthening of the executive and the restriction of individual freedoms. He emphasized,

> If one hopes to see Nicaragua reach the destiny reserved for it by Providence, it is indispensable to exercise caution in the concession of individual guarantees. Do not forget that the imprudent profusion of them is one of the most notable and harmful imperfections in the constitution which you have gathered here to alter. . . . We urgently need to strengthen the principle of authority so weakened and neglected by us. This can be achieved by giving the executive greater power, authority, and consistency; and by surrounding that office with a certain pomp and majesty which will command the respect due the office. [83]

While such words soothed the Conservatives, they inflamed the Liberals.

At the request of Chamorro, the Assembly, on February 28, 1854, changed the title of the chief executive from the somewhat cumbersome, although rather sonorous, "supreme director" to the more conventional "president." At the same time and for identical reasons, the official name of the nation was altered from the "State of Nicaragua" to the "Republic of Nicaragua." What is in a name? Apparently, President Chamorro opined, quite a bit. He pushed hard to bring about those two changes because he felt the new nomenclature lent both greater dignity and authority. As he emphasized while announcing the novelty, "Words are always the expression of ideas and sometimes they lend value to intentions. Nicaragua believes that the title of Republic will shield it from some of the incalculable harm it has experienced in international relations because it has not properly expressed its status. . . . The new designation reflects reality and will benefit the nation."[84] Those words and particularly those changes displeased the Liberals. They interpreted the new "expression of ideas" to mean that Nicaragua was distancing itself from the ideal of the reunification of Central America. They, too, believed in the symbolism of words, and the new titles meant to them greater centralization of power and the concomitant erosion of individual liberties.

President Chamorro promulgated the constitution on April 30, 1854, although events restricted its implementation to Granada. The constitution holds interest primarily as the statement of Conservative ideals. It enhanced the powers of the president, extending his term from two to four years. It invested him with impressive powers to protect order and prevent rebellion: search, seizure, arrest, imprisonment, and exile were but some of them. It increased his power over the military. It further restricted the electorate by raising the property requirements to vote. Very significantly—a real sign of changing times—the document did not mention the communal lands, thereby denying the folk a protection lodged in the Constitution of 1838.

The promulgation of the constitution sounded a trumpet call to battle for the Liberals. On May 5, 1854, a group of Liberals commanded by Máximo Jerez landed at Realejo. Their invasion triggered what appeared to be just one more civil war, but in the increasing political complexity of Nicaragua it resulted eventually in a conflagration Central American history texts universally call La Guerra Nacional (The National War), actively involving every one of the five nations. It lasted until May of 1857, an orgy of anarchy, war, foreign intervention, and social distress. It ranked as the bloodiest war in nineteenth-century Nicaraguan history, perhaps even in Central American history.[85]

While the new constitution might well be given as the immediate cause of conflict, in reality the intense rivalry between León and Granada had been building for a long time with a few respites, most notable of which were the joint campaigns against the popular rebellions and the reception of Minister Squier in 1849. Apparently the foreign threats had done little thus far to unify the two city-states. One gage of enmity is the vitriolic prose and poetry through which citizens of the two cities vilified each other. After the Conservatives (Granada) began to win elections for the office of supreme director, the Leonese peppered their political adversaries with bitter accusations: antipatriotic, divisive, destroyers, self aggrandizing, abusive, criminal, an exhaustive catalog.[86]

Nicaraguans frequently communicated political messages through poetry. After the printing press arrived in 1829, those who could afford it ordered their pronouncements, poetic or prose, printed. In a society with few and irregular newspapers and inhabitants addicted to Apollo, such broadsides served as an effective means of communication. The Leonese one morning contemplated this crude "Arithmetic in Verse" affixed to their doors:

> To add is to create from many
> Homogeneous quantities one single quantity;
> Also homogeneous is the sum total,
> Or more simply termed just the sum.
> [An Example]
> 30 pounds of ignorance
> 20 skins of mules
> 0 quantity of judgment and talent
> 1000 pounds of petulance
> 100 yards of arrogance
> 900 assassins
> 10 cart loads of indignity
> 0 public spirit
> 1 ton of scorn
> And what does it all
> Add up to:
> The inhabitants of Granada.[87]

The poetasters of Granada answered in kind. One energetic Granadan composed a lengthy parody of a Mass offered to the "Trinity of Democratic Savages," to which he signed the name of R. P. F. Aji, "Religious of the Order of the Nude and Shoeless of Democracy:"

Hated Provisional Government, trinity and one, Castellón, Jerez, and Guerrero, Father, son, and cursed spirit of the revolution, in whom we do not believe, from whom we expect only evil, and whom we hate with all our body, soul, and spirit because they are not our legitimate government, because they are infinitely evil and worthy of the hatred of all. Cursed be the horrible trinity of dragons, Castellón, Guerrero, and Jerez, who seek to govern our Republic now and forever, but public opinion rejects them as murderers, arsonists, and thieves.[88]

The poetry and prose in broadside and pamphlet etch the sharp emotional profile of the period. Artists also contributed to the profile as the illustration of the Granadan eagle pulling the tail of the Leónese lion attests. They constitute crude political statements in which passion overshadowed talent. Those passions rose with the intensity of the civil war.

The opening campaign of the civil war moved with lightning rapidity. The Liberals won spectacular victories, largely owing to some lucky breaks, the ineptitude of the Conservative army, and miscalculations of President Chamorro, who personally led the government's army. The Liberal forces seized Chinandega and then León before sweeping southeasterly to the very gates of Granada by May 26, 1854. At the citadel of conservatism, Chamorro finally checked their advance. The Liberals lay siege to Granada. With their blue banner and cry of "Liberty or Death!" they spared no atrocity. They shot anyone with a rifle in hand, including the surrendering prisoners. The Conservatives beneath a white banner and the motto of "Legitimacy or Death!" were no less brutal.[89] José María Estrada labeled the Liberal army "the modern Huns led by the modern Attila" and likened the siege to a return to the "barbarism of the fifth century."[90] A poet writing within the besieged city lamented,

> How desolated lies that wondrous city
> Where once happy people now live cloaked by pity!
> That city whose name
> From east to west gained fame!
> Cascading tears of sadness and pain
> The face of the Lady of the Great Lake stain.
> Ah, how the impact of fratricidal war
> Has sown in you destruction evermore.[91]

Failing to take the city after eight and one-half months of effort, the Liberals lifted the siege in February 1855. The Conservative army immediately advanced to reclaim all of Nicaragua except the area around León. A second military stalemate set in.

Chamorro died on March 12, 1855, shortly after the siege of Granada had been lifted. José Maria Estrada assumed the presidency for the Conservatives. Chamorro's death did not diminish the intensity of the prolonged, bloody struggle. Perceived ideological differences seemed to be more entrenched than ever. The Constitution of 1854 codified those beliefs defended by the Conservatives.[92] The government of Chamorro and later of Estrada showed no hesitation in implementing them.

In the meantime, the Liberals had established in León their own government. The municipal council elected Francisco Castellón as supreme director. He swore loyalty to the Constitution of 1838 and recalled General José Trinidad Muñoz to command the army.

Jerez already had issued the Liberal manifesto, the banner under which the Liberals waged war. Its five points sounded bland and expected: (1) removing Chamorro from office in order to return power "to the people"; (2) treating the supporters of Chamorro as traitors; (3) requiring all government employees to join the new government; (4) recognizing no other political party; and (5) respecting property. The Liberals' determination to defend the Constitution of 1838 constituted the real agenda and highlighted their ideological program.

The two constitutions differed fundamentally. The differences centered on the degree of concentration of political power and the extent of per-

Figure 6. The Granadan Eagle. The mid-nineteenth century drawing of the Granadan eagle pulling the tail of the Leonese lion provides a visual dimension to the bitterness that characterized the relations between León and Granada. Source: The Bancroft Library, Nicaraguan Miscellany, 1851–1858 (redrawn by John Page).

sonal liberty; on the concepts of land ownership (and more vaguely on land use, since the Liberal recognition of communal ownership would give some emphasis to subsistence agriculture, while the Conservative desire to privatize land would encourage commercial production for export at the expense of subsistence agriculture); and on the level of enthusiasm for the ideal to reunify Central America. The Liberals regarded the Constitution of 1854 as the negation of that ideal. At that moment in Nicaraguan history, noticeable ideological differences separated the two parties. The two constitutions gaged the degree of that separation.

In June 1855, Castellón tried to reach an agreement with Estrada to end the thirteen-month civil war. Among other things, he worried that Granada might ally with Guatemala, a country that already had intervened in El Salvador and Honduras, to insure Conservative ascendancy.[93] Confident of impending victory, the Conservative leaders rebuffed him. They typically misjudged the situation. The civil war was about to assume international proportions disastrous for Nicaragua. In August 1854 the Liberals had entered into discussions with Byron Cole, and Castellón signed a contract with the North American on December 28, 1854. In return for generous land grants, Cole promised to enlist 300 Americans under the command of their countryman William Walker to fight with the Liberal army. The agreement referred to Walker and his men as "colonists, thus avoiding a challenge to the U.S. neutrality laws. The hiring of mercenary soldiers was a common practice throughout Latin America. Central Americans followed it in their frequent wars, both internal and isthmian.[94] The Granadans' protest against this arrangement sounded a note of nationalism in an accusation and lament that would echo eerily across the succeeding century and a half:

> Sad, it is extremely sad for the true Nicaraguan, for the citizen of Central American convictions, for anyone who knows how to esteem and is devoted to his nation, for anyone who manifests pride in being a part of a free people to watch as fellow citizens prepare the ruin of the common Fatherland by facilitating the entry of greedy foreign adventurers who will seize our land to extinguish its sovereignty and independence. It is surprising and upsetting to learn that there are Nicaraguans so perverse and so unnatural that they want to see their own land enslaved by men who were not born on its soil. Those Nicaraguans themselves invite in their own executioner, who will enchain them before marching them off to their deaths. It is unacceptable to see that, when the nation faces an eminent danger, they do not put aside personal ambitions to join in a common fight against the outside enemy.

They, too, face a great danger; they, too, will be adversely affected by the outsiders. Yet they persist in their crime of keeping the nation divided by weakening the Republic through the continuation of this unjust and barbarian war.

Who would have ever believed it? The party that calls itself Democratic, composed of Nicaraguans themselves, has signed a contract with foreigners to deliver our country to them. Those monsters have not hesitated to sell our holy Fatherland. . . . Those miserable creatures hold ambition more dearly than ties of blood, than the life of their nation Nicaragua.[95]

The accusation delineated the significant qualitative difference between Walker and his "army" and the previous outside interventions in Nicaragua. In no way was the diminutive "grey-eyed man of destiny" the ordinary mercenary officer.

Earlier British interventions occurred in marginal areas, low in population, isolated, and not integrated into the political and economic life of the nation. In contrast, Walker strode into the national heartland that was high in population, politically active, and economically productive. Furthermore, at least initially, the North Americans allied with some Nicaraguans. The far more serious threat posed by Walker elicited, eventually, a more energetic response.

William Walker had no intentions of fighting for the Liberals only to retire to a farm generously given him by the Nicaraguans. He, too, shared the vision of Nicaragua as agriculturally prosperous and as the vital commercial link for the world. What is more, he envisioned himself as the president of a thriving Nicaragua, indeed, eventually of all of Central America to quote his own slogan "Five or None!" Walker posed the greatest threat Nicaragua faced in the nineteenth century. While Castellón was attempting unsuccessfully to come to terms with Estrada, Walker and fifty-eight North American riflemen disembarked in Realejo on June 13, 1855. Their mission, according to one of his officers, was to rescue Nicaraguans "from the thraldom of despotic darkness and unintentional neglect."[96] At that crucial moment in Nicaraguan history, Colonel Kinney lay claim to a vast area of eastern Nicaragua including San Juan del Norte, Nicaragua's most important port; Commodore Vanderbilt owned and operated the Accessory Transit Company encompassing Nicaragua's most valuable geographical assets; and General Walker initiated his conquest of western Nicaragua, the center of the nation's population and agriculture. That North American impact altered Nicaragua forever.

Little wonder that dismayed Nicaraguans could lament: "Oh, civilization! Oh, culture! How distant you are from this poor fatherland of ours, now fallen into an abyss of misfortunes and on the verge of being eradicated from the map of nations!"[97] U.S. Minister Wheeler observed just a few weeks later, "It is a lamentable spectacle that so lovely a country should be torn by internal dissensions and deluged in the blood of her own citizens."[98] Internal dissensions had abounded for nearly half a century. During the 1850s, at least until 1856, foreign interventions both fed them and fed on them.

The Reaction

The year 1855 recorded the deaths of three well-established and highly influential political leaders: Fruto Chamorro sickened and died on March 12; General José Trinidad Muñoz fell on a battlefield near León on August 18; and Francisco Castellón succumbed to cholera on September 2. Each matured politically during the most intense period of anarchy; each contributed to that anarchy. Their deaths represented the passing of a generation.

The next generation, no less associated with the politics of anarchy, was more inclined, or perhaps more pressed, to compromise. Máximo Jerez spoke forcefully for the Liberals but eventually demonstrated willingness to come to terms with historical reality. Tomás Martínez (1820–1873) entered politics relatively late. A merchant who traveled extensively throughout Central America, he had held only one significant political post, that of prefect, prior to 1854. His family resided in León, but he maintained ties to the Conservatives of Granada through his mother. He joined Chamorro's army in 1854. Although the Conservatives for a time came to terms with William Walker, Martínez never laid down his arms against the filibuster. His nationalism and military tenacity propelled him to the forefront of the Conservatives by 1857. Adamant in expelling the foreigners, he demonstrated flexibility in his relations with the Liberals. The ability of the rivals to compromise signaled a new political reality, resulting partly from converging economic goals, partly from the threat of Walker and foreigners, and partly from the resultant nationalism. The parties demonstrated some cooperation, a sign of change in the new political generation.

The third figure to shape the 1850s and succeeding decades was the American William Walker. Educated as a lawyer and later as a physician, the restless Walker followed the flag of Manifest Destiny first to California, then to Mexico, and finally to Central America. He correctly understood the potential of Nicaragua as the site of an international transportation route and as an agricultural exporter. In that respect, he shared the historic vision of the patriarchs. A combination of adventure, chaos, and challenge attracted him. A complex personality, he united unpredictable bursts of insight with blatant disregard of reality. Bluster and determination carried him amazingly far, but a penchant for making the wrong decisions and attracting questionable allies contributed to his ultimate failure. Walker steered Nicaragua from the turbulent waters of civil war into the stormy seas of international conflict. Yet he played a role of transcendental historical significance. For good or for bad, he coalesced amorphous trends into active forces that would reshape Nicaragua after 1857. His presence forced the conclusion of one historical period and the advent of another. National consolidation replaced anarchy.

The civilian leaders of the Liberal party welcomed Colonel Walker to León.[99] The military chiefs, General Muñoz and his staff, immediately backed away from the American Phalanx. Given his ambitions, Walker wisely understood that his future bypassed those politicians and generals but depended on the power he would gain from the transit route to the southeast, an umbilical cord to North American money, supplies, and recruits. If he were to control Nicaragua, he must dominate that route. Moving to seize it from the Conservatives, he departed León to attack Rivas. Word leaked to Granada of the impending arrival of the American Phalanx and its Nicaraguan allies. The Conservative army and the residents of Rivas barricaded the town and waited. In an action that became his military hallmark, Walker ordered a frontal attack. On June 29, 1855, the first battle of Rivas ended in Walker's defeat and rout, a disastrous beginning for his Central American obsession. He learned not just of the political factionalism between the parties but within them as well. In Rivas men of *both* parties, Liberal and Conservative, fought against him, a cooperation termed by one historian as "an unmistakable sign of patriotism" and a "national triumph." Someone in León had informed the Conservatives of his plans. Walker suspected Muñoz. Clearly the Liberal military chief opposed Walker. In a letter of July 2, 1855, to President José María San Martín of El Salvador, he stated his refusal to "accept the Yankees." Others suggest that Tomás Manning, the powerful English merchant who disliked Walker and opposed the U.S. mercenaries, might have informed the Conservatives of the impending attack.[100]

Walker licked his wounds near León for a couple of months. The death of Muñoz in a battle on August 18—rumors of assassination circulated— freed Walker of his Nicaraguan military rival, making the Liberals more dependent on him than ever. Most of them, still mistakenly believing that Walker fought for their cause, supported him and enlisted in his ranks. Even the old populist bandit chief José María Valle, El Chelón, now a colonel, fought alongside the American Phalanx. He proved to be Walker's most valuable ally. In late August, Walker landed at San Juan del Sur and moved immediately to capture Virgin Bay in order to control the vital Western segment of the transit route. A skirmish at Virgin Bay gave Walker his first taste of victory. With reinforcements of Nicaraguan volunteers from León and more U.S. mercenaries, Walker then undertook his most audacious plan. He commandeered a lake steamer to invade Granada from the water, while the Conservative army awaited him in Rivas. The capture of Granada on October 13, 1855, ranked as Walker's major military victory in Nicaragua, and he achieved it by a skillful maneuver and correct timing rather than by fighting. With the families of the Conservative officers and officials as his hostages, Walker demanded the surrender of the army in Rivas. That tactic also succeeded.

Thanks to these successes Walker emerged by mid-October as the master of Nicaragua. He dictated a treaty on October 23 for the Conservatives and Liberals to sign. His newspaper, *El Nicaragüense*, crowed, "A peace is about to be framed between the so-called Legitimate and Democratic Parties of Nicaragua."[101] Walker's policy aimed to amalgamate the two political parties under his control.[102] He did eventually unite them, but, ironically, not quite in the fashion he intended. The treaty momentarily ended the war, and it established a provisional, "nonpartisan" government with Patricio Rivas, a political nonentity, as chief executive and Walker as commander-in-chief of the Nicaraguan army. Another North American, Parker H. French, also served in the cabinet as minister of the treasury.

While Walker enlisted a few able officers in his cause—C. C. Hornsby and Frank Anderson were examples—he also acted as a magnet which attracted scoundrels. French typified that group. Putting him in charge of the treasury was akin to inviting the fox to guard the hen house. He had left a trail of bad debts and forged drafts in Missouri and Texas, and committed robbery in Mexico and "sharp deals" in California before arriving in Nicaragua to serve Walker, who eventually dismissed him as much for incompetence as for shady behavior.[103] The foremost Liberal, Máximo

Jerez, assumed the portfolio of foreign relations in the Rivas cabinet, while a leading Conservative, Ponciano Corral, served as minister of war.

The U.S. diplomat John Hill Wheeler immediately called upon Rivas, thereby extending North American recognition to the government contrived by Walker. As the diplomatic dispatches of Wheeler readily reveal, the minister unabashedly favored the adventurer, reporting to Washington of Nicaragua's need for Walker, the enthusiasm for his government, and the excellent job he was doing.[104] Wheeler's dispatches complemented the surging spirit of Manifest Destiny of those years. They also suggest incompetence. Nearly all of Wheeler's judgments proved to be wrong. The Secretary of State scolded him for his precipitous recognition of the Rivas government but did not disavow the action. As November 1855, dawned, Walker stood at the pinnacle of his power in Nicaragua. He governed a country through a puppet president assisted by a bipartisan—and binational—cabinet.

A portion of the abundant broadside literature of 1855 naively exalted Walker. In one pronouncement, "a Liberal" praised Walker and El Chelón as leaders who crowned the nation with honor. Obviously the Liberals relished the capitulation of Granada as their victory.[105] A printed poem circulated which announced the advent of liberty and the end of Conservative tyranny. It mentioned only one individual:

> Long live the illustrious Walker,
> Long live the united Fatherland,
> Death to the Aristocracy!
> Join the ranks of
> William, the wise,
> Who leads us to victory
> Over the Conservatives
> Who inhabit America.
> Long live Liberty!
> Death to Conservatism![106]

In 1855 Walker clearly attracted some Nicaraguan partisans, most of whom, but by no means all, affiliated with the Liberals.

Whatever euphoria Walker might have created quickly dissipated. Minister Corral, for one, distrusted and disliked the Yankee general. The North American occupation of Granada repelled him. He secretly dispatched letters to Honduras requesting military intervention to overthrow the filibuster. The letters fell into the hands of an angry Walker, who tried and executed his minister for treason. The execution of a distinguished Nicaraguan and patriarch at the hands of the foreigners on November 8, 1855, shocked his countrymen. The execution, Walker's grave psychological error, conferred hero status on Corral. Opposition to Walker quickly intensified. The principal Granadan families slipped away to their outlying estates or to other towns, eloquent testimony to their disdain for the foreigner and his troops. [107]

Nicaraguan support for Walker disintegrated, with one significant exception. A part of the Church hierarchy continued to applaud him, perhaps acknowledging a political reality, but also perhaps hoping he would impose peace, no matter how restrictive, on Nicaragua. Prior to Walker's capture of Granada, the Conservative government urged priests to preach against the Yankee invaders. It reminded the clergy that the foreigners neither professed Roman Catholicism nor respected the religious beliefs of the Nicaraguans. [108] Walker, however, respected the power of religion, treating the Church and the clergy with deference, maintaining

Figure 7. The Execution of Corral. The brutal execution of Minister of War Porciano Corral in the central plaza of Granada on November 8, 1855, sobered the Nicaraguan patriarchs and alienated most of them from William Walker. Source: *Frank Leslie's Illustrated Newspaper,* December 22, 1855.

that he needed the endorsement of the Roman Catholic Church to achieve stability. He courted it with some success. Father José Hilario Herdocia congratulated Walker on his victories and the peace he envisioned for Nicaragua. [109] The Church donated and loaned money to Walker. [110]

For some years Granada's finest orator, Father Agustín Vijil, had expressed his strong admiration for the United States. [111] With Walker residing in Granada, Vijil took to praising him, often from the pulpit, calling him "the Guardian Angel of Nicaragua" and the "North Star" that would guide Nicaragua to its destiny. Minister Wheeler corroborated the ideological bias of Vijil: "He expressed much desire that the U.S. should own Nicaragua and prevent their sanguinary revolutions. I replied that under the Treaty with England the U.S. could not protect or own Nicaragua. He then hoped that North Americans would come and settle and finally possess the country."[112] A public defense of General Walker written by Vijil appeared in León in 1856. [113] Eventually the priest served as Walker's minister to Washington. In May of 1856, Secretary of State William L. Marcy received him, thus according further recognition to President Rivas and the regime of Walker. Rationalizing that recognition, President Franklin Pierce announced, "It is the established policy of the United States to recognize all governments without question of their source, or organization, or of the means by which the governing persons attain their power. . . . We do not go behind the fact of a foreign government's exercising actual power to investigate questions of legitimacy."[114] Vijil encountered such ridicule and scorn in Washington, particularly from other Latin American diplomats who looked with horror on what was happening in Nicaragua and with special disdain on a collaborator, that after six weeks he returned to Granada. He remained identified with the "North Star," and after his defeat, the government of Nicaragua exiled him to a small, distant parish. [115]

Isolated from the Nicaraguans, Walker made a major, nay, a fatal blunder that would also isolate him internationally. On February 18, 1856, Walker handed President Rivas for his signature a proclamation revoking the charter of the Accessory Transit Company. Walker claimed, quite correctly, that the company owed Nicaragua ten percent of its profits, which he figured for the period 1851–1856 to total US$412,489. He seized the company's property as collateral on the debt. That action might have pleased the Nicaraguans, whose disenchantment with the company had grown at the same pace as the company's rapacity and high-handed behavior, but they soon learned Walker acted purely for his own convenience and in no way complemented their emerging nationalism. Walker transferred the concessions of the Accessory Transit Company to Charles Morgan and C. K. Garrison, archrivals of Vanderbilt. Those two promised more money and greater attention to Walker's needs. The action nearly gave the imperious Commodore apoplexy. Too rich and powerful a man to be tampered with and certainly not to be tricked, he virtually declared war by proxy on Walker, supplying the willing Costa Ricans with funds, the latest weapons, and military advice. Unexpectedly he served as Central America's useful ally.

On March 1, 1856, Costa Rican President Juan Rafael Mora declared war on Walker. Understanding the danger on his southern flank, Walker dispatched an army there. The two armies met at the Hacienda de Santa Rosa within Costa Rican territory, and on March 20 the Costa Ricans soundly defeated the North Americans. Santa Rosa marked the beginning of Walker's fall. The Costa Ricans followed up that victory by invading Nicaragua. They seized Virgin Bay and Rivas, holding the all-important transit route for two months, a bitter blow to Walker. At the second battle of Rivas in April 1856, Walker failed to dislodge the Costa Ricans, but later the scourge of cholera forced the sick and dying army to return home. At Rivas and thereafter, disease won as many victories as arms, and it showed no mercy to any flag.

Militarily, Walker's record in Nicaragua was weak. On the one hand, the Central Americans outnumbered the North Americans, but on the other hand, with the single exception of the Costa Rican army, the North Americans possessed far better weaponry. Walker's knowledge of military strategy was nil; nor did he always heed the advice of his few competent officers. With some notable exceptions, his officers showed more bravado in the barroom than on the battlefield. Not a few of them qualified in dress and demeanor for comic opera roles. Attracted by the "romance of the tropics," they ended up being ridiculed. The Nicaraguans enlisted three formidable allies: aguardiente, dysentery, and cholera. In their own ways, they decimated the North American ranks more effectively than bullets.

As the months passed, the other Central American governments, increasingly anxious about Walker's presence in Nicaragua, resolved to respond to the pleas from Nicaraguan Conservatives and Liberals to dispatch forces to dislodge the filibusters. Walker's "election" to the presidency hastened their response. Having endured many months of Walker's outrageous behavior, the usually pliable President Rivas declared

Commander-in-Chief Walker a usurper, traitor, and enemy on June 25, 1856, and extended those epithets to all who served the North American. In a not unexpected response, Walker deposed Rivas and scheduled an election in which he ran for the presidency. For his part, Rivas made an impassioned call for the two political parties to "bury once and for all our ignoble party sentiments" and to unite against the common enemy:

> For the past two years, we spoke and acted in the name off two parties, Liberal and Conservative. Now, fortune seems to have joined those two parties guilty of fostering so much unhappiness and to have created yet a third party that is both anti-national and anti-religion. The appearance of this new [foreign] party causes us to forget once and for all the names of Liberal and Conservative and to join together in eternal unity. Our love for the religion of Christ as our love for the independence of our Fatherland are eternal. [116]

Further, he urged Guatemala, El Salvador, and Honduras to help expel the Yankees.

In the territory controlled by the North Americans, principally around Granada, Masaya, and Rivas, elections took place on June 29, with Walker proclaiming his victory with 15,835 of the 23,236 votes cast. [117] A rather pathetic inauguration took place on July 12 with only the most obsequious of the Nicaraguan minions present. Long before that event, all Nicaraguans of any significance had turned their backs on Walker. [118] The new "president" of Nicaragua, who spoke very little Spanish and that with great difficulty, read his inaugural address in English.

Even as President Walker spoke, the two parties, after one last violent clash, carried forward the project to unite under President Rivas. Tomás Martínez played the instrumental role in the delicate and protracted process of hammering out a compromise that freed Nicaraguan energies to combat the common enemy. Martínez's political star continued its rapid ascent.

The very day of Walker's inauguration, General Ramón Belloso arrived in León with 800 Salvadoran troops, to be joined within the week by General Mariano Paredes and more than 500 Guatemalans. At the same time, 600 Honduran soldiers were marching toward León. The Central American generals converging on that city, like the governments they represented, swore to defeat the common enemy: William Walker. Nonetheless, despite a common goal, national jealousies burned fervently. A folk caudillo *sui generis*, Rafael Carrera, ruled Guatemala. Conservative presidents presided over El Salvador and Honduras. Despite some ideological similarities, political tension characterized relations between El Salvador and Guatemala and, by extension, between their armies in Nicaragua.[119]

In summoning the Hondurans to take up arms against the filibusters, President Santos Guardiola reminded his fellow citizens and all Central Americans of the threat posed to the sovereignty of the isthmus and the outrages perpetrated against the nation: "The leader of those usurpers has tried to seize the presidency of that republic; to give away to foreigners immense areas of land; to introduce dangerous political and religious innovations; to confiscate private property as a means of dispossessing Nicaraguans of their major inheritance, leaving their owners in the tragic state of slaves in their own country."[120] Walker alarmed the Central American ruling classes by tampering with fundamental institutions, land and labor, to the potential detriment or impoverishment of the elites. That threat may have agitated them more than questions of sovereignty and national dignity.

In the matter of collective Central American involvement in Nicaragua, Costa Rica continued to act on its own—although with the advice, encouragement, and material support of Great Britain and Commodore Vanderbilt. Costa Ricans pursued some special items on their own agenda, such as a boundary dispute with Nicaragua by which they hoped to project themselves into the transit route. Free of the stress and complications of the prickly Central American alliances, Costa Rica acted more decisively, accrediting itself with impressive victories.

The allied armies exerted strong pressures on the Nicaraguan political parties to accelerate their conciliation. The Guatemalans believed the politicians no longer commanded authority, confidence, or respect among a citizenry exhausted by sterile political struggles.[121] The Liberals and Conservatives finally signed a pact on September 12, 1856, to unite their efforts "to save the independence and the freedom of our common Fatherland threatened by the adventurers led by Walker." While Rivas continued in the figurehead role of provisional president, Martínez assumed the post of commander-in-chief of the army. The leaders of the two parties further agreed that a new constitution would be written; a general amnesty proclaimed for past political offenses; and all debts, regardless of which party had contracted them, would be recognized as part of the national debt.[122] That pact marked a significant step toward the formation of the nation-state. Concurrently, but in an unrelated action, the United States withdrew its recognition of Walker.

The fortunes of Walker sagged. On September 14, 1856, Nicaraguan troops under the command of General José Dolores Estrada dealt him a bitter blow. Leading some three hundred men, Lt. Col. Byron Cole, a long-time associate of Walker, attacked Estrada's force of about half their number, sixty of whom were Matagalpa Indian archers encamped on a hacienda on San Jacinto hill. Met with spirited resistance, the Yankees retreated. Cole fell into the hands of local peasants who hung him. From that battle emerged a major popular national hero for Nicaragua. When his rifle jammed, Sergeant Andrés Castro "began throwing rocks at an American, who imprudently jumped out of his trench only to be struck and killed."[123] The victory of a small, all-Nicaraguan force over the larger number of better equipped North Americans; the presence and valor of an Indian contingent; the singular action of Castro, conjuring up comparisons with David and Goliath; and the death of Cole who had introduced Walker into Nicaragua provided fertile patriotic soil from which seeds of nationalism could sprout.

Much tribute also cascaded over the Nicaraguan commander, General Estrada. The Nicaraguans raised him, like Castro, to the status of a national hero. Jerónimo Pérez composed a poem to honor the man and the occasion:

A Tribute to General José Dolores Estrada on the Victory
He Won Over the Filibusters on September 14, 1856

> The sun whose light today you see
> Turning silver the yonder horizon
> Is the same sun which at San Jacinto
> Witnessed the outrage of the threatening Yankee.
> There you resolute general
> With one-hundred peasants in glorious combat,
> Brave and invincible warriors,
> Made the Yankees run with fear.
> That same sun flashed on your sword
> And fearsome was the reflection of its brilliance
> To that vile swine who, defeated,
> Felt your sharp displeasure.
> Today your face reflects the splendor
> Of the light that shone so brightly
> On that day of glory, honor, and eternal fame
> For your Fatherland and for your valorous leadership.[124]

Pérez's poem joined the others pouring from patriotic pens. That poetry dramatically documented the rising spirit of nationalism, an attitude and an emotion that weakened the localism so prevalent in the age of anarchy.

The North Americans attacked Masaya in November 1856 and were beaten back in fierce fighting. Later that month, the allies besieged Granada. Both sides fought furiously. In early December the Central Americans drove their adversaries out, but not before the Yankees blew up and burned down the once prosperous and proud city. Meanwhile, the Costa Ricans captured San Carlos and Castillo, closing the eastern section of the transit route.

Disease, death, desertion, dismay, and defeat encircled Walker and the remnants of his army as 1857 dawned. The bedraggled Phalanx held only Rivas and the route from San Juan del Sur to Virgin Bay. As Rivas was Walker's first defeat, so was it his last. The allied armies besieged it. Captain Charles H. Davis of *St. Mary's*, a U.S. warship at anchor in San Juan del Sur bay, arranged for Walker's surrender on May 1, 1857. As one U.S. senator, James R. Doolittle of Wisconsin, observed, "It was the Government of the United States which rescued General Walker and his command at Rivas, from the people of Nicaragua, and snatched him from the very jaws of inevitable death."[125] Walker continued to torment the Central Americans, trying to invade their lands in 1857, 1858, and 1859. In his fourth attempt in 1860, a British warship caught him and turned him over to Honduran officials. A military firing squad executed him.

Walker scripted and directed his own tragedy. He committed fatal errors. Bad judgment plagued him. He surrounded himself with a cast of malodorous characters, many of them inveterate "losers" who had rejected or been rejected by society, incapable of contributing anything but mistakes and sorry impressions. Like all mercenary groups, they valued plunder over any other consideration, although they were not adverse to dressing avariciousness in garments of patriotic or even moralistic prose. When Walker ordered the execution of General Corral, he not only horrified the Nicaraguans, he initiated their unification. He gratuitously added Vanderbilt to the lengthening list of adversaries by revoking the transit company contract. In many respects, Walker swam against the historical currents of his time.[126] To reinstitute slavery showed a reckless disregard of the temper of time and place. To ignore the rising force of incipient nationalism demonstrated a fatal historical myopia.

Yet on another level, Walker fully grasped the meaning of other potent historical forces. He even helped them along within the flow of Nicaraguan history. Walker contributed significantly to the introduction of modern capitalism based on export production by suggesting or accelerating the institutional adjustments necessary for its triumph.

Walker shared the patriarchs' vision of a productive Nicaragua utilizing its geography both to produce exports and to facilitate international trade. More clearly than the patriarchs, he understood that only readily available capital, proper use of land, and an abundant work force would transform that vision into a reality. Walker believed that trade and investment, particularly foreign investment, would provide the capital Nicaragua lacked. He threw up his hands in dismay at the Nicaraguan neglect and misuse of land. Land lying idle obviously did not produce. To flourish, Nicaragua must cultivate its soil. On November 23, 1855, the government issued a decree granting 250 acres to individual immigrants and 350 to families, under the stipulation that the land be used.[127] In 1856 Walker began to confiscate the land of "enemies of the state," that is those patriarchs who opposed him, and there were plenty of them.[128] A decree mandated the quick sale of confiscated lands and authorized "military script" as legal payment. In short, the decrees facilitated the transfer of land owned by Nicaraguans into North American hands.[129] Other decrees required that *all* land titles be registered and permitted documents to be in either English or Spanish. Both languages enjoyed equality and legality in court cases. Many Nicaraguans did not hold a legal title—or any title—to their land; others were unable to meet the six-month deadline to complete the legal registration of their titles; none was familiar with the registration process. Thunderstruck, the patriarchs watched as some of their peers lost land. Dismayed, they witnessed ever greater acreages accruing to English-speaking settlers.[130] The land laws challenged the patriarchs, and if nationalism did not prompt them to curse Walker, the increasing threats to their lands did. Land rendered profit, prestige, and power. It set the tone and established the patterns for life-styles. The patriarchs readily understood the ultimate consequences of the loss of land. Although no divestment of an Indian community is presently known, Walker's land decrees and action theoretically threatened those communities as well. The potential for immense mischief existed.

Walker realized the uselessness of land without labor. He witnessed and experienced the perennial problem of the dearth of labor in agriculture. To solve these chronic and endemic shortages, he encouraged immigration, decreed forced labor, and reinstituted slave labor. Walker let it be known that his government would enforce all contracts, imposing heavy penalties on all workers who failed to fulfill them.[131] A vagrancy law of 1856 forced all unemployed to work on public projects.

Walker intended the reestablishment of slavery to be the economic and philosophical centerpiece of his government. By declaring "null and void" all laws passed by the federal government of the United Provinces of Central America in a decree issued on September 22, 1856, he reinstituted slavery in Nicaragua.[132] In this matter, he boldly—recklessly—defied history. He himself declared:

> By this act must the Walker administration be judged; for it is the key to its whole policy. In fact the wisdom or folly of this decree involves the wisdom and folly of the American movement in Nicaragua; for on the reestablishment of African slavery there depended the permanent presence of the white race in that region. . . . The Spanish American States, after their independence, aimed to establish Republics without Slavery; and the history of forty years of disorder and public crime is fertile in lessons for him who hath eyes to see and ears to hear. . . . In Nicaragua whole tracts which were cultivated under the Spanish dominion have gone to waste since the independence; and the indigo of the Isthmus, which even ten years ago was a valuable article of export, has disappeared almost entirely from trade.[133]

The partnership of slave and master would destroy the power of the mestizo, characterized by Walker as the "bane of the country." The North American praised the Indian as a hard worker and above all else "submissive." Walker's social scheme ranked Indians and Blacks as a labor force to be exploited for their own good.[134]

Walker's arguments favoring slavery drew from the customary sophistry of the age. Slavery, he affirmed, was a type of "benevolence and philanthropy," a benefit for "inferior" peoples. Walker noted in passing that the slaves of Cuba and Brazil lived better than the Blacks in Africa. Naturally, he offered no evidence to support such claims. In sum, he rationalized slavery in the same terms as its Southern apologists. Not coincidentally, he openly courted the support of the Southern slave states.[135]

The reinstitution of slavery not only stunned the Nicaraguans, it repulsed much of the western world. However, it did find favor in the southern United States and with some U.S. officials. Minister Wheeler believed Nicaragua could "never be developed without slave labor. This therefore is an important and necessary decree."[136] Fortunately, the decree of September 22 served only as a statement of intentions, since events prohibited any implementation.

Walker's apologists turned a blind eye to his retrograde tendencies. They depicted quite a different leader. One claimed he "enjoyed struggling for the rights of man . . . he is honor itself personified in the most chivalrous manner and with the most honorable motive . . . he is a man of the people."[137] Another identified him with "the energy, the enterprise and the free spirit of the American people."[138] Various vociferous endorsements of Walker at various times in history demonstrated a selective treatment of a man who publicly and frequently claimed slavery to be a major commitment.

Nicaragua was the only country in which Black slavery, once abolished, was legally reinstituted. Ironically, Nicaragua had led the campaign in the Americas to abolish slavery. In 1811 Father Benito Soto persuaded the municipal government of Granada to do away with the institution.[139] No written evidence suggests that any Central American ever advocated its reestablishment.

Understanding that military conquest could be all too tenuous, Walker placed extreme importance on his labor and land laws. Not an army of soldiers but rather an army of farmers, he preached—no doubt having learned a history lesson from Texas and California—conquered permanently: "The general tendency of those several [land] decrees was the same; they were intended to place a large portion of the land of the country in the hands of the white race. The military force of the State might, for a time, secure the Americans in the government of the Republic, but in order that their possession of government might be permanent, it was requisite for them to hold the land."[140]

In the face of Walker's objectives most patriarchs opposed his political and military control of their nation, and all feared the consequences of his land and labor policies. Under Walker's program, they correctly understood their destiny to "be thrust aside, their nationality lost, their religion destroyed, and common classes converted into hewers of wood and drawers of water," to borrow the phraseology of Minister Mirabeau Buonaparte Lamar.[141] For them, Walker constituted much more than the threat of an occupying army. He represented a basic restructuring of society in favor of the new arrivals.[142] Little wonder, then, that the foreigner eventually succeeded in unifying the fractious patriarchs once they found their very life-styles at stake. The unified struggle against the filibuster blurred their previous divisions, and victory conferred a common achievement on all. Thereafter, economic pursuits minimized struggle and emphasized common interests: first, the switch to a coffee economy; then, the actual growing, processing, and exporting of the beans; and finally, the expenditure of coffee profits to modernize the state and society. Each step toward greater coffee prosperity diminished incentives for political conflict among the patriarchs, just as it minimized whatever differences remained between the two parties.

Walker's land and most particularly his labor laws also threatened the folk. His authority declined too rapidly for him to have been able to impose his new economic order on them. It must be emphasized, however, that in Walker the folk gained a sharp perception of impending threat to themselves and to their communities.

The Walker intrusion demonstrated, at least at that moment in time, that foreign intervention could unite the quarrelsome Central Americans. The five small nations cooperated sufficiently to fight together to protect not just the independence of one of their number but to reaffirm common institutions. None welcomed a change in landowning patterns that would favor aggressive foreigners over local patriarchs. Even if momentarily, Central Americans acted in unison; hopes for a common *patria*, a reunified Central America, flickered, however faintly. For the Central Americans, the war had "as its principal objective to defend and save the honor of our race." Defeat of the "invincible Yankees" infused pride.[143] The Central Americans rejoiced in their victory and celebrated it thereafter as a major historical event.

"The Sweet Name of the Fatherland"

Beside delaying the creation of the nation-state, the rivalry between the two city-states also frustrated the emergence of nationalism. Both concepts require definitions. For Nicaragua, the nation-state signifies a unified geographic space over which a recognized government rules with some degree of authority and effectiveness. An emotional force, nationalism contributes mightily to the creation and strength of the nation-state. Important as this emotion, concept, or force is, it defies easy definition. On an elementary level, it symbolizes a love for or devotion to one's nation coupled with a disregard for other nations. An outside threat can create, intensify, or sustain that devotion. Such a sense of nationalism springs from a basic "us" versus "them" mentality. A more sophisticated definition focuses on a group consciousness that assigns great value to the nation-state and identifies with it. Individuals identifying with the nation feel that their own welfare depends to a large extent on its well-being.[144]

Nicaraguans wrote little about the concepts of the nation-state or nationalism prior to 1840. Probably their inclusion within the wider Central American federation until 1838 and the bitter relations between León and Granada inhibited such expressions. Separation from the federation followed by British aggression in the 1840s and U.S. aggression during the following decade turned their attention to both concepts.

The elites and intellectuals expressed their views in print, so it is easier to study the evolution of their feelings of nationalism; moreover, during this period under study they might well have been the only ones with any concept of the nation rather than the community. However, their vision, too, was limited. They spoke and wrote about the nation when obviously they meant their own minute groups, their needs, objectives, and aspirations. They transmogrified their own interests into national ones. Their minimal consensus focused on an appreciation of the geographical importance of Nicaragua as a canal or transit route, a realization of the potential of the natural wealth, vague concepts of sovereignty and national indivisibility, and a fear of foreign attack or intervention. As they gained experience, their perceptions began to disengage from the past, a way of life bequeathed by Spanish colonial structures and shaped by the immediate environment, to grasp for a different future, increasingly materialistic and Europeanized.

No single event intensified nationalist expression more than the drama imposed by William Walker. In general, foreign presence played (and plays) a significant role in the emergence and honing of Nicaraguan nationalism. To the extent that foreign aggression disturbed and even disrupted folk communities, it prepared the foundation upon which a popular nationalism could later be constructed. The prolonged drama of foreign intervention shook Nicaragua. The folk could neither remain indifferent nor ignore it.

The roots of economic nationalism burrowed into the tobacco monopoly English merchants enjoyed in the early 1840s, a consequence of loans contracted and constant fiscal insolvency. The Nicaraguans accused the English of earning unconscionable profits at their expense. The *Redactor Nicaragüense* was blunt: "Foreigners impoverish our country, while enriching themselves."[145] Such complaints of the impoverished and dependent would become the standard cry of economic nationalism in the succeeding century and a half, not just in Nicaragua but throughout Latin America.

In his *Revista Política*, Pedro Francisco de la Rocha subsumed the two concepts of nation-state and nationalism under ample discussions of *nacionalidad* (nationality or, given the context, even nationalism), the Spanish word Nicaraguan writers frequently employed during the decades of the forties and fifties in their intellectual explorations of nation-state and nationalism. While de la Rocha lamented the scant overt evidence of nacionalidad among Nicaraguans, he affirmed that "buried deep in the heart" of Nicaraguans throbbed "the immortal and eternal devotion" to a nation. "It is impossible to stifle or eradicate it because it permeates our customs, strengthened by our community of interests, religion, way of life, language, and civilization. We share one piece of territory which binds us together in brotherhood. We share three centuries of common experience and common memory."[146] Thus he exemplified and articulated an intellectual's preoccupation with nationalism. In the official acts of nation-building, the intellectuals play a significant role as high priests officiating in the temple of nationalism. They conjure up or elaborate an "official" nationalism.

In an essay in 1849 entitled "Patriotismo," a Leonese newspaper discussed the terms *patria* (fatherland) and *patriotismo*, whose English translation ordinarily would be "patriotism" but within the context of this particular essay should be rendered "nationalism." The essay observed that everyone evoked "the sweet name of the Fatherland" but few, if any, helped to transform the vague idea into a reality. It called for the subordination of selfish interests to the greater well-being of the nation-state. Within nine months, the newspaper returned to that theme in two essays. It proclaimed that "Nationalism ought to be the source of our well being." From it would spring progress, prosperity, and liberty.[147] Given the political-economic context in which those essays appeared—the alliance of the Liberals and Conservatives to defeat the popular rebels, the beginning of the transit route across Nicaragua, and the presence of Squier—they assumed significance as ideological statements attuned to patriarchal thought and to new, if fleeting, national realities.

In an intriguing display of nationalism in 1853, another newspaper juxtaposed two contrasting yet complementary essays. The first, by the omnipresent S.C., attacked the series of articles "Civilization versus Barbarism," written by Domingo Faustino Sarmiento in 1845 in Chile. S.C. criticized the Argentine intellectual for his eagerness to copy the modes of Europe and the United States and to denigrate the Indo-Hispanic cultures. He posited an unusually early statement of cultural nationalism. The second, unsigned, bore the title "One September Afternoon on the Volcano of Masaya," a whimsical *costumbrista* piece. Mixing science, history, and folklore, it sang of the wonders and forces of nature in Nicaragua.[148] It lauded the local. It even poked a bit of fun at European greed. That praise of Americana subtly reproached Sarmiento. Were the timing and placement of the two essays a coincidence? If so, it was a remarkable one.

While the intellectuals conducted genteel discussions related or tangential to nationalism, foreigners boldly provoked the Nicaraguans, thus fanning glowing intellectual embers into torrid emotional flames. The British encroachments after 1841, the misbehavior of the transit company and many of its passengers after 1849, but, most importantly, the threat posed by William Walker in the mid–1850s energized that most basic of all nationalist responses, "us" versus "them." As John Stuart Mill suggested, a foreign presence facilitates the consolidation of patriotic feelings and accelerates nation building.[149] The Nicaraguans forged their nationalism in the fires of war against Walker.

If nationalism be an emotional identification of the individual with the nation-state and its well-being, then it matured during the difficult years of 1855–1857. Nearly all Nicaraguans participated to some degree in the struggle. Indians too fought against Walker. Probably many of them were dragooned into taking up arms, but other evidence suggests their antipathy toward the foreigner. For example, when Walker established a military garrison of approximately sixty men and a hospital for sick and wounded on Ometepe Island in Lake Nicaragua in late 1856, the Indians acted spontaneously, spurred by their historic suspicion of outsiders, to attack the North Americans and drive them off the island, inflicting heavy losses on Walker during his final months in Nicaragua.[150] Recognizing the contributions of another ethnic group, the Nicaraguans conferred hero status on the mulatto sergeant Andrés Castro. The warring folk were effective; Walker himself confessed that the rural guerrillas bothered his forces more than the armies.[151]

The attitude of Emanuel Mongalo might serve to demonstrate how the struggle against Walker aroused the nationalism of an ordinary citizen. Mongalo served as a common soldier in the struggle against Walker. The service strengthened his identity with the nation-state. After the war, while teaching primary school, he wrote in 1861 a short geography book for children: *Compendio de Geografía Hecho Esprofesamente para la Juventud Nicaragüense* (A Short Geography Written Expressly for Nicaraguan Young People). The teacher confided that he wrote the book "to serve my country, which I want to see ranked among the enlightened nations. It seems just it should be dedicated to my own dead father, who made a thousand sacrifices for my education and who always reminded me that in addition to teaching my younger brothers I also have a fatherland to serve."[152] Duty, service, education, and a concept of nation combined into a potent force to create and sustain Mongalo's nationalism.

Not just bullets but the anger of an injured and aroused people fell on the invaders. Walker himself recalled that "no epithet of hatred or contempt for the race of the North was left unuttered."[153] Joseph Clarence Tucker confided to his brother his feelings in Nicaragua in 1856 as "an American of a race *hated* and *cursed* from the *bottom of their hearts*."[154] Private David Deaderick III remembered a small incident, somewhat amusing but still revealing, of the young lad who jumped out of the bushes at the side of a road on which an American cavalry detachment was riding near Rivas and shouted, "Quieren por Walker?" (Are you for Walker?) and then added, "Yo no quiero al filibustero god-damn!" (I don't like the god-damn filibuster!), before scampering off into the undergrowth. [155] The boy's insertion of English words into his statement doubtless reflected the vocabulary to which the filibusters exposed the Nicaraguans.

Popular tales circulating among Nicaraguans revealed their attitudes toward the North American invaders. Those tales, like the Indian stories they paralleled, wryly told how savvy locals got the best of foreigners. A popular short story later emerged, "The Sale of the Negro," that both attacked Walker's pro-slavery stance and poked fun at the less than sagacious general. At any rate, the Nicaraguans definitely outwitted and outmaneuvered him in that story. [156]

Popular songs, the *corridos*, reflected similar preoccupations. One of the most frequently sung throughout much of the century, entitled "Song of the Widow," derived from the frequent wars troubling Nicaragua. In it, the woman laments the absence of her husband who has gone off to fight a war and has not been heard from. [157] Lusty voices in 1856 joined together to sing the popular, rowdy song "Mamá Ramona," whose lyrics were:

> Ah! Poor Mamá Ramona,
> She's been screwed.
> By laying with the Yankees
> She showed the devil she's no prude!
>
> Ah! Poor Mamá Ramona,
> With the Yankees she felt whorey.
> They grabbed her tits
> And now we can't complete the story.
>
> From faraway came the Yankees,
> From faraway came those bastards

To screw our Nicaragua,
Those thieves are really dastards.

From faraway came the Yankees
In their fancy dress overjoyed,
Yelling "Hurrah! Hurrah!
"It's Granada we've destroyed!"

For all those Yankees,
We gave a grand reception,
Flashing the blades of our machetes
And firing our cannon were no deception.

In Guadalupe Street
Let's build a road
Paved with the bones of the Yankees
And the blood of our men so bold.

On the road to Mombacho,
Plenty of pairs of ears you'll see,
Not from the heads of brave men,
But of sons of bitches who fight for a fee!

Ah! Poor Mamá Ramona,
She's been screwed.
So shamelessly did she behave
That the devil carried her off as lewd. [158]

The Mamá Ramona of that *corrido* probably was Ramona Barquero, who ran a boarding house in Masaya. [159] Words of pride in local valor mixed with crude humor, castigating the foreign invader and also the fraternizing Nicaraguan, Mamá Ramona. The lyrics emphasized that basic nationalistic dichotomy, 'us' versus 'them,' with insulting language expressing hatred of the outsider and the collaborator. These sentiments, expressed by the ordinary public least exposed to the formal concepts of the nation-state and nationalism, prepared it to accept both.

Clearly the most egregious offense to a sense of nationalism, no matter how latent, is the imposition of foreign rule. All groups evinced a sensitivity to the foreign presence. White foreigners with scant linguistic skills were easily identifiable in an Indian or mestizo, Spanish-speaking environment. No movement went unnoticed or unreported. By their very visibility, those intruders inevitably created impressions. To the extent these were negative impressions, the contrast with the Nicaraguans' own ideals, preferred modes of behavior, or sense of fairness caused psychological reactions that distanced them from the outsider. That reaction nurtured sentiments akin or leading to an elementary nationalism. Scholars only now are turning their attention to the impact of foreign armies upon the creation of feelings of nationalism among the folk. The conclusions thus far are mixed. [160]

It would be premature to conclude that the Nicaraguan folk who fought Walker and the American Phalanx were nationalists, at least in any conventional Western sense. The folk maintained a loyalty to their local community rather than to an abstract nation. They suspected, disliked, and feared outsiders, and most especially when they brought disruptive violence to their communities. In the mid–1850s nationalism touched them probably only in the basic challenge of "us" versus "them." A national program, if such existed, offered them little. Their cultural and economic concerns remained distinct from those of the patriarchs. Not until the twentieth century would nationalist programs speak directly to the needs and desires of the humble. In the nineteenth century, local considerations absorbed the folk. At various times and for a variety of reasons, those considerations might coincide with expressions of patriarchal nationalism.

It was a party of patriarchs, not the folk, that invited Walker and his American Phalanx into Nicaragua. Only through threat and violence did the Conservatives formally and reluctantly work with Walker during a brief period at the end of 1855. As for his Liberal hosts, Walker in time disillusioned and frightened them. As 1856 opened, nearly all the patriarchs had deserted him. While they fought among themselves, their fear of the foreign intervention eventually united them against Walker. Though drawn to their city-states, they were capable of a national vision and hence of expressing nationalism, particularly during the trauma characteristic of mid-nineteenth century Nicaragua.

The educated often expressed themselves through poetry, the literary form most cultivated in the nineteenth century. The patriotic poetry of the mid–1850s contrasted sharply with verses in that genre of the mid–1840s. The contrast reveals the emergence of a more recognizable form of nationalism. The so-called patriotic poetry of the mid–1840s sang the praises of either León or Granada, depending from whence hailed the poet. A decade later, it took up the cause of an increasingly unified struggle against the Yankees. It carried a more transcendental patriotic cast. In short, it became *national*!

In an early example of patriotic verse, Gregorio Juárez and Francisco Castellón greeted José de Marcoleta, the diplomat who had worked strenuously in Washington and at the European courts to protect "the cause most sacred," Nicaragua's geographic integrity, with a poetic salute to his patriotic battle "against the capricious British who want to mutilate our beautiful land." [161]

From the National War poetic tributes increased in numbers. The brutal destruction of Granada sobered all Nicaraguans, and that wanton act symbolized to many the fate that befell the country. In 1856, the poet and general José del Carmen Díaz y Renazco composed one of the best of those symbolic tributes to Granada, "To the National Flag on the Ruins of Granada." In a way it paralleled the first stanza of the national anthem of the United States because both voice the pride and joy of seeing the flag still flying after a devastating battle. The poem responds directly to the sign written and posted among the ruins by Henningsen, "Here was Granada." The poem proclaims, "Granada lives!" It opened with these lines:

> In the midst of fire, explosion, and shots,
> You rise up holy banner with brilliance and majesty.

Carmen Díaz reminded his readers: "There you continue to wave as the North Americans flee to their homeland." These "brothers" who fell died for Fatherland, honor, and religion, three strong motivating forces for nationalism. The poem closed by celebrating national rebirth after the defeat of the North American invaders.

In another poem, Díaz compared the filibusters to "bandits" and reminded them:

> Horde of Bedouins,
> You crossed the sea to seek your fortune,
> But in Nicaragua you found only the path to your tomb.

In a burst of nationalism, he vowed, "My Fatherland is noble. It would struggle to its destruction rather than witness one son on bended knee before a foreign invader!" That poem, "Canción," alternated between expressing love for Nicaragua and hatred for the "mean and loathsome Yankee."[162] The three poems in the triptych "Songs of War" by Juan Iribarra also revealed bitter feelings toward the Yankees amid appeals to nationalism. They went beyond denouncing Walker to decry foreign exploitation, calling on Nicaraguans to expel all foreigners.[163] Such poetry served as a prototype of nationalist sentiment, proud verbal challenges to foreign intervention that echoed and re-echoed across the decades. The poet punctuated a reality: internecine civil wars frustrated the creation of the nation-state, while foreign invasion accelerated that complex process.

The poetry glorified the hero and the nation or its symbols such as the flag or a well known geographic landmark. It instilled feelings of attachment for locale and of pride in the achievements of other Nicaraguans against a common enemy. To the extent it spoke to and accomplished those ends, poetry transmitted thought, emotion, and ideals about the nation of birth; it focused attention on Nicaragua as a political and emotional concept.

Most Nicaraguan historiography acknowledges the struggle against Walker as the emergence of a "national consciousness." The historiography of the 1980s emphasized the defeat of Walker as the "first significant victory" over "imperialism."[164] The experience reversed Nicaraguan attitudes toward the United States. The good will, hope, and friendship, all so vividly characteristic of Nicaraguans during the visit of Minister Squier, disappeared. Disappointment, bitterness, and suspicion replaced those positive qualities. William Carey Jones, a special U.S. diplomat dispatched to Central America, reported from Nicaragua in 1858:

> The few Americans who remain in the country . . . find themselves under the necessity to be . . . "very humble." . . . Any suggestion that [the Nicaraguans] desire an emigration from the United States, or in any considerable numbers from Europe, or will willingly see it, in any form whatever, is deceptive. The dominant idea of all Spanish America is the preservation of the domain and ascendancy of what they are pleased to call the *raza latina* or latin race. . . . [Y]ou may be assured that our countrymen are regarded only with feelings of bitterness and our prosperity and advancement as an impending calamity to these states.[165]

In 1849, during the visit of Squier, the Nicaraguans feared English invasion or encroachments. Less than a decade later, they feared U.S. intervention more than English threats. Worse, they saw in the Clayton-Bulwer Treaty an agreement between the two Anglo powers to determine the fate of their country without even consulting the inhabitants. Those fears, coupled with the experiences of British and North American interventions, contributed to diminish political fighting between Conservatives and Liberals, to the consolidation of the nation-state, and to the forging of nationalism as a significant ideology.

Foundations of the Nation-State

At the liberation of Granada the poet described the Nicaraguan flag waving bravely from its mast, but the domain over which it fluttered lay in ruins. While Nicaragua as a juridical entity existed, the nation in any real functional sense did not. The National War, climaxing a third of a century of intermittent civil wars, had devastated it. The Minister of Public Works, Education, and Public Credit, Jesús de la Rocha, noted sadly that his country was awakening from a long nightmare to find its economy in shambles: commerce languished in a "pathetic state of nonexistence and inertia"; agriculture suffered from a lack of labor, roads, capital, and adequate laws; and the destruction of public records erased the government's knowledge of the public debt.[166] The transit route, once the centerpiece of the patriarchs' hope for an economically vigorous Nicaragua, remained closed, a sour reminder of a sweet dream.[167] U.S. Minister Mirabeau Buonaparte Lamar concluded, "Nicaragua is in a most reduced and deplorable condition."[168] The Peruvian diplomat Francisco S. Astaburuaga concurred. He observed a population reduced by war and cholera, capital diminished by forced loans, cities in ruins, and homes emptied by repeated sackings.[169] Nearly a decade after the defeat of Walker, the traveler Frederick Boyle gloomily described the ruins still characteristic of most populous regions. He apologized, "I am hoping and trying to paint the downfall of Nicaragua without exaggeration, but I have no words for the squalid misery of its smaller towns. Everywhere are mounds that tell of fallen buildings; great porches and pillars of stone yet stand, all solitary, by the roadside."[170] Wars, national and international, clearly had thwarted economic growth and prevented development.[171]

Remarkably, the patriarchs still could muster up optimism in the face of that grim reality. Minister de la Rocha paused in his litany of disasters to reaffirm the patriarchal vision: "The geographical situation of Nicaragua puts it into contact with all the nations of the world. Soon it will convert this nation into a commercial emporium and one of the contributors to world civilization."[172] The minister, like the poet, predicted the phoenix Nicaragua would take wing from the ashes of destruction. Whether he understood the reasons for it or not, that prediction materialized. The cumulative effect of generations of war had turned the tide of events: an exhausted, frightened, sobered patriarchy eschewed recourse to arms, accepting political compromise. The temptations of the North Atlantic capitalist marketplace beckoned—by then, an irresistible siren. Nicaragua stood at one of those historical junctures where the future took leave of the past.

A new generation of patriarchs agreed on political conciliation. When challenged by popular rebellion, the patriarchs coalesced to defeat the threat in 1849. Later, in 1856–57, they again united to expel the foreign interlopers and to reassert national independence. The brutal experience of foreign intervention strengthened nationalist instincts sufficiently to reduce rivalry between the two city-states. The immensity of political and economic disaster weakened Granada and León, toning down party rhetoric.[173] Indeed, a major obstacle to the creation of the nation-state collapsed during the National War. León lost political prestige because of its early association with Walker; the war virtually destroyed Granada. Managua filled the vacuum, and after 1857 began to play in earnest the role of capital it had taken in name in 1852. Neither León nor Granada possessed the prestige, confidence, or power after the National War to challenge its increasingly effective leadership over the populous regions of Nicaragua. Comparatively uncompromised by the city-state rivalries that prolonged the age of anarchy, Managua represented more innovation than tradition. At any rate, its emergence as an increasingly effective political center symbolized the new psychological foundations upon which to begin to construct the nation-state.

Economic necessities also contributed to party cooperation. Bitter experience with the Accessory Transit Company made it abundantly clear to all Nicaraguans that the immediate future did not lie with a foreign transportation company. A more realistic hope to turn their vision into an economic reality sprang from agrarian exports. A hope for new markets in California and steamship access to major U.S. ports propelled them in their economic quest. Inspired by the example of neighboring Costa Rica's coffee prosperity, the two rival political parties wanted their country to emulate it. One group of patriarchs called the government's attention to the fact that Costa Rica's public revenues had risen from 1,000 pesos in 1827 to 500,000 in 1852, largely owing to coffee prosperity.[174] The patriarchs finally acknowledged the obvious: their economic interests coincided rather than clashed. Those interests dictated, first, the imposition of order, and, second, a readjustment of national institutions to further complement export agriculture. Members of the elite sought institutionalized means to facilitate the acquisition of capital, land, and labor in order to realize their economic vision. They wanted a government that would play an active economic role complementing their export-oriented objectives. Such a Positivist formula of political order and economic prosperity guided the Latin American elites throughout the last half of the nineteenth century.

The patriarchs, in particular the Liberals enfeebled by their closer links to Walker, compromised politically in their desire to fulfill the economic vision. The way was now open for the establishment of a defined institutional construct for effective government. The process toward the creation of the nation-state could move forward. Possibly for the first time, the ability to exercise power over large areas accompanied the claim to such power.

The formal cooperation between the Liberals and the Conservatives dated from September 12, 1856, when they signed an agreement to fight together to defeat Walker. That pact facilitated the transition from war to peace, from Walker to a national unity government. It propelled Nicaragua into a new era of relative or comparative party cooperation.[175]

Thanks to such cooperation, the two parties settled some thorny economic issues. They agreed on the vital but contentious financial questions of how the customs duties would be levied and collected, eliminating an advantage that Granada previously had enjoyed in collecting those important duties on the San Juan River, a major source of government funding. They further adjusted the commercial advantages of Granada by promoting the opening of new ports on the Pacific at Corinto and El Barquito, a response to the California trade. Indeed, the rapidly rising trade in the Pacific promised León economic advantages rivaling those Granada extracted from the Atlantic trade. The promise and later achievement of relative economic balance between the two preeminent cities contributed to greater political order and to the nation-building process. The parties consolidated and regularized the internal debt to the general satisfaction and benefit of the patriarchs. Such agreements contributed to national economic integration, a marked characteristic of the remainder of the century.

Political accommodations also characterized the relations between the Liberals and Conservatives. Patricio Rivas served as president until June 24, 1857, when generals Máximo Jerez and Tomás Martínez assumed the "bipartisan presidency," the transitional government from war to reconstruction. The last public speech of President Rivas pleaded for party cooperation: "They [Jerez and Martínez] promise to reconcile the parties, to uphold the dignity of the nation, and to protect the political and civil rights of all Nicaraguans. I urge all of you to support the new chief executives, to give them your cooperation, and to help them in carrying out their duties."[176] The bipartisan executives guaranteed peace, encouraged national unity, reconstituted the judiciary system, conducted elections for a constituent assembly and a president, and, by example, contributed to political reconciliation. A Constituent Assembly convened on November 8, 1857, promptly elected Martínez—endorsed by Jerez—as the president of Nicaragua. He took office on November 15.

The embodiment of patriarchal political consensus, the constitution promulgated in 1858 drew part of its inspiration and much of its innovation in the deliberations of the constituent assemblies of 1848 and 1854. It impressively strengthened the powers of the president, doubling his term of office from two to four years and making him commander-in-chief of the armed forces. More stringent property and income qualifications further restricted male participation in both voting and office holding. Elections remained indirect; only a tiny fraction of the population participated.[177] As previously pointed out, this constitution enshrined the Biblical dictum to honor one's parents as requisite for citizenship. All these provisions characterized the constitution as a major instrument of patriarchal governance, prompting José Luis Velázquez to conclude that it permitted the oligarchy to run the nation as it would a rural estate.[178] New political structures marked significant steps toward the creation of a well-ordered nation-state. The government in Managua emerged after 1857–58 with the instrumentalities to govern effectively and to monopolize violence.[179] The patriarchs demonstrated sufficient unity of "common sympathies" to promote cooperation.

While the patriarchs might profess "common sympathies," considerable doubt remained whether they shared such sympathies with the folk. The nation-state as perceived and created in 1857–58 depended not just on the acquiescence and cooperation of the patriarchs, its authors, but also on their ability to subordinate the inwardly oriented rural communities to the larger "national" goals. The patriarchs faced the challenge of convincing the folk communities to embrace the nation-state and its economic goal of agrarian exports. Otherwise, they would be forced to restructure these communities to make them fit the new nation-state. In sum, the proposed export economy might require their lands and most certainly would need their labor. Liberals and Conservatives approved a constitution whose silence on the issue of communal lands threatened the folk.

The patriarchs cloaked their goals and their nation-state with an ideology of nationalism as they understood and patterned it. Some cynics might suggest that the patriarchs believed the Fatherland was created to serve them and acted accordingly. The identity they fostered for the nation obviously harmonized with their ideals, values, and experiences.

Their confident behavior in 1857–58 reflected their emerging political consensus and, quite frankly, their victories, first over the folk and then over the filibusters. Behaving as though their own well-being was synonymous with the public good, the patriarchs found little difficulty in concluding, for example, that communal landowning was retrograde, a barrier to progress and to the fulfillment of their vision, and hence to the greater glory of Nicaragua. As important as their consensus was, however, it should not be confused with a popular consensus.

Under the new constitution, the Conservatives dominated politics and power until the final decade of the nineteenth century. A dynasty of six presidents "from the tertulia in Granada—the cabal of oligarchs who, from that city, generally shape the policy, if not control the action of this government" followed Martínez into the presidential palace of Managua.[180]

Martínez rode a wave of popularity into the presidency. In many ways, he embodied the emerging nationalism. At no time had he compromised himself with Walker. He had fought steadfastly against the filibuster and revealed himself to be a reputable military commander in the field. Further, he remained virtually untainted by the acrimonious civil struggles prior to the National War. His very distance from that past represented a new hope to many Nicaraguans. Momentarily setting aside partisan preference, even Liberals endorsed him, at least during his early years in office.

The new president harbored no illusions about the challenges confronting him when he took the oath of office on November 15, 1857. A tall, rather plain, self-educated, and reserved man, Martínez read a simple and somber inaugural address: "Our fields lie bleached by the ashes of our dead; our cities lie ruined, a reminder for many years to come of the horrors wrought by foreign invaders; even now, agriculture and commerce remain paralyzed as a consequence of a recent Costa Rican invasion; the public treasury is empty; private property is destroyed; the schools remain closed. Such is the present picture, sad as it may be, of Nicaragua. At this moment and under these circumstances, I take control of the destiny of our nation".[181] Martínez then turned from the past to contemplate the future. He promised a government of "peace, reconciliation, and justice" that would promote agriculture, commerce, education, and Central American unity. Rightly or wrongly, isthmian unity had been associated with Liberal goals. Aware of the Central American contributions to the defeat of Walker, Martínez strongly endorsed the goal Jerez had long championed: "I have supported and I will continue to support

Central American unity. I do not know the form or shape it will assume, but I do know that unity is the only way to prevent intervention in the individual small nations. Unity will command the respect of those foreign powers which have belittled us until now."[182] On another occasion, he warned that division invited foreign intervention: "Our great family, divided into five nationalities, thus presents itself to the cupidity of those who envy the fertility of our soil and the geographic location of our precious Isthmus."[183]

Action accompanied his words. On April 15, 1858, Martínez signed a treaty in San José to define the troublesome boundary between Nicaragua and Costa Rica. In it Nicaragua recognized the 1824 secession of Guanacaste from Nicaragua and its inclusion into Costa Rica as Nicoya Province. While Nicaragua retained control of the transit route, it allowed Costa Rica access to the waterway. By settling the disputes peacefully and realistically, Nicaragua recognized the immense Costa Rican contribution to the defeat of Walker. Also, the settlement united the two nations as they faced new threats from Walker and other foreign adventurers. The treaty with Costa Rica, logical as it might have been, required both confidence and courage on the part of the Nicaraguan signer because it recognized the loss of approximately 4,000 square miles of territory, no small tract in Central American terms. It was a measure of the strength and rationality of Martínez that he assumed the responsibility of signing it. In the meantime, the two nations joined forces to thwart foreign interlopers, of whom there were many.[184] The Treaty of Managua signed by Great Britain and Nicaragua in 1860 recognized Nicaraguan sovereignty over the Mosquito territory, although for complex reasons Nicaragua did not exercise it for another three decades.[185]

Martínez appreciated the longing of his fellow countrymen for public order. In late 1858, he spoke to the painfully sensitive but omnipresent question of "national betrayal" and "traitors" to the fatherland, posed by the presence of Walker and his various internal political alliances and arrangements of convenience. A new Penal Code Concerning Traitors defined "national betrayal" as any acts of "making war detrimental to the national security of the Republic, whether it compromise independence, the constitution, or liberty." It castigated as "traitors" any Nicaraguan who aided, abetted, or allied with foreigners in making such wars.[186] This issue was destined to remain sensitive in Nicaraguan history.

Ideologically favorable to the new constitution, Martínez both drew strength from it and strengthened it. He enforced it rigorously. In 1859, his government completed the compilation of civil, penal, and procedural codes for the nation. He also reconstituted the courts and commanded the enforcement of the laws. The president was able to introduce a period of effective respect for and implementation of law, until then novel in Nicaraguan national history.

For a decade, 1857–1867, Martínez energetically exercised the considerable powers conferred on the presidency by the constitution. He both demonstrated and strengthened the effectiveness of the newly emergent nation-state. He ably administered that state; levied and collected taxes; encouraged education; built a social, economic, and administrative infrastructure; judged and enforced laws; and exercised a monopoly over violence. In effect he acted as a caudillo cloaked in the mantle of a constitution. In comparison with the historical experiences of Latin America, the institution of caudillo appeared late in Nicaragua.

Responding to these achievements, the patriarchs saluted effusively the peace, order, and good government of the early years of the Martínez administration. Their words radiated hope. The foremost poet of the period, Carmen Díaz, summarized the tribute in a poem published in 1860:

> Blood bathed the Fatherland.
> It was both a Tower of Babel and an abyss.
> It was the scene of crimes and cynicism.
> All was darkness; all, confusion.
> A wild storm broke over the Fatherland
> Menacing one and all with death;
> Might reigned supreme and force prevailed,
> Shaking the Fatherland with the tumult.
> But a light pure and radiant prevailed;
> A voice strong and reassuring spoke;
> The sky cleared serene and limpid;
> And the Fatherland raised its eyes in triumph.
> A sword flashed. It was your sword.
> It was your voice that prevailed.
> It was your brave look, your confidence
> That the Fatherland gratefully acknowledged!
> Martínez! In one voice, all the people
> Shout out this glorious name;
> They call you hero of the Fatherland
> And your brow they crown with laurel.
> Your name, writ large, will remain
> To guarantee the future, to recall the past.

> You live eternally. Your memory
> Endures so long as the Hispanic race will last.[187]

Such poetry in praise of the caudillo was by no means uncommon in nineteenth-century Latin America; this one probably rang with a little more conviction than most.

A broadside circulated in 1862 celebrated the half-decade of peace and order, attributing to it the emergence of economic prosperity: "Since June of 1857, the brilliant dawn of peace illuminates Nicaragua. . . . This beautiful part of Central America awaits a promising future if this peace continues. . . . We repeat: do not disturb our peace; do not cause us to lose our harvests or reverse the impressive expansion that agriculture experiences."[188] A few years later, commemorating the forty-fourth anniversary of Central American independence, Juan E. de la Rocha spoke glowingly of Nicaragua's "prosperity and progress," words expressing the satisfaction of the patriarchs with the new historical experience.[189] Nicaraguan historiography generally acknowledged positively the advent of that new period. Even Liberals tended to praise Martínez, particularly early on. Enrique Guzmán concluded in 1878, "[The Conservative Party] governed under the administration of General Martínez from 1858 to 1862 and during those five years Nicaragua enjoyed freedom and happiness to a degree that had never been possible up to that time, just like the best governed nation on earth."[190] The hyperbole made its point: Nicaragua stood at the threshold of a new era.

Radical Discontinuity

The defeat of William Walker, the cooperation between the Liberals and the Conservatives, the promulgation of the Constitution of 1858, and the efficient and effective governance of President Martínez created the conditions to build Nicaragua as a nation-state. The agonizing age of anarchy ended. The period of the Martínez presidency witnessed remarkable political changes, particularly during the early years of his decade-long administration. In turn, those changes heralded inevitable social and economic innovations. Within their historical context, the changes stand out as radical discontinuities. Nicaragua clarioned its entry into a new historical period.

In 1849 Ephraim George Squier viewed Nicaragua just before changes noticeably nudged it into the nineteenth century. Until then, Nicaragua had lacked extensive contact with the world at large. Society looked inward. The patriarchs and the populace led distinctive local lives, in the city as well as in the countryside. Social and economic needs were modest, although a persistent vision of another orientation caused some patriarchal hopes to soar. By all accounts, everyone enjoyed access to land, a reality that made society look deceptively simple. Squier resided in a Nicaragua still more attuned to its colonial past than inclined toward the modernity of Western Europe, still more original than homogenized into Western capitalism. Appreciating the uniqueness of what he witnessed, Squier paused from time to time in his observations to reflect on their meaning, to penetrate the implications of what he saw. Such reflections constitute the few efforts foreigner visitors made to understand the society that enveloped them.

A sensitive observer, Squier detected in the lively streets of Granada individual exuberance combined with social harmony: "The streets were thronged with noisy children, and the señoras and señoritas were all seated in the doorways or in the balconied windows, in quiet enjoyment of the cool evening breeze, which swung the lamps, suspended in front of each house, slowly to and fro. There seemed to be a sense of the luxury of mere existence among the inhabitants, which the traveller looks for in vain except under the tropics, and which there appears to be in perfect harmony with nature." Those streets of Granada intrigued Squier, probably because so much of the daily life was lived in the outdoors. The streets were less lanes of communication and transportation and more extensions of living quarters, open parlors of social encounter where domestic and public discourse, mingled to the apparent satisfaction of the residents:

> As I rode through the streets [of Granada] and witnessed the apparent absence of want, of care for the present, or concern for the future, I could not resist the impression that probably no equal number of people in the world enjoyed more real happiness than these. With the mass of men, those whose higher powers of enjoyment have never been developed, and whose happiness depends chiefly upon the absence of physical wants, or upon the ease with which they may be gratified, the life of the people of Granada must come very near to their ideal of human existence.

Squier lauded the simple but fulfilling quality of everyday life. Attending a public festival in León sparked other thoughts in the young diplomat as he contrasted the scene before him with the cities he knew in the United States:

I sat on my horse for a quarter of an hour, listening to the music and merriment, and speculated whether, after all, in spite of unstable governments, and destitute of all those accessories which, according to our utilitarian ideas, are necessary to the popular welfare—whether the people of León were not on the whole happier and more contented than those of any city of equal size in our own country? Here were no crowded workshops, where youth and age toil on, on, during the long day and by the pale gas light, amidst foul vapors, or in a corrupted atmosphere, that trade may thrive, and arrogant commerce strut in the Exchange! No thundering machines to disturb the calm of evening, to drown the murmurs of the night winds and the gentle melody of the falling dews, with hoarse, unearthly clangor![191]

Moments like those seem to have made the small cities of Nicaragua seem romantically ideal.[192] Squier understood that the world offered more than one social pattern. Unlike so many of the other foreign travelers, he did not impose his values on an unknown society so much as he tried to understand different values within another cultural context. Even while the young diplomat observed and interpreted those street activities, the historical dynamic of Nicaragua was changing in a way unprecedented in depth and pace since the sixteenth century.

Ten extremely dramatic years, 1849–1859, encapsulated Nicaragua's emergence from an amorphous geographic collective of folk and patriarchs into a recognizable nation-state firmly controlled by a handful of patriarchs who, with contradictions indicative of a society in flux, insisted on the modernization of society. The reality that the patriarchs created, namely a satisfactory contractual arrangement for governance, undermined the essence of the patriarchy, the genetic mandate. Ironically but inevitably, the national government and nation-state they advocated challenged them to conform to the new sociopolitical construct or to surrender themselves to others attuned to change. The growing separation of political and social authority eventually would weaken Nicaragua's patriarchal foundation.[193] Cracks in it appeared during the long Martínez administration. A more powerful, modernizing state with its emphasis and dependence on an export economy eventually doomed the patriarchate of the past just as it had folk society.[194] Within the broadest context of Nicaraguan history, the events of that decade marked a visible change in national behavior, a radical discontinuity with the past. The emerging nation-state subverted the patriarchal and folk inheritances.

Some of the historical discontinuities were obvious. Nicaragua fought its first major war against foreigners; a vitriolic anti-United States sentiment engulfed the nation; and the Nicaraguans opposed the reopening of the transit route. Those three discontinuities intertwined intimately. While Nicaraguans had fought countless civil wars and engaged freely in broader Central American struggles, the National War pitted them against English-speaking Protestants from a geographically distant and culturally different United States. While Walker acted as a free agent, the embittered Nicaraguans resented the support citizens of the United States accorded him, the failures of Washington to enforce its own neutrality laws, and ambiguous actions on the part of the Department of State—the reception of Walker's envoy, Father Agustín Vijil, for example. They argued that Walker could not have succeeded without at least the tolerance of Washington.[195]

The devastation of the war changed the attitudes of most Nicaraguans toward the United States from the outpouring of friendship that Squier experienced in 1849 to various shades of reserve and even of hostility. If Squier encountered effusively friendly Nicaraguans who looked to Washington for leadership and protection, his successors found suspicion and distrust[196] and —little wonder. Both Borland and Lamar harbored not very well concealed desires to see Nicaragua incorporated into the United States.[197] Lamar had helped wrest Texas from the Mexicans and his every action indicated that he would like nothing better than also to incorporate the valuable geographic assets of Nicaragua into the Union. He enjoyed none of the Nicaraguan exuberance that had overwhelmed Squier. For that matter, Lamar demonstrated none of the finesse and exhibited little of the intellectual insight of Squier. He complained bitterly about his treatment and never disguised his low esteem of the Nicaraguans: "They are poor and ignorant and exceedingly prejudiced against the Americans. Their prejudices are founded upon their fears. They think their destiny is to be overrun by our race, whose influx into their country will be the death of their nationality."[198] He expanded on that theme in other dispatches: "The great trouble with Nicaragua may be easily explained. She saw in the melancholy results of the Walker War, how near she was to being conquered by a handful of Filibusters—and from that day to the present moment, she has been oppressed with a sense of insecurity, so long as an American is allowed to tread her soil. . . . The dread of being thus denationalized and her people degraded is the great and probably sole impediment to a good understanding with her."[199] His successor, Alexander Dimitri, corroborated the unfriendly attitudes. He reported that the wealthy and powerful Fulgencio Vega had advised President Martínez that "it is better for all true and patriotic Nicaraguans to go down together into the tomb than yield one inch to the arrogant demands of the United States."[200] On another occasion, the minister referred to Granada as "that nursery of prejudice and hostility to everything that bears the semblance of American interests."[201] He also spoke of President Martínez's "unfriendly disposition towards American interests."[202]

It was not paranoia that drove Nicaraguan attitudes and actions. Threats were real enough. Until his execution before a Honduran firing squad in 1860, Walker repeatedly tried to return to Nicaragua. Other foreign adventurers also tormented Nicaragua. U.S. naval vessels sailed in and out of Nicaragua's harbors. Minister Lamar urged Washington to occupy the transit route and administer it.[203]

Although a transit route had once signified to the Nicaraguans the realization of their fondest hope for lucrative international trade, it menaced them after 1855 as an open door for foreign intervention in the Walker mode. They remembered how he used it to recruit soldiers and to receive supplies. "There is not a patriotic Nicaraguan who desires to see it reopened," Minister Dimitri concluded, "because all are convinced that its active operations must infallibly result in the sweeping of the country by hordes of filibusters, under pretense of emigration."[204] The Nicaraguan president adamantly refused to sign a treaty with the United States to reopen the route under U.S. protection.

Martínez believed not only that the reopening constituted a security threat to the nation, but also, along with many knowledgeable Nicaraguans, that the route bestowed few or almost no economic benefits on their country. The president was discovering—with Latin Americans everywhere—that the region's abundant natural resources served foreign capitalist instead of the locals. Minister Dimitri unexpectedly agreed with Martínez that the route infused few benefits and perhaps even exercised a negative influence over the national economy. The minister confided,

> The best men of Nicaragua . . . are fairly convinced and maintain that the transit is of no benefit to the generality of the Republic. In this, I can bear him [Foreign Minister Zeledón] witness; for conversing with some of those men, they have invariably advanced the stereotyped idea that its advantages, though they might be reaped at the extremities of the route, are not diffused through the country and outside of those points. They express, on the contrary, that when the transit was in operation the labor required to keep it up; the higher wages given for that labor, than the usual rates of the country; the business of transporting passengers and freight on mules

across the portion of the land route; all of these called off the hands, already too scarce, from the cultivation of the soil and materially reduced the sum of the agricultural products of the country. These views . . . are invariably rounded off with the dangers of the transit, as a means of flooding the country with lawless marauders and of its re-aperture's being the signal for the reappearance of the same lawless men. [205]

Deprived of the profits from their own resource, which foreigners turned into a major security threat, Nicaraguans wanted to control and operate the transit route themselves. [206] If that proved impossible, they hoped to use other powers to check the U.S. presence.

Nicaraguan diplomacy somersaulted. Totally reversing the diplomatic goals of the end of the 1840s when they courted Washington to counter English threats, Nicaraguans looked to London and Paris in the final years of the 1850s for protection from U.S. aggressions. Nicaragua was learning through trial and error a vital diplomatic strategy for a small and weak state: to play off the major nations against each other in order to enjoy security in the shadow of their conflicts. Britain and France responded in the sense that they occasionally dispatched warships. Their presence in Nicaraguan waters annoyed Washington. When the Frenchman Félix Belly appeared in Costa Rica and Nicaragua in 1858 with the draft of a treaty for a canal concession, the Department of State exploded with anger. At that very moment it was pressing President Martínez to sign the Cass-Irisarri Treaty, which would permit the United States to protect all transit routes across Nicaragua, using force if necessary to insure the safety of the "lives and property" of U.S. citizens. Martínez considered the proposed treaty as an open invitation to intervention, a surrender of Nicaragua's sovereignty. He therefore welcomed Belly royally, hoping the Frenchman did in fact command the means to protect Nicaragua from U.S. pressures. [207]

Belly's presence offered the Nicaraguan and Costa Rican presidents an opportunity to confer in Rivas on the matter of future transit route arrangements. Together, presidents Juan Rafael Mora and Tomás Martínez issued the powerful Rivas Manifesto, a major nationalistic statement on May 1, 1858. [208] The date was symbolic: it marked the first anniversary of the surrender of Walker. The manifesto denounced U.S. intervention and the Cass-Irisarri Treaty, while calling on France, England, and Sardinia to guarantee the sovereignty of Central America. Karl Bermann labels the manifesto "a sort of Monroe doctrine of Europe against the United States." [209] The manifesto gave the Department of State apoplexy.

Instead of yielding to the pressure to sign the Cass-Irisarri Treaty, Martínez gave vent to his nationalism. Under unremitting pressures from Washington, both presidents finally backed off and withdrew their manifesto. The contract with Belly did not materialize[210]; neither did the Cass-Irisarri Treaty. In the final analysis, Managua, not Washington, won. There was no treaty and the route did not immediately reopen. Maintaining his position that the transit route created more problems than it resolved, Martínez successfully stalled the reopening until 1864, when Nicaragua received slightly better contractual terms. The project never regained vigor. The last crossing took place in April of 1868.[211] The Rivas Manifesto remains one of the most revealing documents of the period. It parted the curtain of diplomatic decorum to reveal a profound, even visceral nationalism peppered with anti-Yankee sentiments while looking to Europe for protection.

The 1850s marked a major diplomatic discontinuity. In 1849, Nicaraguans extended a warm embrace to the United States and declared their gratitude for Washington's protection and leadership. They interpreted the events of the mid–1850s as a betrayal of their trust and friendship. That sense of betrayal interacted with a surge of nationalism to reinforce each other. Thereafter, no matter how close relations with Washington might superficially appear, the Nicaraguan experience with Walker, the transit company, and the U.S. government in the mid–1850s had created a barrier which inhibited broad-based intimacy with the metropolis.

With the transit route less than an economic success story, the government turned its attention to export agriculture. President Martínez energetically supported the growth and export of coffee, building in part on previous trends.

Apparently the first law to encourage coffee production dated from 1835. It exempted coffee producers from taxation for ten years.[212] However, scant information about the planting of coffee trees or the harvesting of the beans appeared until the mid–1840s. The historian José D. Gámez believed that the first coffee trees came from Costa Rica for use in gardens as ornamental plants. He dated the first coffee plantations from 1845–46 and located them in the hills near Managua and Granada.[213] A law of August 1847 exempted Nicaraguan coffee plantations of 2,000 or more trees from all taxes and their owners and workers from military service.[214] The German traveler Alexander von Buelow spoke of coffee as a significant product in 1846.[215] He visited a small coffee estate near Granada owned by the Prussian emigrant Gerkowsky de Koeningsberg and another owned by the French emigrant Paillereau in that same region. The Frenchman cultivated 5,000 trees that produced no less than two pounds of coffee each and 15,000 two-year-old trees, still too young to bear beans.[216] Von Buelow mentioned coffee exports via San Juan del Norte in 1846, but he failed to specify whether the fifty *quintales* originated in Nicaragua or Costa Rica.[217] Squier noted in 1849 the expanding sea of green coffee trees rippling over the hills from Lake Managua to the ocean.[218] No one took Squier's words praising the quality of the coffee and the limitless potential for its expansion more seriously than Supreme Director Chamorro. In 1853 his government offered subsidies to new coffee growers.[219] Meanwhile, coffee was becoming more popular than chocolate in the local diet so that by the mid–1850s many Nicaraguans insisted on coffee as the first and final drink of the day.[220]

These preferences facilitated the task of President Martínez as he guided Nicaragua along the coffee road to riches, using a map provided by the experience of neighboring Costa Rica. On May 28, 1858, he began to issue a long series of new laws encouraging coffee culture. It excused coffee producers and their workers from military service for twelve years during peace time; it exempted coffee from any taxes; very significantly it facilitated the acquisition of land to raise coffee trees.[221] A year later, a Law for Uncultivated Lands offered a wide variety of incentives to farmers: an exemption of agricultural machinery from import duties; prizes for improvements in agriculture and transportation; the distribution of seeds, plants, and agricultural manuals at cost; and subsidies for the introduction of new crops.[222] To facilitate exports, the government built the new port of Corinto in 1859. Not coincidentally, Corinto enjoyed an ideal geographical location to facilitate coffee shipments. It grew so rapidly that two decades later it handled fully three-quarters of all of Nicaragua's foreign trade.[223] Coffee composed 10 percent of the value of Nicaragua's exports in 1871 and rose rapidly thereafter.[224]

Discontinuity lay not in the government's encouragement of the growth and export of coffee but rather in the land and labor laws devised and, very importantly, enforced to achieve those ends. Coffee culture altered the relation of the population to the land. Coffee production began during a period of rapid population increase and in the most populous region of Nicaragua. Because land that could produce coffee became a primary source of wealth, it was eagerly sought after by the patriarchs, other investors, and foreigners. They planted coffee trees on vacant land as well as on fields that once produced food for local consumption. Those who wanted to grow, process, and export coffee encroached upon the life-styles of peasants, ending their ready access to the preferred lands and enlisting their labor on the estates. The new enterprise threatened to destabilize folk communities. The export goals of the would-be coffee producers did not coincide with the subsistence patterns of the rural majority. The contradiction contained the seeds of future struggles.

A stronger nation-state favored patriarchs both politically and economically. They monopolized political power. They used it to benefit themselves by facilitating their acquisition of lands, particularly those suitable to grow export crops, by regulating labor in such a way as to meet the work demands of their estates, and by using the government to construct complementary infrastructures—ports, roads, and later railroads.[225]

The Constitution of 1858 on the one hand protected individual owner-ship of land, thereby strengthening the patriarchs; on the other hand, its silence concerning communal and ejido lands signified the withdrawal of former protection for communal ownership, thereby dooming the folk communities. That the collective ownership of land no longer enjoyed constitutional protection was of grave importance for both plebe and patri-cian. The state's efforts to weaken the communal landholding and land management systems assaulted fundamental folk values and eroded the organization of the folk society. The promotion of individualism fostered a change of revolutionary proportions. It challenged historical patterns that had been established in the pre-Columbian past.

The government drove the first wedge into the solidarity of those com-munities in early 1859 with a law permitting an individual to acquire own-ership of land he had worked within the communal holdings for four con-secutive years.[226] The patriarchs had learned in Nicaragua, as their counterparts had learned elsewhere in Latin America, that it was extremely difficult to divest the communities of their lands but compara-tively easy to bamboozle or bully the individual small landowner. Disband-ing communal landholding harmonized with the patriarchs' economic con-victions attuned to a type of neocapitalism. Of course, the process also worked to their advantage in acquiring or expanding landholdings in the relatively populous regions favorable to coffee culture as well as in aug-menting an always tight labor market.

From long experience, the patriarchs well knew that land without labor was useless. Labor shortages historically plagued them. They resolved in 1858 to regiment labor better, thereby insuring a readily available work force for their estates. They advocated laws to control labor and the force to implement them.[227] In 1858–59, President Martínez signed several laws to require Nicaraguans to work three days per year on roads, an effort to improve the transportation and communication infrastructures.[228] The government took a major step in 1859 to regulate rural labor in its Law of Uncultivated Lands, which professed to protect both employer and employee. It required an agrarian judge to oversee, approve, and adjudicate all work contracts in agriculture, ranching, construction, and mining. The law limited the work day to eight hours and was intolerant of an employer's failure to pay promptly, doubling the worker's salary if the pay was over three days late. At the same time, it stringently regulated the worker's payment of debt to the employer with rigid punishments on the defaulting debtor.[229] Another law in 1862 vastly expanded the role of the agrarian judge and almost all of the forty-three articles of that law dealt with regimenting labor. [230] The labor laws passed in the years after the promulgation of the Constitution of 1858 increasingly regulated peasants and rural workers. Such regulations benefited the large producers. The mechanisms of rural labor control served as social control as well.

As the number of patriarchal estates engaged in commercial and particularly export agriculture grew, pressures on the peasants and folk communities mounted. The nation-state had three primary motives for displacing the folk communities from their land. First, the patriarchs coveted lands suitable for export agriculture. Second, they wanted to create a labor force over which they exercised control. To deny or to limit access to land facilitated the creation of surplus labor. Third, the communities detracted from the creation of a viable nation-state. So long as the communities existed, the folk gave them rather than the nation their primary loyalty. Dissolving the communities was a means of "nationalizing" the folk, forcing them to turn from the historically and culturally important community to the newly invigorated nation. [231]

The reluctance of the folk to embrace the nation-state voluntarily was understandable. It conferred no visible benefits and presented quite a few disadvantages. Without the vote, with scant access to education, and subjected to foreign cultural values, the folk suffered a status loss in the transition. The state squeezed taxes and services out of the common people whenever and however it could and required the men to serve in the army. Subject to forced labor and increasingly limited in their access to land, they suffered economically from the emergence of the nation-state with its agrarian export orientation. Actions that tended to undermine the vigor and importance of the folk societies set in motion a significant historical divergence from the past. In truth, the trends toward concentration of land ownership and the shift from subsistence to export agriculture together constituted the major radical discontinuity with the past.

Once the political momentum to create the nation-state and the accompanying economic momentum to accelerate agricultural exports, most particularly coffee, got under way, the patriarchs moved as quickly as was practical and possible to consolidate their gains and to achieve their goals during the remainder to the nineteenth century, first under Conservative governments but after 1893 under a Liberal government. Political labels after 1858 proved increasingly meaningless since the political and economic programs of both parties became alike. By the end of the nineteenth century, the society was quite different from that at mid-century. Communal lands and ejidos had disappeared. Large estates grew in size and number. Export agriculture limited subsistence agriculture. Some peasants lost their land and became day workers; others made new claims on frontiers or on more marginal lands; still others found it increasingly necessary to alternate between working their own land and hiring out to the large landowner for part of the year; some exchanged agrarian pursuits for urban. Wealth concentrated in fewer hands. In general, those trends threatened the quality of life of the majority.

Part of Martínez's skill in the challenging task of governing Nicaragua in 1857 and the years immediately following derived from an ability to recognize changes, subtle as some of them might have appeared at first, already introduced or under way in Nicaraguan society. He strengthened, expanded, and directed political order, coffee culture, labor laws, control over the transit route, and boundary settlements. In the process he honed patriarchal preferences into neocapitalist trends, embarking on a transition that characterized the last four decades of the century. The government strengthened itself partly at the expense of family structures. In the process, the foundations of the patriarchate wobbled.

Inescapably, psychological changes accompanied the process of creating the nation-state and emphasizing export agriculture. The patriarchs drew ever more heavily from the North Atlantic experiences, using the United States, Great Britain, and France as models for cultural preferences and behavior. For the sake of "progress" the patriarchs imposed a cultural model on Nicaragua alien to popular preference and, ironically, in the long run threatening to their own life-styles.[232] The ever wider adoption of those foreign models eroded the individuality and uniqueness of Nicaragua after 1857.[233]

The creation of the nation-state was cataclysmic for the ordinary person and for the folk communities of Nicaragua. It changed fundamentally the relations of people with their communities and environment; it imposed an increasingly strong authority, the centralizing government, over their lives; it threatened their quality of life. At the historical juncture of Nicaragua beginning in the mid–1850s, an increasingly effective nation-state obliterated much of the communal past and charted a new capitalist future. [234]

Decades of anarchy dissolved into years of radical discontinuities. Turbulence had characterized those decades between the disintegration of the Spanish Empire, 1798, and the defeat of William Walker, 1857. At the same time it was a period of compromise and enforced tolerance between the patriarchs and the folk. It was a time of neither extreme wealth nor poverty, when everyone enjoyed access to land and to food. By 1841 foreign intrusion had begun in earnest. Pressures first from Great Britain and then from the United States weighed increasingly on the young, underpopulated, and impoverished nation.

The clash between national entity and imperial imposition sharpened the Nicaraguan search for identity. "The contradictions between Nation and Empire," Alejandro Serrano Caldera convincingly asserts, "intensify the search for the complex nature of the Latin American being as an individual, as a people, and as history."[235] Nowhere was that search more intense or more brutal than in Nicaragua. In many respects, the age of anarchy previewed the future rather than concluded the past. The search and struggle for national identity during those years yielded new complexities rather than solutions. Two significant trends appeared by the end of the 1840s: the rise of nationalism and the pressure on the folk societies to conform to the patriarchal and increasingly neocapitalist image of the nation-state. Both set in motion powerful historical forces whose consequences were unforeseen, perhaps unforeseeable, in the nineteenth century. Events, internal and external, converged to crown triumphant the patriarchs, at least for the remainder of the nineteenth century. They consolidated their control over the folk just as they consolidated the nation and, for the moment, held at bay the empires. They would have the remainder of the nineteenth century to shape Nicaragua, to seize or squander their opportunities. Clearly, the Nicaraguan phoenix that arose from the ashes of the National War bore only a partial resemblance to its predecessor.

Chronology

1798   Patriarchs set forth their economic vision for Nicaragua.

1814   Provincial delegates petitioned the crown to separate Nicaragua from the kingdom of Guatemala and to raise its rank to an intendency.

1821   *September 15.* Central America declared independence. *September 28.* In León, Nicaraguans declared their adherence to independence.

1823   *July 1.* Five provinces of Central America federated under the name of the United Provinces of Central America. Civil war erupted between León and Granada.

1824   The first sacking of León during the civil wars. Nicoya/Guanacaste region of Nicaragua seceded and asked to be annexed to Costa Rica.

1826   *April 8.* Promulgation of the constitution of the Federal State of Nicaragua. *August 14.* First meeting of state legislature.

1830–1833   The federal government dispatched Dionisio Herrera to govern Nicaragua in an effort to impose peace.

1830–1845   Period of political domination of Nicaragua by León and the Liberals

1838   *April 30.* Nicaragua left the Central American federation. *November 12.* Promulgation of first constitution.

1841   British expanded their protectorate over the Mosquito coast. Pablo Buitrago selected as the first supreme director.

1845   *January.* Second sacking of León. *April 4.* José León Sandoval elected supreme director, the first chief executive with defined Conservative ideas.

1845–1846	Coffee culture introduced into Nicaragua.
1845–1849	Period of popular rebellions.
1846	*July 24.* The Villa de Managua raised to the rank of city.
1847	Publication of the *Revista Política* by Pedro Francisco de la Rocha, the first historical-Political study by a Nicaraguan. U.S. steamship service established to east and west coasts of Central America.
1848	*January 1.* British occupied San Juan del Norte. Direct steamship service between that port and Southampton established. Conservatives tried to replace Constitution of 1838.
1849	*March 19–July 20.* Gordon expedition, the first organized group of North Americans, traveled to California by crossing Nicaragua. *June 22.* Minister E. G. Squier arrived in Nicaragua. *July 17.* Government executed the populist caudillo Bernabé Somoza. *August 26.* Cornelius Vanderbilt signed contracts with Nicaragua for a canal and transit route.
1850	*April 18.* Clayton-Bulwer Treaty signed. *July 25.* Spain recognized Nicaragua. *November.* British renamed San Juan del Norte "Greytown" and declared it a free port.
1851	*January 1.* First steamship crossed Lake Nicaragua. *July 14– August 30.* First trip of Vanderbilt Steamship Line, New York-San Francisco via Nicaragua.
1852	*August.* Opening of new transit route: San Juan del Norte-Virgin Bay-San Juan del Sur. Managua named the national capital.
1853	*April 1.* Fruto Chamorro took office as supreme director. *May 9.* Law passed to encourage coffee culture.
1854	*January 22.* Constituent Assembly convened. Liberal leaders in exile. *February 28.* Constituent Assembly changed name of State of Nicaragua to Republic of Nicaragua; of supreme director to president. *April 30.* New constitution sanctioned but only enforceable in Granada. *May 5.* Liberals landed at Realejo and civil war began. *May 8.* Liberals issued their program. July 13. U.S. sloop-of-war *Cyane* shelled and burned San Juan del Norte. *December 28.* Francisco Castellón entered into a contract with Byron Cole to enlist 200 Americans under command of William Walker.
1855	*June 16.* Walker and 58 U.S. mercenaries disembarked in Realejo. *June 29.* First battle of Rivas, defeat of Walker.

October 13. Walker captured Granada. *October 23*. Treaty between Walker and Ponciano Corral to end civil war and to invest Patricio Rivas with presidency. *November 8*. Walker executed Corral as traitor. Nicaraguans began to unify in opposition to Walker. U.S. Minister Wheeler presented his credentials to Rivas.

1856–1858   The National War in which all five Central American nations allied to fight Walker.

1856   *February 18*. Walker revoked the charter of the Accessory Transit Company. *March 1*. President Mora of Costa Rica declared war on Walker. *March 20*. At the Battle of Santa Rosa, Costa Ricans defeated Walker. *April 10*. Second battle of Rivas. Costa Ricans defended Rivas from Walker attack. *June 25*. President Rivas declared Walker a usurper and enemy. *July 12*. Walker inaugurated as "president" of Nicaragua. *September 12*. Liberals and Conservatives signed an agreement of cooperation against Walker and for national reconstruction. *September 14*. Battle of San Jacinto. Nicaraguan army defeated forces of Byron Cole. Andrés Castro and José Dolores Estrada emerged as national heroes. *September 22*. Walker reinstituted slavery.

1857   *May 1*. Third battle of Rivas. Walker surrendered. The National War ended. *June 23*. Patricio Rivas ended his administration as chief executive. *June 24–October 19*. Máximo Jerez and Tomás Martínez, governed as bipartisan dual executive. *November 8*. Constituent Assembly convened in Managua. *November 15*. Martínez inaugurated president.

1858   *April 15*. Treaty signed by Nicaragua and Costa Rica to establish boundaries. Nicaragua ceded Guanacaste to Costa Rica. *August 19*. New constitution promulgated.

Notes

1. City-States

1. "Informe Dirigido al Señor Marqués de la Hornaza por los Comerciantes y Hacendados de la Villa de Nicaragua [Rivas] en Junio de 1798," reprinted in *Boletín Nicaragüense de Bibliografía y Documentación*, 2 (October-December 1974), pp. 28–29.

2. José Coronel Urtecho, "La Familia Zavala y la Política de Comercio en Centroamérica," *Revista del Pensamiento Centroamericano*, special no. 141–142 (June-July 1972), pp. 55, 27–28, 30.

3. Alberto Lanuza Matamoros, "Comercio Exterior de Nicaragua (1821–1875)," *Estudios Sociales Centroaméricanos* (San José), 14 (May-August, 1976), p. 118.

4. Miguel González Saravia, *Bosquejo Político Estadístico de Nicaragua, Formado en el Año de 1823* (Guatemala City: Beteta, 1824), p. 12; for further data on colonial exports see Germán Romero Vargas, *Las Estructuras Sociales de Nicaragua en el Siglo XVIII* (Managua: Editorial Vanguardia, 1988), p. 371.

5. Jaime Wheelock Román, *Nicaragua: Imperialismo y Dictadura* (Mexico City: Editorial Siglo Veintiuno, 1975), p. 54.

6. Juan Carlos Solórzano Fonseca, "Centroamérica en el Siglo XVIII: Un Intento de Explicación Económica y Social," *Estudios Sociales Centroamericanos* (San José), 11:32 (May-August, 1982), pp. 13, 14, 18.

7. Romero Vargas, *Las Estructuras*, pp. 74 and 129.

8. Ibid., pp. 146–148.

9. Ibid., p. 296.

10. Ibid., p. 343.

11. Ibid., p. 309.

12. Ibid., pp. 324–340.

13. Ibid., p. 375.

14. David R. Radell and James J. Parsons, "Realejo: A Forgotten Colonial Port and Shipbuilding Center in Nicaragua," *Hispanic American Historical Review*, 51:2 (May 1971), p. 310.

15. Lanuza Matamoros, "Comercio Exterior de Nicaragua," p. 120.

16. Rodolfo Cardenal C., "Acerca de las 'Reflexiones' de Coronel Urtecho," *Revista del Pensamiento Centroamericano*, 151 (April-June 1976), p. 34.

17. Pedro Joaquín Chamorro Zelaya, *Fruto Chamorro* (Managua: Editorial Unión, 1960, p. 12. Complaints against Guatemalan merchants abounded. Hector Lindo-Fuentes succinctly summarized their power over Central American commerce in "Weak Foundation: The Economy of El Salvador in the Nineteenth Century, 1821–1898," (Ph.D. diss. University of Chicago), pp. 14–19.

18. Solórzano Fonseca, "Centroamérica en el Siglo XVIII," p. 16.

19. The document from the Archivo General de las Indias is reproduced in the *Revista de la Academia de Geografía e Historia de Nicaragua*, 7:2 (August 1945), pp. 27–29.

20. Mario Rodríguez, *The Cádiz Experiment in Central America, 1808 to 1826* (Berkeley: University of California Press, 1978), p. 118.

21. "La Diputación Provincial de Nicaragua y Costa Rica Pide a la Regencia del Reino la Erección de una Audiencia y Capitanía General en Estas Dos Provincias, con Independencia de Guatemala." This document from the Archivo General de las Indias is reprinted in the *Revista de la Academia de Geografía e Historia de Nicaragua*, 7:3 (November 1945), p. 2.

22. Romero Vargas reflected on the repetition of past economic patterns as an explanation for Nicaragua's subsequent failure to develop economically: *Las Estructuras*, pp. 373–374.

23. Examples are many. The early conclusions of John Hale were typical: "It [Nicaragua] will shortly become the emporium of vast and extensive commerce. . . . The products of the country are so various; the animal kingdom so multifarious in its species, and game so abundant, that it is capable of sustaining the wants of an hundred times its present number of inhabitants. The articles of exportation are so numerous, that it would be presumptious of me to endeavour to give an enumeration of them. Suffice it to say, in general terms, that nature has exerted herself here." *Six Months' Residence and Travels in Central America through the Free States of Nicaragua, and Particularly Costa Rica* (New York: J. Hale, 1826), p. 30. Alphonse Dumartray and Pedro Rouhaud reinterated the encouragement on the European continent: *Opúsculo sobre la República de Centro-América y Particularmente sobre los Estados de Nicaragua y Costa Rica* (Paris: Librería Americana, 1833), pp. 12–16.

24. González Saravia, *Bosquejo Político*, p. 16. In the same year that González Saravia wrote his study, Manuel Antonio de la Cerda presented a plan to the Constituent Assembly of Central America to rehabilitate the port of San Juan del Norte and to construct a canal across Nicaragua. The documents are reproduced by Franco Cerutti, "Documentos sobre el Proyecto del Canal por Nicaragua," *Revista del Pensamiento Centroamericano*, 172–173 (July-December 1981), pp. 101–105.

25. *Mentor Nicaragüense* December 11, 1841.

26. *Nicaragua: Its People, Scenery, Monuments, Resources, Condition and Proposed Canal* (New York: Harper, 1860), pp. xiii-xiv. For another afirmation of the "vision," see "Squier Notes on Nicaraguan Debt," Squier Papers, Box 2, Folder 9, Latin American Library, Tulane University.

27. Juan Cruz Ruiz de Cabañas, *Carta Pastoral que el Ilustrísimo Señor Don Juan Cruz Ruiz de Cabañas, Obispo de León de Nicaragua, Dirige a Todos los Fieles de*

Su Diócesis (Madrid: La Imprenta de Don Benito Cano, 1795), pp. 32, 38.

28. Ibid., pp. 51–52.

29. *Discurso Pronunciado por el Licenciado D. Juan E. de la Rocha, Alcalde 1° Constitucional en el Aniversario XLIV de Nuestra Independencia* (León: Imprenta de Justo Hernández, 1865).

30. Miles L. Wortman, "Government Revenue and Economic Trends in Central America, 1787–1819," *Hispanic American Historical Review*, 55:2 (May 1975), pp. 279–280.

31. Orlando W. Roberts, *Narrative of Voyages and Excursions on the East Coast and in the Interior of Central America* (Edinburgh: Constable, 1827), p. 229.

32. Romero Vargas, *Las Estructuras*, pp. 296–307, 376–377.

33. Miles L. Wortman, *Government and Society in Central America, 1680–1840* (New York: Columbia University Press, 1982), p. 230.

34. Alejandro Marure, *Bosquejo Histórico de las Revoluciones de Centro América desde 1811 hasta 1834* (Paris: Bouret, 1913), I, 20 and 68.

35. This judgment of Ayón can be found in Anselmo H. Rivas, "Los Partidos Políticos de Nicaragua,"*Revista Conservadora del Pensamiento Centroamericano*, 70 (July 1966), pp. 2–3.

36. Carl Scherzer, *Travels in the Free States of Central America: Nicaragua, Honduras, and San Salvador* (London: Longman, 1857), I, 113–114.

37. "Documentos Posteriores a la Independencia,"*Revista de la Academia de Geografía e Historia de Nicaragua*, 7:2 (1936), pp. 255–257.

38. Ibid., pp. 293 and 295.

39. Lanuza Matamoros, "Comercio Exterior de Nicaragua," p. 114; Pablo Levy, *Notas Geográficas y Económicas sobre la República de Nicaragua* (Paris: Librería Española de E. Denne Schmitz, 1873), p. 515; Squier, *Nicaragua*, p. 648.

40. Humberto Belli, "Un Ensayo de Interpretación sobre las Luchas Políticas Nicaragüenses," *Revista del Pensamiento Centroamericano*, 157 (October–December 1977), p. 52.

41. Levy, *Notas Geográficas*, p. 250.

42. George Byam, *Wild Life in the Interior of Central America* (London: Parker, 1849), p. 20.

43. Dan Stanislawski, *The Transformation of Nicaragua, 1519–1548* (Berkeley: University of California Press, 1983), pp. 141–142.

44. David R. Radell dates the rivalry from the early colonial period. "Historical Geography of Western Nicaragua: The Spheres of Influence of León, Granada, and Managua, 1519–1965" (Ph.D. diss. University of California, Berkeley, 1969), p. 176; Virgilio Rodríguez Beteta, "Transcendencia de la Guerra Nacional de Centro America contra William Walker,"*Anales de la Sociedad de Geografía e Historia de Guatemala*, 30:1–4 (1957), p. 23; Edgardo Buitrago, "León y Granada en el Destino Histórico de Nicaragua,"*Boletín Nicaragüense de Bibliografía y Documentación*, 60 (February–April 1989), pp. 1–11.

45. Romero Vargas, *Las Estructuras*, p. 178.

46. Max Harrison Williams, *Gateway through Central America: A History of the San Juan River-Lake Nicaragua Waterway, 1502–1921* (La Paz, Bolivia: Empresa Editor Urquizo, 1976), pp. 47–48.

47. Lanuza Matamoros, "Comercio Exterior de Nicaragua," p. 132; José Luís Veláz-quez, "La Incidencia de la Formación de la Economía Agroexportadora en el Intento de Formación del Estado Nacional en Nicaragua (1860–1930)," *Revista del Pensamiento Centroamericano*, 158 (October-December 1977), pp. 11–13; Coronel Urtecho, "La Familia Zavala," pp. 76–77; and Alejandro Reyes Huete, *Estampas de Nuestra Historia* (Granada: El Correo, 1956), p. 35.

48. *Gaceta Oficial de Nicaragua* (Granada), February 12, 1853.

49. "Oriente y Occidente,"*El Nicaragüense* (San Jose: EDUCA, 1978), pp. 119–123.

50. Chamorro Zelaya, *Fruto Chamorro*, p. 257 *passim*. Most foreign travelers observed and commented on municipal rivalries as a source of disunity. Accord-ing to Carl Scherzer, 'nobody likes to have any other than one of his own relations for the head of state, or that any other town than the one he was born in should become the seat of government, and enjoy the material advantages appertaining to that position. This political narrow-mindedness and egotism will afford a key to many of the deplorable events of which Central America has been the theatre almost ever since the Spanish rule was thrown off: one town has envied another, one village owed a grudge to its neighbor on account of certain advantages to which it deemed itself entitled." *Travels*, I, 114. Frederick Boyle commented, "Granada is the seat of the aristocratic, anti-foreign party, while its rival, León, is the headquarters of the democratic or progressive party. These two towns have sacked one another again and again without in any way settling the ques-tions at issue. The fact is that Granada wishes to destroy León, and León to destroy Granada; and thus no progress is made towards consolidation and no progress ever can be made." *A Ride Across a Continent: A Personal Narrative of Wanderings through Nicaragua and Costa Rica* (London: Bentley, 1868), I, 93–94.

51. Mario Sancho, *La Jóven Literatura Nicaragüense* (San José: Alsina, 1919), p. 22.

52. "Every one of the five States was separately divided into two hostile camps as to which of their two principal towns should be the Capital. Thus in Costa Rica blood was spilt as to whether it should be Cartago or San José, in Salvador the dispute lies between the towns of San Salvador and Santa Anna, in this Republic between Guatemala and Quetzaltenango, in Honduras Comayagua and Teg-ucigalpa are rivals, and in Nicaragua as Your Lordship is aware the inhabitants of León and Granada are at this moment endeavoring to exterminate each other in the same quarrel." Foreign Office 15/85 No. 38 (London), Charles L. Wyke to Clarendon, Guatemala City, July 29, 1855.

53. Diana Balmori, Stuart F. Voss, and Miles L. Wortman, *Notable Family Networks in Latin America* (Chicago: University of Chicago Press, 1984), p. 59 *passim*.

54. Cardenal, "Acerca de las 'Reflexiones,' " pp. 34 and 45.

55. *Gaceta Oficial de Nicaragua* (Granada), March 19, 1853.

56. "Informe del Jefe del Estado de Nicaragua, Manuel Antonio de la Cerda, al Con-greso Federal, sobre la Situación de Nicaragua en 1825,"*Revista de la Academia de Geografía e Historia de Nicaragua*, 10:2 (October 1950), p. 135.

57. Jacobo Haefkerns,*Viaje a Guatemala Centroamérica* (Guatemala City: Editorial Universitaria, 1969), p. 167.

58. Scherzer, *Travels*, I, 114. In a letter dated May 12, 1931, Augusto César Sandino denigrated the parties in these words, "Our people have been so degraded by ignorance that neither Liberals nor Conservatives know what they are arguing about, to the extreme that there are many Liberals in name who are more Conservative in fact than those who call themselves Conservatives." See Karl Bermann, ed., *Sandino without Frontiers. Selected Writings of Augusto César Sandino* (Hampton, Va.: Compita Publishing, 1988), p. 91.

59. Letter to Dionisio de la Quadra, November 12, 1822. Printed in "Documentos Posteriores a la Independencia,"*Revista de la Academia de Geografía e Historia de Nicaragua, 4:2 (August 1942), p. 13.*

60. *Mentor Nicaragüense* (Granada), December 4, 1841.

61. Pedro Francisco de la Rocha, *Revista Política sobre la Historia de la Revolución de Nicaragua en Defensa de la Administración del Ex-Director Don José León Sandoval* (Granada: Imprenta de la Concepción, 1847), reprinted in the *Revista del Pensamiento Centroamericano*, 180 (July-September 1983), p. 33.

62. Juan E. de la Rocha, *Discurso Pronunciado*.

63. Lanuza Matamoros, "Comercio Exterior de Nicaragua," pp. 110–111.

64. The speech appears in Chamorro Zelaya, *Fruto Chamorro*, p. 117.

65. Rivas, "Los Partidos Políticos," p. 8.

66. Ibid., p. 3.

67. Ibid., p. 4.

68. Jorge Eduardo Arellano, "El Garibaldi Frustrado de Nicaragua (Perfil de Máximo Jerez: 1818–1881)," *Cuadernos Centroamericanos de Historia* (Managua), 1 (January-April 1988), p. 14.

69. Quoted in Jorge Eduardo Arellano, "El Primer Historiador de Nicaragua: Pedro Francisco de la Rocha y su *Revista Política sobre la Historia de la Revolución de Nicaragua,*"*Revista del Pensamiento Centroamericano*, 180 (July-September 1983), p. 10.

70. *Mensaje de S. E. el General Director Supremo Fruto Chamorro a la Asamblea Constituyente del Estado de Nicaragua, Instalada el 22 de Enero de 1854* (Managua, 1854).

71. Chargé d'Affaires of Peru, Felipe Barriga Alvarez, to Minister of Foreign Relations, Lima, from León, August 31, 1850. Reprinted in the *Revista de la Academia de Geografía e Historia de Nicaragua, 9:2* (August 1947), p. 86.

72. Quoted in Chamorro Zelaya, *Fruto Chamorro*, p. 114.

73. Rivas, "Los Partidos Políticos," p. 8.

74. José Coronel Urtecho, "Introducción a la Epoca de Anarquía en Nicaragua, 1821–1857," *Revista Conservadora del Pensamiento Centroamericano*, 134 (November 1971), p. 45.

75. The initials S. C. are encountered frequently in the 1830s, 1840s, and 1850s, but no one has been able to attribute them to any specific intellectual, the author of "Estado de los Pueblos al Establecerse la República Democrática." The articles in this collection were originally published in the *Registro Oficial* of 1847 and collected and reprinted in the *Revista de la Academia de Geografía e Historia de Nicaragua* 11:1 (April 1951), pp. 73–75. (*Registro* and *Rejistro* spellings were interchangeable. In this and similar cases I have retained the spelling at the time

of the original publication.)

76. Amaru Barahona, "Análisis y Significado de Nuestra Independencia de España,"*Revista Nicaragüense de Ciencias Sociales* (Managua), 2:3 (December 1987), p. 27.
77. S.C., "Estado de los Pueblos," pp. 67–75.
78. González Saravia, *Bosquejo Político*, p. 8.
79. Squier, *Nicaragua*, p. 648.
80. Levy, *Notas Geográficas*, p. 240. Frederick Boyle left this ethnic description in the mid-1860s: "For it should be remembered that the population of Nicaragua is not white. Two-fifths are Indians of unmixed blood, two-fifths mestizos, or Indian half-breeds, and the remaining fifth negro, or mulatto, or Sambo. Possibly there may be ten families in the whole country whose geneological tree, if they possessed one, could show an ancestry of European blood unmixed; but of those we saw judging from their outward appearance only, which is the lightest test of all, one stock alone, the Chamorro, seemed to us to present sufficient signs of purity."*A Ride*, I, 63-64.
81. Romero Vargas, *Las Estructuras*, pp. 238-239.
82. Jorge Eduardo Arellano, *El Padre-Indio Tomás Ruiz, Prócer de Centroamérica* (Managua: Ediciones Nacionales, 1979).
83. Byam, *Wild Life*, p. 12.
84. Ibid., p. 19
85. Ibid., p. 24.
86. Ibid., p. 25.
87. Chamorro Zelaya, *Fruto Chamorro*, p. 129.
88. Letter from Sandoval to Pablo Buitrago, León, February 18, 1846, printed in the *Revista de la Academia de Geografía e Historia de Nicaragua*, 7:3 (November 1945), p. 48.
89. Ministerial report submitted to the legislature of Nicaragua, February 16, 1853, reprinted in Scherzer, *Travels*, I, 115.
90. José Dolores Gámez, *Historia de Nicaragua* (Managua: Tipografía Nacional, 1889), p. 472.
91. Belli, "Un Ensayo de Interpretación," p. 50.
92. Ibid., p. 51.
93. De la Rocha, *Revista Política*, p. 25.
94. *Travels*, I, 209–210; for his similar experiences elsewhere in Nicaragua, see pp. 143–144 and 207.
95. *Rejistro Oficial* (Managua), June 5, 1847; de la Rocha, *Revista Política*, p. 25.
96. The first edition of John Stuart Mill's *Considerations on Representative Government* bears the date 1861. These citations come from the later edition (New York: Liberal Arts Press, 1958), p. 229.
97. "One of the strongest hindrances to improvement [of representative government], up to a rather advanced stage, is an inveterate spirit of locality. Portions of mankind in many other respects capable of and prepared for freedom, may be unqualified for amalgamating into even the smallest nation. Not only may jealousies and antipathies repel them from one another and bar all possiblity of voluntary union, but they may not yet have acquired any of the feelings or habits

which would make the union real, supposing it to be nominally accomplished. . . . I am not aware that history furnishes any example in which a number of these political atoms or corpuscles have coalesced into a body and learned to feel themselves one people, except through previous subjection to a central authority common to all. It is through the habit of deferring to that authority, entering into its plans and subserving its purposes, that a people such as we have supposed receive into their minds the conception of large interests common to a considerable geographical extent. Such interests, on the contrary, are necessarily the predominant consideration in the mind of the central ruler; and through the relations more or less intimate, which he progressively establishes with the localities they become familiar to the general mind." Ibid., pp. 61–62.

98. Ibid., pp. 59 and 61.
99. De la Rocha, *Revista Política*.
100. Ibid., p. 26.
101. S.C., "Estado de los Pueblos," pp. 67-75.
102. Gámez, *Historia de Nicaragua*, p. 518.
103. Library of Congress, Manuscript Division, The Papers of John Henry Wheeler. MS 16,736.1. Diary of Wheeler, December 23, 1854.
104. Scherzer, *Travels*, I, 68.
105. This quotation comes from Arellano, "El Primer Historiador," p. 10.
106. The list of historians contributing to this interpretation of the Nicaraguan past is lengthy. For another example see Chamorro Zelaya, *Fruto Chamorro*, p. 8.
107. Cardenal, "Acerca de las 'Reflexiones,'" pp. 23–47; Ileana Rodríguez, *Primer Inventorio del Invasor* (Managua: Editorial Nueva Nicaragua, 1984); and Jaime Wheelock Román, *Raíces Indígenas de la Lucha Anticolonialista en Nicaragua* (Managua: Editorial Nueva Nicaragua, 1981).
108. Ibid., p. 7.
109. Solórzano Fonseca, "Centro América en el Siglo XVIII," pp. 11–22; see particularly p. 18.
110. De la Rocha, *Revista Política*, p. 43.
111. Nicolas Buitrago Matus, *León: La Sombra de Pedrarias* (Managua: n.n., 1966), p. 196.
112. *Travel in Central America Being a Journal of Nearly Three Years Residence in the Country* (London: Longman, 1847), p. 161.
113. Thomas L. Karnes, *The Failure of Union. Central America, 1824–1960* (Chapel Hill: University of North Carolina Press, 1961), p. 47.
114. Coronel Urtecho *"Introducción a la Epoca de Anarquía."* p. 41.
115. Sara L. Barquero, *Gobernantes de Nicaragua. 1825–1947*, 2nd ed. (Managua: Ministerio de Instrucción Pública, 1945), p. 33.
116. "In Medieval feudalism, as in many class-divided societies . . . courts were usually peripatetic. . . . The lack of a capital city . . . both contributed to, and expressed, the low degree of territorial integration." Anthony Giddens, *The Nation-State and Violence. Volume Two of a Contemporary Critique of Historical Materialism* (Berkeley: University of California Press, 1985), p. 117; also see Gratus Halftermeyer, *Managua Através de la Historia, 1846–1946* (León: Edi-

torial Hospicio, 1946), p. 13.

117. Chamorro Zelaya, *Fruto Chamorro*, pp. 90–94; de la Rocha, *Revista Política*, p. 59; "La Controversia que Decidió," *Revista de la Academia de Geografía e Historia de Nicaragua*, 7:3 (November 1945), pp. 43–58.

118. Radell, "An Historical Geography," p. 179.

119. "A los Habitantes del Mismo Estado," April 7, 1830, reprinted in the *Revista de la Academia de Geografía e Historia de Nicaragua*, 10:3 (December 1950), p. 258.

120. General Minister Agustín Vijil to the Federal Government, April 5, 1830. Reprinted in Huete, *Estampas*, pp. 45–46.

121. *La Opinión Pública* (León), May 9, 1833.

122. Gámez, *Historia de Nicaragua*, pp. 471–472.

123. The Conservatives freely and frequently published their criticisms of the constitution. *Mentor Nicaragüense* (Granada), November 6, 1841, lamented the excessive liberty it bestowed. Felipe Sáenz thought too much power went to the legislature. *Manifiesto que Hace el que Suscribe a los Pueblos de Centro-América, del Motivo por que Fué Arrojado con Otros Fuera de Su Patria la Ciudad de Rivas; en el que se Propone Contestar el Papel Llamado Vindicación, Suscrito por Doce Indivíduos, sobre la Calumnia que se Hace a Su Familia con Motivo de los Atentados del 3 de Diciembre de 1848* (San José: Imprenta de la Paz, 1849), reprinted in the *Revista de la Academia de Geografía e Historia de Nicaragua*, 6:1 (April 1944), pp. 41–61. Rafael Lebrón complained that the constitution tied the hands of the executive, depriving him of the power necessary to govern. Isidro Urtecho, "Galería de Notables Rivenses: Rafael Lebrón," *Revista de la Academia de Geografía e Historia de Nicaragua*, 2:1 (September 1937), pp. 357–361. Both Fruto Chamorro and José María Estrada summarized before the Constituent Assembly of 1854 the reasons why Nicaragua required a more "pragmatic" constitution. *Mensaje del Director Supremo de Nicaragua Jeneral Don Fruto Chamorro a la A. C. del Estado Instalada el 22 de Enero del Año de 1854; y Discurso Pronunciado por el Presidente de la Misma Asamblea Lic. Don José María Estrada en el Acto de la Instalación* (Managua: Imprenta de la Libertad, 1854).

124. Emilio Alvarez L., *Ensayo Biográfico del Prócer José León Sandoval* (Managua: Editorial Atlántida, 1947).

125. De la Rocha, Revista Política, pp. 64–65.

126. *Registro Oficial* (Managua), September 26, 1846.

127. The Constitution of 1838 provides the most authoritative statement on the conduct of elections. A better understanding of its requirements will be found in Rafael Chamorro Mora, "Las Constituciones Políticas de Nicaragua," *Encuentro* (Managua), 21 (1984), p. 41; Alvarez L., *Ensayo Biográfico*, pp. 52–53; *Registro Oficial*, April 12, 1845. For a brief description of local elections in the nineteenth century see Juan Manuel Mendoza, *Historia de Diriamba* (Guatemala City: Imprenta Electra, 1920), p. 45.

128. José Dolores Gámez, *Historia Moderna de Nicaragua: Complemento a Mi Historia de Nicaragua* (Managua: Banco de América, 1975), p. 684.

129. *Mentor Nicaragüense*, (Granada), December 4, 1841.

130. Ibid., December 11, 1841
131. Chamorro Zelaya, *Fruto Chamorro*, p. 249.
132. Peter F. Stout provided a verbal portrait of Chamorro, whom he met and liked, in *Nicaragua: Past, Present, and Future* (Philadelphia: Potter, 1859), pp. 120–121. Jerónimo Pérez made the historical judgment: *Memorias para la Historia de la Revolución de Nicaragua en 1854*, reprinted in *Obras Históricas Completas* (Managua: Editorial San José, 1975), I, 6.
133. His inaugural address is reprinted in ibid., pp. 6–8.
134. Chamorro Zelaya, *Fruto Chamorro*, p. 214.
135. Domingo Lacayo et al. (22 signatures), *Supremo Director del Estado* (León: Imprenta del Orden, 1853); Gregorio Juárez et al. (18 signatures), *Supremo Director del Estado* (Granada: Imprenta del Orden, 1853); Fernando Guzmán et al. (18 signatures), *Supremo Director del Estado* (Granada: Imprenta del Orden, 1853).
136. In his study of Nicaragua's constitutional history, Emilio Alvarez concluded that the Constitution of 1838 had high ideals but little pragmatism. He criticized it for failing to invest the executive with sufficient powers to govern. His conclusions concurred with Chamorro's complaints. *Ensayo Histórico sobre el Derecho Constitucional de Nicaragua* (Managua: La Prensa, 1936), I, 51. For a brief comparative study of Nicaragua's constitutions see Chamorro Mora, "Las Constituciones Políticas," pp. 31–59.
137. Fruto Chamorro, *El Director Supremo a los Pueblos del Estado* (Managua: Imprenta de la Libertad, 1853).
138. Fruto Chamorro, *Al Público* (Managua: Imprenta de la Libertad, 1853).
139. National Archives. Diplomatic Dispatches, Nicaragua. Minister Solon Borland to Secretary of State William Marcy, December 10, 1853.
140 Ibid., November 10, 1853.
141. From an essay entitled "A Don León Alvarado," included in Pedro Ortiz and Pedro González, eds., *Frutos de Nuestro Huerto* (Managua: El País, 1888), reprinted in *Revista Conservadora del Pensamiento Centroamericano*, 123 (December 1970), pp. 51–52.
142. Thomas Belt, *The Naturalist in Nicaragua* (London: Bumpus, 1888), pp. 327–328.
143. Roberts, *Narrative*, p. 325.
144. G. A. Thompson, *Narrative of an Official Visit to Guatemala from Mexico* (London: John Murray, 1829), p. 462.
145. Von Buelow is quoted in "Emigración y Colonización en Interés del Comercio Alemán," *Revista de la Academia de Geografía e Historia de Nicaragua*, 28–29:1–4 (1964), pp. 25–26.
146. Roberts, *Narrative*, pp. 222–223.
147. John L. Sephens met Bridge in 1840: "My stopping place was the house of Mr. Bridge, an Englishman from one of the West India Islands, who had been resident in the country many years; he was married to a lady of León, but, on account of the convulsions of the country, they lived on his hacienda. The soil was rich for cotton and sugar, and Mr. Bridge said that here fifty men could manufacture sugar cheaper than two hundred in the islands: but the difficulty was, no reliance

could be placed upon Indian labor." *Incidents of Travel in Central America, Chiapas and Yucatan* (New Brunswick: Rutgers University Press, 1949), II, 20.

148. Von Buelow, "Emigración y Colonización," p. 13; Arellano, "El Primer Historiador," p. 11; Lanuza Matamoros, "Comercio Exterior de Nicaragua," pp. 120–121. Information on the lucrative tobacco monopoly the English merchants enjoyed is found in Andrés Vega Bolaños, *1840–1842: Los Atentados del Superintendente de Belice* (Managua: Editorial Unión, 1971), pp. 48–59; *Registro Oficial* (San Fernando), July 12, 1845.

149. Lanuza Matamoros, "Comercio Exterior de Nicaragua," p. 125; von Buelow, "Emigración y Colonización," p. 13.

150. Ibid.

151. Ibid.; "I started for Realejo. On the way I met Mr. Foster, the English vice-consul, coming to see me. He turned back and took me first to the *máquina*, or cotton factory, of which I had heard much on the road. It was the only one in the country." Stephens, *Incidents of Travel*, II, 21.

152. Robert Glasgow Dunlop, *Travel in Central America, Being a Journal of Nearly Three Years Residence in the Country* (London: Longman, 1847), pp. 55–56; *Registro Oficial* (San Fernando), July 12, 1845.

153. Squier to Secretary of State John M. Clayton, June 10, 1849. House of Representatives, 31st Congress, 1st Session, Executive Document No. 75. *Tigre Island and Central America. Message from the President of the United States, July 22, 1850*, p. 134.

154. Lanuza Matamoros, "Comercio Exterior de Nicaragua," pp. 125–131.

155. Ibid., p. 131.

156. Squier, *Nicaragua*, p. 653. George Byam spoke pessimistically of gold and silver production in 1840. *Wild Life*, pp. 52–55.

157. *Alberto Lanuza Matamoros*, "La Minería en Nicaragua (1821–1875)," *Anuario de Estudios Centroamericanos* (San José), 3 (1977), pp. 215–216 and 219.

158. Lanuza Matamoros, "Comercio Exterior de Nicaragua," pp. 114–115; 120; 121; 122.

159. *Mentor Nicaragüense* (Granada), November 13, 1841.

160. Von Buelow, in "Emigración y Colonización," pp. 9–11. Five piastres equaled one peso. Usually the peso was on a par with the dollar.

161. Dunlop, *Travel*, p. 11.

162. Jacob B. Stillman, *An 1850 Voyage: San Francisco to Baltimore by Sea and by Land* (Palo Alto, Calif.: Lewis Osborne, 1967), p. 26.

163. Dunlop, *Travel*, p. 11.

164. Adolphe Boucard, *Travels of a Naturalist* (London: Pardy, 1894), p. 109.

165. Squier, *Nicaragua*, p. 656.

166. Ibid., p. 633. Squier commented on the potential of the California markets in "Squier Notes on the Nicaraguan Debt."

167. Foster to Frederick Chatfield, Realejo, December 31, 1850. Foreign Office 15/70.

168. Import duties collected at San Juan del Norte in 1847 amounted to $48,655 pesos; in 1848, $35,728. *Correo del Istmo de Nicaragua* (León), September 16, 1849.

169. Scherzer, *Travels*, I, 116–117.

170. For 1845, see Chamorro Zelaya, *Fruto Chamorro*, pp. 81–82; for 1851, see "Squier Notes on the Nicaraguan Debt."

171. Ibid.

172. *Mentor Nicaragüense* (Granada), February 5, 1842.

173. Von Buelow, in "Emigración y Colonización," p. 29.

174. Squier, *Nicaragua*, p. 258. References to the use of cacao as a medium of exchange are frequent. Romero Vargas, *Las Estructuras*, p. 246; "The lower class of people have also another use for the cacao nuts: they make them serve as currency, one nut being considered equal to the fortieth part of a medio. In small trading transactions they are so regularly employed as money that you sometimes see scarcely any other in the fruit markets, so that in Nicaragua it is literally true that money grows upon trees." Scherzer, *Travels*, I, 124; "Although silver money circulated, wax candles and cacao beans served to buy small items." Mendoza, *Historia de Diriamba*, p. 31.

175. Alberto Lanuza Matamoros, "Nicaragua: Territorio y Población (1821–75)," *Revista del Pensamiento Centroamericano*, 151 (April—June 1976), pp. 3 and 9.

176. Blas A. Real Espinales, "Dinámica de Población y Estructura Agraria en Nicaragua," *Estudios Sociales Centroamericanos* (San José), 3:9 (September-December 1974), pp. 170–172.

177. "The population of Central America, all speculations and assertions to the contrary notwithstanding, is increasing with a rapidity not exceeded by that of our own country, leaving out our gains from emigration. The statistics of Costa Rica and El Salvador (the only States of which we possess the official data) show that in Costa Rica the proportion of births is 1 to 20, and of deaths 1 to 54 of the population. In El Salvador the births are 1 to 22, deaths 1 to 51 of the population. This is a greater proportion of births than in any country of Europe, and a less proportion of deaths than in any country in Europe, excepting Norway, where the deaths are 1 to 55. In other words, there are more births and fewer deaths in Central America, and a more rapid increase in population, and augmentation of labor, than in any country of Europe." Letter of E. G. Squier to U.S. Senator H. B. Anthony, New York, January 25, 1861. Printed in the *Providence Journal* (Providence, R.I.), February 2, 1861.

178. Wortman, *Government and Society*, p. 271.

179. Squier, *Nicaragua*, p. 649. Objective studies of traditional farming techniques are extremely rare, since most of the few studies use "Western" criteria of judgment, always under the assumption that more technology is better. A thoughtful study by Gene C. Wilken, *Good Farmers. Traditional Agricultural Resource Management in Mexico and Central America* (Berkeley: University of California Press, 1987), provides unusually sensitive insights into traditional agricultural resource management, concluding that much of it is highly effective. At one point, the author notes, "Traditional farmers respond much like their industrialized counterparts: they identify goals, minimize costs (most of which are labor), and maximize gains by careful use of available resources." (p. 263).

180. Squier, *Nicaragua*, p. 649.

181. Ibid., p. 441.

182. Ibid., p. 188.

183. Ibid., p. 431.
184. Mrs. Henry Grant Foote, *Recollections of Central America and the West Coast of Africa* (London: Newby, 1869), pp. 19–20.
185. Stout, *Nicaragua: Past, Present, and Future*, p. 98.
186. Ibid., p. 77. Carl Scherzer joined the chorus of praise for Masaya, calling it the "most industrious, peaceful, and prosperous of all the towns." He also cataloged the crafts. *Travels*, I, pp. 68, 70.
187. Charles Parke, "Journal of a Trip Across the Plains . . . and a Voyage from San Francisco to New Orleans via Nicaragua, 1849–50," Huntington Library (San Marino, Calif.). Manuscript HM 16996.
188. Wheelock, *Nicaragua: Imperialismo y Dictadura*, pp. 59–60.
189. Lanuza Matamoros, "Comercio Exterior de Nicaragua," p. 114.
190. Roberts, *Narrative*, p. 237.
191. Ibid., pp. 208, 212, and 215.
192. Ibid., p. 224.
193. Ibid., p. 225.
194. Dunlop, *Travel*, p. 251.
195. Von Buelow, "Emigración y Colonización," p. 28.
196. Bailey, *Central America*, pp. 122–123.
197. Scherzer, *Travels*, I, 68.
198. Von Buelow, in "Emigración y Colonización," p. 28.
199. Squier, *Nicaragua*, p. 258.
200. Ibid., pp. 292–293.
201. Lucien McLenathan Wolcott, "Journal of a Trip across the Plains . . . and Return Voyage to Ohio via Nicaragua," Huntington Library. Manuscript HM 26614.
202. Squier, *Nicaragua*, p. 259
203. Ibid., p. 258.
204. "The blind, the lame, and the sick are the only beggars I ever saw in Nicaragua. The necessaries of life are easily procured. Very little clothing is required. And one may plant maize or bananas; and there is plenty of work for all who are willing or obliged to labor; so the healthy and strong amongst the poorer classes lead an easy and pleasant life." Belt, *Naturalist*, pp. 160–161.
205. Squier, *Nicaragua*, pp. 652 & 134.
206. *El Nicaragüense* (Granada), November 24, 1855.
207. Lacayo, *Supremo Director del Estado* and Guzmán, *Supremo Director del Estado*.
208. Ibid.
209. Nicaragua. *Código de la Lejislación de la República de Nicaragua* (Managua : El Centro Americano, 1873), I, 206–207. An example of a case made for tax reductions appeared in the *Gaceta Oficial de Nicaragua* (Granada), March 27, 1852.

2. Father

1. Thomas Manning, an English merchant resident in Nicaragua, received frequent mention by travelers and in government accounts from the early 1820s to at least the early 1850s. He grew rich in León, where he owned an export firm and estates. Robert G. Dunlop, who met him in 1844, reported that he "turned

Roman Catholic to marry a mulatto lady, who is almost white, and very good looking. His house is the best in León." *Travel in Central America, Being a Journal of Nearly Three Years of Residence in the Country* (London: Longman, 1847), pp. 7–8.

2. Priests might marry young eloping couples when the woman was pregnant. Verena Martínez-Alier, *Marriage, Class and Colour in Nineteenth-Century Cuba. A Study of Racial Attitudes and Sexual Values in a Slave Society* (New York: Cambridge University Press, 1974), p. 44.

3. The Pragmatic Sanction issued by the Spanish monarch in 1776 and extended to the Americas two years later sought to strengthen parental authority over marriages to prevent ones that would "gravely offend family honor and jeopardize the integrity of the State." It decreed disinheritance as the penalty for breaking the law. Annulment was possible. Ibid., p. 11; Elizabeth Kuznesof and Robert Oppenheimer, "The Family and Society in Nineteenth-Century Latin America: An Historiographical Introduction," *Journal of Family History* (Fall 1985), p. 218; José Mata Gavidia affirmed that Spanish family organization with all the laws pertaining to it was transplanted to the New World, including the requirement of parental consent for marriage. *La Influencia de España en la Formación de la Nacionalidad Centroamericana* (Guatemala City: Unión Tipografía, 1943), p. 23.

4. Class and racial differences were legitimate reasons for parents to seek annulment of unapproved marriages. Martínez-Alier, *Marriage*, pp. 1 and 83.

5. Los Discípulos de Confucio (pseud.), *Primera Amonestación* (León: Imprenta de la Libertad, 1851).

6. Thomas Belt, *The Naturalist in Nicaragua*, 2nd ed. (London: Bumpus, 1888), p. 344.

7. "In Central America every State has a small number of soldiers, ill paid, worse fed and clothed, and of the lowest order of scoundrels; the officers being hardly a shade better, but with a little more method in their general conduct." George Byam also used the words "dissolute" and "ruffians" to describe the Nicaraguan army. *Wild Life in the Interior of Central America* (London: Parker, 1849), pp. 15–16.

8. Nicaragua. Ministerio de Guerra, *Reglamentos para la Organización, Réjimen, Disciplina y Conservación del Ejército del Estado de Nicaragua* (León: Imprenta de la Libertad, 1850).

9. José María Estrada, *Defensa del Poder Legislativo del Estado de Nicaragua* (Granada: Imprenta del Orden, 1851).

10. Jorge Eduardo Arellano, *Breve Historia de la Iglesia en Nicaragua, 1523–1979* (Managua: Editorial Manolo Morales, 1986), pp. 51–54.

11. *Oración Fúnebre, que en las Solemnes Exequias del Señor Presbítero Beneficiado Dr. D. J. Desiderio de la Quadra, Provisor, Vicario Capitular y Gobernador del Obispado de Nicaragua y Costa Rica, Pronunció el Señor Presbítero Dean D. Remijio Salazár en la Santa Iglesia Catedral el día 5 de Octubre de 1849* (León: Imprenta de Minerva, 1849).

12. An anonymous biography of him appears in "Apuntes Biográficos del Pbro. Don Pedro Solís," *Revista de la Academia de Geografía e Historia de Nicaragua*, 2:1

(September 1937), pp. 145–155.

13. Nicaragua. Ministerio de Relaciones del Supremo Gobierno, *Tenemos la Complacencia de Dar a la Luz Pública la Carta Respetable que la Santidad de Pío IX, Dirige al Excmo. Sr. Dr. Don Jorje de Viteri y Ungo, Dignísimo Obispo de Nicaragua* (León: Imprenta de la Paz, 1850).

14. *Esposición que S. E. el Illmo. Sr. Obispo Dr. D. Jorje de Viteri y Ungo, Dirijió a las Cámaras Lejislativas del Estado en Su Reunión del Presente Año* (León: Imprenta de la Paz, 1852) and *Para Conocimiento de los Estados Confederados Se Imprimen los Documentos Siguientes* (Comayagua: Imprenta de José M. Sánchez, 1852).

15. Pavón to Jorge Viteri, letter dated August 22, 1851. Ibid.

16. Arellano, *Breve Historia de la Iglesia*, pp. 57, 59; Manzar Foroohar, *The Catholic Church and Social Change in Nicaragua* (Albany: State University of New York Press, 1989), pp. 7–8.

17. Pavón to Tomás Manning, letter dated August 22, 1851. *Para Conocimiento de los Estados*.

18. José Coronel Urtecho, "La Familia de Zavala y la Política del Comercio en Centroamérica," *Revista del Pensamiento Centroamericano*, 141–142 (June–July, 1972), p. 2.

19. Diana Balmori, Stuart F. Voss, and Miles L. Wortman, *Notable Family Networks in Latin America* (Chicago: University of Chicago Press, 1984), pp. 4, 8, 23 *passim.* "In the nineteenth century the absence of effective government after independence and the disappearance of other corporate organizations created a vacuum into which the family moved as the dominant political and economic actor." Kuznesof and Oppenheimer, "The Family and Society," p. 219.

20. André Bourgiére, "Introduction," to Robert Foster and Orest Ranum, eds., *Family and Society: Selections from the Annales: Economics, Societies, Civilizations* (Baltimore: The Johns Hopkins University Press, 1976), pp. viii–ix.

21. Gordon J. Schochet, *Patriarchalism in Political Thought: The Authoritarian Family and Political Speculation and Attitudes Especially in Seventeenth-Century England* (New York: Basic Books, 1975), pp. 55 and 64.

22. Ibid., pp . 7–8; St. Thomas Aquinas, *De Reimine Principum* in Alessandro Passerin d'Entreves, *Aquinas: Selected Political Writings* (Oxford: Blackwell, 1978), p.9.

23. Schochet, *Patriarchalism*, pp. 20, 22–23; Hannah Arendt, *Between Past and Future: Six Exercises in Political Thought* (New York: Viking Press, 1961), p.117.

24. Gerald R. Leslie, *The Family in Social Context* (New York: Oxford University Press, 1967), p. 170.

25. The examples are many in Nicaraguan history. The most notorious case involved the Somoza dynasty. See José A. Alonso, "Elites Gobernantes y 'Familismo' en Nicaragua," *Estudios Centroamericanos* (San Salvador), 28:296 (June 1973), pp. 331–334.

26. José Dolores Gámez, *Apuntamientos para la Biografía de Máximo Jerez* (Managua: Tipografía Nacional, 1893), p. 26; Berta Corredor, *La Familia en América Latina* (Bogotá: Centro de Investigaciones Sociales, 1962), p. 17.

27. Coronel Urtecho, "La Familia Zavala," p. 1.
28. Francisco Pérez Estrada, *Ensayos Nicaragüenses* (Managua: PINSA, 1976), p. 147; Pablo Antonio Cuadra and Francisco Pérez Estrada, *Muestrario del Folklore Nicaragüense* (Managua: Fondo de Promoción Cultural Nicaragüense, 1978), p. 345.
29. Juan Manuel Mendoza, *Historia de Diriamba* (Guatemala City: Imprenta Electra, 1920), p. 33.
30. David Leverenz, *The Language of Puritan Feeling: An Exploration in Literature, Psychology, and Social History* (New Brunswick: Rutgers University Press, 1980), p. 11.
31. Manuel Castrillo Gámez, *Estudios Históricos de Nicaragua* (Managua: Editorial Asel, 1947), p. 3.
32. Pedro Joaquin Chamorro Zelaya, *Fruto Chamorro* (Managua: Editorial Unión, 1960), pp. 194–195.
33. Belt, *The Naturalist,* p. 177.
34. "Causa contra Bernardo Méndez por Considerársele Autor de la Revolución del 25 de Enero de 1837," *Revista de la Academia de Geografía e Historia de Nicaragua,* 1:3 (February 1937), p. 362
35. Castrillo Gámez, *Estudios Históricos*, p.3.
36. E. G. Squier, *Nicaragua: Its People, Scenery, Monuments, Resources, Condition and Proposed Canal* (New York: Harper, 1860), p. 253.
37. Ibid.
38. Belt, *The Naturalist,* p. 213.
39. Castrillo Gámez, *Estudios Históricos,* p. 3.
40. To compare her role with that of a Mexican woman see Larissa Adler Lomnitz and Marisol Pérez-Lizaur, *A Mexican Elite Family, 1820–1980: Kinship, Class, and Culture* (Princeton University Press, 1987), pp. 212–214.
41. *Travels,* I, 75.
42. Entitled "Composición Poética de una Sra. Vecina del Sauce en el Departamento Occidental." The poet used the pseudonym "La Patriota del Sauce" and remains anonymous. Patriotism in this poem meant support of Granada in the war with León. *Defensor del Orden* (Granada), November 10, 1854.
43. *Integridad de Centro América* (Granada), January 8 and February 5, 1850.
44. *Gaceta Oficial de Nicaragua* (Granada), February 21, 1852.
45. Franco Ccrutti, "Gregorio Juárez: Apuntes y Documentos para Su Mejor Ubicación en la Historia Literaria Nicaragüense," *Revista Conservadora del Pensamiento Centroamericano,* 129 (June 1971), pp. 12–15.
46. An unused source for the study of women and, indeed, of society in general is the epitaph. I am grateful to Jorge Eduardo Arellano for generously sharing with me his xeroxed copy of "Colección, [de] Epitafios en Prosa y Verso Recogidos por José Domingo Zapata desde el Año de 1854 a 1876. León, 1877."
47. Carl Scherzer, *Travels in the Free States of Central America: Nicaragua, Honduras, and San Salvador* (London: Longman, 1857), I, 145.
48. Belt, *The Naturalist,* p. 361.
49. Dan Stanislawski, *The Transformation of Nicaragua: 1519–1548* (Berkeley: University of California Press, 1983), pp. 7–8.

50. Mendoza, *Historia de Diriamba,* pp. 52–53.
51. Jorge A. Blanco G ., *Diriamba* (Managua : Editorial Atlántida, 1938), pp. 17-19.
52. *Gaceta Oficial de Nicaragua* (Granada), April 2, 1853.
53. Los Amigos del Progreso, *Paralelo de las Revoluciones* (Rivas: Imprenta Nueva, 1849).
54. *Eco Popular,* (Granada), July 13, 1854.
55. Pedro Francisco de la Rocha, *Revista Política sobre la Historia de la Revolución de Nicaragua en Defensa de la Administración del Ex-Director Don José León Sandoval* (Granada: Imprenta de la Concepción, 1847), reprinted in the *Revista del Pensamiento Centroamericano,* 180 (July-September 1983), p. 38. Jerónimo Pérez lamented common crime and rowdiness in the Masaya of this period: see "Mis Recuerdos" in *Obras Históricas Completas* (Managua: Colección Cultural Banco de America, 1975), pp. 778-779. The *Registro Oficial* (Managua; June 5, 1847) fretted about the deteriorating state of society: "Lack of respect for the fatherland, law, and authority has created confusion."
56. "El Estado Libre de Nicaragua en Centroamérica," *Revista de la Academia de Geografá e Historia de Nicaragua,* 30 (January-June 1965), p. 102.
57. *Mentor Nicaragüense,* December 4, 1841.
58. Chamorro Zelaya, *Fruto Chamorro,* p. 85. Thomas Belt noted the drinking and the fights it engendered: "In their drinking bouts they often quarrel among themselves, and slash about with their long heavy knives, inflicting ugly gashes and often maiming each other for life. . . . Fortunately even at these times they do not interfere with foreigners, their quarrels being amongst themselves, and either faction [party] fights or about women, or gambling losses." *The Naturalist,* p. 296.
59. Chamorro Zelaya, *Fruto Chamorro,* p.82
60. Francisco Díaz Zapata, *Muy Honorable Cámara* (Managua: Imprenta de la Paz, 1852).
61. "Datos de Curia de la Ciudad de Granada durante el Año de 1846. Granada, Enero 1, 1847. Agustín Vijil," *Revista del Archivo General de la Nación,* :l (January-March 1964), pp. 5–7
62. Juan Cruz Ruiz de Cabañas, *Carta Pastoral que el Ilustrísimo Señor Don Juan Cruz de Cabañas, Obispo de Nicaragua, Dirige a Todos los Fieles de su Diócesis* (Madrid: Imprenta de Don Benito Cano, 1795), pp. 41–42.
63. Four issues of the *Mentor Nicaragüense* carried the letter: January 15 and 22; February 5; and April 16, 1842.
64. Schochet, *Patriarchalism in Political Thought,* p.6.
65. "Galería de Notables Rivenses," *Revista Conservadora del Pensamiento Centroamericano.* 88 (January, 1968), p. 22. In a poetic salute to Nicolás de la Rocha upon his death in 1846, his son, Juan Eligio, praised his education of his children, his obedience to his own father, faithfulness as a husband, devotion and love as a father, virtue as a citizen, and a zealous Christian commitment. *Rejistro Oficial* (Managua), December 5, 1846.
66. Registro Oficial (León), February 7, 1846.
67. *Correo del Istmo de Nicaragua* (León), December 1, 1849.
68. *Gaceta Oficial de Nicaragua* (Granada), January 24, 1852.

69. De la Rocha, *Revista Poltíca*, p. 53.
70. Norberto Ramírez, *Nicaragüenses* (León: Imprenta de Minerva, 1849); *Correo del Istmo de Nicaragua* (León), July 1, 1849.
71. *Graceta Oficial de Nicaragua* (Granada), October 4, 1853.
72. Ibid., April 2, 1853.
73. *Proclama del Director Supremo Fruto Chamorro sobre el Complot y su Represión* (Managua, November 21, 1853). For other similar remarks see *Gaceta Oficial de Nicaragua* (Granada), April 23, 1853.
74. Fernando Guzmán et al., *Supremo Director del Estado* (Granada: Imprenta del Orden, 1853).
75. Anonymous, *Oración Suplicatoria* (Granada: Imprenta del Orden, ca. 1854).
76. Paul Levy, *Notas Geográficas y Económicas sobre la República de Nicaragua* (Paris: Librería Española de E. Denne Schmitz, 1873), p. 274.
77. "The Patriarchal Theory, stated in its simplest form, represents society as the enlargement of the family, and the family as a group composed at first of a man and his wife and children . . . all of these would acknowledge the authority of the First Father, as chief or patriarch, as long as he lived." Donald McLennon, ed., *The Patriarchal Theory: Based on the Papers of the Late John Ferguson McLennan* (London: Macmillan, 1885), p. 1.
78. Humberto Belli, "Un Ensayo de Interpretación sobre las Luchas Políticas Nicaragüenses," *Revista del Pensamiento Centroamericano,* 157 (October-December 1977), pp. 51–53. The continuity in Nicaraguan history of tribute to and faith in the patriarchate is very impressive. In announcing its political platform in 1989, the National Opposition Union (UNO), the coalition opposing the Revolution, proclaimed its determination to strengthen the family and to pay homage and respect to parents as two of its planks.
79. Mark D. Szuchman, *Order, Family and Community in Buenos Aires, 1810-1860* (Stanford: Stanford University Press, 1988), p. 230.
80. Ibid., p. 231.
81. Ibid., p. 232.
82. Gilberto Freyre, *The Masters and the Slaves: A Study in the Development of Brazilian Civlization* (Berkeley: University of California Press, 1986) and *The Mansions and the Shanties* (Berkeley: University of California Press, 1986). Darrell E. Levi studied a dominant elite family across time in his *The Prados of São Paulo, Brazil: An Elite Family and Social Change, 1840-1930* (Athens, Ga.: The University of Georgia Press, 1987). On pp. 5-9, he defined and discussed "the old patriarchal model." José Murilo de Carvalho convincingly argues the general unity of the political elites as a major contribution to the political order. "Political Elites and State Building: The Case of Nineteenth-Century Brazil," *Comparative Studies in Society and History,* 24 (July 1982), pp. 378-399.
83. In his Christmas message for 1988, the heir and pretender to the Brazilian throne, Prince Luíz de Orleans e Bragança, spoke of his ancestor Emperor Pedro II as "the respected and loved patriarch of that immense family that was then Brazil." A copy of that message is in the library of the author.
84. On a much smaller scale, this reality coincides with the observation Maurice Zeitlin and Richard Earl Ratchiff make about Chile: "To belong to a landed cap-

italist family is thus also to belong to one of the nation's reigning political families." *Landlords and Capitalists: The Dominant Class of Chile* (Princeton: Princeton University Press, 1988), p. 10.

85. Byam, *Wild Life*, p. 14.
86. Scherzer, *Travels*, I, 52.
87. Squier, *Nicaragua*, p. 557.
88. Levy, *Notas Geográficas*, p. 160.
89. Squier, *Nicaragua*, pp. 517–520.
90. Scherzer, *Travels*, I, 120.
91. Squier, *Nicaragua*, pp. 125–127; 134–139.
92. David Richard Radell, "An Historical Geography of Western Nicaragua: The Spheres of Influence of León, Granada, and Managua, 1519–1965," (Ph.D. diss., University of California, Berkeley), p. 167.
93. Scherzer, *Travels*, I, 123.
94. Dunlop, *Travel*, pp. 6, 12, 13.
95. Squier, *Nicaragua*, p. 344.
96. Ibid., p. 343.
97. Radell, "An Historical Geography of Western Nicaragua," pp. 154–156.
98. Julius Froebel, *Seven Years' Travel in Central America, Northern Mexico, and the Far West of the United States* (London: Bentley, 1859), p. 122.
99. Belt, *The Naturalist*, p. 49.
100. Orlando W. Roberts, *Narrative of Voyages and Excursions on the East Coast and in the Interior of Central America* (Edinburgh: Constable, 1827), p. 187.
101. Froebel, *Seven Years' Travel*, p. 192.
102. Squier, *Nicaragua*, p. 409.
103. Belt, *The Naturalist*, p. 189.
104. John Baily, *Central America: Describing Each of the States of Guatemala, Honduras, Salvador, Nicaragua, and Costa Rica* (London: Trelawney Saunders, 1850), p. 121.
105. Blas A. Real Espinales, "Dinámica de Población y Estructura en Nicaragua," *Estudios Sociales Centroamericanos* (San José), 3:9 (September-December 1974), p. 168.
106. Alphonse Dumartray and Pedro Rouhaud list the seven most populous cities in 1833 as: León (30,000); Masaya (20,000); Rivas (20,000); Managua (12,000); Granada (10,000); Chinandega (5,000); and Nanadaime (3,000). *Opúsculo sobre la República de Centro-América y Particularmente sobre los Estados de Nicaragua y Costa Rica* (Paris: Librería Americana, 1833), p. 8.
107. For thoughtful generalizations on the town plan in nineteenth-century Nicaragua, see Levy, *Notas Geográficas*, p. 265. To a remarkable degree the Nicaraguan cities conformed to the generalities posited by Gideon Sjoberg, *The Preindustrial City. Past and Present* (Glencoe, Ill.: The Free Press, 1960).
108. Roberts, *Narrative*, p. 234.
109. Scherzer, *Travels*, I, 59.
110. Froebel, *Seven Years' Travel*, p. 33.
111. John L. Stephens, *Incidents of Travel in Central America, Chiapas and Yucatan* (New Brunswick: Rutgers University Press, 1949), II, 14.

112. Squier, *Nicaragua* p. 241.
113. Roberts, *Narrative*, p. 224.
114. Stephens, *Incidents of Travel*, II, 17.
115. Jacob D. B. Stillman, *An 1850 Voyage: San Francisco to Baltimore by Sea and by Land* (Palo Alto: Lewis Osborne, 1967), p. 39.
116. Scherzer, *Travels*, I, 70.
117. Frederick Boyle, *A Ride Across a Continent: A Personal Narrative of Wanderings through Nicaragua and Costa Rica* (London: Bentley, 1868), I, 142–143.
118. Belt, *The Naturalist*, p. 49.
119. Scherzer, *Travels*, I, 90–91.
120. Ibid., p. 61.
121. The elite engaged directly in commerce. When Orlando Roberts called on the Governor of Granada in 1820, Crisanto Sacasa, he found him and his wife at work: "On calling next day at the Governor's, I found him and all his household, assorting a large quantity of cocoa and indigo, which had that morning arrived from Nicaragua [Rivas] . . . The principal people consider it no degradation to be employed in the meanest offices of trade. The produce of a farm, for instance cheese, butter and milk, were retailed under the immediate superintendance of the Governor's lady; who also sold coarse checks [doubtless a reference to crude, brown cakes of sugar], and some other articles, the manufacture of the country." *Narrative*, p. 240. In 1865, Boyle commented, "With the solitary exception of the Chamorro family, every man of wealth or birth in Nicaragua keeps a shop, whatever may be his other avocations; and this is the case throughout Central America, except Guatemala. All the booted class keep a shop, or have an interest in that of some one else; therefore they are aristocratic. After all, if there must be distinctions of class, this seems to be a very proper line to draw, and it has the advantage of being easily recognizable."*A Ride*, I, 121–122.
122. *Mentor Nicaragüense*, November 31, 1841.
123. Bedford Pim, *Dottings on the Roadside in Panama, Nicaragua and Mosquito* (London: Chapman and Hall, 1869), p. 43.
124. Radell, "An Historical Geography of Western Nicaragua," p. 233.
125. Squier, *Nicaragua*, p. 241.
126. Ibid. p. 242; many commented in a similar fashion. For another example see Stillman, *An 1850 Voyage*, p. 36.
127. *Don Dionisio de Herrera Propone a la Asamblea del Estado de Nicaragua un Plan de Estudios. Año 1831*, reprinted in the *Revista de la Academia de Geografía e Historia de Nicaragua*, 10:3 (December 1950), pp. 263–264.
128. Jesús de la Rocha, *Informe Presentado por el Ministro Interino de Relaciones Interiores y Exteriores a las Cámaras Legislativas de Nicaragua* (Granada: Imprenta del Orden, 1853), p. 28.
129. *Mentor Nicaragüense*, November 6, 1841.
130. José Luís Romero, *A History of Argentine Political Thought* (Stanford University Press, 1963), p. 145.
131. Pérez, "Mis Recuerdos," *Obras*, pp. 765–816.
132. De la Rocha, *Revista Política*, p. 43.

133. Ibid., p. 44.
134. Sebastián Salinas, *Informe Presentado al Cuerpo Legislativo por el Secretario del Despacho de Relaciones Interiores y Exteriores* (León: Imprenta de la Libertad, 1850), p. 22
135. Jesús de la Rocha, *Informe Presentado por el Ministro Interino*, p. 28.
136. Squier, *Nicaragua*, p. 378.
137. Ibid., p. 216.
138. Jesús de la Rocha, *Informe Presentado por el Ministro Interino*.
139. *Gaceta Oficial de Nicaragua* (Granada), March 26, 1853.
140. Scherzer, *Travels*, I, 119.
141. *Nicaragua: Past, Present, and Future* (Philadelphia: Potter, 1859), pp. 108–109.
142. Scherzer, *Travels*, I, 118.
143. Pedro Francisco de la Rocha, "Reforma de la Instrucción Pública," published in the *Gaceta de Nicaragua* (Granada, 1850), reprinted in the *Revista del Pensamiento Centroamericano*, 180 (July-September 1983), p. 82.
144 Ibid., p. 81.
145. *Memoria Presentada al Primer Congreso Legislativo de Nicaragua por el Sr. Ministro de Fomento, Instrucción y Crédito Público. El Día 14 de Enero de 1859* (Granada: Imprenta de El Centro-Americano, 1859).
146. De la Rocha, "Reforma de la Instrucción," p. 80.
147. The intellectuals included in this study are: Francisco Barberena (1822–1888); Pablo Buitrago (1807–1882); Francisco Castellón (1815–1854); Fruto Chamorro (1806–1855); Rosalío Cortés (dates unknown); Carmen Díaz (1835–1892); Francisco Díaz Zapata (1812–1865); Juan Iribarren (1827–1854); Máximo Jerez (1818–1881); Gregorio Juárez (1800–1879); Jerónimo Pérez (1828–1884); José Laureano Pineda (1802–1852); Anselmo H. Rivas (1826–1904); Jesús de la Rocha (1812–1881); Juan Eligio de la Rocha (1815–1873); Pedro Francisco de la Rocha (c1820–1881); José Benito Rosales (17??-1850); Sebastián Salinas (18??–1866); Buenaventura Selva (1820–1900); Toribio Tijerino Pomar (1808–1850); Agustín Vijil (1801–1867); Juan José Zavala (1797–1849).
148. This anonymous intellectual wrote well-organized and convincing essays that revealed a considerable breadth of knowledge.
149. For a useful discussion of these topics within the context of European history, consult Miroslav Hroch, *Social Preconditions of National Revival in Europe: A Comparative Analysis of the Social Composition of Patriotic Groups among the Smaller European Nations* (New York: Cambridge University Press, 1985).
150. Jorge Eduardo Arellano, *Bibliografía General de Nicaragua. Primera Entrega: 1674–1900* (Managua: Dirección General de Bibliotecas y Archivos, 1981), pp. 6–7.
151. Instituto Centroamericano de Historia, Universidad Centroamericana, *Catálogo de la Exposición Treinta Años de Periodismo en Nicaragua, 1830–1860* (Managua: n.n., 1971). pp. 2–9.
152. Jorge Eduardo Arellano, "El Primer Historiador de Nicaragua (Pedro Francisco de la Rocha y su *Revista Política sobre la Historia de la Revolución de Nicaragua*)," *Revista del Pensamiento Centroamericano*, 180 (July-September 1983), pp. 7–21.

153. Jorge Eduardo Arellano, *Panorama de la Literatura Nicaragüense. Epoca Anterior a Darío (1503–1881)* (Managua: Editora Alemana, 1968), p. 47.
154. Manuel Ignacio Pérez Alonso offers a brief peek into a late colonial library in his essay "Una Biblioteca Granadina del Siglo XVIII," in the introduction to Pedro Ximena, *Reales Exequias por D. Carlos III y Real Proclamación de D. Carlos IV* (Managua: Banco Central de Nicaragua, 1974), pp. xxiii–xxxviii.
155. Jorge Eduardo Arellano, *Diccionario de las Letras Nicaragüenses. Primera Entrega: Escritores de la Epoca Colonial y el Siglo XIX* (Managua: Biblioteca Nacional Rubén Darío, 1982), p. 111.
156. Stillman, *An 1850 Voyage, pp. 48–49.*
157. Arellano, *Panorama de la Literatura Nicaragüense, p. 50.*
158. Jorge Eduardo Arellano, *Historia de la Universidad de León. Epoca Colonial* (León: Editorial Universitaria UNAM, 1973), p. 124.
159. Chester J. Zelaya Goodman, *El Bachiller Osejo y la Introducción de las Ideas Ilustradas en Costa Rica* (San José: Ciudad Universitaria, 1967), pp. 4–6; Arellano, *Historia de la Universidad de León*, p. 125.
160. Arellano, *Panorama de la Literatura Nicaragüense, p. 45.*
161. Arellano, "El Primer Historiador," pp. 13–14.
162. *Pérez,"Mís Recuerdos,"Obras*, pp. 773–774.
163. Carlos Cuadra Pasos, "Apuntes Biográficos," in Anselmo H. Rivas, *Nicaragua. Su Pasado. Ojeada Retrospectiva* (Managua: La Prensa, 1936), p. iv.
164. Squier, *Nicaragua*. pp. 342–343.
165. Norberto Ramírez, *Honorables Senadores Y Representantes* (Managua: Imprenta de la Paz, 1849).
166. Lowell Gudmundson ably described and analyzed the complexities of Costa Rica in *Costa Rica before Coffee: Society and Economy on the Eve of the Export Boom* (Baton Rouge: Louisiana State University Press, 1986). The Costa Rican historian Clotilde Obregón provides a meaty study of the Carrillo period in her *Carrillo: Una Epoca y un Hombre, 1835–1842* (San José: Editorial Costa Rica, 1989). The abundant data of Gudmundson and Obregón allow a useful contrast and comparison between Costa Rica and Nicaragua during the early years of independence. For some Nicaraguan observations on the Costa Rica situation, see José Coronel Urtecho, "Introducción a la Epoca de Anarquía en Nicaragua, 1821–1857," *Revista Conservadora del Pensamiento Centroamericano*, 134 (November 1971), p. 41.
167. S.C., "Estado de los Pueblos al Establecerse la República Democrática," articles published in the *Registro Oficial* of 1847, collected and republished in the *Revista de la Academia de Geografía e Historia de Nicaragua*, 11:1 (April 1851), pp. 67–75.
168. Carlos Monge Alforo, *Historia de Costa Rica*, 9th ed. (San José: Imprenta Trejos, 1959), p. 160.
169. Ibid., p. 157. To contrast the land policies of Guatemala and Costa Rica, consult for Costa Rica Obregón, *Carrillo*, pp. 93–95; and for Guatemala see Ralph Lee Woodard, Jr., *Social Revolution in Guatemala: The Carrera Revolt* (New Orleans: Tulane University, 1971), p. 68; Manuel Coronado Aguilar, *Apuntes Históricos Guatemalenses* (Guatemala City: Editorial José de Pineda Ibarra,

1975), pp. 482–486; and E. Bradford Burns, *The Poverty of Progress. Latin America in the Nineteenth Century* (Berkeley: University of California Press, 1980), pp. 97–105.
170. Stephens, *Incidents*, I, 219.
171. Ibid., II, 20.
172. Squier, *Nicaragua*, p. 508.
173. Boyle, *Ride across a Continent*, I, 60.
174. Joaquín Elizondo, La Infraestructura de Nicaragua en 1860 Examinada por un Hijo de Rivas, el Agricultor Joaquín Elizondo," *Revista Conservadora del Pensamiento Centroamericano*, 57 (June 1965), p.56.
175. Hebe Maria Mattos de Castro, "Beyond Masters and Slaves: Subsistence Agriculture as a Survival Strategy in Brazil during the Second Half of the Nineteenth Century," *Hispanic American Historical Review*, 68:3 (August 1988), pp. 485, 489; Maria Sylvia de Carvalho Franco, *Homens Livres na Ordem Escravocrata* (São Paulo: Universidade de São Paulo, Instituto de Estudos Brasileiros, 1974), p. 92 *passim*.
176. José Coronel Urtecho, "La Familia Zavala y la Política del Comercio en Centroamérica," *Revista del Pensamiento Centroamericano*, 141–142 (June-July 1972), p. 68.

3. Folk

1. The spelling varies, Güegüence or Güegüense. Authorities seem about equally divided in their preferences. I will spell it with a "c," apparently the historical spelling, unless it appears in a printed title with "s."
2. Daniel G. Brinton, *The Güegüence; A Comedy Ballet in the Náhuatl-Spanish Dialect of Nicaragua* (Philadelphia: Brinton, 1883), pp. xviii-xix.
3. Ibid., p. xlii; Francisco Pérez Estrada, *Estudios del Folklore Nicaragüense* (Managua: Brenes, 1968), pp. 39–40.
4. Enrique Peña Hernández includes *El Güegüence* among those "currently" danced in Nicaragua. *Folklore de Nicaragua* (Managua: n.n., 1986), p. 200; Pablo Antonio Cuadra, "El Güegüence, Comedia-Bailete Anónima de la Epoca Colonial,"*Revista Conservadora del Pensamiento Centroamericano*, 74 (November 1966), p. 7. In April 1989, a sophisticated, stylized puppet production of *El Güegüence* was given in Managua. Commenting on that production, Franz Galich wrote, "It is the foundation stone of Nicaraguan idenity, and its psychological influence continues to this day." "El Güegüence Vuelve a las Andanzas," *Ventana: Barricada Cultural* (Managua), April 8, 1989, p. 16.
5. Alberto Ordóñez Argüello, "'El Güegüence' o el Primer Grito Escénico del Mestizaje Americano,"*Boletín Nicaragüense de Bibliografía y Documentación*, 5 (May-June 1975), p. 19. "Macho-ratón" in the rural Central American vocabulary means "little mule." Quadra, "El Guëgüence," p. 15. In 1984 I observed an elaborate staging of this dance in Managua.
6. See particularly the "Introduction: Interpretations of the Dance in Anthropology" by Paul Spenser and the "Epilogue: Anthropology and the Study of Dance" by Peter Brinson in Paul Spenser, ed., *Society and the Dance* (New York: Cam-

bridge University Press, 1985). The Peruvian José María Argüedas referred to the significance of dance to Indians and mestizos in his novel *Deep Rivers* (Austin: University of Texas Press, 1978). On p. 193, for example, he spoke of dance as a means of "recognition" and "communication."

7. Nathan Wachtel, "The Vision of the Vanquished: The Spanish Conquest of America Represented in Indian Folklore," in Marc Ferro, ed., *Social Historians in Contemporary France: Essays from Annales* (New York: Harper, 1972), p. 232. Paul Connerton presents a convincing case of how ritual performances convey and strengthen social memory of the past. *How Societies Remember* (New York: Cambridge University Press, 1989). In his "Estudio Preliminar," Jorge Eduardo Arellano provides an outstanding sociohistoric interpretation: *El Güegüence o Macho Ratón. Bailete Dialogado de la Epoca Colonial* (Managua: Ediciones Americanas, 1984), pp. 7–75. The "encoded" meanings of folk dances seem to have attracted the attention of folklorists and social scientists only during the last half of the twentieth century. The distinguished Brazilian scholar Maria Isaura P. de Queiroz wrote about the "latent functions" of the folk dance in her *Sociologia e Folclore. A Dança de São Gonçalo num Povoado Bahiano* (Salvador, Bahia: Libraria Progresso Editora, 1958), pp. 71–74.

8. Brinton, *The Güegüence*, pp. 16–17.

9. Ordóñez Argüello, "El Güegüense, o el Primer Grito," p. 19. Franco Cerutti concurs. *El Güegüence y Otros Ensayos de Literatura Nicaragüense* (Rome: Bulzoni, 1983), p. 16.

10. Pablo Antonio Cuadra emphasized the dance-drama's "intention to criticize authority and to make fun of society." *El Nicaragüense*, 7th ed. (San José: Editorial Universitaria Centroamericana, 1976), p. 91.

11. Cerutti, *El Güegüence*, p. 23.

12. Galich, "El Güegüence Vuelve a las Andanzas," p. 16; see the commentary of Salvador Cardenal Argüello in Arellano, ed., *El Güegüence o Macho Ratón*, p. 18.

13. Ibid., p. 46. In 1977, Dávila Bolaños termed *El Güegüence* a "revolutionary epic drama" that was "anti-Spanish, anti-Catholic, anti-colonialist, and anti-slavery." *Indice de la Mitología Nicaragüense* (Estelí, Nicaragua: La Imprenta, 1977), p. 16.

14. Brinton, *The Güegüence*, p. xlii. According to Enrique Peña Hernández, a dance called *Moros y Cristianos* has been performed only in Boaco. *Folklore de Nicaragua*, p. 169.

15. "Teatro Popular 'Original del Jigante,' " *Cuaderno del Taller San Lucas* (Granada), 3 (1943), pp. 93–104.

16. Quoted in Wachtel, "The Vision of the Vanquished," n. 3, pp. 318–319.

17. Brinton, *The Güegüence*, p. xxiii.

18. Wachtel, "The Vision of the Vanquished," p. 231.

19. Ibid., pp. 249 and 257.

20. Froebel, *Travels*, pp. 78–79.

21. Juan M. Mendoza, *Historia de Diriamba* (Guatemala City: Imprenta Electra, 1920), p. 31.

22. E. Bradford Burns, *The Poverty of Progress: Latin America in the Nineteenth*

Century (Berkeley: University of California Press, 1980), p. 45.

23. José Coronel Urtecho, *Reflecciones sobre la Historia de Nicaragua* (León: Editorial Hospicio, 1962), I, 17–19 *passim*.

24. In her Introduction, Jo Anne Engelbert emphasizes both the significance and meaning of Indian story telling. Rosario Santos, ed., *And We Sold the Rain: Contemporary Fiction from Central America* (New York: Four Walls Eight Windows, 1988), pp. ix-xi. Not only Indians use the tale, in verse or prose, to affirm pride. In their vast popular poetic literature, *literatura de cordel*, the ordinary people of the Brazilian backlands often relate how the local outsmarts the "city slicker." An example of that poetry is José Bernardo da Silva, *Discussão de um Praciano com um Matuto* (Juázeiro do Norte, Ceará: São Francisco, 1965).

25. Gregorio Smutko, "La Psicología de Algunos Chistes Campesinos de Nicaragua," *El Pez y la Serpiente* (Managua), 20 (Winter 1977), p. 129.

26. Julius Froebel, *Seven Years' Travel in Central America, Northern Mexico, and the Far West of the United States* (London: Richard Bentley, 1859), p. 78.

27. Pablo Antonio Cuadra and Francisco Pérez Estrada, *Muestrario del Folklore Nicaragüense* (Managua: Fondo de Promoción Cultural Banco de America, 1978), p. 97.

28. Smutko, "La Psicología," p. 129.

29. Brinton, *The Güegüence*, p. xliii.

30. Cuadra and Pérez Estrada, *Muestrario*, pp. 105–108. A shorter story, "El Cerro y el Cargador" also pits the Indian against the king. Smutko, "La Psicología," p. 136.

31. Cuadra and Pérez Estrada, *Muestrario*, p. 97.

32. El Buen Sentido, (pseud.) *Opinión del Estado del Salvador con Relación a los Sucesos de Nicaragua* (San Salvador: Imprenta del Triunfo, 1851).

33. Frederick Boyle, *A Ride across a Continent: A Personal Narrative of Wanderings through Nicaragua and Costa Rica* (London: Bentley, 1868), I, 63–64.

34. E. G. Squier, *Nicaragua: Its People, Scenery, Monuments, Resources, Condition and Proposed Canal* (New York: Harper, 1860), p. 268.

35. Paul Levy, *Notas Geográficas y Económicas sobre la República de Nicaragua* (Paris: Librería Española de E. Denne Schmitz, 1873), pp. 214 and 240.

36. Arellano, "Estudio Preliminar," *El Güegüence*, p. 43.

37. Boyle, *A Ride*, II, 179.

38. Mendoza, *Historia de Diriamba* pp. 47, 82–83.

39. Germán Romero Vargas, *Las Estructuras Sociales de Nicaragua en el Siglo XVIII* (Managua: Editorial Vanguardia, 1988), p. 367. Linda Newsom provides a useful introduction to the Indians in her *Indian Survival in Colonial Nicaragua* (Norman: University of Oklahoma Press, 1987).

40. Thomas Belt, *The Naturalist in Nicaragua*, 2nd ed. (London: Bumpus, 1888), p. 293.

41. Cuadra and Pérez Estrada, *Muestrario*, p. 345.

42. Levy, *Notas Geográficas*, p. 215.

43. Squier, *Nicaragua*, p. 514.

44. Orlando W. Roberts, *Narrative of Voyages and Excursions on the East Coast and in the Interior of Central America* (Edinburgh: Constable, 1827), p. 214.

45. Squier, *Nicaragua*, pp. 190–191.

46. Ibid., p. 102.
47. Froebel, *Seven Years' Travel*, p. 89.
48. Jacob D. B. Stillman, *An 1850 Voyage: San Francisco to Baltimore by Sea and by Land* (Palo Alto, Calif.: Lewis Osborne, 1967), pp. 51–53.
49. Squier, *Nicaragua*, p. 503.
50. Froebel, *Seven Years' Travel*, p. 50.
51. Boyle, *A Ride*, II, 6–7.
52. Froebel, *Seven Years' Travel*, p. 91. Subsequent literature throughout Latin America shrouded the Indian village in Romanticism, a trend well exemplified by the Mexican novel *La Navidad en las Montañas* (1871) by Ignacio M. Altamirano. Even so realistic a masterpiece as Ciro Alegría's *El Mundo Es Ancho y Ajeno* (1941) idealized the Indian community.
53. Robert Redfield, *The Little Community and Peasant Society and Culture* (Chicago: University of Chicago Press, 1971), p. 130.
54. Squier, *Nicaragua* p. 242.
55. George M. Foster, "What Is Folk Culture? *American Anthropologist*, 55:2, Part I (April-June 1953), p. 171.
56. Conclusions concerning folk culture and society derive in part from Robert Redfield, *The Folk Culture of Yucatan* (Chicago: University of Chicago Press, 1941); Redfield, "The Folk Society," *The American Journal of Sociology*, 52:4 (January 1947), pp. 293–308; Gideon Sjoberg, "Folk and Feudal Societies," *The American Journal of Sociology*, 58:3 (November 1952), pp. 231–239; George M. Foster, *Tzintzuntzán: Mexican Peasants in a Changing World* (Boston: Little, Brown, 1967); and Miroslav Hroch, *Social Preconditions of National Revival in Europe: A Comparative Analysis of the Social Composition of Patriotic Groups among the Smaller European Nations* (New York: Cambridge University Press, 1985). Folk culture and society are by no means limited to Latin America in this hemisphere. Both flourished in the United States, and folk culture continues to this day, even in the largest modern urban centers. Occasional intellectual movements, such as "regionalism" in the Midwest during the 1920s and 1930s, so evident in the art of Grant Wood, John Steuart Curry, and Thomas Hart Benton, emphasized it: "There is much scurrying about the country in automobiles these days, and much accumulation of superficial ideas. The sophistication which is the goal of this kind of life is precisely the opposite of that true culture whose roots go deep into tradition and the ancient handiworks and the life of the race. These things root and grow in places. There is a kind of integrity of an old man who belongs to a certain environment and nowhere else that is not found in the cosmopolite who bears a dozen veneers one imposed on another; one feels that the old man with roots is more perfect and complete. And it is because of this integrity and perfection that all the materials belonging to unspoiled places in the United States are of the highest value for painting, sculpture, poetry, fiction, and all of all of the more fundamental arts." Frank Luther Mott, "Literature with Roots," *The Midland* (Chicago), 19:3 (May-June 1931), pp. 82–83.
57. Carl Scherzer, *Travels in the Free States of Central America: Nicaragua, Honduras, and San Salvador* (London: Longman, 1857), I, 168; Brinton, *The üegüence* p. xi.
58. Squier, *Nicaragua*, p. 92.

59. Stillman, *An 1850 Voyage*, p.57.
60. Squier, *Nicaragua* p. 180.
61. Boyle, *A Ride*, II, 48.
62. Belt, *The Naturalist*, pp. 278–282.
63. Squier, *Nicaragua*, p. 520.
64. Belt, *The Naturalist*, pp. 286–287.
65. George Byam, *Wild Life in the Interior of Central America* (London: Parker, 1849), p. 24.
66. Benjamin I, Teplitz, "The Political and Economic Foundations of Modernization in Nicaragua: The Administration of José Santos Zelaya, 1893–1909," (Ph.D. diss., Howard University, 1973), pp. 344–354.
67. Barrington Moore, Jr., *Social Origins of Dictatorship and Democracy: Lord and Peasant in the Making of the Modern World* (Boston: Beacon Press, 1972), p. 497.
68. Pierre Clastres, *Society Against the State* (New York: Zone Books, 1987), p. 207.
69. Miles L. Wortman, *Government and Society in Central America, 1680–1840* (New York: Columbia University Press, 1982), p. 271; Auguste Myionnet-Dupuy estimated 65% in *Deux Ans de Séjour dans l'Etat de Nicaragua (Amérique Centrale). 1850, 1851, 1852* (Paris: Poussielgue Masson, 1853), pp. 28-29; Alberto Lanuza Matamoros accepted the figures of Myionnet-Dupuy. *Estructuras Socioeconómicas, Poder y Estado en Nicaragua, de 1821 a 1875* (San José: Programa Centroamericano de Ciencias Sociales, 1976), p.53.
70. Squier, *Nicaragua*, p. 649.
71. "Informe Dirigido al Señor Marqués de la Hornaza por los Comerciantes y Hacendados de la Villa de Nicaragua [Rivas] en Junio de 1798," *Boletín Nicaragüense de Bibliografía y Documentación*, 2 (October-December 1974), pp. 28–30.
72. Anne MacKaye Chapman, *Los Nicarao y los Chorotega según las Fuentes Históricas* (San José: Universidad de Costa Rica, 1960), pp. 25–32.
73. Francisco Pérez Estrada, "Breve Historia de la Tenecía de la Tierra en Nicaragua," in his *Ensayos Nicaragüenses* (Managua: Banco de America, I976), p. 147 *passim*.
74. Romero Vargas, *Las Estructuras*, pp. 92–105.
75. Squier, *Nicaragua*, pp. 274–275.
76. Romero Vargas, *Las Estructuras*, pp. 93–95.
77. José Mata Gavidia, *La Influencia de España en la Formación de la Nacionalidad Centro Americana* (Guatemala City: Unión Tipográfica, 1943), pp. 30–31.
78. Alexander Moore, "Peoples of the Old World Revisited: The Cultures and Communities of Spain," in Owen M. Lynch, ed., *Culture and Community in Europe* (Delhi: Hindustan Publishing Corporation, 1984), pp. 41–43; also see William Schell, Jr., *Medieval Iberian Tradition and the Development of the Mexican Hacienda* (Syracuse, N.Y.: Maxwell School of Citizenship and Public Affairs 1986), pp. 40–42.
79. "Un Documento Excepcional: El Realejo, Chinandega y El Viejo a Finales del S. XVIII," *Boletín Nicaragüense de Bibliografía y Documentación*, 7 (September–

October 1975), p. 84.

80. Romero Vargas, *Las Estructuras*, pp. 93–100.

81. Ibid., p. 96.

82. Jaime Wheelock Román. *Nicaragua: Imperialismo y Dictadura: Crisis de una Formación Social* (Mexico City: Siglo Veintiuno, 1975), p. 76.

83. In his memoires of nineteenth–century Diriamba, Juan M. Mendoza recalled, "One could acquire land by simple occupation, without any other title." *Historia de Diriamba*, p. 28.

84. Pérez Estrada, "Breve Historia," p. l58; Nicaragua. *Código de la Legislación de la República de Nicaragua* (Managua: El Centro Americano, 1873), I, 190–191.

85. Squier, *Nicaragua*, p. 274.

86. Pérez Estrada, "Breve Historia." p. 186.

87. Wheelock Román, *Nicaragua. Imperialismo y Dictatura*, *p. 76.*

88. Jesús de la Rocha, *Informe Presentado por el Ministro Interino de Relaciones Interiores y Exteriores a las Cámaras Legislativas de Nicaragua* (Granada: Imprenta del Orden, 1853), p. 7.

89. *Gaceta Oficial de Nicaragua* (Granada), April 30. 1853.

90. All of the laws mentioned in this paragraph can be found in Nicaragua, *Código*, I.

91. Vol. I. of the Index was published in 1900; Vol. II, in 1916. (Managua: Tipografía Nacional).

92. Ibid., II, 72.

93. Ibid., p. 276.

94. José Reyes Monterrey, "Algunos Antecedentes Históricos de la Lucha de Clases en Nicaragua," *Taller* (León), 9 (November 1973), p. 56.

95. *Gaceta Oficial de Nicaragua* (Granada). February 28. 1852.

96. Wheelock Román, *Nicaragua. Imperialismo y Dictadura*, pp. 57–59.

97. Ibid., p. 25; Carl Bovallius, "Viaje por Centroamérica, 1881–1883," *Revista Conservadora del Pensamiento Centroamericano*, 39 (December 1963), p. 56.

98. Squier, *Nicaragua*, p. 274.

99. Belt, *The Naturalist*, p. 288.

100. George Byam, *Wild Life in the Interior of Central America* (London: Parker, 1849), pp. 24–25.

101. Belt, *The Naturalist*, pp. 198–199.

102. Levy, *Notas Geográficas*, p. 441.

103. Germán Romero Vargas noted that by the second half of the seventeenth century, governors of Nicaragua were complaining to the crown about the lack of laborers to work the land. *Las Estructuras*, p. 290.

104. Squier, *Nicaragua*, p. 414.

105. Sanford A. Mosk, "Indigenous Economy in Latin America," in Dwight B. Heath and Richard N. Adams, eds., *Contemporary Cultures and Societies of Latin America* (New York: Random House, 1965), p. 155. Generally speaking, economists have paid far greater attention to the export sectors rather than to the subsistence sectors of the Latin American economies. Anthropologists tend to provide the most insight into the subsistence sectors. A thoughtful and laudatory example of an anthropological study of the folk economy can be found in Stephen Gudeman and Alberto Rivera, *Conversations in Colombia: The Domes-*

tic Economy in Life and Text (New York.: Cambridge University Press, 1990). On pages 18–38, the authors discuss the concepts of land use in terms of the needs, desires, and goals of the ordinary rural inhabitant.

106. Mendoza, *Historia de Diriamba,* p. 83.
107. John L. Stephens, *Incidents of Travel in Central America, Chiapas and Yucatan* (New Brunswick: Rutgers University Press, 1949), II, 18–19.
108. "The Experience of Samuel Absalom, Fillibuster," *The Atlantic Monthly,* part I, 4:26 December 1859), pp. 658–659; part II, 5:27 (January 1860), p. 59.
109. Alexander von Buelow, "Emigración y Colonización en Interés de Comercio Alemán," *Revista de la Academia de Geografía e Historia de Nicaragua* 28–29: 1–4 (January–December 1964), p. 28.
110. Scherzer, *Travels,* I, 194.
111. Belt, *The Naturalist,* p. 282.
112. *Discurso Pronunciado por el Licenciado D. Juan E de la Rocha, Alcalde 1° Constitucional en el Aniversario XLIV de Nuestra Independencia* (León: Imprenta de Justo Hernandez, 1865).
113. "The system adopted of recruiting is very simple indeed. A few soldiers with fixed boyonets are sent out to bring in fresh men, or, to use their own expressive term, to 'catch' men. When the unfortunate recruit is 'caught,' a musket is put in his hands, and he becomes a soldier. Soldiering is by no means a popular occupation: during a revolution, at the approach of forces of either party, the peace-loving native, in order to escape being 'caught' and forced into service, will remain hidden in the woods till they are nearly starved." "Nicaragua and the Filibusters," *Blackwood's Magazine* (Edinburgh), March 1856, p. 318.
114. Robert Dunlop, *Travel in Central America, Being a Journal of Nearly Three Years Residence in the Country* (London: Longman, 1847), pp. 56–57.
115. Christie wrote to Palmerston from San Juan del Norte on September 5, 1848: "There will however be great difficulty in getting labor. . . . At present no labor is to be got here." Foreign office 53/11.
116. Belt, *The Naturalist,* pp. 160–161.
117. "La Infraestructura de Nicaragua en 1860 Examinada por un Híjo de Rivas, El Agricultor Joaquín Elizondo," *Revista Conservadora del Pensamiento Centroamericano* 57, (June 1965), pp. 55–56.
118. The majordomo of an excellent cacao estate near Granada complained to Squier in 1849 about the lack of workers: "now was the time for collecting the cacao, but no men were to be had." *Nicaragua,* p. 135. The newspaper *El Nicaragüense* (Granada) reported a shortage of house servants; March 22, 1856. Peter F. Stout revealed in 1858 that the Sandoval indigo estate outside of Granada was for sale, largely because of the difficulty in hiring dependable workers. *Nicaragua. Past, Present, and Future* (Philadelphia: Potter, 1859), p. 69. Belt complained in the late 1860s and early 1870s, "It has been for some time difficult to obtain sufficient laborers for our mines." *The Naturalist,* p. 191. As late as 1870, Paul Levy devoted considerable discussion to the problems created by the scarcity of labor. *Notas Geográficas* p. 477 *passim.* See also Wheelock Román, *Nicaragua. Imperialismo y Dictadura,* pp. 58–59.
119. Wortman, *Government and Society,* p. 271. In 1849, Squier reported that indigo

production on an estate he visited near Chinandega had been abandoned because of "the impossiblity of securing permanent laborers." *Nicaragua*, p. 341.

120. Squier, *Nicaragua*, p. 278.

121. Levy, *Notas Geográficas*, p. 446.

122. Ibid., p. 447.

123. *Correo del Istmo de Nicaragua* (León), October 4, 1849.

124. Executive Decree of October 17, 1843. Nicaragua, *Código*, I, 158.

125. Paul J. Vanderwood, *Disorder and Progress: Bandits, Police, and Mexican Development* (Lincoln: University of Nebraska Press, 1981), p. xi.

126. Clastres, *Society Against the State*, p. 218.

127. *Eco Popular* (Granada), July 13, 1854. Concerning the Indians of the Colombian Andes, José María Samper observed, *circa* 1860, "For the Indian of the Andine countryside, the ties of society are perilous, the schoolteacher is an incomprehensible myth, the alcalde a useless personage, the parish priest a demigod, and the tax-collector little less than the pest or thunderbolt. His life is concentrated upon his primitive hut and half acre farm." Quoted in Phanor James Eder, *Colombia* (New York: Scribner's, 1913), p. 224.

128. *El Defensor del Orden* (Granada), October 5, 1854.

129. Hroch, *Social Preconditions of National Revival*, p. 179

130. *Correo del Istmo de Nicaragua* (León), December 16, 1849.

131. Mateo de Mayoraga, Minister of Foreign Relations, discussed the masses in relation to elitist and "official" values in *Gaceta Oficial de Nicaragua* (Granada), September 24, 1853.

132. *Manifiesto que Hace el que Suscribe a los Pueblos de Centro-América, del Motivo por que Fué Arrojado con Otros Fuera de su Patria la Ciudad de Rivas: y en el que se Propone Contestar el Papel Llamado Vindicación, Suscrito por Doce Individuos, sobre la Calumnia que se Hace a su Familia con Motivo de los Atentados del 3 de Diciembre de 1848* (San José: Imprenta de la Paz, 1849), reprinted in the *Revista de la Academia de Geografía e Historia de Nicaragua*, 6:1 (April 1944), pp. 41–61.

133. (Granada), February 5, 1842.

134. Letter to Prbo. Agustín Vijil, January 13, 1852, in Pedro Joaquín Chamorro Zelaya, *Fruto Chamorro* (Managua: Editorial Union, 1960), p. 164.

135. Burns, *The Poverty of Progress*, pp. 23, 26, 29, 31.

136. Fruto Chamorro, *Mensaje del Director Supremo de Nicaragua General Don Fruto Chamorro a la A. C. del Estado Instalada el 22 de Enero del Año de 1854* (Managua: Imprenta de la Libertad, 1854).

137. S.C., "Estado de los Pueblos al Establecerse la República Democrática," articles published in the *Registro Oficial*, 1847, collected and reprinted in the *Revista de la Academia de Geografía e Historia de Nicaragua*, XI (April 1951), pp. 67–75.

138. Elizondo, "La Infraestructura," pp. 55–56.

139. Froebel, *Seven Years' Travel*, p. 33.

140. Squier, *Nicaragua*, pp. 268–269

141. Ibid., p. 279

142. Belt, *The Naturalist*, pp. 64–65.
143. Levy, *Notas Geográficas*, pp. 214–215.
144. Scherzer, *Travels*, I, 62.
145. Bedford Pim, *Dottings on the Roadside in Panama, Nicaragua, and Mosquito* (London: Chapman and Hall, 1869), p. 43.
146. Scherzer, *Travels*, I, pp. 91, 95, 97.
147. Belt, *The Naturalist*, p. 282.
148. Ibid., pp. 282–283.
149. Boyle, *A Ride*, II, 89.
150. The observation appeared in the essay "Nicaragua and the Filibusters," p. 318.
151. Rodolfo Cardenal, "Acerca de las 'Reflexiones' de Coronel Urtecho," *Revista del Pensamiento Centroamericano*, 151 (April–June, 1976), p. 41.
152. Jaime Wheelock Román outlines those rebellions and their causes in *Raíces Indígenas de la Lucha Anticolonialista en Nicaragua* (Managua: Editorial Nueva Nicaragua, 1981), pp. 86–99. His useful bibliography, pp. 119–123, lists important sources for the study of the rebellions. Chester Zelaya provides a fuller synthesis in his *Nicaragua en la Independencia* (San José: Editorial Universitaria, 1971), pp. 65–78; 143–147; 189.
153. "The Indian in Nicaragua was slowly undergoing a progressive transformation. He was being converted into a peasant, acquiring the conscience and the interests of the small property owner, increasingly shaped by class and economic outlooks rather than, before, ethnic and religious." Wheelock Román, *Raíces Indígenas*, p. 89.
154. *Gaceta Oficial de Nicaragua* (Granada), February 12, 1853.
155. Those who did not receive a local monopoly complained. Hermenejildo Reyes published a broadside pointing out that the monopoly in León "has brought about the total ruin of the sugar plantations." *Protesta Pública al Gobierno* (León: Imprenta de la Paz, 1853).
156. Orlando Cuadra Downing, *Bernabé Somoza (1815–1849). Vida y Muerte de un Hombre de Acción* (Managua: Imprenta Nacional, 1970), pp. 89–90. In the realm of comparative history, certain issues involved in the aguardiente protests in Nicaragua had already surfaced in the Whiskey Rebellion in western Pennsylvania in 1791. In both cases, rural folk protested government regulation of a popular liquor, an interference in popular economic activities. In both cases, the governments used force to strengthen their political positions and public order.
157. Dunlop, *Travel*, p. 251; José Dolores Gámez, *Historia Moderna de Nicaragua. Complemento a Mí Historia de Nicaragua* (Managua: Banco de América, 1975), pp. 344–345. That nineteenth-century historian referred to Somoza as a "revolutionary", p. 344, while the government insisted upon calling him a "bandit." In 1970, Orlando Cuadra Downing mounted a defense of Somoza in an effort to understand his actions. *Bernabé Somoza*, pp. 16–18 *passim*.
158. Gámez, *Historia Moderna de Nicaragua*, pp. 463–464.
159. Isidro Urtecho, "Galería de Notables Rivenses. Rafael Lebrón," written in 1907 and printed in the *Revista de la Academia de Geografía e Historia de Nicaragua*, 2:1 (September 1937), p. 359.
160. Nicaragua. Asamblea Constituyente, 1847–1848, *Para Conocimiento del Público*

se Dan a Luz los Nuevos Documentos Relativos a las Dificultadades que se Presentan para la Sanción del Proyecto de una Constitución que Ha Formado la A. C. (León: Imprenta de la Paz, 1848). José Mará Estrada, a delegate to the Constituent Assembly, concluded, "What I think about all this is that so many mutual rebukes, just or unjust, have the effect of dividing us into squabbling groups to the further agony of the State." *Juício Particular Formado sobre las Cuestiones Políticas que se Han Suscitado con Relación a la Nueva Carta Constitutiva del Estado de Nicaragua* (Granada: Imprenta de la Concepción, 1848).

161. *Registro Oficial* (Masaya), March 22, 1845.

162. Ibid., July 19, 1845.

163. Pedro Francisco de la Rocha, *Revista Política sobre la Historia de la Revolución de Nicaragua en Defensa de la Administración del Ex-Director Don José León Sandoval* (Granada: Imprenta de la Concepción, 1847), reprinted in the *Revista del Pensamiento Centroamericano*, 180 (July-September 1983), p. 49.

164. Scherzer, *Travels*, I, 167–168; Froebel, *Seven Years' Travel*, pp. 74–75; Chamorro Zelaya, *Fruto Chamorro*, p. 73.

165. Boyle, *A Ride*, II, 58; Froebel, *Seven Years' Travel*, p. 93.

166. Pedro Francisco de la Rocha, *Revista Política*, pp. 49–51. For information on the attack on Chinandega see the *Registro Oficial* (San Fernando), August 16, 1845.

167. The report of Prefect of the Department of the Oriente, Ponciano Corral, February 9, 1847, is reprinted in the *Revista del Archivo General de la Nación* (Managua), 1:1 (January–March 1964), pp. 8–10.

168. *Revista Política*, p. 60.

169. *Al Público* (Granada), August 13, 1848, reprinted in the *Revista de la Academia de Geografía e Historia de Nicaragua*, 7:3 (November 1945), pp. 87–88.

170. Chamorro Zelaya, *Fruto Chamorro*, pp. 133; 137–138; Los Amigos del Progreso, *Paralelo de las Revoluciones* (Rivas: Imprenta Nueva, 1849).

171. Sáenz, *Manifiesto que Hace el que Suscribe*. Another source, the same year, charged the leaders of León were "communists." Los Amigos del Progreso, *Paralelo de las Revoluciones*.

172. *Correo del Istmo de Nicaragua* (León), July 1, 1849.

173. Urtecho, "Galería de Notables Rivenses," p. 360.

174. De la Rocha *Revista Política*, p. 60.

175. Luís Alberto Cabrales, "El Tránsito, los Filibusteros, y la Guerra Nacional," *Centro* (Managua) (March-August 1940), p. 56.

176. De la Rocha, *Revista Política*, p. 2.

177. Dunlop, *Travel*, p. 8.

178. *Eco Popular* (Granada), July 13, 1854.

179. De la Rocha, *Revista Política*, pp. 60 and 62

180. Enrique López Albujar, *Los Caballeros del Delito. Estudio Criminológico del Bandolerismo en Algunos Departamentos del Perú* (Lima: Compañía de Impresiones y Publicidad, 1936), p. 40.

181. Vanderwood, *Disorder and Progress*, p. 15.

182. As early as 1930, Hildebrando H. A. Castellón called for revisionist studies of Somoza. He felt too much myth surrounded the man. The time had arrived to take a dispassionate look at him. He suggested that Somoza was "a caudillo of his

time and not a bandit chief" *Biografía de Bernabé Somoza. Apuntes Históricos,* 1815–1849 (Paris: n.n., 1930). A second edition appeared in Managua in 1963. In 1970, Orlando Cuadra Downing, who wrote the longest and most lauded study of Somoza, characterized him as a "chief of an agrarian revolutionary movement." *Bernabé Somoza,* p. 18.
183. Castellón, *Biografía,* p. 16.
184. Ibid., pp. 13 and 16; Cuadra Downing, *Bernabé Somoza,* p. 23 *passim.*
185. *Registro Oficial,* July 26, 1845.
186. Miguel Angel Ramos, *Reseña Histórica de Nicaragua desde el Descubrimiento hasta la Invasión de Walker* (Tegucigalpa: Imprenta Calderón, 1956), pp. 26–27. Nicaraguan historiography fails to incorporate the Indian and folk rebellions, 1845–1849. When they are mentioned, they are treated as insignificant. For example, Julián N. Guerrero C. and Lola Soriano de Guerrero concluded, "During the administration of Chief of State Don José León Sandoval, 1845 and 1846, armed movements broke out in the West and North of Nicaragua characterized by mere depravation and vandalism, without either political motivations or party affiliations." *Caciques Heróicos de Centroamérica. Rebelión Indígena de Matagalpa en 1881 y Expulsión de los Jesuitas* (Managua: n.n., 1982), p. 79.
187. Chamorro Zelaya, *Fruto Chamorro,* p. 152.
188. Squier, *Nicaragua,* p. 131.
189. *Boletín Oficial* (León), June 14, 1849.
190. Squier, *Nicaragua,* p. 110.
191. Ibid., p. 142.
192. *Gaceta del Gobierno* (León), December 16, 1848.
193. *Boletín Oficial* (León); July 12, 1849.
194. Ibid., June 12, 14, 19, and 29, 1849; José Trinidad Muñoz used similar language in his *El Jeneral en Jefe del Ejército del Estado a sus Subordinados y a los Amigos de la Sociedad* (León: Imprenta de Minerva, 1849).
195. *Boletín Oficial* (León), June 14, 1849.
196. Ibid., June 14, 15, and 19, 1849.
197. Ibid., June 25, 1849.
198. Gregorio Díaz, *Compatriotas* (León: Imprenta de Minerva, 1849).
199. Jorge Eduardo Arellano wrote a short novel, *Timbucos y Calandracas* (Managua: Silvio Mayorga, 1982), the theme of which was Somoza's potential threat to the elites.
200. Jorge Eduardo Arellano, "El Primer Historiador de Nicaragua. Pedro Francisco de la Rocha y su *Revista Política sobre la Historia de la Revolución de Nicaragua," Revista del Pensamiento Centroamericano,* 180 (July-September l983), p. 11.
201. *Boletín Oficial* (León), June 19, 1849.
202. Ibid., June 28, 1849.
203. Muñoz, *El Jeneral en Jefe.*
204. Los Amigos del Progreso, *Paralelo de las Revoluciones.*
205. Sáenz, *Manifesto que Hace el que Suscribe,* pp. 43 and 57.
206. Domingo Faustino Sarmiento, *Life in the Argentine Republic in the Days of the Tyrants; Or, Civilization and Barbarism* (New York: Hafner Publishing

Company, n.d.), p. 42.

207. Anselmo H. Rivas, *Nicaragua. Su Pasado. Ojeada Retrospectiva* (Managua: La Prensa, 1936), p. 131. Originally published in the *Diario Nicaragüense de Granada,* November 6, 1895–February 16, 1896.

208. José Coronel Urtecho, "Introducción a la Epoca de Anarquía en Nicaragua, 1821–1857," *Revista Conservadora del Pensamiento Centroamericano,* 134 (November 1971), p. 40; Castellón, *Biografía,* p. 23.

209. Cuadra Downing, *Bernabé Somoza,* p. 114.

210. Sáenz, *Manifiesto que Hace el que Suscribe.*

211. *Boletín Oficial Extraordinario* (León), July 5, 1849.

212. Sebastián Salinas, *Informe Presentado al Cuerpo Legislativo por el Secretario del Despacho de Relaciones Interiores y Exteriores* (León: Imprenta de la Libertad, 1850).

4. Fatherland

1. *Gaceta del Gobierno* (León), December 16, 1848.

2. Gregorio Díaz, Compatriotas (León: Imprenta de Minerva, 1849).

3. Martin de la Bastide, *Mémoire sur un Nouveau Passage de la Mer du Nord à la Mer du Sud* (Paris: Didot, 1791); Alphonse Dumartray and Pedro Rouhaud, *Opúsculo sobre la República de Centroamérica y Particularmente sobre los Estados de Nicaragua y Costa Rica* (Paris: Librería Americana, 1833).

4. John L. Stephens, *Incidents of Travel in Central America, Chiapas and Yucatan* (New Brunswick: Rutgers University Press, 1949), I, 323–339. Stephens met Baily in Granada and discussed his survey with him.

5. Ibid., pp. 334–335.

6. Alejandro Marure, *Memoria Histórica sobre el Canal de Nicaragua* (Guatemala City: Imprenta de la Paz, 1845). A summary of negotiations for a canal across Nicaragua appears in the section "Historical Sketch of the Various Negotiations Which Have Been Made in Respect to Opening the Canal," E. G. Squier to Secretary of State John M. Clayton, October 10, 1849, contained in *Tigre Island and Central America. Message from the President of the United States. July 22, 1850.* House of Representatives. 31st Congress, 1st Session. Ex. doc. 75, pp. 204–207.

7. Napoleon Louis Bonaparte, *Canal of Nicaragua: or a Project to Connect the Atlantic and Pacific Oceans by Means of a Canal* (London: Misle and Son, 1846), p. 6.

8. *Alcance al Número 21 de Registro Oficial* (Masaya), June 16, 1845.

9. Letter of Fruto Chamorro to the Minister of War of El Salvador, July 22, 1844, reprinted in Pedro Joaquín Chamorro Zelaya, *Fruto Chamorro* (Managua: Editorial Unión, 1960), p. 354.

10. "Muñoz and the whole democratic party, activated by patriotic as well as sectional views, were opposed to the granting of the transit contract, while their political adversaries at Granada and Rivas, situated so as to derive immediate advantage from the transit through the southern section of the country, were inclined to yield to the arguments of the friends and agents of the Company."

Julius Froebel, *Seven Years' Travel in Central America* (London: Richard Bentley, 1859), pp. 148–149.

11. Ephraim George Squier, *Nicaragua: Its People, Scenery, Monuments, Resources, Condition and Proposed Canal* (New York: Harper, 1860), p. 559; Mario Rodríguez has written the definitive study of Chatfield and his activities, *A Palmerstonian Diplomat in Central America: Frederick Chatfield, Esq.* (Tucson: University of Arizona Press, 1964).

12. Bing Clark, *A Geographical Sketch of St. Domingo, Cuba, and Nicaragua with Remarks on the Past and Present Policy of Great Britain Affecting those Countries* (Boston: Eastburn's Press, 1850), pp. 29–32.

13. A letter of Pepe Batres (José Batres Montúfar), November 30, 1837, in José Arzu, *Pepe Batres Intimo. Su Familia, Su Correspondencia, Sus Papeles* (Guatemala City: Sánchez, 1940), p. 186.

14. Documentation of British expansion into Nicaragua during this period appears in Andrés Vega Bolaños, *Los Atentados del Superintendente de Belice. 1840–1842* (Managua: Editorial Unión, 1971), see particularly pp. 62–199.

15. Castro Fonseca, *Para Conocimiento del Público se Publica la Acta Siguiente* (Granada: Imprenta de la Universidad de Granada, 1841); *Mentor Nicaragüense* (Granada), November 6 and 20, 1841.

16. *Memoria Dirigida por el Ministerio del Estado y del Despacho de Relaciones de Nicaragua* (León: Imprenta de la Paz, 1847).

17. The quotation comes from Díaz, *Compatriotas*. The figures come from "Squier Notes on Nicaraguan Debt," Squier Papers. Box 2, folder 9. Latin American Library, Tulane University.

18. *Correo del Istmo de Nicaragua* (León), December 16, 1849.

19. Fruto Chamorro, *Mensaje de S.E. el General Director Supremo Fruto Chamorro a la Asamblea Constituyente del Estado de Nicaragua, Instalada el 22 de Enero de 1854* (Managua: Imprenta de la Libertad, 1854).

20. On the role of perception in history, consult Donald M. Lowe, *The History of Bourgeois Perception* (Chicago: University of Chicago Press, 1982).

21. House of Representatives, Thirtieth Congress, Second Session, Report No. 145. *Report: Canal or Railroad between the Atlantic and Pacific Oceans* (Washington, D.C., February 20, 1849), p. 1.

22. The population of 129 included "men, women, and children." "Nicaraguan inhabitants who had left, when possession was taken by the Mosquito government, have been gradually returning." William D. Christie to Palmerston, San Juan del Norte, September 5, 1848. Foreign Office 53/11.

23. Charles Parke, "Journal of a Trip across the Plains . . . and a Voyage from San Francisco to New Orleans via Nicaragua, 1849–50." Huntington Library, Manuscript HM 16996.

24. An anonymous correspondent for *Harper's* vividly recounted the impressive growth of San Juan between 1850 and 1854. "San Juan," *Harper's,* 10 (December 1854), pp. 50–61.

25. National Archives. Diplomatic Dispatches. Nicaragua. Walsh to Secretary of State Daniel Webster, May 28, 1852.

26. Chargé d'Affaires of Peru, Felipe Barriga Alvarez, to Minister of Foreign

Relations, Lima, from León, August 31, 1850, reprinted in the *Revista de la Academia de Geografía e Historia de Nicaragua*, 9:2 (August 1947), pp. 86–87.

27. John Foster, British Vice-Consul, Realejo, to Frederick Chatfield, December 31, 1850. Foreign Office 15/70.

28. For the full account of the journey see the diary of William Franklin Denniston, "Journal of a Voyage from New York to San Francisco via Nicaragua . . . 1849–50," Huntington Library, Manuscript HM 50660. The quotation comes from that diary. Max Harrison Williams provides details of the Gordon expedition in *Gateway through Central America. A History of the San Juan River, Lake Nicaragua Waterway, 1502–1921* (La Paz, Bolivia: Empresa Editora Urquizo, 1976), pp. 73–79. The British took note of Gordon's presence. William D. Christie to Palmerston. Greytown, March 27, 1849. Foreign Office 53/17, No. 13.

29. *Boletín Oficial Extraordinario* (León), July 5, 1849.

30. A.H. Rivas, *Nicaragua. Su Pasado. Ojeada Retrospectiva* (Managua: La Prensa, 1936), p. 19.

31. Squier, *Nicaragua*. All the quotations come from pages 225–229.

32. Ibid., pp. 230–231.

33. Ibid., pp. 231–233.

34. Ibid., pp. 233–234.

35. Ibid., pp. 235–236.

36. Ibid., p . 235.

37. *Boletín Oficial Extraordinario*(León), July 5, 1849. U.S newspapers reported the enthusiastic reception of Squier: "The arrival of Mr. Squier, as Minister from the United States, seems to have been regarded as an event of remarkable importance. It is heralded in all the journals as a new era for Nicaragua." *National Intelligencer* (Washington, D. C.), October 12, 1849.

38. John Crampton reported to Palmerston that Secretary of State John Clayton had informed him of Squier's supervision of the negotiations for the canal and transit treaties. Washington, October 15, 1849. Foreign Office 5/501, no. 89.

39. Letter to Squier from Sebastián Salinas, Minister of Foreign Relations, Casa de Gobierno, June 22, 1850. Reprinted in U.S. Congress Executive Document 75, 31st Congress, 1st Session, p. 327. Squier was aware of his own importance to the Nicaraguans: "I must observe at the risk of sounding a little egocentric, that, rightly or wrongly, I am regarded in Nicaragua as their fastest friend in the United States, and although I am only a private citizen, its Government keeps me informed of all its movements and has instructed its Minister to advise with me in all that concerns its interests. "Squier Notes on Nicaraguan Debt."

40. *Integridad de Centro-America* (Granada), January 1, 1850.

41. Squier, *Nicaragua*, p. 388.

42. Sebastian Salinas, *Informe Presentado al Cuerpo Legislativo por el Secretario del Despacho de Relaciones Interiores y Exteriores* (León: Imprenta de la Libertad, 1850), p. 24.

43. "The improvement in the trade of this country . . . has been the result of the recent discoveries in California . . . almost every article of its produce for exportation has advanced one hundred per cent in value, by the increased demand to supply the San Francisco and Panama Markets." Vice-Consul John Foster to

Frederick Chatfield, December 31, 1850. Foreign Office 15/70.

44. Lucien Mcleanthan Wolcott, "Journal of a Trip across the Plains . . . and Return Voyage to Ohio via Nicaragua," Huntington Library. Manuscript HM 266614.

45. *New York Herald,* May 1, 1858.

46. Quoted in Chamorro Zelaya, *Fruto Chamorro,* p. 163. Some North Americans Strongly criticized the behavior of their compatriots. Jacob Stillman commented, "It is with pain that I think of the brutal conduct of many of my countrymen, as it was exhibited during the whole route through Central America. The character which the nation enjoys they arrogate to themselves, and abuse the confidence which it inspires. With less claims as individuals to a character for refinement, they perpetrate the most indecent outrages upon a people whom they call unenlightened, but who really are greatly their superiors in every virtue that gives value to civilization." *An 1850 Voyage: San Francisco to Baltimore by Sea and by Land* (Palo Alto: Lewis Osborne, 1967), pp. 30–31.

47. Luís Alberto Cabrales, "El Tránsito, los Filibusteros, y la Guerra Nacional," *Centro* (Managua) (March–August 1940,) pp. 57–58. The foreign presence grew rapidly. Some North Americans in Granada published one issue of an English-language newspaper, *Nicaragua Flag* (July 26, 1851). It contained news of the foreign colony: " we suppose some 300 or more Americans and other foreigners at present are residing in the State of Nicaragua. Most of these are engaged in business, commercial or agricultural. Their numbers will be greatly increased in a few months."

48. Crampton to Malmesbury. Washington. November 21, 1852. Foreign Office 5/548, no. 189.

49. Parke,"Journal of a Trip"

50. Quoted in Chamorro Zelaya, *Fruto Chamorro,* p. 228. British Vice-Consul John Foster provided some useful details about the Realejo-San Juan del Norte journey in 1850. Foster to Frederick Chatfield, Realejo, December 31, 1850. Foreign Office 15/70.

51. Information from an advertisement of the Vanderbilt Line (Huntington Library.)

52. Joseph Warren Wood, "Diary of an Expedition to California. . . and Return East (1852) via Nicaragua," Huntington Library. Manuscript HM 318.

53. John Pratt Welsh, "Diary. Vol. 3 . . . Return from San Francisco to Illinois via Nicaragua . . . in 1852," Huntington Library. Manuscript HM 30628.

54. Alonzo Hubbard, "Journal of a Voyage from New York to San Francisco by way of Nicaragua . . . 1852." Huntington Library. Manuscript HM 27237.

55. James A. Clark, "Journal . . . Account of Trip East as far as Grey Town, Nicaragua, 1852–54," Huntington Library. Manuscript HM 18962. Although Mark Twain later became a sharp critic of imperialism, this is not the tone of his letters written as he crossed Nicaragua in early 1867. At best, he offered a brief, all-too-conventional view of the scenery and "natives" as observed from the transit route. *Mark Twain's Travels with Mr. Brown Being Heretofore Uncollected Sketches* (New York: Knopf, 1940), pp. 38–57.

56. Wolcott, "Journal of a Trip across the Plains."

57. Parke, "Journal of a Trip."

58. Ibid.

59. James T. Wall, "American Intervention in Nicaragua, 1848–1861"(Ph.D. diss. University of Tennessee 1974), p. 181.
60. An Officer in the Service of Walker (pseud.), *The Destiny of Nicaragua: Central America as It Was, Is, and May Be* (Boston: Beat, 1856), p. 38.
61. Williams, *Gateway*, p. 84.
62. David L. Folkman, Jr., *The Nicaragua Route* (Salt Lake City: University of Utah Press, 1972), p. 59.
63. Auguste Myionnet Dupuy, *Deux Ans de Séjour dans l'Etat de Nicaragua (Amérique Centrale). 1850, 1851, 1852* (Paris: Poussielgue Masson, 1853), p. 7.
64. National Archives. Diplomatic Dispatches. Nicaragua. Robert Walsh to Secretary of State Daniel Webster, May 28, 1852.
65. Mrs. H. G. Foote, *Recollections of Central America and the West Coast of Africa* (London: T. Cautley Newby, 1869), pp. 3, 7, 8.
66. National Archives. Diplomatic Dispatches. Nicaragua. Wheeler to Secretary of State William Marcy, February 19, 1855.
67. John Foster to Frederick Chatfield, Realejo, December 31, 1850. Foreign Office 15/70.
68. The advertisements and the recommendations of businessmen in the *Nicaragua Flag* (Granada), July 26, 1851, suggest the impressive presence of U.S. entrepreneurs.
69. Carl Scherzer, *Travels in the Free States of Central America: Nicaragua, Honduras, and San Salvador* (London: Longman, 1857), I, 53.
70. "The money which has lately been thrown into circulation has been in a great measure amongst the poorer classes" British Vice-Consul John Foster to Frederick Chatfield, Realejo, December 31, 1850. Foreign Office 15/70.
71. Williams, *Gateway*, p. 84.
72. Chamorro Zelaya, *Fruto Chamorro*, pp. 233–234.
73. Karl Bermann, *Under the Big Stick. Nicaragua and the United States since 1848* (Boston: South End Press, 1986), pp. 42–43.
74. *Gaceta de Guatemala*, (Guatemala City), July 18, 1854.
75. Quoted in Wall, "American Intervention in Nicaragua," p. 314.
76. Library of Congress. Manuscript Division. The Papers of John Hill Wheeler, Manuscript 16,736.1. Diary, entry for December 21, 1854.
77. *Sacramento Daily Union*, November 5, 1855.
78. *New York Times*, December 15, 1854.
79. Message of the President of the United States, May 15, 1856. Senate. 34th Congress. 1st Session. Ex. doc. 68, pp. 1 and 6.
80. July 28, 1852. William R. Manning , ed., *Diplomatic Correspondence of the United States, Inter-American Affairs. 1831–1860* (Washington D.C.: Carnegie Endowment for International Peace, 1934), IV, pp. 295–300.
81. National Archives. Diplomatic Dispatches. Nicaragua. November 10, 1853.
82. "El Año de 1854 en la Noche del 31 de Diciembre de 1853," is signed "The Editors." *Boletín del Ejército Democrático de Nicaragua* (León), July 1, 1854.
83. Fruto Chamorro, *Mensaje de S. E. el General Director Supremo Fruto Chamorro a la Asamblea Constituyente del Estado de Nicaragua, Instalada el 22 de Enero de 1854* (Managua: n.n., 1854).

84. Fruto Chamorro, *Circular a Todos los Gobiernos, Dándoles Conocimiento de los Motivos que Ha Tenido Nicaragua para Tomar el Nombre de República* (Managua: n.n., 1854).
85. José Dolores Gámez, *Apuntamientos Para la Biografía de Máximo Jerez* (Managua: Tipografía Nacional, 1893), p. 26.
86. Examples among the broadside literature of the period abound: Francisco Díaz Zapata, *Breve Compendio* (León: Imprenta de la Paz, 1852); Los Leoneses, *Centro-Americanos* (León: Imprenta de la Paz, 1851); *Pronunciamiento y Acta de Organización de un Gobierno Provisorio en el Estado de Nicaragua* (León: Imprenta de la Paz, 1851); and José Trinidad Muñoz, *El General que Suscribe a los Nicaragüenses* (León: Imprenta de la Paz, 1851).
87. *Aritmética en Verso* (León : Imprenta de la Paz, 1851).
88. *Trisajio* (Granada: Imprenta del Orden, 1854) . Some poetical broadsides were: *Al Público* (Granada: Imprenta del Orden, 1854); *Canción Patriótica* (Granada: Imprenta del Orden, 1854); *Canción* (Granada, n.n., 1854); *A Los Libres* (without place, publisher, or date, but of this same period). The Bancroft Library, University of California, Berkeley, preserves copies of these and other poems.
89. Library of Congress. Manuscript Division. The Papers of John Hill Wheeler. Manuscript 16,736.1. Diary, entry for January 31, 1855.
90. These remarks are excerpts from a speech before the deputies assembled in Granada, April 8, 1855. The speech is reprinted in Orlando Cuadra Downing, "La Voz Sostenida," *Revista Conservadora del Pensamiento Centroamericano*, 6 (January 1961), p. 78.
91. *Eco Popular* (Granada), July 13, 1854.
92. For another insight into those beliefs see Jesús de la Rocha, *Informe Presentado por el Ministro Interino de Relaciones Interiores y Exteriores a las Cámaras Legislativas de Nicaragua* (Granada: Imprenta del Orden, 1853).
93. Letter of Castellón to President José María San Martín of El Salvador, June 30, 1855, reprinted in Ofsman Quintana Orozco, *Apuntes de Historia de Nicaragua* (Managua: Editora Mundial, 1968), p. 130.
94. Already in 1851, the Liberals of León were accused of hiring California filibusters. *Gaceta Oficial de Nicaragua* (Granada), November 29, 1851. Max Weber characterized the recruitment of mercenaries as a widespread practice of patrimonial rule. Reinhard Bendix, *Max Weber: An Intellectual Portrait* (Berkeley: University of California Press, 1977), p. 343.
95. *El Defensor del Orden* (Granada), June 11, 1855.
96. An Officer, *The Destiny of Nicaragua* p. vi.
97. *El Defensor del Orden* (Granada), December 7, 1854.
98. National Archives. Diplomatic Dispatches. Nicaragua. Wheeler to Secretary of State Marcy, January 2, 1855.
99. The Liberals later rationalized that had the Conservatives been reasonable and negotiated with them there would have been no cause to invite Walker. Los Leoneses, *Declaración Imparcial sobre Yankees en Nicaragua* (León: Imprenta del Gobierno Provisorio, 1856).
100. Francisco Vigil, *Muñoz en 1855: Guerra Civil de 17 Meses, del 5 de Mayo de 1854 al 23 de Octubre de 1855* (Granada: n.n., 1935), pp. 8, 26, 29, 36–37, 40.

101. *El Nicaragüense* (Granada), October 27, 1855. Although the title of the newspaper was in Spanish, most of the Copy was in English.

102. "In order, however, to consolidate a general peace, we were willing to bury past differences and endeavor to amalgamate the two parties into one. For this purpose we have, since the Treaty of October last, held in check our old friends the Democrats, and have attempted to conciliate the men formerly attached to the Government of Estrada." William Walker, *To the People of Central America* (Granada: n.n., 1856). This broadside, like many of the decrees and statements of Walker, was printed in English. Wheeler wrote to Secretary of State Marcy, "The policy of the present Government is to amalgamate both parties." National Archives. Diplomatic Dispatches. Nicaragua. May 15, 1856.

103. Edward McGowan, *The Strange Eventful History of Parker H. French* (Los Angeles: Glen Dawson, 1958).

104. Typical of the minister's judgments was this statement: "I am certain that the influences of Americans from the North will tend to purify their [the Nicaraguans'] principles and elevate their conduct. With this idea it will prove a blessing if the whole of Central America becomes Americanized by the industrious and interprising men from the North." National Archives. Diplomatic Dispatches. Nicaragua. Wheeler to Secretary of State Marcy, June 15, 1856. Given the prevalent mood of expansion in the United States and the low opinion North Americans held of Latin Americans, it was not surprising that Walker enjoyed public support at home. Lewis Cass, who became Secretary of State in 1857, admired Walker: "I am free to confess that the heroic effort of our countrymen in Nicaragua excites my admiration, while it engages all my solicitude. I am not deterred from the expression of these feelings by sneers, or reproaches, or hard words. He who does not sympathize with such an enterprise has little in common with me. The difficulties which General Walker has encountered and overcome will place his name high on the roll of the distinguished men of his age. . . . That magnificent region, for which God has done so much and man so little, needs some renovating process, some transfusion by which new life may be imparted to it. Our countrymen will plant there the seeds of our institutions, and God grant that they may grow into an abundant harvest of industry, enterprise, and prosperity. A new day, I hope, is opening under the States of Central America." *New York Times*, May 24, 1856. Quoted in Bermann, *Under the Big Stick*, pp. 87–88.

105. Un Liberal (pseud.), *El Laurel Democrático* (León: Imprenta del Gobierno de Nicaragua, 1855).

106. El Centinela Demócrata (pseud.), *A Los Libres*. This broadside contains no information on place of publication, publisher, or date. The Bancroft Library houses the copy I read.

107. Isidro Urtecho, "Fisionomía de una Epoca Legada," *Revista Conservadora del Pensamiento Centroamericano*, 88 (January 1968), p. 40; José Dolores Gámez, *Historia de Nicaragua* (Managua: Tipografía Nacional, 1889), p. 634.

108. "Circular del Gobierno a los Padres Curas Recomendándoles la Predicación contra la Expedición Filibustera que se Ha Intentado o Intenta sobre Esta República," printed in the *Boletín Oficial* (Granada), July 14, 1855.

109. Hubert H. Bancroft, *The Works of Hubert Howe Bancroft*, vol. VIII, *History of Central America*. Vol. III, *1801–1887* (San Francisco: The History Company, 1887), p. 338.

110. Gámez, *Historia de Nicaragua*, pp. 620–622.

111. "Among the Rev. clergy of Granada, who have signalized themselves by a warm welcome of Americans and other foreigners passing through and sojourning in the State of Nicaragua, we are gratified in announcing the name of Rev. Father Vijil, curate of this city. This distinguished prelate has not only personally extended the civilities and hospitalities of polished life to foreigners, but took occasion in his clerical capacity, from the pulpit, to impress upon his countrymen the duty of treating strangers with kindness. Such manifestations of regard are worthy of commendation, and we revert to the fact with feelings of mingled pleasure and gratification." *Nicaragua Flag* (Granada), July 26, 1851.

112. Library of Congress. Manuscript Division. The Papers of John Hill Wheeler. Manuscript 16,736.1. Diary, May 6, 1855.

113. Augustín Vijil, *A Pedimento* (León: Imprenta del Gobierno Provisorio, 1856).

114. Message of the President of the United States, May 15, 1856. Senate. 34th Congress. 1st Session. Ex. doc. 68, p. 5.

115. For a sympathetic biography of Vijil, see Francisco Vijil, *El Padre Vijil. Su Vida* (Granada: El Centro-Americano, 1930).

116. Rivas's call, dated July 1, 1856, is reprinted in Sara L. Barquero, *Gobernantes de Nicaragua, 1825–1947* (Managua: Ministerio de Instrucción Pública, 1945), pp. 106–107. Calls for party unity had already circulated. José María Estrada, a former chief of state, affirmed that opinion was turning against Walker. He was losing his Nicaraguan allies. "Now, matters have assumed a different aspect. Some became gradually convinced that the usurper of Sonora and the murderer of [Minister of State Mateo]. Mayorga could not be the friend of order; others have seen with their own eyes, that the adventurer to whom they entrusted their destinies and fate of their country only thinks of himself and of those belonging to him. This undeceiving of oneself is sad, but useful. It is yet time to find a remedy for the evil. This remedy is union. Will those who have declared themselves against the legitimate government still treat this union with contempt? However great and manifold may be the errors of the past, all Nicaraguans who, abjuring their errors on the altar of public interest, shall rush with detemination upon the foreigners who now oppress Nicaragua, will show that they are not entirely strangers to the ideas of morality, religion, and country." José María Estrada, Comayagua, January 25, 1856, "Manifesto to the Legitimate President of the Republic of Nicaragua, to the Governments and People of Central America." Reprinted in English translation in Message of the President of the United States, May 15, 1856. Senate. 34th Congress, 1st Session. Ex. doc. 68. Walker himself acknowledged growing Nicaraguan hostility. Walker, *To the People of Central America*.

117. *El Nicaragüense* (Granada), July 12, 1856.

118. David Deaderick III, "The Experience of Samuel Absalom, Filibuster," *The Atlantic Monthly*, 4:26 (December, 1859), p. 664.

119. A Guatemalan view of the tension among the allies is cogently stated in *La*

Situación de Nicaragua durante la Guerra con los Filibusteros en 1856 y 1857 (Guatemala City: Imprenta Nueva, 1857). The book is a collection of articles that appeared in the *Gaceta de Guatemala* of that period. Virgilio Rodríguez Beteta rendered a historical judgment of the relations among the allies in his "Trascendencia de la Guerra Nacional de Centro América contra William Walker," *Anales de la Sociedad de Geografía e Historia de Guatemala,* 30:1–4 (January-December 1957), p. 23. For the views of Honduran General Trinidad Cabañas, see his long interview with John Hill Wheeler. Library of Congress, Diary, December 16, 1855.
120. Santos Guardiola, *El Presidente del Estado de Honduras a Sus Habitantes* (Comayagua: n.n., 1856).
121. *La Situación de Nicaragua,* p. 19.
122. Adán Selva, *Hacia Donde Vamos?* (Managua: ASEL, 1968), pp. 246–247.
123. Quotation from the battle report of General José Dolores Estrada, September 20 1856, reprinted in Gustavo Alemán Bolaños, *Como Ganó Nicaragua Su Segunda Independencia* (Managua: Editora Atlántida, 1944), p. 29.
124. Managua, September 14, 1857. Reprinted in Francisco Pérez Estrada, *José Dolores Estrada. Héroe Nacional de Nicaragua* (Managua: ASEL, n.d.), p. 99.
125. Speech of James R. Doolittle of Wisconsin, delivered in the U..S. Senate on January 21, 1858.
126. Charles W. Doubleday, *Reminiscences of the "Filibuster" War in Nicaragua* (New York: Putnam's, 1886), pp. 89–90.
127. The decree dated November 23, 1855, and signed by Patricio Rivas was constantly reprinted thereafter in El Nicaragüense (Granada). The original decree as well as the newspaper reprints were in English. It reads as follows:

DECREE

The Supreme Goverment of the Republic of Nicaragua, to encourage the immigration of persons of thrift and industry to become settlers and inhabitants within its territorial limits, to the end that its resources may be more fully developed and its commerce increased, and to promote the general welfare of the State has decreed:

Art. 1. A free donation or grant of 250 acres of public land shall be made to each single person who shall enter the State (during the continuance of this decree) and settle and make improvements upon the said tract, the same to be located by the Director of Colonization thereafter to be named, and immediate possession given.

Art. 2. Each family entering the State and settling upon its territory shall receive 100 acres of land in addition to the 250 granted to single settlers.

Art. 3. A right to occupy and improve shall be issued to applicants, and at the expiration of six months, upon satisfactory evidence being presented to the Director of Colonization of compliance with the provisions of this decree, title will be given.

Art. 4. No duties shall be levied on the personal effects, household furniture, agricultural implements, seeds, plants, domestic animals, or other imports for the personal use of the colonists or the development of the resources of the land donated, and colonists shall be exempt from all extraordinary taxes, and contributions, and from all public service except when the public safety shall otherwise demand.

Art. 5. The colonists being citizens of the Republic cannot alienate the land granted to any foreign government whatever, and shall not alienate the said land or their rights thereunto until after an occupancy of at least six months.

Art. 6. A Colonization office shall be established and a Director of Colonization appointed, whose business it shall be to attend to the petitions of emigrants, to collect and dispense seeds, plants, etc., and to keep the Registry Books of the Department.

Done in Granada, the 23rd day of November 1855.

Patricio Rivas.

President of the Republic.

128. "Indeed, intelligence of some act of disaffection was continually coming to General Walker; and thereupon he would outst the offender, confiscate his estate to the government, and perhaps grant it to some one of his officers, or pawn it to foreign sympathizers for military stores. The neighborhood of Rivas was dotted with ranch-houses, decimated by these means, rank grass growing in the court yards, and cactus hedges gapped, and the crops swept away by the foragers." Deaderick, "The Experience of Samueal Absalom," I, p. 664.

129. William Walker, *The War in Nicaragua* (Tucson: The University of Arizona Press, 1985), pp. 252–253.

130. As early as June 7, 1855, just prior to Walker's arrival, Minister Wheeler noted the increasing hostility of the government to foreign ownership of land. Library of Congress. Manuscript Division. The Papers of John Hill Wheeler. Manuscript 16, 736.1. Diary, June 7, 1855.

131. The first and basic labor decree was issued on September 6, 1856, in English:

DECREE

Art. 1. Any contract made for labor for a term of months or years shall be binding on the parties to it.

Art. 2. Any person who shall make a contract to perform labor and shall fail to fulfill the contract, shall be sentenced by the Judge of First Instance, Prefect, Subprefect, Agricultural Judge, or Local Alcalde, to forced labor on the public works, for a term of not less than one, nor more than six months; or until the party to whom the labor is due may ask for the release of the laborer.

Art. 3. Any laborer who shall contract to do work for a longer period than six months and shall fail to fulfill his contract, may be sentenced, by either of the before-mentioned authorities, to forced labor on the public works for the time of his unexpired service, or until the party to whom his labor is due may ask for his release.

A copy of this decree appears in the National Archives. Diplomatic Dispatches. Nicaragua. Wheeler to Secretary of State Marcy, September 30, 1856.

132. The decree reads:

Inasmuch as the Constituent Assembly of the Republic, on the 30th day of April, 1838, declared the State free, sovereign, and independent, dissolving the compact with the Federal Constitution established between Nicaragua and the other States of Central America:

Inasmuch as since that date Nicaragua has been in fact free from the obligations of the Federal Constitution imposed:

Inasmuch as the act of the Constituent Assembly, decreed on the 30th of April, 1838, provides that the Federal decrees given previous to that date shall remain in force, unless contrary to the provisions of that act:

Inasmuch as many of the decrees theretofore given are unsuited to the present condition of the country, are repugnant to its welfare and prosperity, as well as to its territorial integrity:

Therefore, the President of the Republic of Nicaragua, in virtue of the power in him invested,

DECREES

Art. 1. All acts and decrees of the Federal Constituent Assembly, as well as of the Federal Congress, are declared null and void.

Art. 2. Nothing herein contained shall affect rights heretofore vested under the acts and decrees hereby repealed.

Among the decrees which the foregoing repeals is an act by the Federal Constituent Assembly, of 17th April, 1824, abolishing slavery in Central America. The repeal of the repealing statute revives the original law, and, therefore, the right to hold slaves is acknowledged by the Government of Nicaragua. Of course the acknowledgment of the right to hold slaves imposes the obligation to secure owners in the enjoyment of their property. (That decree bore the date September 22. 1856. Ibid.)

133. Walker, *The War in Nicaragua*, pp. 256, 260.
134. Ibid., pp. 261, 262.
135. For his complete rationalization of slavery see "Letter from Gen. William Walker," *New York Herald*, September 17, 1857.
136. National Archives. Diplomatic Dispatches. Nicaragua. Wheeler to Secretary of State Marcy, September 30, 1856.
137. An Officer, *The Destiny of Nicaragua*, p. 47.
138. George W. Peck, *Nicaragua and General Walker. Speech of Hon. Geo. W. Peck of Michigan Delivered at the Mass Meeting Held in the Park, New York May 23, 1856* (Washington, D.C.: The Union Office, 1856).
139. Alejandro Reyes Huete, *Estampas de Nuestra Historia*, (Granada: El Correo, 1956), p. 19.
140. Walker, *The War in Nicaragua*, pp. 253–254.
141. National Archives. Diplomatic Dispatches. Nicaragua. Lamar to Secretary of State, February 26, 1858.
142. The history of Hawaii in the nineteenth century offered a thought-provoking example of how U.S. citizens peacefully changed land structures in another country to their benefit. The historian Gavan Daws recorded one significant result: "By the end of the nineteenth century white men owned four acres of land for every one owned by a native, and this included chiefs." *Shoal of Time: A History of the Hawaiian Islands* (Honolulu: The University Press of Hawaii, 1974), p. 128.
143. *La Situación de Nicaragua*, pp. 19, 29.
144. Anthony Giddens offers this short, simple, and useful definition of nationalism:

"A phenomenon that is primarily psychological—the affiliation of individuals to a set of symbols and beliefs emphasizing communality among members of a political order." *The Nation-State and Violence. Volume Two of a Contemporary Critique of Historical Materialism* (Berkeley: University of California Press, 1985), p. 116. While César Graña seemed to separate "popular" and "intellectual" nationalism, he ascribed similar goals to both: "Actually nationalism, as a popular feeling or as an ideology begotten by propagandists or intellectuals, has always tended to assume the voice of a mandate of history vindicated by its self-evident justice and rationality." "I. Cultural Nationalism: The Idea of Historical Destiny in Spanish America," *Social Research*, 29:4 (Winter 1962), p. 397.

145. *Redactor Nicaragüense* (León), January 18, 1841. The *Registro Oficial* (San Fernando) repeated the charges, evincing antiforeign sentiments. (July 12, 1845).
146. Pedro Francisco de la Rocha, *Revista Política sobre la Historia de la Revolución de Nicaragua en Defensa de la Administración del Ex-Director Don José León Sandoval* (Granada: Imprenta de la Concepción, 1847), p. 40.
147. *Correo del Istmo de Nicaragua* (León), September 16, 1849; May 9 and May 23, 1850.
148. *Gaceta Oficial de Nicaragua* (Granada), October 15, 1853.
149. John Stuart Mill, *Considerations on Representative Government* (New York: The Liberal Arts Press, 1958), p. 64.
150. Concerning the Indian attack, Jerónimo Pérez concluded,"Thus those original inhabitants taught lessons in patriotism to all Central Americans." *Memorias para la Historia de la Revolución de Nicaragua en 1854*, p. 294.
151. Walker, *The War in Nicaragua*, p. 290.
152. Orlando Cuadra Downing, "La Voz Sostenida. Antología del Pensamiento Nicaragüense," *Revista Conservadora del Pensamiento Centroamericanco*, 6 (January 1961), p. 80.
153. Walker, *The War in Nicaragua*, p. 298.
154. Tucker was describing his experiences as he left Nicaragua for Honduras. Letter from Joseph Clarence Tucker, Tegucigalpa, May 26, 1856, to his brother (unnamed). Joseph Clarence Tucker (1821–1891) Papers. Bancroft Library no. 69/6M.
155. "The Experiences of Samuel Absalom, Filibuster," *The Atlantic Monthly*, 5:27 (January 1960), p. 38.
156. Anselmo Fletes Bolaños, "La Venta de un Negro," included in Jorge Eduardo Arellano, ed., *Cuentistas de Nicaragua* (Managua: Ediciones Distribuidora Cultural, 1984), pp. 31–32.
157. Ernesto Mejía Sánchez, "Romances y Corridos. Fuentes Históricas para los Romances y Corridos Nicaragüenses," *Revista Conservadora del Pensamiento Centroamericano*, 74 (November 1966), p. 31.
158. Pablo Antonio Cuadra and Francisco Pérez Estrada, *Muestrario del Folklore Nicaragüense* (Managua: Editorial San José, 1978), pp. 176–177.
159. Mejía Sánchez, "Romances y Corridos," pp. 29, 33.
160. In the Iberian world, perhaps the best and certainly the earliest example occurred in Portugal in 1640, when the masses played a major role in terminating the "Babylonian captivity," Spanish domination, and reasserting Portuguese

independence. A. H. de Oliveira Marques *History of Portugal,* Vol. I: *From Lusitania to Empire* (New York: Columbia University Press, 1972), pp. 322 and 327. Writing about Paraguayans battling the invading armies of Argentina, Brazil, and Uruguay, Barbara J. Ganson observed: "A broadly based sense of nationalism appeared to have developed among them due to particular circumstances." "Following Their Children into Battle: Women at War in Paraguay, 1864–1870," *The Americas,* 46:3 (January, 1990), p. 371. In the case of Chile's invasion of Peru during the War of the Pacific (1879–1883), scholars differ on its effect on the emergence and growth of Peruvian nationalism among the folk. On the one hand, Heraclio Bonilla believes that little evidence of sustained nationalism emerged. "The Indian Peasantry and 'Peru' during the War with Chile," Steve J. Stern, ed., *Resistance, Rebellion, and Consciousness in the Andean Peasant World* (Madison: The University of Wisconsin Press, 1987), pp. 219–231. On the other hand, basing herself on two geographical case studies, Florencia E. Mallon concluded that under particular circumstances peasants joined in a common, broad-based struggle against the invader expressive of a distinctive nationalism. Those particular circumstances did not exist in Cajamarca; they did in Junín. "The Comasinos formed theirs [national consciousness], in reaction to a Chilean invasion that attacked them in their very homes, building off a protonational Andean tradition, and in the context of a resistance movement organized by communities and given a great deal of local autonomy. Despite their continuing existence in a precapitalist economy, therefore, the Comasinos were indeed able to develop nationalism." "Nationalist and Antistate Coalitions in the War of the Pacific: Junín and Cajamarca, 1879–1902", in ibid., pp. 232–279.

161. Franco Cerutti included the poem "Felicitación" in his "Documentos para la Historia de Nicaragua a través de la Versificación del Siglo XIX. II Tomo. Poemas Ocasionales de Distinta Inspiración. Poemas de Carácter Cívico-Político," *Revista Conservadora del Pensamiento Centroamericano,* 114 (March/ 1970), p. 79.

162. All these poems are contained in Franco Cerutti, *Dos Románticos Nicaragüenses: Carmen Díaz and Antonino Aragón* (Managua: PNSA, 1974), pp. 38, 44–45.

163. Jorge Eduardo Arellano, "Poesía y Testamento de Juan Iribarren," *Revista Conservadora del Pensamiento Centroamericanco,* 69 (June 1966), pp. 6–7.

164. *Apuntes de Historia de Nicaragua* (Managua: Universidad Nacional Autónoma de Nicaragua, 1982), I, 23; Instituto de Estudio de Sandinismo, *Pensamiento Anti-Imperialista en Nicaragua. Antología* (Managua: Editorial Nueva Nicaragua, 1982), p. 11

165. William Carey Jones, Special Agent of the United States to Central America to Secretary of State Lewis Cass, January 30, 1858, reprinted in William R. Manning, ed., *Diplomatic Correspondence of the United States. Inter-American Affairs, 1831—1860.* Volume IV, *Central America* (Washington, D.C.: Carnegie Endowment for International Peace, 1934), pp. 649–650.

166. *Memoria Presentada al Primer Congreso Legislativo de Nicaragua por el Sr. Ministro de Fomento, Instrucción y Crédito Público el Día 14 de Enero de 1859* (Granada: Imprenta de El Centro-Americano, 1859).

167. "Already greatly hindered by the allied war against Walker, the seizure of the river steamers by Vanderbilt's agent in January 1857 brought an end to transportation across the isthmus. Seven years of contention intervened before the route resumed continuous operation. By then it as too late to really hope for success." Folkman, *The Nicaragua Route*, pp. 124–125.

168. National Archives. Diplomatic Dispatches. Nicaragua. Lamar to Secretary of State Cass, March 27, 1858.

169. *Repúblicas de Centro-América. Idea de Su Historia y de Su Estado Actual* (Santiago: Imprenta del Ferrocarril, 1857), p. 68.

170. Frederick Boyle, *A Ride across a Continent: A Personal Narrative of Wanderings through Nicaragua and Costa Rica* (London: Bentley, 1868), I, 55–56, 67–68; II, 110, 117–118.

171. Jaime Wheelock Román, *Nicaragua: Imperialismo y Dictadura* (Mexico City: Siglo Veintiuno Editores, 1975), p. 25.

172. Jesús de la Rocha, *Memoria . . . 1859*.

173. Scherzer observed, "Since the reign of Walker, it [Granada] has lost its almost exclusive privilege of choosing the members of the government from its own patrician families—a privilege that was divided between it and León; but it may console itself with the reflection that its rival has fallen far lower in power and prosperity." *Travels*, I, 54.

174. Domingo Lacayo et al., *Supremo Director del Estado* (León: Imprenta de Orden, 1853); *El Nicaragüense* (Granada) of January 19, 1856 also pointed out the substantial profits Costa Rica reaped from coffee. Frederick Boyle contrasted Costa Rican prosperity with Nicaraguan poverty in the mid-1860s. *A Ride*, II, pp. 200–201 *passim*.

175. José Luís Velázquez, "La Incidencia de la Formación de la Economía Agroexportadora en el Intento de Formación del Estado Nacional en Nicaragua: (1860–1890)," *Revista del Pensamiento Centroamericano*, 157 (October-December 1977), p. 13.

176. Speech given in León, June 24, 1857, quoted in Barquero, *Gobernantes de Nicaragua*, p. 111.

177. Velázquez, "La Incidencia de la Formación," p. 14.

178. Ibid., p. 15.

179. I draw on the ideas about the nation–state put forth by Giddens, *The Nation-State and Violence*.

180. The quotation originates in a U.S. diplomatic dispatch. National Archives. Diplomatic Dispatches. Nicaragua. Dimitri to Secretary of State Cass, February 28, 1860.

181. "Mensaje del Excmo. Senor General Presidente don Tomás Martínez en el Acto de Su Inauguración el 15 de Noviembre de 1857," reprinted in the *Revista de la Academia de Geografía e Historia de Nicaragua*, 10:2 (October 1950), p. 168. For a more complete analysis of the status of public education immediately after the National War consult the *Memoria Presentada. . . el Día 14 de Enero de 1859*. For a summary of economic conditions consult *Memoria Leída por el Señor Ministro de Hacienda D. José Miguel Cárdenas al Congreso Legislativo de Nicaragua en su Reunión Ordinaria de 1861* (Managua: Imprenta del Progreso,

1861). The *Memoria* emphasized problems. It noted that in 1859 and 1860 governmental expenses slightly exceeded income; it called for new taxes. Jubilantly it noted that exports outnumbered imports.
182. "Mensaje . . . Martínez . . . 1857," pp. 168–169.
183. Quoted from his "Manifesto to the People of Central America," dated April 10, 1858, and included in National Archives. Diplomatic Dispatches. Nicaragua. Lamar to Secretary of State Cass, May 26, 1858.
184. Gámez, *Apuntamientos* pp. 45–46; William O. Scroggs, "William Walker and the Steamship Corporation in Nicaragua," *American Historical Review,* 10:4 (July 1905), p. 810; Alberto Quijano Quesada, *Costa Rica Ayer y Hoy. 1800–1939* (San José: Editorial Borrase Hermanos 1939), pp. 197–230.
185. The complete text of the treaty in English and Spanish appears in Gunter Kahle and Barbara Potthost, *Der Wiener Schiedsspruch von 1881* (Koln: Bohlau Verlag, 1983), pp. 73–79.
186. Ministerio de Relaciones Exteriores, *Circular a los Prefectos Gobernadores Departamentales Y Demás Autoridades Superiores* (Managua: n.n., 1858).
187. Cerutti, *Dos Románticos Nicaragüenses,* p. 53.
188. Unos Amigos de la Paz (pseud.), *Al Público* (León: Imprenta de Minerva, 1862).
189. *Discurso Pronunciado por el Licenciado D. Juan E. de la Rocha, Alcalde 1° Constitucional en el Aniversario XLIV de Nuestra Independencia* (León: Imprenta de Justo Hernández; 1865).
190. Quoted in Anselmo H. Rivas, "Los Partidos Políticos de Nicaragua," *Revista Conservadora del Pensamiento Centroamericano,* 70 (July 1966), p. 3.
191. Squier, *Nicaragua,* pp. 154, 443–444, 327.
192. Other travelers shared the Romantic reaction to what they beheld. Jacob Stillman rhapsodized, " how much I longed for the power to convey a correct impression of the interesting scene, combining all that was picturesque in nature with the innocent simplicity of a people but little removed from the pastoral state." *An 1850 Voyage,* p. 47.
193. "In a culture that was beginning to make a fundamental distinction between political and social authority, a theory such as patriarchalism that presupposed their identity was bound to become outmoded, irrelevant, and therefore unacceptable." Gordon J. Schochet, *Patriarchalism in Political Thought: The Authoritarian Family and Political Speculation and Attitudes Especially in Seventeenth-Century England* (New York: Basic Books, 1975), p. 57.
194. For a study of this process in another Central American nation, see E. Bradford Burns, "The Modernization of Underdevelopment: El Salvador, 1858–1931," *The Journal of Developing Areas,* 18:3 (April 1984), pp. 293–317.
195. National Archives. Diplomatic Dispatches. Nicaragua. Dimitri to Secretary of State Cass, April 30, 1860. José de Marcoleta illustrated how in the eyes of the Nicaraguans the actions of individual U.S. citizens and of the United States appeared indistinguishable, in "La Piratería Convertida en Derecho de los Estados Unidos de América" (1857); the "Unos Cien Nicaragüenses. Al Pueblo de los Estados Unidos" (1858) made the same equation. Both are reprinted in Instituto de Estudio de Sandinismo, *Pensamiento Antimperialista,* pp. 28–52.
196. Wall, "American Intervention in Nicaragua, 1848–1861," pp. 305–306.

197. "Mr. Henry Foote our new Vice-Consul in Salvador was lately present at a dinner given to Mr. Borland in Granada when that functionary stated publicly that it was his greatest ambition to see the State of Nicaragua forming a bright star in the Flag of the United States." Charles Lennox Wyke to Clarendon, November 27, 1853. Foreign Office 15/79, No. 37

198. National Archives. Diplomatic Dispatches. Nicaragua. Lamar to Secretary of State Cass, March 27, 1858.

199. Ibid., June 24, 1858.

200. Ibid., Dimitri to Secretary of State Cass, February 28, 1860.

201. Ibid., April 30, 1860.

202. Ibid., September 19, 1859.

203. Ibid., Lamar to Secretary of State Cass, June 24 and July 4, 1858.

204. Ibid., Dimitri to Secretary of State Cass, December 7, 1859.

205. Ibid., December 29, 1859.

206. Ibid., April 30, 1860.

207. Bermann, *Under the Big Stick,* pp. 96, 98, 100–101; Folkman, *The Nicaragua Route,* pp. 96–97; James T. Wall, *Manifest Destiny Denied: America's First Intervention in Nicaragua* (Washington, D.C.: University Press of America, 1981), pp. 168–170; Scroggs," William Walker and the Steamship Corporation," pp. 810–811; José Ramírez M. *José de Marcoleta. Padre de la Diplomacía Nicaragüense* (Managua: Imprenta Nacional, 1975), I, 61–84.

208. An English translation of the Rivas Manifesto appears in Manning, *Diplomatic Correspondence,* IV, 692–693.

209. Bermann, *Under the Big Stick,* p. 96.

210. Cyril Allen, "Felix Belly: Nicaraguan Canal Promoter," *Hispanic American Historical Review,* 37:1 (February 1957), pp. 46–59; Edward W. Richards, "Louis Napoleon and Central America," *The Journal of Modern History,* 34:2 (June 1962), pp. 178–184; Thomas Schoonover, "Imperialism in Middle America: United States, Britain, Germany, and France Compete for Transit Rights and Trade, 1820s–1920s," in Rhodes Jeffreys-Jones, ed., *Eagle Against Empire* (Aix-en-Provence: Université de Provence, 1983), chap. 2.

211. Interest switched to planning a canal across the isthmus following much the same path as the transit route. In mid–1989 an official expedition of Nicaraguan scientists journeyed down the San Juan River from El Castillo to the ruined and deserted San Juan del Norte. They made ecological studies as a background for canal proposals. Japan manifested a vague interest in building a canal. "Scientific Expedition Explores the San Juan River," *Barricada Internacional* (Managua), June 3, 1989.

212. Nicaragua. *Código de la Legislación de la República de Nicaragua* (Managua: El Centro Americano, 1873), I, 206–207.

213. Gámez, *Historia de Nicaragua,* pp. 526–527; for speculation on early coffee planting see Dionisio Martínez Sáenz, "Quíen Fué el Primer Sembrador de Café en Nicaragua?" *El Café en Nicaragua,* 2:17 (April 1946), pp. 6–9.

214. An 1849 book on Nicaragua by Alexander von Buelow was translated from German into Spanish, "El Estado Libre de Nicaragua en Centroamérica," and published in the *Revista de la Academia de Geografía e Historia de Nicaragua,* 30

(January-June 1965), pp. 40–139. Information concerning the 1847 law comes from page 110.

215. Ibid., p. 107; A. von Buelow, "Capítulo V de Imigración y Colonización en Interés del Comercio Alemán por el Baron A. von Buelow," *Revista de la Academia de Geografía e Historia de Nicaragua,* 38–39 (January-December 1964), pp. 25–26.

216. Ibid., p. 30.

217. Ibid., p. 9.

218. Squier, *Nicaragua,* p. 403.

219. Chamorro promulgated the decree on May 8, 1853. *La Gaceta Oficial de Nicaragua* (Granada), May 21, 1853; Pedro Joaquín Chamorro, "Fruto Chamorro. Apuntes Biográficos," *Revista de la Academia de Geografía e Historia de Nicaragua,* I:3 (1937), p. 372.

220. Scherzer, *Travels,* I, 124.

221. Nicaragua. Código I, 207.

222. Nicaragua, *Ley de las Tierras Incultas* (Managua: n.n., 1859).

223. David R. Radell and James J. Parsons, "Realejo: A Forgotten Colonial Port and Shipbuilding Center in Nicaragua," *Hispanic American Historical Review,* 51:2 (May 1971), p. 312.

224. Wheelock Román, *Nicaragua. Imperialismo y Dictadura,* p. 14.

225. "The development of a domestic export-oriented agrarian oligarchy results in the strengthening of the role of the state, increasing its capacity for repressive action and for exclusion of the poorer classes from the political dialogue. A strong state apparatus is in the interests of the domestic export oligarchy, first because it allows them to socialize some of the costs of marketing their crop, and may even allow them to develop policies which subsidize imputs or prices of their product. A second objective of the strong oligarchical state is to assure access to and control of land for the oligarchy. A third objective of the strong oligarchy is to keep labor's share of income low." Jan L. Flora, *Roots of Insurgency in Central America* (Meadville, Penn.: Allegheny College, 1988), pp. 36–37.

226. Francisco Pérez Estrada, "Breve Historia de la Tenencia de la Tierra," in his *Ensayos Nicaragüenses* (Managua: PINSA, 1976), pp. 184–186.

227. "Low labor density implied ease of access to land and it became an article of faith among both the colonial and republican administrations that no one would work for wages as hired labor unless he or she was compelled; the clear implication was that the development of an export sector depended on restricting access to land and the use of force in controlling the labor supply." Victor Bulmer-Thomas, *The Political Economy of Central America since 1920* (New York: Cambridge University Press, 1987), p. 11.

228. *Gaceta Oficial de Nicaragua* (Managua), July 17, 1858; July 31, 1858; and June 25, 1859. Alberto Lanuza Matamoros, "Comercio Exterior de Nicaragua (1821–1875)," *Estudios Sociales Centroamericanos,* 14 (May-August 1976), p. 111.

229. Nicaragua, *Ley de las Tierras Incultas.*

230. Nicaragua. *Ley de Agricultura de 18 de Febrero de 1862* (Managua: Imprenta de Miguel Robelo, 1862).

231. Ernest Gellner discusses the antithesis of local community and nation in *Nations and Nationalism* (Ithaca: Cornell University Press, 1983), p. 14.

232. Foreign visitors often commented on European influences on Nicaraguan life-styles. For example, Scherzer recorded, "Among the opulent inhabitants of Gra-nada the French fashions have also of late years replaced the simple national cos-tume, though not so entirely with women as with men. The high, equable tem-perature of the climate makes a light and easy costume indispensable; and the ladies in Granada appear in their ordinary domestic life with arms and neck bare. The tight-fitting fashions of Europe would be, one would suppose, intoler-able here; and yet some fair ladies of patrician families have condemned them-selves to this torture. The propaganda of the fashions makes many more con-verts than that of religious faith." *Travels*, I, 61–62. Sergio Ramírez wrote a succinct and critical history of the shaping of Central America's imported culture in the nineteenth century: "Cultura y Caficultura," *Balcanes y Volcanes y Otros Ensayos y Trabajos* (Managua: Editorial Nueva Nicaragua, 1983), pp. 15–43.

233. Concern with that loss of national identity and the later search for it are major themes of Alejandro Serrano Caldera, *Entre la Nación y el Imperio* (Managua: Editorial Vanguardia, 1988).

234. Pierre Clastres has written a thoughtful, provocative, and convincing essay to argue, "The true revolution in man's prehistory . . . is the political revolution, that mysterious emergence—irreversible, fatal to primitive societies—of the thing we know by the name of the State." *Society against the State* (New York: Zone Books, 1987), p. 202.

235. Serrano Caldera, *Entre la Nación y el Imperio*, p. 12.

Index